The Motor Car 1946–56

Contents

For Helen
who prefers driving them

First Published 1979
© Michael Sedgwick 1978

ISBN 0 7134 1271 2

Printed in Great Britain by
Redwood-Burn Ltd
Trowbridge & Esher
for the Publishers
B. T. Batsford Ltd
4 Fitzhardinge Street
London W1H 0AH

The Motor Car
1946–56

Michael Sedgwick

B T Batsford Ltd London

Acknowledgment

The real credit for this book must go to the people who hold the keys to specialist knowledge, without whom the scribe merely becomes a mixture of parrot and précis merchant.

First of all I must single out the staff of the National Motor Museum Library at Beaulieu—the late Eric Bellamy and his successor Peter Brockes—who endured a flood of visits, requests and wholesale withdrawal of material into the reading-room, over a period of three years.

I have also drawn greatly on the assistance of my good friend Nick Georgano, recognized as world-ranking number one in the realm of automotive history. Nick will by no doubt be heaving a sigh of relief now the frantic appeals for help have ceased, especially as he consented to read the manuscript in the rough-draft stage and weeded out countless howlers. The mini-car jungle was penetrated only with help from David Filsell and Andrew Woolley, whose knowledge is equalled only by their forbearance. Two other people to whom I owe a debt of gratitude are Peter Mayer and Roger Gloor of the Swiss *Automobil Revue*, who let me spend a whole day among their archives and never complained.

When writing about a period during which virtually no foreign cars were imported into Britain, one relies heavily on hearsay evidence and also on foreign historians who drove and owned these vehicles. Thus for the American chapters I appealed for help to a whole panel of experts—Dave Brownell of *Cars and Parts*, Maurice D. Hendry, Beverly Rae Kimes of *Automobile Quarterly*, Richard M. Langworth and Keith Marvin. I must also pay tribute to the memory of a good friend, the late Charles Lam Markmann, whose astringent recollections of imported sports models in the early 1950s enlivened my researches.

The French automobile industry is much better documented than it used to be, thanks to the efforts of Serge Pozzoli, Lucien Loreille and others, but I owe a debt of gratitude to Paul Badré for guiding me through the uncharted maze of early post-war Paris Salons and their strange exhibits. J. A. Grégoire introduced me to his excellent *50 Ans d'Automobile*, the only authentic guide to the complex Aluminium Française–Grégoire saga which runs like the 'Harry Lime Theme' through our period.

Across the border in Switzerland, Ferdinand Hediger was of immense help in sorting out not only the products of his own country but also many of the rarities which could be bought within the Confederacy between 1946 and the early 1950s. Halwart Schrader was a tower of strength on cars produced by East and West Germany: answering countless questions, introducing me to other specialists and finally reading my chapters on the German makes. Milos Skorepa and Marian Suman-Hreblay gave generously of their vast knowledge on Czechoslovakian cars, and Björn-Eric Lindh performed the same service in respect of Sweden. On Russian cars, Margus-Hans Kuuse was another tireless source of information; almost nothing has been written on Denmark's cars, and I could not have ventured two consecutive words on the subject without the unstinting help of Anders Ditlev Clausager and Ole Riisager. Eddie Ford of *Restored Cars* put me right on Australian matters, and for South America generally I have relied on the knowledgeable and helpful Alvaro Casal Tatlock.

As always, the public relations departments of almost every surviving maker have been bombarded with questions, often about vehicles that they (and we) might prefer to forget. Few of them have failed to respond to such appeals, and my thanks go to all these ladies and gentlemen. I have also received unstinting help from my fellow scribes and from one-make historians, several of whom contributed research destined for their own books. Their names are legion, but the following must be singled out for their patience and kindness: Angelo Tito Anselmi, John Bolster, Richard Crump, John Davy, Sigvard Heringa, David Kinsella, Ivan Mahy, Ian Morton, F. Wilson McComb, Cyril Posthumus, C. P. Read, Gerry Simonds, R. A. Southgate, D. J. True, Michael Worthington-Williams and Eric Wooddin—my thanks to you all.

Finally, my thanks go to my friend, former partner and favourite co-driver Helen Marshall. She has shared the wheel of many cars of the 1950s with me and owned not a few herself. To Helen, I also owe the inimitable description of the Triumph Mayflower, and her humour and compassion sustained me through yet another long labour.

M.C.S.
Midhurst 1978

Illustrations

Introduction

'You can't write this book,' said a colleague; 'Your period isn't even a proper period.' There is some substance in this remark; 1946–56 represents a convenient span of ten years, and not much else. While VE-Day is an obvious starting point, what, one may ask, makes 1956 a watershed? To Americans, the first post-war phase begins with the development of the 1947-model Studebakers and ends with the birth of the compacts in 1960. In Europe, the Mini, a 1959 débutante, marks the breach with the shibboleths of the *système* Panhard. The contraction of industry into large international groups is a phenomenon of the 1960s: Chrysler, for instance, consolidated their European empire between 1964 and 1967. Badge engineering, though common enough in our period, had yet to reach its zenith: even in 1956 quite a few makes clung to identities of dubious merit or commercial value. Unified design, where it existed, did not cross frontiers. There were similarities between American, German and British Fords; Opel and Holden had features in common with Chevrolet and Vauxhall, but T-cars and Fiestas would have been unthinkable. The motorway age had already begun in Germany and Italy but had yet to penetrate Britain. Perhaps the only real watershed that can be associated with 1956 was the Suez Crisis; the mini-cars it bred had no lasting effect, but suddenly the world was awakened to what might happen if the taps were turned off.

In effect, this book deals with three periods. Essentially, the cars that could be bought between 1946 and 1948 were warmed-over 1939 themes; even the Volkswagen had been visible, if not on general sale, by the winter of 1938. This breathing space after the Second World War was needed, not only to allow the development of a new generation but also to cope with a world-wide shortage of vehicles.

The second phase runs from 1948 to 1955. Though not everyone in the motor-car industry plunged into unitary construction, they thought unitary. Chassis and body were no longer two 'strangers in the night', meeting for the first time on the assembly line. The car had become an entity, though its development followed two different schools of thought. In America, painless motoring was the order of the day; having achieved a clashproof gearchange in 1929, Detroit now went all out for automatic transmission, backed by power assistance for steering, brakes, windows, seats and even radio antennae. In Europe, such amenities were less important; instead, greater attention was paid to brakes, steering, suspension and road behaviour. Not that gimmickry was absent—radios and heaters, rarities in 1939, had become commonplace by the mid-1950s, when indeed we were all wondering how we had ever managed without the humble screenwash. Yet one may search in vain for mention of such a device in the accessory catalogues of 1946, and few makers outside America offered it as a regular extra even in 1950.

The third phase—the last stage of unrestricted development the automobile was to enjoy—was just unfolding at the end of our period. Seat belts were rarely seen, and there is no mention of the energy-absorbing bumper. In the excitement of America's horsepower race, nobody bothered about the high emission levels of huge vee-eights with twin quadrajet carburation, and *lebensraum* was more important than compact dimensions; but European and American concepts were being fused to provide both painless driving and good handling qualities, with Citroën's Déesse in the role of harbinger. Chronologically, it falls within our terms of reference, but historically it is an integral part of the 1960s scene.

Thus, if our period has significance, it must be assessed as the age of the stylist, of the 'intelligent buyer' and of global thinking.

The first two were almost incompatible. The stylists and the press departments told the customer what he ought to want, and he took it, tending to pass up anything that was old fashioned without always realizing why. Confronted initially with higher cruising speeds (65–70 mph as against the 50–55 mph of 1939) he was quite happy to accept the mediocre road holding of an earlier era, and words such as oversteer and understeer were bandied about uncomprehendingly. In any case, until 1952 one took what was available, which explains why the new freedom led to a reawakened interest in the sporting type of car, which was *designed* to do 90 mph or more. Fortunately this interest was backed by the industry, which went to work on tyres and brakes to enable this performance to be used to the full. Alfa Romeo were fitting radial-ply tyres as early as 1952, and four years later Citroën and Triumph headed the list of models which were available with disc brakes—although only at the front—as standard.

Nor did everyone think globally. America, economically self-sufficient, could afford to design exclusively for Americans, and her wares were as insular as those of Britain had been in the 1930s. The spread of motoring bred 'national' makes such as Russia's Moskvitch, Australia's Holden and Sweden's Volvo. Though all three were being sold abroad by the mid-1950s, only Volvo as yet catered for foreign requirements. Britain might aspire to the role of general provider, but the incubus of purchase tax led to a new race of kit cars. Japan, still somewhat undeveloped, built primitive vehicles peculiar to the country, and unacceptable anywhere else.

However, these were the exceptions. Everyone wanted cars, and the majority of car-producing nations suffered from balance-of-payments problems which dictated a brisk export trade. First Britain and then West Germany entered the fray in a cut-throat struggle where mistakes and delays could be catastrophic. The latest masterpiece had to withstand the dirt roads of South Africa, the stewing heat of a Queensland summer, the sustained high speeds of American freeways and the sub-Arctic temperatures of northern Sweden. The safest way to ensure this was to test a model in all these conditions, which firms of the calibre of Austin and Fiat habitually did. Others could not afford the expense.

Sales had to be backed by service. There was no point in printing literature in French or Spanish and in appointing a concessionaire, unless spares were readily available and carefully distributed. A further hazard was encountered when selling in countries with an established industry: one tended to be fobbed off with third-rate dealers.

This was a daunting prospect, rendered all the tougher by the spread of unitary construction. Before the war, a £30,000 tooling bill underwrote an acceptable degree of change, perhaps sufficient to finance a manufacturer for two years. Now a complete changeover cost twenty times as much, and its success relied on rapid amortization. To expand meant attention must be paid to dealer networks as well as to factory capacity, and only 'the big battalions' could afford both. For others, the choice was effectively between the gallows and the firing squad. Borgward and Jowett died of over expansion, Singer and Hudson of a desperate loyalty to outmoded shapes.

Finding a model 'for the world' was a problem that dogged the established makers throughout the post-war period; it was not until the end of the 1950s that such firms as BMC, Fiat and Renault attained this objective, though Volkswagen scored a bull's-eye from the start. Often a miscalculation could have mortal results, as in the case of the 'Vanguarditis' prevalent in the early 1950s.

Standard were not the only supporters of this thesis: Renault's Frégate and Fiat's 1400 were variations on the same theme. The difference was that the French and Italian cars were junior leads: the Vanguard had to put on a Ruth Draper act which it could not sustain. Its makers picked the wrong size of car; they committed themselves to a one-model policy with no escape route; and they picked a design of remarkable inflexibility. The theory was excellent, since it constituted the Model A Ford formula brought up to date: in effect a car of American characteristics and appearance, but smaller, more compact and more frugal on fuel. The only trouble was that the world no longer wanted anything as large as this. Greater engine efficiency meant that a 2-litre staple car was, in Powel Crosley's words, a case of 'building a battleship to cross a river'. The true outback motorist wanted four-wheel drive, available on Jeeps and Land Rovers. Those unworried by fiscal problems preferred a true American car, while by the end of the period customers in the 2-litre class were looking for six cylinders and more refinement. The Vanguard was not a bad car—it merely fell between every possible stool.

Such global thinking, of course, bred more stereotypes. Thus by 1950 a mass-produced car with a capacity of under 2 litres was likely to have a four-cylinder pushrod engine, coil ignition, mechanical pump feed, a synchromesh gearbox, a single-plate clutch, hydraulic brakes and independent front suspension, usually (though by no means always) of the short-and-long-arm type. To these would soon be added hypoid rear axles and full unitary construction.

On the other hand, once a shibboleth was shattered, 'the big battalions' would tend to follow. If the trend towards 'putting all the works up both ends' dates from the early 1960s, the wind of change was already evident. Renault had followed Volkswagen with a rear-engined light car, while new recruits to front-wheel drive included Panhard in France, Goliath and Lloyd in Germany, SAAB in Sweden and sundry DKW derivatives in countries as diverse as Poland and Argentina.

I have tried to survey this complicated decade against the social and economic background of the era. This has involved a certain caution, for pitfalls attend the historian of the recent past. One tends to judge the mundane in terms of its decline. The Austin Sheerline and Princess, for instance, have acquired reputations of 'breaker's yard specials', but, while it is true that many an aged Rolls–Royce owes its P100s to a discarded Sheerline and that Princesses made £20–30 as scrap when one paid to have lesser cars towed away, it is also true that they spearheaded Longbridge's new school of design. As for the collectables, these also must be placed in perspective. Few of the European exotics were made in sizable numbers, if only because, in 1952, £3,000 represented a large amount of money. Had my office not been a few blocks away from Harold Radford's showrooms, I doubt if I would ever have encountered a Pegaso outside Earls Court.

There is also the problem of how to present one's findings. Some people will no doubt feel that the global thinking of the 1940s and 1950s warrants a treatment by category rather than by nation. The case of the mini-cars, certainly, makes one wonder if this would not be the best method, since the ideas behind a Bond, an Isetta, a Messerschmitt and a Rovin were essentially similar, and so were the economic circumstances that bred them. The snag is, of course, that a 'buyer's guide' treatment tends to be totally unreadable, and I feel that national backgrounds are more important than mere cars.

There is also the vexed question of what to include and what to omit. I have to confess to the omission of some of the more obscure mini-cars, on the grounds that they displayed few individual traits and were known only to a few show goers. A name without a background is not only boring but also a means of airing one's own ignorance. Four-wheel drive vehicles have received only cursory attention, and I have steered firmly off the whole army of mobile homes that emerged towards the end of the period: the SMMT and the tax authorities alike may regard these as private cars, but their origins are light van. As for sports racing models, I have applied the same rule as in *Cars of the 1930s*: a model merits inclusion only if it was intended for street use, if it was actually used for this purpose or if its design history was relevant to subsequent touring-car developments by the same house.

Production figures are as accurate as it has been possible to procure. However, an American factory which claims to make 75,000 vehicles in a given year might be referring not only to calendar-year or model-year production but also to home registrations of the make in question. Some manufacturers were not above counting in foreign licence production in a bad year or excluding it when the home results were good enough to stand on their own. The statistics quoted are, however, valid on a comparative basis to show how one make stood in relation to another, and I trust readers will be indulgent in the case of minor inconsistencies.

Finally, Americans, Britons and Germans may well complain that I have oversimplified and that some subvariants have been omitted. This applies especially to the American chapters, since with the advent of convenience and performance options in the mid-1950s the variations available from Chevrolet, Ford and Plymouth alone were legion, and I feel that in such cases trends are more important than the minutiae better suited to a one-make history. It is worth remembering that even in 1958 Jaguar could have maintained their full output for four years without duplicating a single vehicle.

1 America

1.1 The Psychomatic Paradise

An unkind critic once compared the front end of a 1950 Buick with that ill-tempered American native, the buffalo. So, indirectly, did the car's makers, who boasted of 'nine brute-strong vertical grid bars, making it impossible to lock horns with the car ahead of you'!

This type of image emphasized the American automobile industry's isolation during the first post-war decade. However, the American motorist did not cut himself off from European ideas: he started to take an interest in them for the first time since 1914. Even in 1946, Standard Eights could be seen in the streets of New York, and, while the TC MG exerted an influence out of all proportion to the 2,001 actually sold in the country, about 20,000 examples of Austin's A40 reached American customers during 1948. Where Britain led, others followed. The first Volkswagen had crossed the Atlantic by 1950, and six years later Volvo, Fiat and Renault were jostling the established English *marques*. (In those days Hillman Minxes were promoted as cheaper per pound weight than sirloin steak!) The effects of this invasion were not yet apparent. Neither the Chevrolet Corvette nor Henry Ford II's Thunderbird 'personal car' were competitive with Jaguar, much less Ferrari, while the true American sports cars, such as Cunningham and Kurtis, were scarcely known outside club circles; but the continuing, if modest, penetration of the foreigners revealed a less-than-uniform acceptance of what Detroit offered.

In 1952 the late Ken Purdy wrote that 'any American manufacturer could duplicate the Delahaye, Cotal box and all, to sell at going American rates'. None of them did. They had problems of their own, whether it was keeping up with the horsepower race or just plain survival.

Because America was never in the front line, it is tempting to assume that after 1945 she could easily return to producing 4,500,000 motor-cars a year. Her automobile industry had built 92% of the Allies' wheeled AFVs, 75% of their aero engines and 47% of their tanks. Ford alone had contributed 3,945 B24 bombers and 4,276 troop-carrying gliders. Unlike France's factories, America's were up to date. The country had two years' headstart on anyone: a 1939 Oldsmobile was already more modern in concept and appearance than a 20CV Renault or a Series III Wolseley, but the 1941 edition with its automatic gearbox belonged to a different generation. Further, Detroit's wares were firmly entrenched in markets as diverse as Belgium and New Zealand.

Reconversion was, however, a painful process. Petrol was not rationed, but tyres were. Steel, zinc and chromium were in short supply. Throughout 1946, scarcely a week passed without a halt in deliveries of some vital component. There was no glass in January or September, seat cushions were difficult to obtain right up to October, and door locks disappeared from the market in March. Though this last bottleneck had been overcome by June, a shortage of bonnet locks had supervened. By October there were plenty of locks, but no doors.

The Trade Unions likewise took a hand. Their demands for a guaranteed minimum wage and a 40-hour week were reasonable enough: indeed, Walter Reuther's United Auto Workers accepted and honoured a pay structure geared to the cost of living, with the consequence that Studebaker workers actually took a voluntary cut during 1948.

Unfortunately, a strike at Ford or General Motors did not stop there. Accessory plants would come out in support, closing rival factories where nothing was in dispute. In the winter of 1945–6, General Motors were shut down for 121 days, and the ramifications of this stoppage meant no bearings for Packard. At the same time the glass industry came out, bringing Chrysler and Nash to a halt. Because everything in Detroit was on a large scale, the losses were formidable: 360,000 cars in the short 1945 calendar year, and 48,000 in February 1946 alone. It took over a year to sort all these problems out, but after this American production settled down to an inexorable tempo that nothing—not even the Korean War—could disturb for long. Reporting threatened cuts in strategic materials at the end of 1950, *The Motor* said, 'After the first quarter [of 1951] there is no uniform expectation, and indeed few expectations of anything. . . . They don't know where their copper, aluminium and steel are coming from for that period.' Hire-purchase restrictions were imposed, cast iron pistons found their way into some of the new vee-eights, and the Unions rebelled again—against the $80 deposit on even the cheapest Chevrolet, which would hit their members worst of all. Although output slipped from a new high of 6,665,863 in 1950 to less than 4,500,000 in 1951 and 1952 alike, it was back at the 6,000,000 level before the last shots were fired in Korea. By 1955 it was to increase dramatically to 7,920,186 units (equivalent to almost thirty years' output of Volkswagens at the rate they were then sold).

The performance in 1950 represented about 75% of the world's total, and even five years later America still commanded a 67% share, but most of it stayed at home. No longer was Detroit the general provider *par excellence*. She still exported a lot of cars—280,000 in 1949—but this was less than 5% of the national output. This change is highlighted by the record of

Ford's Canadian operation, which sent 43.5% of its cars abroad in 1938 but only 15% eleven years later.

Much of this was due to the dollar crisis. In free markets such as Belgium, Detroit held on, launching new models—the Hudson Jet, for instance—at the Brussels Salon. American cars still outsold German cars—by 24,572 to 23,868—in 1952, though the Volkswagen had edged them out of first place. In the early post-war years they led in Switzerland also, their 1949 contribution of 8,787 units being only fractionally less than the combined efforts of Britain, Germany and Italy. More typical, however, was the situation of Australia, once a Ford and Chevrolet preserve. In 1955 the Commonwealth registered only 17,228 new American cars. Even if one counted the Holden, 'Australia's own car', as being based on American designs, the grand total came nowhere near Britain's sales of 99,213 units.

While currency problems deprived many motorists of their Ford vee-eights, Cast Iron Wonders and Chrysler Windsors, the sheer size of these vehicles was a sufficient deterrent. This was not a post-war phenomenon but more a result of the two extra years of peace. Between 1936 and 1942 Pontiacs increased by about 18 inches in length, but the 1956 cars were not significantly longer than their 1946 counterparts. They merely looked larger, because of a lower build, slab-sided styling and—latterly—the unattractive tail fins. If we take three different breeds from three different strata—the General Motors Chevrolet, Ford's Mercury and the Chrysler Eight—we find that the Chevrolet and Chrysler actually lost 1 inch of wheelbase, which the Mercury gained in the same period. As for length, against a growth of 18 inches on Chryslers between 1949 and 1956 must be set the Chevrolet's record—a consistent 195–197 inches throughout. The weight, likewise, changed little, though only Chevrolet remained loyal to their familiar six. The new type of overhead-valve vee-eight, adopted by Chrysler in 1951 and by Mercury in 1954, was actually a weight saver: in Chrysler's case the differential was in the region of 100 lb. Cars were, however, wider, Chryslers spreading by an impressive 7 inches in six years. They were also far more powerful—and more expensive.

The growing tempo of production, of course, offset the rising cost of material. Americans might opt for yearly model changes, but they seldom changed both mechanics and sheet metal simultaneously. Chevrolet offered only three basic types of engine during our period—the old Cast Iron Wonder dating back to 1929, the redesigned pressure-lubricated six that had supplanted it by 1953, and the 265-cubic-inch (4.3-litre) vee-eight of 1955. The 1941–2 body shape remained unchanged until 1948, its all-new successor had a four-season run, and a revised edition with wrapround windscreen was used in 1953 and 1954, before 1955 ushered in the 'dog's leg' screen. Many a faithful flathead soldiered on for years. Of the cars made in 1941, the splash-lubricated Hudson Eight had departed by 1953, but still listed were the straight-eight Packard, the small Nash and the longest-lived of them all, Studebaker's diminutive Champion, launched in 1939 and not destined to have overhead valves until 1961. Thus prices, though 30% up on 1942 levels when production resumed, rose only about 20% during the change to true post-war models, stabilized briefly in 1949 and 1950 and then resumed a gentle upward spiral. A 1956 Chevrolet cost its owner 64% more than its 1946 counterpart, but the annual increase never exceeded 13%.

The most remarkable change was in the horsepower. Quoted increases of 200% in ten years are misleading, since they are based on comparisons between the regular 1946 model and the most powerful of a wide range of 1956 'power packs', but the fact remains that the first post-war Chrysler Saratogas disposed of 135 bhp and 90–95 mph, whereas in 1956 a stock Windsor four-door sedan ($2,870 fob Detroit) would comfortably exceed 100 mph on 225 bhp thanks to its vee-eight engine. If the customer wanted less power, he had to buy a Dodge, still available with the old 230-cubic-inch six. Top-line Chryslers had discarded this engine eighteen months previously. Up to 1950, Chrysler had been content with a straight-eight, but for 1951 they decided on a slightly smaller vee-type which gave an impressive 180 bhp. The horsepower race was on.

Not only did the short-stroke vee-eights open up new horizons of performance, but they also had other advantages. The latest high-octane fuels demanded rigidity: crankshaft failures were exceptional. Four-throw cranks with five mains and staggered banks of cylinders gave better balance, eliminating the 'wuffle' familiar to owners of old-school Ford vee-eights. Finally, the new generation of engines, though wide, were also short, which meant that makers could dispense, once and for all, with different chassis for sixes and eights. Steps in this direction had already been taken by 1940 but were defeated by the length of the straight-eights then in fashion. The results of such rationalization were often a sedate six and an eight with lethal handling characteristics, but it helped to cut development costs, which were formidable.

Tooling up for the new 1949 models cost General Motors and Ford about $90,000,000 each, and even the smaller independents had to foot impressive bills. Hudson spent $18,000,000 on their Step-Downs, and Nash $15,000 on the Airflyte. Later, the pace would quicken. $40,000,000 was set aside in 1955 for the expansion of the Plymouth plant, as against a mere $9,000,000 in 1932 for converting from four- to six-cylinder engines. At this time Ford had just voted $600,000,000 on long-term production and distribution plans. General Motors also had invested $500,000,000 in order to bring Buick's potential up to 1,000,000 units a year, a target that had yet to be achieved in 1976.

By 1955 only Kaiser—who were in any case about to close down—lacked a vee-eight. Cadillac and Oldsmobile led in 1949, in 1951 the first Chrysler contender had been introduced, and Ford had switched to overhead valves two years later. Nobody, however, deserted sixes immediately: there was still a market for more frugal automobiles. Chevrolet's sales indicated the way the market was to go: in 1955, their first year in the game, sixes outsold eights by three to two, but within a year the ratio had been reversed. As for the straight-eight, it simply disappeared. Buick, long a devotee of the old configuration, remained undecided for a year in 1953, but 1954 was the last season for Pontiac and Packard, leaving the Russian ZIS and a few special-ized competition machines to carry a once-popular banner.

The horsepower race had an element of comedy. Chrysler opened the batting in 1951 with their 180-bhp hemi but did not develop it further, whereupon Cadillac took over the race by introducing quadrajet carbura-tion, giving 195 bhp. They added another ten horses in 1953, only to be matched by the new Lincoln. A year later Chrysler had regained the lead, but five other makes (including, surprisingly, the last of Packard's huge nine-bearing straight-eights) had passed 200 bhp. In 1955 it became a month-by-month contest. Cadillac led first with twin quadrajets and 270 bhp, but soon Packard had improved on this, and by the summer Chrysler had attained 300 bhp, although only on their limited-edition 300 hardtops. By 1957, a Chevrolet had one unit of brake horsepower per cubic inch—283 each way—while Ford were offering 245 bhp.

The vee-eight was one more blow to the independents. It was hard enough that makers had to sell more to stay solvent. In 1923, a small firm could manage on sales of 5,000 a year, and, in 1939, sales of 35,000 had been just about viable. After the Second World War the break-even point was around 80,000, though the head of one of 'the big battalions' would reconsider if a middle-class make dropped below 250,000 cars. In 1956, not an outstand-ing season, all the top ten manufacturers accounted for over 100,000 units apiece, and of these only two—Cadillac and the recently constituted Ameri-can Motors—failed to sell 200,000.

The tragedy of the independent manufacturers has been brilliantly told in Richard M. Langworth's *Last Onslaught on Detroit*, the saga of Kaiser–Frazer; and, although Kaiser–Frazer committed a fatal error in trying to enter the industry in 1946, their story is essentially that of Nash, Hudson or Studebaker. General Motors could not be competed with—or Ford, once Young Henry set himself the task of edging General Motors out of first place. Such basic expenses as tooling and advertising were the same, whether the car were a Chevrolet or a Henry-J, but slower production meant a slower return and, of course, slower progress towards amortiza-tion. During their nine-year life, Kaiser had three basic shapes—one fewer than Chevrolet—but they could not afford even this. With (in the early days) only one assembly plant at Willow Run, the young company's shipping costs were higher than those of Chevrolet—cars in a completely knocked-down state could be shipped eleven to a box-car, as against four complete examples. When the vehicles reached their destination, there were fewer dealers to handle them. While the independents were quicker to come to terms with the Unions, they could make hay only while General Motors and Ford haggled. Once agreement was reached, wages were uniform and had to be related to sales. In 1948, their best year, Kaiser–Frazer made 181,316 cars, which put them in eighth place, ahead of Mercury and De Soto. However, this figure is small compared with General Motors' 1,500,000 cars or with Ford's 750,000 cars. By 1955, the independents were in trouble: they had enjoyed 20% of the market in 1929, and just under 10% in 1941, but now they had dropped to 5–6%. General Motors and Ford, by contrast, shared almost 80% of the market.

The smaller firms fought hard. Kaiser offered a four-door convertible, Hudson's Step-Down was the best-handling American car of the era, and Packard's Torsion-Level suspension was nearly as good—if. not so advanced—as Citroën's Hydropneumatics. Raymond Loewy's team gave Studebaker two dramatic breakthroughs in styling—in 1947 and again in 1953. Though Nashes were lacking in aesthetic appeal, the company produced America's first successful modern compact and also a successful unitary-construction convertible. There were free insurance schemes and some frantic cost cutting. Studebaker tried saving 10 cents on door latches, with the result that the doors burst open. Nash transferred their specialist lines to British factories, initially with the Nash–Healey sports car and then with the Austin-built Metropolitan.

Unfortunately, any maker anxious to stay in business had to cover the two lower echelons of the market, which meant competing with Ford and Mercury if not Lincoln. This was not as easy as it sounded, for, though there were gradations of styling to distinguish a Buick from a Pontiac, the lines of demarcation were becoming blurred. The Chevrolet Corvette had neither a working-class image nor a working-class price tag, the Ford Victoria Sun-liner had the Lincoln look (intentionally), and even the staid Plymouth was transformed in 1956 into the Fury, finished in 'eggshell white, with a gold anodized aluminium colour sweep'. It was like marking an invisible centre-forward.

The middle-class sector, above all, was capricious. After 1955, De Soto's outputs fell to five figures and never recovered; even Mercury had some difficulties. The independents' coverage was less than adequate even before Ford's legendary Edsel warned of what might happen. After the mergers, American Motors (Nash–Hudson) still offered no convertible, and Studebaker–Packard produced only the expensive Packard Caribbean. Yet they had to persevere, often with unhappy results: American Motors' Rambler sold 27% more cars in 1956 than in 1955, but their Nash and Hudson lines were an unmitigated flop because of competition from Mercury, Pontiac and Dodge.

The mergers themselves were at best a palliative. The Kaiser–Willys marriage may be dismissed as a deathbed ceremony, but in both the other contemporary cases one make had to be discarded—and probably the wrong one. Packard's cash reserves gave Studebaker an eighteen-month respite, but the termination of Packard's traditional line in the summer of 1956 lost 3,000 workers their jobs. The concentration of Nash and Hudson activities at Kenosha undoubtedly saved money; it also displeased Hudson fans, who now had a choice between a Packard-engined Nash and a Hudson-engined Nash. They wanted neither.

As always in America, the safe way was the known way. The country as a whole did not require small cars and would not require them until the energy crisis of the 1970s. This fact is highlighted by the saga of the General Motors and Ford projects initiated in 1944.

Ford eventually unloaded their subcompact on their French house, where it was produced as the Vedette. Chevrolet were less fortunate. Their projects, under the direction of Earl McPherson, included an interesting little sedan of unitary type, with an all-independent suspension (of McPherson strut type) and an unusual oversquare six-cylinder engine with twin flywheels. Plans were laid for a new Light Car Division based on Cleveland, Ohio, and the Cadet survived its trials with flying colours. However, the cost accountants calculated that, at $1,000 (which was very close to the $1,059 then asked for a full-size Chevrolet), the new car would have to sell 300,000 a year. This in itself was a problem, but in addition the demand for a standard car dictated that any expansion would have to be centred on this. The Cadet was killed.

This should have discouraged other experimenters. After all, if Kaiser's $54,000,000 investment was doomed to failure, there did not appear to be any hope for smaller outfits, who had to raise their funds by preselling franchises. Even if the Securities Exchange Commission did not like these practices, the Playboy and the Keller—if not some of their contemporaries—were viable motor cars.

It was the same sad story of the American Austin (Bantam) in the 1930s. The lower end of the market was where Ford and Chevrolet prices began. Chevrolet could not make the Cadet pay, because it cost nearly as much to make as a regular Stylemaster. The Playboy at $995 offered less for the same money, while by the time the Keller was ready in 1949 the proposed list price of $1,245 was uncomfortably close to a Chevrolet at $1,429. Further, the Chevrolet had a six-cylinder engine, whereas the Keller was only a four, and it was backed by a nationwide service and not just by agencies who had money to invest. Even the Crosley, with sound finances behind it, had disappeared by the summer of 1952; and it had been around since 1939.

American production methods were not completely inflexible. Within their chosen parameters, the factories could make almost anything the public might want. Chrysler persevered with cheap eight-seaters until 1954, while the war scare of 1950–1 produced special 'Civil Defense' editions of regular station wagons, convertible into ambulances. The demise of those strange hearse-makes with Lycoming and Continental engines did not worry the morticians. The 163-inch Cadillac commercial chassis was just as suitable, accounting for 88% of all 'professional car' sales in 1956.

Even in the days before rally packs, four-on-the-floor and low-emission engines with a California-only label, the customer had a wide choice. In 1952, Hudson offered only the 1948 Step-Down shape, but the permutations were interesting—two wheelbases, two tyre sizes, four engines (three sixes and the indestructible straight-eight), three gearboxes (manual, manual-with-overdrive and automatic), six axle ratios (not all available with every combination of engine and transmission), five body styles and twenty-six exterior colours. If interior trim and factory-approved accessories are added, it can be seen that Hudson, who delivered 76,000 cars that season, need never have duplicated a single vehicle.

The American stereotype, of course, remained. In 1946 it was exactly the same as it had been in 1942: a side-valve six of 3½–4 litres' capacity with a three-speed gearbox offering synchromesh on its two upper ratios (Americans seldom used bottom gear). These ratios were selected by a column-mounted lever; this arrangement was tolerable because Detroit never tried four speeds, and thus spared their customers the memorable nastinesses of Hillmans or Peugeots. Mechanical pump feed and 6-volt electrics were general practice: 12-volt systems did not reach America until 1955. A separate chassis was retained, and the brakes were hydraulic: the coil-and-wishbone independent front suspension was usually of the short-and-long arm type, with semiellipties at the rear. Alongside the six was ranged a straight-eight, of capacity from 4.2 to 5½ litres.

There were, of course, exceptions. Buick, Chevrolet and Nash preferred overhead valves, Nash used unitary construction, and Studebaker's front suspension was of transverse-leaf type. Up to 1948, Fords were also transversely sprung, with beam axles at both ends. Other manufacturers favoured live axles and coils at the rear, which were nearly as unpleasing. Cadillac and Ford concentrated on vee-eights, although Ford had adopted a companion six in 1941. Further, General Motors' fully automatic transmission was available on Cadillacs and Oldsmobiles, while some Chrysler cars were produced with semiautomatic transmissions incorporating a fluid coupling.

Unitary construction was really superfluous when a year's run alone accounted for some 300,000 cars, and General Motors utilized one body for a variety of makes and models. Buick, Oldsmobile and Pontiac often had points in common, while similarities between Ford and Mercury were not always appreciated by owners of the latter *marque*. The art of the stylist was important, but his principal task was to alter the detailed execution of next year's body, so that it looked different and could thus postpone retooling. Sometimes retooling was delayed too long: Chrysler's sales fell catastrophically in 1954, the result of interminable juggling with the 1949 shape. Nor was Henry Ford the only High Tory of the boardroom: so, too, was K. T. Keller of Chrysler, and Hudson's A. E. Barit insisted on 'a European type of car you can step into'. Even if such facelifts worked, the chromium-plated 'side-spears' were a headache, working loose and becoming the finest rust traps in the business since the demise of the sidemount.

Automatic transmission was as important as the new vee-eight. Already, by Pearl Harbour, it had won acceptance: from 30% in 1941, the proportion of automatic Cadillacs had doubled by 1942. Though manual transmission was still available as late as 1950, hardly any synchromesh-equipped examples were produced after 1948.

Others followed—Buick and Pontiac in 1948, Lincoln and Packard a year later. Ford's own automatic transmission was not ready, so General Motors' Hydramatic was adopted as an interim expedient: it was also fitted to Hudson, Kaiser–Frazer and Nash, though Studebaker preferred the Borg–Warner system, and Packard made their own. The big breakthrough came in 1950, when Chevrolet launched their two-speed Powerglide, which added only $150 to the retail price of a car. One-fifth of all Chevrolets made in 1951 were automatics, while on more expensive models synchromesh was on its way out: it was fitted to only 20% of Packards, 22% of Buicks and 30 % of Hudsons. By 1954, 57% of the nation's new cars were equipped with the new transmissions, and during 1954 Buick delivered their two millionth Dynaflow unit. By the end of our period it was difficult, if not impossible, to obtain any species of Chrysler, Oldsmobile or Packard with a manual box; Cadillac and Lincoln had long since given up altogether.

Automatic cars took all the discomfort out of driving: properly handled, they neither jerked nor 'hunted'. The disadvantages, however, were inherent power losses (though a reduction of 1 second in the 0–60-mph acceleration time did not matter to the average American), higher fuel consumption, a tendency to change gear more often than the driver wished and towing problems in the event of a breakdown. Early boxes even went 'bad' when the fluid curdled.

The worst snag was, of course, the strain placed on braking systems that were often already less than adequate. This was particularly evident with the cheaper two-speed systems, for low, the only alternative to drive, offered a maximum of about 50 mph. This did not matter when the engine was a 140 bhp six, but it was murderous when the engine was a vee-eight with all the performance options. I rate a tuned 1960 Chevrolet Impala with Powerglide as the most alarming vehicle I have ever driven.

Another vexed question with automatics was the control layout. Five different quadrants were in use in 1955, and the advent a year later of Chrysler's push buttons made it six. Drivers were not always aware of the dangers inherent in the common P–N–D–L–R (park–neutral–drive–low–reverse) layout which had no stop between forward and backward movement. This, of course, would later be prohibited by law.

Having dispensed with gear changing, America turned to power steering, a more questionable asset, since Detroit offered full-time assistance without raising the ratio, thus depriving the driver of all feel. In spite of this the system, first found on Cadillacs and Chryslers in 1951, had reached about 40% of the more expensive models by 1953. Power brakes, of course, were not new, though there was very little that could be done to remedy the low standards of retardation endemic to an overall speed limit (even the horse-power race had standing-start acceleration as its main objective). Further, indifferent brakes were not improved by the narrow wheel arches and wheel spats then in fashion, and fade was a serious factor. True, American brakes had yet to reach their nadir and did not do so until the 14-inch wheel came into fashion in 1957. The 15-inch wheels of the 1955–6 period could still take a 12-inch drum, although even the rapid Ford Thunderbird was content with the 11-inch size. However, few cars of the first post-war decade could cope with more than one crash stop from speeds of about 60 mph.

Nor was this the limit of power assistance. Power hoods on convertibles had been fairly general practice in 1942, Lincolns and Cadillacs could be bought with power-assisted windows by 1946, and Cadillacs also had power seats by 1950. A power-operated boot lid was a 1955 option. Curiously, though, heaters tended to be extras even in 1956, and radios invariably were. Record players were beginning to feature in factory accessory catalogues. So-called compulsory extras remained a nuisance, but, as the list of permutations increased, it was sometimes difficult to decide just what was standard!

Many American innovations were practical. Tubeless tyres were perfected by Goodrich as early as 1948, though manufacturers avoided using them for another eight years on the grounds of the specialized repair facilities they needed. Key starting originated on the 1949 Chryslers: it was a welcome relief from the old 'pedomatic' methods, which were as hazardous as the early automatics, since the industry never decided which pedal to use. Buick preferred the accelerator, and Nash the clutch. A questionable asset was Buick's foot-operated parking brake. Generally believed to be a byproduct of the automatic era, it had in fact been standard equipment since 1942 and was used with the manual as well as with Dynaflow. Oldsmobiles had the same device by 1953.

There were other less justifiable gimmicks. The prime fad of 1953 was the wire-wheel trim ($79.50 a set, to fit over your discs and to eliminate the small amount of brake cooling that existed), although the Continental spare-wheel kit was also a very popular craze. This vertical mounting at the rear was harmless and was offered as a factory extra on Kaisers. The name commemorated the Lincoln Continental Mark I of 1940–8.

Safety was played down, though padded instrument panels and child-proof door latches were in evidence by 1956, and seat belts could be found in accessory catalogues as early as 1953: the Lincoln-engined Muntz Jet had them as standard equipment. Makers avoided overemphasizing safety for fear that this might suggest that cars were crashprone. However, the general use of one-piece curved screens and wrapround rear windows from 1953 onwards, made the American car much safer in traffic: the claustrophobic days of the 1935 'turret-top' were over.

The four-door sedan commanded a good 50% of the market until 1952, with two-door versions trailing it at 20–25%. By 1956, however, the traditional American closed body had a low 34.6%—still in the lead, but only just. The new hardtops were attracting just over 33% of buyers.

In its own way the hardtop was as important as automatic transmission or tubeless tyres. The Americans did not invent it—it was merely the *faux cabriolet* of the 1920s with rear quarter lights. Its fixed roof made it more practical than a convertible, and by finishing the top in a contrasting colour it was possible to break up solid areas of sheet metal. Buick were first in 1949 with their Riviera, and within two years a whole army of Capris, Holidays and Hollywoods had followed. In 1955 Oldsmobile offered a four-door edition, and, by 1956, the rest of the industry was rapidly following.

Convertibles contributed a steady 2–3%. However, the style was still a long way from its peak in the 1960s, and, when Buick sold a record 35,000 ragtops in 1948, the event was still worth a press release. No new styles made their appearance, the standard article being a two-door four-light six-seater. The sporty versions of 1953–4 (the Oldsmobile Fiesta and the Buick Skylark) were taken seriously only by latter-day collectors, though some of them boasted genuine wire wheels. Roadsters were confined to the short-lived Dodge Wayfarer of 1949, but sales of less than 10,000 in three seasons showed that nostalgia as yet attracted no buyers.

By contrast, the station wagon had shaken off its non-U image, as strong in America as in Britain, even if Americans never called it an estate car or associated it directly with the servants' hall. The pre-war woody had been classified as a commercial vehicle. Its full-timbered construction, which extended as far as the front doors and the screen pillars, was not adaptable to assembly-line methods, and wagons were often contracted out to specialist builders such as Cantrell and Mifflinburg. Already in 1940 Ford, 'the nation's wagonmaster', had sold over 13,000 in a year; they were still in the lead in 1955, furnishing 47% of the market's requirements.

With their new social status came a larger demand, and the woodwork receded, first to external strakes and finally altogether, as the latest generation of metal wagons changed to sedan-type front doors—and rear doors also on the 1956 Rambler Cross Country (also available as an extended four-door hardtop). Sales climbed steadily, from 28,757 car-type wagons in 1946 to nearly 300,000 in 1953. This type accounted for 11% of new-car sales in 1956.

Sporty car-type pickups had yet to appear, although Ford's 1957 catalogue did contain one—the elegant Ranchero. The half-timbered cars of the 1946–8 period are perhaps best forgotten. Chrysler's Town and Country sedan and convertible attained quite a wide usage, although they had some competition from Ford and Nash with their Sportsman and Suburban. Manufacturing costs rather than good taste proved their downfall. The Fords were adapted from a stock convertible, each piece of maple trim being shaped from a solid block of wood. A price of about $2,000 was tailored round the Ford badge, and the two did not add up. The all-time low in this cow opera came (literally) when actor Leo Carrillo adorned the bows of his 1948 Chrysler with a stuffed steer's head.

Automobile advertising still consisted mainly of tendentious nonsense. Convertibles and near-convertibles, such as Mercury's glass-topped Sun Valley, received the Edward S. Jordan treatment, 'The sky seems closer, friendlier, when you're cruising easily up a mountain highway in a Sun Valley.' Other banalities relied on the ignorance of the customer, who could easily be persuaded that a commonplace feature either was new or reflected a manufacturer's personal concern for his public. In 1947, General Motors offered an optional-extra radio 'specially designed for the acoustical properties of the Buick body'. A year earlier Plymouth had seriously informed the public that 'the rear-wheel brakes are designed to operate in conjunction with the front', which makes one wonder what Argyll, Henri Perrot and J. M. Rubury had been doing in 1912! Perhaps the depth of ineptitude was Crosley's 1948 reinvention of jewellescent cellulose, in 'light metallic blue–grey ... reminiscent of the wings of the mourning dove'.

No account of Detroit in the first post-war decade would be complete without considering the dream cars. However alarming the 1955 Lincoln Futura, 'a $25,000 laboratory on wheels', might seem with its twin protruding cockpit covers and power assistance for everything, many of these vehicles actually ran—I remember encountering a previous Ford creation motoring through Ewell on trade plates one autumn evening—and were used for serious development work. Much of General Motors' success with high-compression vee-eight engines and high-octane fuels came from the trials of the Buick-built XP300 and Le Sabre of 1950, both featuring 335 bhp supercharged power units and Dynaflow transaxles. Chrysler produced 50 of their 1953 GS family for the *haut monde* of Europe, and Virgil Exner's lovely 1952 K310 coupé and convertible all but made the Corporation's catalogue. Unfortunately, the cost-conscious K. T. Keller discovered that the economic list price would be $20,000, more than twice the sum asked for the specialized Cunningham sports car.

Canada also possessed a sizable industry, which turned out a record 375,028 cars in 1955. In pre-war days Canadian car production had boomed because of the Empire and a great demand for right-hand drive models. Now, of course, the Dominion was in the dollar area, and the Empire was forgotten. Fortunately for Canadian manufacturers, the import duty stayed at a high 17½% until 1955, and, although this did not warrant the assembly of Cadillacs or Lincolns across the border, it made certain that Canadian assembly plants would be reopened after the Second World War. By 1950, Hudson, Nash and Studebaker were all producing cars in Canada. Studebaker's Ontario operation would, indeed, be the last refuge of a once-proud *marque* after 1963.

The few specifically Canadian cars that were available were produced at the behest of the dealers. When Ford made Lincoln–Mercury a separate division, the latter's agents naturally suffered in a poorer country such as Canada. Hence they were offered the Meteor, a Ford with a Mercury grille, while Ford dealers had the Monarch, a slightly up-market edition of their regular wares. The cross-bred Pontiac–Chevrolets of pre-war days were revived in 1955, when Pontiac stopped making a six in America. Chrysler pursued their time-honoured but baffling practice of making Canadian Plymouths under the Dodge name. These local variants were expanded into a complex three-model range from 1953 onwards.

1.2   The Chevy Chase

As Chevrolet goes, so goes America.

America's—and the world's—best-selling automobile followed the national norm for our period: a genuine post-war edition in 1949, hardtops and automatics in 1950, wrapround screens and rear windows, key starting and power steering in 1953, power seats and windows in 1954, vee-eights, 12-volt electrics and tubeless tyres in 1955 and seat belts in 1956. As befitted a cheap car, the driving aids were optional extras.

The 1946 range was the same as that of 1942. The misleadingly titled sport sedan was of orthodox six-light type, but also carried over from before the war, was the four-light Sportmaster (descended from the Cadillac Sixty Special) and the two-door fastback Aerosedan (with roots going back to the Australian General Motors–Holden 'slopers' of 1935–40). Also offered were a two-door sedan, a power-top convertible and a four-door woody. Prices ranged from a little over $1,000 to $1,604.

Under the bonnet, everything dated back to 1937: the faithful six-cylinder overhead-valve Cast Iron Wonder still had only semipressure lubrication, the crankshaft ran in four bearings, the downdraught carburetter was fed by the usual mechanical pump, and the output from 3,548 cc (216.5 cubic inches) was an adequate 90 bhp. The three-speed synchromesh gearbox (the column shift had been standardized in 1940) and hypoid rear axle were copybook, as was the torque tube drive; 11-inch brake drums sufficed, since the 16 inch wheels were fully exposed. The front suspension was of an improved knee action type. With a weight of around 3,200 lb a 1946 Chevrolet could reach 80 mph and would cruise at the maximum legal limit of 70 mph. There were three models—the cut-price Stylemaster, the better-equipped Fleetmaster and the flashy Fleetline—but the same chassis and engine were used for all cars. Only subtle alterations—mainly the removal of the superfluous chromium trim—distinguished the 1947 and 1948 versions.

1949 was generally a year of change; on the GJ and GK Chevrolets this meant spatted rear wheels, the demise of separate wings and a bonus for the crash-repair shops. Windscreens, though curved, retained a central divider, and the wheel diameter was down to 15 inches. The car, however, looked more different than it actually was—this also applied to the 1950 models as well, apart from the introduction of the first really cheap automatic, the two-speed Powerglide exclusive to Chevrolet. 'Set the pilot control lever,' instructed the catalogue, as though discussing a domestic heating appliance, 'Press the accelerator. And that is all there is to it,' which was quite true until one had to stop in a hurry from 60 mph. Nor was *The Motor* entirely fair in regarding the £57 charged for the latest driving aid as 'quite substantial': by the time low-priced automatics reached Britain, the increment was to be nearer £200! Acceleration times were not significantly inferior, for Powerglide-equipped Chevrolets used a more powerful 3.8-litre engine with hydraulic valve lifters. Since this pressure-lubricated 235 unit was already fitted to trucks, it cost the Division no more and helped to sell over 1,000,000 cars in this season, and 456,000 automatics alone in 1951. There was still a choice of trunkback or fastback sedans: the latter, which carried the Fleetline label, sold poorly and were discontinued after 1952.

After two years of minimal change, Chevrolet adopted wrapround screens and rear windows on their 1953 models, though the result was unhappy. 'It looked,' said an unkind American critic, 'as though it had been designed by Herbert Hoover's haberdasher.' The 235 engine was now standard on all cars, automatic editions having aluminium pistons and an extra 7 bhp, while the ancient Cast Iron Wonder still found its way into 'fleet' models of the austere 150 series. This lacked side-trim and cost $1,670 as a four-door sedan, as against $1,761 for the better-equipped 210. The top of the line was the luxurious Bel Air at $1,874. (Range semantics can be confusing—before 1953 this name was exclusive to hardtop coupés. Now it was applied to a whole line.) There was also the Corvette sports car, but, as this carried a price tag that was only $153 lower than that of the cheapest Cadillac, it will be dealt with elsewhere.

Chevrolet increased their cars' horsepower slightly in 1954, but the 1955 version was more dramatic. The frame was reinforced and extended at the front to embrace the bumper mountings, the front track was widened, and recirculating ball steering replaced the worm-and-roller type. A brake servo was optional—though 11-inch drums were still deemed adequate—tubeless tyres were adopted, and there was a new 'dog's leg' screen. Available extras included air conditioning, overdrive and electric wipers, the main range consisted of sixteen models, and prices started at about $1,600. Unusual and attractive was the Nomad, a sporty close-coupled station wagon.

The six was changed very little, but the optional oversquare-dimensioned overhead-valve vee-eight with its wedge-shaped combustion chambers transformed the Chevrolet, dispelling the staid image of recent years. By local standards it was small, with a capacity of 265 cubic inches (4.3 litres). The output was 162 bhp with a manual gearbox, and 170 bhp in automatic form. Various performance options were listed: the 205 bhp Super Turbofire pack with four-barrel carburetter cost only $95. The season's sales jumped to 1,713,478, with tuned versions of the eight accounting for about 65,000 cars. In 1956 Chevrolets were predictably much the same, apart from such extras as Continental spare-wheel kits and sensors for convertibles, which raised the hood at the touch of rain. Compulsory automatics did not as yet feature: all cars were still available with synchromesh boxes and overdrive.

Ford were quicker to reconvert after the war. Thus they outsold Chevrolet by three to one in 1945. However, they fell back to their usual place, 24,000 behind, in 1946. The reason was not hard to find, in the influence of the founder. True, his grandson Henry Ford II had taken over since 1944, but it was one matter to reorganize the River Rouge factories and quite another to create brand-new models from scratch. Further, much time and money were being expended on the subcompact that was to become the French Vedette: as late as September 1944 Henry Ford II was talking of 'a lower-priced car than has been offered the public since the days of my grandfather's Model A'; these researches included an in-line five-cylinder engine which was one of Henry Ford's fancies. Hence the public had to tolerate not only warmed-over 1942 models but also cars very similar to the 1935 Ford.

'Long slow-action springs of new multi-leaf design,' proclaimed the 1946 catalogue, 'smooth the smallest road irregularities, result in a smoother, more level ride,' but nothing could conceal the presence of the old and bouncy transverse arrangements used by Ford since the beginning. A cruciform-braced frame and 12-inch hydraulic brakes represented the most progressive development wrung out of Old Henry, though Ford, unlike Chevrolet, offered a choice of engines. The durable side-valve Ford vee-eight with its twin-pump cooling had grown from 3,622 cc (221 cubic inches) to 3.9 litres (239 cubic inches), and its output of 100 bhp gave it the edge over the opposition. The alternative, introduced in 1941, was a frugal four-bearing in-line six of 3.7 litres' capacity; this model improved on the vee-eight's habitual and daunting 16 mpg. The car's conservative looks were not improved by the ponderous box fenders grafted on for 1942. A standard (or, as Ford described it, De Luxe model) sedan sold for $921 in 1945 and for $1,250 in 1946: in accordance with their usual practice the company offered a Super De Luxe line with a wider choice of bodies, including the ever-popular woody. A two-speed rear axle was an unusual option. This range was carried on into 1948, though Young Henry's determination to introduce a new car led to the Sportsman, an unattractive timbered convertible, with hand-formed panelling over a standard metal body. It cost a lot to produce, and $2,000 Fords were not suitable for 1947. Only 2,487 were sold.

In 1949, however, Harold Youngren's new creations were unveiled—and with them Ford set themselves the goal of beating Chevrolet. Apart from the engines, there were no links with the old days. The 'ploughed-field' suspension was dropped in favour of a coil-spring independent set-up, with semi-elliptics at the rear. Lever-type dampers gave way to the modern tubular version, a ladder-type frame replaced the cruciform type (except on convertibles, which needed the extra bracing) and a hypoid rear axle, used in conjunction with Hotchkiss drive, helped to lower the car. The optional overdrive was now placed behind the gearbox, as on all other American cars. Engines were moved 5 inches further forwards, thus removing rear-seat passengers from uncomfortable proximity to the axle, a well-known Ford weakness. The end product was only 1 inch longer than its 1948 counterpart but was 4 inches lower, 240 lb lighter and 7–8 inches wider inside.

The 'midship' ride was the most important factor in transforming the Ford. Sedan bodies, of the four-light type, were more streamlined than the rival Chevrolets. Even the six could achieve 90 mph, and a year later the company celebrated by adding a coat of arms to the radiator badge! Ford, of course, lagged behind General Motors when it came to automatics: the delay was admittedly a mere eight months, but it was generally noted that the first automatic Lincolns used Cadillac's Hydramatic, *faute de mieux*. Their own Fordomatic was, however, worth waiting for, since it offered three forward speeds to Powerglide's two, even if the permitted maxima on the intermediates were not noticeably higher. With the Fordomatic era came

Ford's contribution to 'missile' styling, the famous twin-spinner grille, which lasted until 1953. The hardtop was also regarded with caution: their 1951 Crestline—like its companions, the Mercury Monterey and the Lincoln Capri—was an ordinary two-door sedan with a vinyl top. The real hardtop was introduced in 1952, and two years later Ford would outdo Chevrolet with the Skyline, incorporating a transparent roof panel. The legendary girl-trapping metal retractable would not be seen until 1957.

Chevrolet were only 217,000 ahead in 1951, and a year later Ford halved the gap, with cars 'styled round the average man', smaller wheels and one-piece curved screens. An extra 10 bhp had been extracted from the Ford vee-eight, but the important news concerned the Mileage Maker six, a short-stroke overhead-valve 3½-litre unit with a useful 101 bhp which made one wonder why an eight was used at all. A power-steering option was added halfway through the 1953 season.

1954 was Ford's year, even if they still failed to catch Chevrolet. On the mechanical side the principal improvements were the McPherson ball-joint independent front suspension already adopted by Lincoln, and two new engines. The six reverted to 3.7 litres (233 cubic inches) with an increase in output to 117 bhp, but at long last Ford had opted for upstairs valves on the vee-eight, which offered 132 bhp from almost the same swept volume. Though the traditional woodies had disappeared, there was still an ornate Country Squire wagon with wood trim, while in the 1955 catalogue was a car which would have made Old Henry wince. The top-of-the-line Fairlanes were ornamental enough, with their 'tiara line', a plated belt moulding incorporating a vee-neck in the middle, but the Crown Victoria outshone any Chevrolet, thanks to 'a crown of chrome sweeping down from roof to belt line at center-pillar level'. A 'dog's leg' screen and tubeless tyres were predictable changes, though Ford retained 6-volt electrics until the following season. Further, their stock vee-eights were more powerful than those of Chevrolet—a year's seniority meant 182 bhp from 4½ litres (272 cubic inches) on the costliest Fairlanes. More powerful units were reserved for the brand-new Thunderbird 'personal car'. The Mainlines were innocent of any ornamentation, came only with the six or the low-compression 272-cubic-inch eight and included a cut-price two-door Ranch Wagon.

Power was increased for 1956—as much as 200 bhp from vee-eights and 137 bhp from sixes. 1955's Thunderbird-only power unit, the 4.8-litre 292, became generally available, bodies were 1 inch lower, and Ford laid more stress on safety features than did General Motors, with deeply dished steering wheels, padded mirrors, reinforced seat mountings and a seat-belt option. The gap between the two great rivals closed to almost zero in 1957, though Ford would not take the lead again until 1959.

Traditionally the 'Old lady's' car, Chrysler's inexpensive Plymouth did not alter its image in the first nine years of peace, because of an unswerving faith in the value of engineering and because of K. T. Keller's mistrust of stylists. Right up to 1954, the Plymouth remained a four-bearing flathead six, though at least it had full-pressure lubrication. The basic 215-cubic-inch (3.6-litre) version saw the breed through to mid-1954 on an output of around 95 bhp, and even then the extra 200 cc and 15 bhp still put it well behind Chevrolet and Ford. All these circumstances explain why Plymouth slipped from their accustomed third place in sales to fifth, behind Buick and Oldsmobile. In any case, the *marque* had always been a bad third. In 1949, 574,734 Plymouths were built, as against 841,000 Fords and well over 1,000,000 Chevrolets.

Like all Chrysler products, the Plymouth was solidly engineered: the power units had a magnificent war record under the stubby bonnets of Dodge's all-wheel-drive trucks. Their hydraulic brakes, among the industry's first, had the reputation of being less fadeprone than most. But, even when the car was redesigned for the 1949 season, the boxy four-light style lacked the flair of its rivals. It did not look much better with 1953's single panel screen, and the disastrous 1954 models were different but nothing else. The car's mandatory improvement record was patchy: self-parking electric wipers were standard as early as 1951, though neither power steering nor an automatic transmission made their appearance until halfway through 1954.

As offered in 1946, the Plymouth represented Chrysler's version of the American stereotype: 2LS hydraulic brakes, a coil-spring independent front suspension, semielliptics at the rear and a hypoid back axle. In the best Chrysler tradition, however, there was a transmission handbrake, an anachronism to which only Fiat clung more tenaciously. On paper, the Plymouth's output placed it midway between Chevrolet and Ford. The wheelbase was 117½ inches, and an unusual gimmick, also found on other Chrysler cars, was the Safety Signal speedometer, with coloured sectors for different speed zones. There were two lines differing only in equipment, and bodies were the usual ones, apart from a 1936-style three-window business coupé common to all Chrysler makes until 1948 and retained by Plymouth for four seasons thereafter. Though the dollar shortage kept Plymouths—with or without Chrysler badges—off the British market for the time being, the old confusion of *marques* could still be obtained elsewhere. Chrysler Canada offered the Dodge Kingsway, a de luxe Plymouth with Dodge badges. This and a De Soto variant, the Diplomat, were also sold abroad, such crossbreeds being current as late as 1959.

1949 Plymouths were completely restyled and given key starting and automatic chokes, but basically there was little change, apart from an austerity version on a 111-inch wheelbase, the P17, made only with two-door coachwork. Sedans, like Chevrolet's Fleetline, were of fastback type, and the range also included America's first all-metal station wagon. A brief flutter was caused in 1950 by the XX500 show car, an attractive slab-sided six-light sedan from Pininfarina, unrelated to the factory-sponsored Exner creations. It would inspire the Lancia Flaminia, and its influences were detectable in Plymouth's own Valiant of 1960, but for the time being nobody at Chrysler took the hint. All that happened in 1951 and 1952 was the introduction of type names. The short-chassis P22 became the Concord, and the longer P23s the Cranbrook and the Cambridge. Also on the options list was overdrive—behind Ford but ahead of Chevrolet. A single 114-inch chassis was specified for 1953, and cars were offered with Hy-Drive, billed as an automatic but in fact the usual four-speed box with fluid coupling which had been used on more expensive Chrysler cars since 1939.

Plymouth's fortunes reached their nadir in 1954, with less than 400,000 cars sold; none of its companion makes managed to produce 280,000, and the unhappy De Soto was down to a mere 70,000. Some frantic midseason efforts produced a larger engine, a real automatic transmission and a power-steering option, though the stylist Virgil Exner summed up the situation when he informed Keller, 'You need a whole new skin on it.' An interesting side-issue marketed by Chrysler of Antwerp was a Plaza sedan with overdrive box in conjunction with a 3.1-litre four-cylinder Perkins diesel engine. This attained 71 mph on the 2.87:1 high top and had a fuel consumption of 36 mpg. Sales were quite brisk; the conversion was still available in 1956.

In 1955 the result of Exner's structures, the Flight Sweep line, was applied to the entire Chrysler range. In terms of dimensions, the new idiom meant an increase in wheelbase of 1 inch, an increase in overall length of 10 inches and an increase in front track of 3 inches: the roof line was 1 inch lower. The chassis was much as before, and the old six soldiered on. But Plymouth, like Chevrolet, had acquired a new vee-eight. This Hy-Fire was a simpler engine than the hemis used in senior models, with polyspherical combustion chambers, and was available in 4-litre and 4.3-litre sizes, with outputs in the 157–177 bhp bracket. Convertibles were now available only with eight-cylinder engines, and prices ($1,490–2,152) were average for this class of car. The new eights were capable of 100 mph, while once again wider wheel arches minimized brake fade.

Four-door hardtops and safety were the principal events of 1956, though another innovation was the Chrysler push-button Powerflite, with the ratios of the automatic gearbox selected by a row of buttons on the dash: hitherto Chrysler had preferred an orthodox lever, albeit facia mounted. The most powerful eight had a capacity of 4½ litres (277 cubic inches) and 200 bhp.

Also new was Plymouth's contender in the sport-car market. Unlike the Thunderbird and the Corvette, it used neither a special chassis nor a special body. The Fury was essentially the regular Belvedere hardtop.

It had, however, been doctored. The engine, still a 'poly', was a tuned edition of the 303-cubic-inch (5-litre) unit fitted to Canadian Dodges, with quadrajet carburation, a fiercer camshaft profile and 240 bhp. The clutch, gearbox, dampers and suspension were all of heavy-duty type, the springs were lowered, and police-type brake linings were specified. A wider track gave better road holding, seat belts were part of the package, and all the usual power options were available. All Furys came in white and gold, with a white trim, while the price, at $2,600, was $500 higher than that of the regular hardtop. It managed a two-way mile at 124.01 mph but should not be confused with later Furys; the name would be applied to untuned prestige models from 1959 onwards.

Of other bargain basement contenders, only Nash made a serious impression, with their pioneer compact, the Rambler, created by N. E. Wahlberg and Ted Ulrich in 1950. It sold a steady 50,000 a year in its early days, working up to 84,000 in 1955: later editions of the 'baby bathtub' would edge Plymouth out of their hard-fought third place in 1960 and 1961. Its popularity also persuaded American Motors to discard the respected Nash and Hudson names after 1957, in favour of a Rambler label. There was a precedent: Nash's precursors, the Thomas B. Jeffery Company, had sold bicycles under the Rambler name in the nineteenth century, perpetuating it on the cars they built between 1901 and 1913.

In the early post-war period, however, Nash's economy car was the 600, a 1941 débutante noted for a welded-up unitary construction and non-independent coil rear springing. The engine, unlike that of larger Nashes, was a four-bearing side valve six with a capacity of only 2.8 litres, developing 82 bhp. Wheelbase was a compact 112 inches, and the car could be bought with Nash's much-publicized 'air conditioning'—this was nothing of the sort, being a controlled heating and ventilating system with twin electric fans. The styling was unspectacular, but the fuel consumption was 25–28 mpg, and prices started at a reasonable $1,298 in 1946. It helped the company to sell over 113,000 units in 1947 and continued unchanged into 1948.

In 1949 the all-new Airflyte, an unattractive tub-like fastback with unrelieved slab sides and no hint of a fender, was introduced. All four wheels were spatted, which made punctures an interesting exercise. Compensations were a wide single-panel curved screen and bench seats 5 feet wide: with Nash's optional bed-seats, the Airflyte became a veritable honeymoon express. A mattress and plastic window screens were listed extras.

Avant-garde thinking had to be paid for in other ways. The presence of inboard rear dampers ensured that the springs would have to be removed when the dampers were serviced, while the crowning nightmare was the Uniscope, a binnacle on the steering wheel which housed the instruments. The electrical spaghetti extending down a column 4 inches in diameter may be imagined. Curiously, the shrouded 2LS front brakes in their 9-inch drums worked quite well, though the spats played havoc with the steering lock, and the car understeered alarmingly. It also suffered from rust, while the inflexibility of unitary construction limited the body styles to a four-door sedan, a two-door sedan and a brougham which was simply the latter with inward-facing rear seats. Overdrive, long available on larger Nashes, was now available on the 600 as well. The car was rather expensive at $1,811, though it continued into 1950 as the Statesman with a 3-litre engine. It had acquired a Hydramatic option (Nash could not afford their own automatic transmission) by 1951.

The Rambler of 1950 was essentially the same car but scaled down to compact proportions, with a wheelbase of 100 inches and a length of only 176 inches. The 2.8-litre engine was retained, though the semielliptic rear springs were a vast improvement on the Statesman's coils. More important, Ulrich had achieved a robust unitary ragtop by making the car a cabrio – limousine à l'Allemande with reinforced side-rails. A simple box-type front-end assembly kept the weight down to 2,430 lb. No attempt was made to compete with Ford or Chevrolet, the Nash being offered as a luxury package at $1,808, complete with 'air conditioning', power top, clock, cigar lighter and even a radio. Sales of 57,555 cars in 1951 showed that the company was on the right tack. True, Kaiser–Frazer turned out 81,000 of their rival Henry-J sedans, but many of these failed to find buyers and had to be retitled as 1952 models.

The Rambler range was extended to embrace a hardtop, a station wagon and even a delivery van, while for 1952 the mainstream Nashes—which included the Statesman—were given a facelift by Pininfarina. Though even he could not make a beauty of the bathtub car, it certainly looked far more acceptable with its notchback bodies, deeper screens, open front-wheel arches, thinner pillars and oval grilles. On these cars the addition of a Continental spare-wheel kit actually helped! A year later the Rambler had also received the Italian treatment, together with a Hydramatic option and a more powerful 3.2-litre engine.

Unfortunately, although the 100-inch cars were continued into 1954 and 1955, in 1954 the 108-inch Cross Country series with four-door coachwork was introduced. After the Nash–Hudson merger of 1954, some Ramblers were sold with Hudson badges—these were invariably used in Britain, where Hudsons had always outsold Nashes. All 1955 cars had larger front-wheel cutouts, 3.2-litre engines and bigger brake drums: the convertible, alas, had been dropped. A speed of 85 mph was possible, and an overdrive-equipped example tested by The Motor could better 30 mpg on long runs. By this time, of course, the Statesman had been promoted to the middle-class bracket.

American Motors celebrated the completion of their two millionth unitary car in 1956 by dropping the original compact Rambler, only to reinstate it two years later. The latest Typhoon engines featured new top ends with overhead valves and wedge-shaped combustion chambers. Though capacity was unchanged, 12-volt electrics and torque tube drive were adopted, there was a reversion to coils at the rear, and the structure was redesigned: the reinforced rear body pillar was cunningly made into a styling feature. All the luxury options such as power steering were available, as was a unique four-door hardtop station wagon.

Unlike Ford and Chevrolet, Nash were not afraid of subcompacts. Further, they did their thinking aloud, exhibiting a two-seater convertible in the Airflyte idiom during 1950. The merger of grille and front bumper was just as infelicitous as Buick's contemporary effort, but the new NXI was a true miniature on an 84-inch wheelbase, weighing only 1,350 lb. The presence of a Fiat 500 engine—the Fiat *millecento* and even the Triumph Mayflower engines were mentioned as possible alternatives—led to some interesting speculation. After a 'surview' which involved interviews with 250,000 visitors, Nash retired to rethink the idea. The result was on sale four years later, at a base price of $1,445.

However, it was not made in Kenosha; it was contracted out to Austin of England, Fisher and Ludlow building the unitary hulls.

The vehicle was, however, authentic Nash. The slab-sided two-seater hardtops and convertibles were Pininfarina type out of Airflyte with two-tone paintwork. Mechanics were Austin but modified to American ideas— cam-and-roller steering and a three-speed box improvized by blanking off the lowest ratio of a standard Austin four-speeder. The engine was Austin's 1,200 cc overhead-valve A40 four, developing 42 bhp. As in the original Rambler, the equipment was comprehensive—radio, heater and twin horns—and the compact dimensions (the Metropolitan, at 149½ inches, was 1 foot shorter than an A40 Sedan) were matched by a modest weight of 1,848 lb. Despite widely spaced gear ratios—4.625:1, 7.1:1 and 11.27:1— the car was a brisk performer, though the handling was non-existent. Not that this mattered on "milady's perfect companion for shopping trips". Metropolitans tended to indicate the proximity of an American air base in Britain. The initial order was for 20,000 cars, but subsequent batches had brought the total up to an impressive 97,000 by 1961, when the model was finally discontinued. From late 1955 the Metropolitan used the 1,489 cc BMC B-type power unit; it proved surprisingly popular when released in Britain in 1957.

Kaiser–Frazer explored the cheap-car market from a different angle, with dreams of a working man's car at $1,195, a price they never quite achieved. *The Motor* might deprecate the peculiar styling, 'The shark-like receding chin bonnet is by Studebaker out of Willys, and the rear wings are Cadillac and soda', but they hit the nail on the head when they summarized the Henry-J as 'a jalopy de luxe'.

Its size apart, the Henry-J, first seen in 1950, represented the American norm. The chassis with its five cross-members shared the Rambler's 100-inch wheelbase. Once again a hypoid axle and open propeller shaft were used, and Kaiser–Frazer, like Nash, offered overdrive as a regular option. Brake drum diameter was more generous than the Rambler's, but Kaiser, who could only afford one engine at a time, bought their smaller ones from Willys: the 2.2-litre side-valve four of Jeep fame, and its companion 2.6-litre six, which disposed of 80 bhp. Even after Howard Darrin's improvements, the two-door fastback sedan with its Cadillac-type tail fins was excessively ugly, and the handling was indifferent. The exposed front wheels gave the Henry-J a better turning circle than that of the Rambler, at 34 feet, and the straight-line performance was comparable: over 70 mph in four-cylinder form and 80 mph with the six, which also returned an even 24 mpg with the optional overdrive. The base price was a mere £8 above the company's original target.

Henry-J production amounted to almost 120,000 units, but they took a long time to sell. Most variants were attempts to disguise last year's models: this went for the 1952 Vagabond with the Continental spare-wheel kit. Apart from an external-access boot adopted early in the model's run, little else was done to it, and the worst the Henry-J did was to absorb money that might have been better expended on a vee-eight programme. A curious side-issue of 1952–3 was the Allstate. Despite its name it was in fact marketed only in Alabama, Arizona, Arkansas, Florida, Mississippi, North Carolina, Tennessee, Texas, Utah and Virginia, but its sale was exclusive to the Sears Roebuck store chain. The tyres, batteries and sparking plugs were Sears's own make, and the grilles were different, but this delectably American idea misfired, and only 2,363 Allstates found buyers. By 1954 Henry-J production was down to barely 1,000 units, and in any case the merger with Willys had given Kaiser a better compact.

After surviving 1933's receivership, Willys had pursued a modest existence until 1941, concentrating on austere little sedans with four-cylinder side-valve engines. What changed all this was, of course, the Jeep. Not that Willys designed it or were even the sole producers, the vast wartime contracts being shared with Ford. But the standard power unit was the 2.2-litre Willys, and it was Willys rather than Ford who elected to continue manufacture after the war. By the end of 1945, civilian Jeeps were on the market, soon followed by a two-wheel drive station wagon on a longer wheelbase with a Studebaker-type transverse-leaf independent front suspension. Next on the agenda, in 1948, was an amusing little sports four-seater, the Jeepster, with a 72 bhp overhead-inlet valve edition of the Willys Four engine, though their 2.6-litre six could be bought in wagons and Jeepsters alike. The Jeepster was somewhat ahead of its time and sold a mere 11,000 units in its three-year run, but the other Jeep models, including the wagons, survived all the vicissitudes of the Kaiser–Willys merger. Later station wagons featured beam front axles and a 4 × 4 option.

Jeep sales were good—over 38,000 in 1950—which may explain why Willys delayed a return to the private-car field. In 1946, the details were released of a two-door sedan on a compact 104-inch wheelbase, styled by Brooks Stevens and Alexis de Sakhnoffski. The engine was the new side-valve six, but the Jeep wagon's independent front suspension was matched to independent rear springing of divided-axle type. Deliveries, promised in 1948, never materialized.

The car that emerged at the 1952 Brussels Salon was more orthodox, though it had landed Willys with a tooling bill for $55,000,000. The designer was Clyde Paton from Ford's old subcompact team, and the new car featured full unitary construction.

This was the only heresy. The rest was the American norm: a three-speed gearbox with column shift, an open propeller shaft, a hypoid rear axle, 9-inch hydraulic drum brakes and a coil-and-wishbone independent front suspension. With a 108-inch wheelbase and a length of 181 inches, the Aero Willys was a larger car than either the Rambler or the Henry-J: at about 2,600 lb, it was also heavier. The engines were, of course, Willys' own in both the L- and the F-head configurations, though fours were seldom seen, being confined to the cheapest Aero Larks and were fitted to a mere 130 of these. By 1953, quite a diversity of models was available, the most expensive Aero Ace sedans and Aero Eagle hardtops using the 90 bhp F-head six and identifiable by their single-panel screens. At a basic price of $1,731 the Willys was a little overpriced, though sales were promising—31,000 in 1952 and over 40,000 in 1953.

With Kaiser, of course, came Kaiser's dead stock, including a sizable supply of 226-cubic-inch (3.7-litre) flathead six-cylinder engines and matching Hydramatic transmissions, and these found their way into the costlier 1954 Willys models. The *marque* struggled on into 1955, now exclusively Kaiser-powered, while 'shark's tooth' grilles replaced the W motif of pre-Kaiser days. The 5,869 cars delivered that year were the last of the American Willys line (Jeeps apart), but this was not the end of the Aero. In 1960 it cropped up in Sâo Paulo, Brazil, where it was destined for a thirteen-year run. Ironically, a fusion of local Ford and Willys interests caused the last Itamaraty sedans—and subsequent Jeeps—to display Ford badges.

Hudson were no strangers to the lower echelons of the American market. Their cut-price Essex had won them a third place in 1929's sales, though since 1940 they had been concentrating on the middle-class sector. The Jet of 1953 marked a belated return to old haunts.

The welded-up unitary construction which had proved so successful on the Step-Down series was retained. The little car might even have repeated this success, if the Hudson board had not decided that they wanted to step into a car rather than *down* into it, insisting on a boxier shape. This was inspired by the Fiat 1400, and looked it.

The engine was a typical Hudson design, a 3.3-litre long-stroke side-valve type with the latest full-pressure lubrication. Another latter-day deviation for this company was the dry-plate clutch, though the coil-and-wishbone front suspension derived directly from the larger cars. The front brakes were of the 2LS type, and there were three transmission options—straight manual, overdrive and Hydramatic. Further, Hudson were already in the power-pack business, and not content with a choice of cast iron or alloy heads, they offered the alloy head type with twin carburetters. Hence the output of the Jet's engine was in the 104–114 bhp bracket, and the maximum speed ranged from the low 80s to well over 90 mph. The wheelbase was 105 inches, and the overall length an average 181 inches. *The Autocar* correctly described the Hudson as 'a car of European character', but this was not what the customers wanted, and the Jet staggered through into August 1954 without making any impression. The new Nash-oriented management, understandably, wanted no part of it, though the engine reappeared in the Nash-shaped hulls of cheaper 1955 models.

By 1942 Studebaker had retrieved their past cheap-car disasters with the Champion, a modest 2.8-litre side-valve six launched three years earlier. This reappeared in 1945 as the 5G-series. Only the Roos-designed transverse-leaf independent front suspension distinguished it from the opposition. The engine developed an adequate 80 bhp, the wheelbase was 110 inches, and the optional extras included Studebaker's well-known Hill Holder, an updated version of the Victorian sprag.

The 5G was, however, destined for a short run of only 20,000 units. In the summer of 1946, Raymond Loewy, Studebaker's consultant stylist, introduced the famous 'coming-or-going' shape. Though the Champion continued, its design would henceforth be integrated with the middle-class Commander line.

1.3   Tubeless Tyres and Lost Causes

In 1946, one paid from $1,450 to $2,300 for a middle-class automobile. One also had a far wider choice than in any other sector of the market. Of the major makers, only Willys abstained: General Motors and Chrysler offered three *marques* apiece. Sales were always capricious: falling demand had wiped out the small assemblers in the early 1920s, and the large assemblers a few years later. De Soto, Hudson, Kaiser, Nash and the yet-unborn Edsel would soon be added to this list.

The General Motors Pontiac was a steady seller which set no rivers on fire. Even in 1956, the hairy world of wide tracks and GTOs lay light years ahead, and a good 80% of traditional Pontiac customers would have deserted them, if they had known what was in the future. The reward for conformity was a gentle fluctuation between fifth and sixth places in the production stakes: the price was a conservatism which kept the Division wedded to straight-eights until 1954, not to mention a lack of identity barely balanced by the plated silver streaks on the bonnet tops. Pontiac themselves must have thought so, for a second streak made its appearance in 1953. Nobody needed to worry: they were fifth again that year, with a cool 414,011 units.

The *marque* lay only one rung up the ladder from Chevrolet, hence Pontiacs used essentially the same chassis, though with longer wheelbases—119 and 122 inches in 1946. From 1949, the bodies were also common to the two breeds. As befitted a conservative house, Pontiac used side valves right up to 1954. Their immediate post-war offerings were a four-bearing six of 239 cubic inches (3.9 litres) and a five-bearing eight (249 cubic inches or 4.1 litres), uncomfortably close to its lesser sister in output and performance alike: even the price differential was a mere $30, and the same body styles sufficed for both. In one respect alone was the Pontiac Eight ahead of its time: the cylinder dimensions were nearly square, at 82.55 mm × 95.2 mm. Pontiac prices started at a low $1,427, and the 1942 themes were continued until 1948, when the Hydramatic became an option.

Subsequent developments (apart from 1952's Dual Range Hydramatic) paralleled Chevrolet at every turn—hardtops in 1950 and wrapround screens in 1953, in which year the six was uprated to 118 bhp. The eight received the same treatment in 1954, revised valves and manifolding boosting power to 127 bhp. A new Star Chief series on a longer 124-inch wheelbase was an attempt to give Pontiac some kind of *cachet*: this model was offered only with the eight-cylinder engine. The Hydramatic was standard, though not compulsory.

Unlike Chevrolet, however, Pontiac scrapped its entire engine programme in 1955, in favour of a 287-cubic-inch (4,706 cc) overhead-valve vee-eight, giving 180 bhp. The wheelbase options were 122 and 124 inches, and the cheaper Chieftain range even duplicated Chevrolet's sporty Nomad station wagon, only with a Safari label. Canadian customers were given the Pontiac six they demanded by the simple expedient of putting the right grille (including the silver streaks) on a Bel Air Chevrolet. The 1956 cars were little changed apart from the mandatory four-door hardtop and a new 5.2-litre engine with a choice of outputs up to 227 bhp.

Oldsmobile's history went back to the nineteenth century, with a personality to suit. The Division had long been used as a forcing house for new ideas—1938's unsuccessful semiautomatic gearbox and 1940's true Hydramatic, several months ahead of Cadillac. Gilbert Burrell's short-stroke vee-eight, new for 1949, would give Oldsmobile the edge on Pontiac. In

1956 they sold nearly 433,000 units as against Pontiac's 332,268.

In 1946, Oldsmobile had little of moment to offer except the Hydramatic. Mechanics were close to Pontiac's, with the same choice of six or eight. The actual engines were not, however, identical; the six-cylinder Oldsmobile, at 238 cubic inches, was fractionally smaller, but more powerful, at 100 hp, while the straight-eight (4,212 cc and 110 bhp) was superior on both grounds. The frame, transmission and brakes followed Chevrolet or Pontiac practice, but Oldsmobile favoured a Buick-type rear suspension, with a live axle and coils. Prices started a mere $50 above those of Pontiac, the cheapest 66 (a companion 68 did not appear until 1947) using Chevrolet-type bodies. Dynamic Cruisers came with either engine and had a hint of Buick Special, while the hefty 98, or Custom Cruiser, on a 127-inch wheelbase, looked as large as a Cadillac and was in fact bigger than some. The Hydramatic was standard equipment on this car, and a year later some 90% of Oldsmobile's customers preferred automatics. A manual Oldsmobile was seldom seen: even when the Hydramatic plant at Livonia burnt down in 1953, the gaps were filled with Dynaflows and Powerglides rather than with synchromesh.

For 1948, the top-of-the-line Futuramic gave Americans a sneak preview of 1949's styling, with curved screens and notchbacks. Not much was done to the mechanics, though dual-choke carburation had squeezed another 5 bhp from the ageing straight-eight, and at 18 feet overall the 98 was the largest Oldsmobile since the legendary Limited of 1911 with its 43-inch wheels. Power seats and windows were already available.

The full treatment came in 1949, when all Oldsmobiles went Futuramic. Though the six was still listed in an enlarged 4.2-litre form, the straight-eight had disappeared in favour of General Motors' first cheap overhead-valve vee-eight, the Rocket. By later standards this had a modest capacity of 303 cubic inches (5 litres), and the output was likewise a conservative 135 bhp. The result was a genuine 100 mph, and wisely the Division reverted to semiellipitics at the rear on 1951's models. Oldsmobile's progressive role was maintained: wrapround screens and rear windows in 1950, the last year of the sixes, power steering during 1952 and 12-volt electrics in 1953. A quadrajet carburetter option boosted output to 165 bhp, and there was a short-lived sporty ragtop, the Fiesta, which offered all the power assistance, plus a fancy plunging belt-line, for an inclusive $5,717. Oldsmobile were a year ahead of Pontiac with 'dog's leg' screens in 1954, though more important were the new wide wheel arches. Engines now disposed of 324 cubic inches (5.3 litres) and 185 bhp, increased to over 200 bhp in 1955. The 1956 versions of the Hydramatic transmission had a 'park' position on their selectors, and the range structure had stabilized. 88s used the 122-inch wheelbase, 98s were 4 inches longer, and the same engine was common to all Oldsmobiles, though the lesser species featured dual-choke carburation and a modest 230 bhp.

Buick, 'the Doctor's Friend', was an established favourite. Always an overhead-valve it had been a straight-eight since 1931, and the image exuded respectability. The sole deviation had been 1936's Century, a classic example of the big engine–small chassis formula. With such a background, it was to be expected that not only an automatic but a Dynaflow system exclusive to the breed would be listed as early as 1948. By 1950 Dynaflow would be compulsory on the big Roadmaster. Power-steered Buicks were first seen in 1952, but within a year this too would become universal at the top of the range.

If Ford was 'the nation's wagonmaster', then Buick was the convertible specialist *par excellence*. Thus it was logical that they should pioneer the hardtop coupé in 1949: their four-door sedan edition, introduced a year later, was less felicitous and not nearly as influential as Oldsmobile's 1955 reinvention of the style. By contrast, 1949's bonnet portholes (retained in later years at the request of Buick dealers) were not original, dating back to the 1934 La Salle, while the less said of 1950's bumper–grille merger the better. Customers obviously disliked it, and on the 1951 models the 'buffalo's tusks' were given a 'frame'. Buick went 'dog's leg' in 1954: they had to, since they shared bodies with Oldsmobile.

They also shared their cruciform-braced chassis and all-coil suspension in 1946, though as yet a foot-operated parking brake with manual release was peculiar to Buick: this meant four pedals on manual-gearbox cars! 12-inch brake drums took care of the considerable weight—even the cheapest two-door Special was 3,670 lb—and all Buicks were bulky as well. The Special on a 121-inch wheelbase was 208 inches long. Styling of Specials was Pontiac-Oldsmobile: that of the Supers and Roadmasters aped the Oldsmobile 98 and the Cadillac. Prices started at $1,522, though the sumptuous Roadmaster convertible was over $2,300. Unlike Cadillac, Buick offered a woody, albeit only in the Super range.

Engines were the familiar overhead-valve five-bearing straight-eights, capacities being 4,064 cc for Specials and Supers and 5,247 cc (with an output of 144 bhp) for Roadmasters; the pre-war twin-carburetter option was no longer listed. The best-selling model was the Super, accounting for well over 50% of the 277,000 cars produced in 1947. The Special was a little too close to the Oldsmobile 78 to have much appeal.

Two-speed Dynaflow made its début on 1948 Roadmasters: like Chevrolet, Buick provided hydraulic valve lifters and more brake horsepower on engines intended for use with the new transmission. By 1950 all Buicks could be had with automatic transmission, and the system was steadily improved, the two-stage 1953 version eliminating much of the 'churning and slipping' hitherto inherent at takeoff. By the end of our period manual gearboxes were confined to the cut-price Specials.

A new cheap Buick was the fastback Special sedan of 1950, selling at just under the \$2,000 mark. In the same year the Super was given a larger 4.3-litre engine, the Special following suit a year later. The real landmark was, however, the Division's first vee-eight with 12-volt electrics, a 1953 innovation. As yet the Special remained a straight-eight, while a single 322-cubic-inch (5.3-litre) unit sufficed for the larger cars: the output in optional quadrajet form was 188 bhp, adequate for speeds of over 100 mph.

There was also a sporty convertible, though Buick's Skylark was less stock than some of its contemporaries, with cutaway body sides, plated wire wheels, power assistance extending even to the radio aerial, and full-width wheel arches. It was no bargain at \$5,000, though 1,690 were sold. From this it was a logical step to 1954's revival of the Century theme, with a short chassis and large engine. A smaller 4.3-litre vee-eight, rated at 143 bhp, had finally supplanted the straight-eights at the bottom of the range.

Four-barrel carburation was standardized on 1955 Buicks, giving as much as 236 bhp on Roadmasters. Almost any 1956 car could reach 110–115 mph, and the power steering was higher geared as a compensation. The 322 was now the staple engine, while emphasis had shifted to the cheaper cars; these accounted for four-fifths of the 572,000 Buicks sold that year. The *marque* sat happily in third place overall, with a 9.1% share of the domestic market.

Labelled by Tom McCahill as 'the car Ford would have been if there was no price competition', the Mercury was still too much like a Ford vee-eight for anyone's comfort. Apart from some heavier chromium plate and an extra 2 inches of wheelbase, there was nothing to justify the additional \$300 the customers—about 71,000 of them in that first year of peace—had to pay. On 3.9 litres and 100 bhp it was, however, a respectable performer and went through three seasons with minimal alteration.

Like the Pontiac, the Mercury lacked a cachet, and from the 1949 models onwards its makers tried to make it a cheap Lincoln rather than an uprated Ford, though this was more by accident than by design. E. T. Gregorie's proposed 1949 Ford had turned out too heavy, so it was upgraded to a Mercury. The 'real' Mercury emerged as a Lincoln!

The engineering, of course, was new-generation Ford—coil-spring independent front suspension, Hotchkiss drive, a hypoid rear axle and the Lincoln's cruciform-braced frame. The vee-eight engine was bigger than the Ford's, at 4.2 litres, and disposed of 110 bhp, while the wheelbase was 4 inches longer. The bodies were more aerodynamic, with rear-wheel spats and different grilles. A speed of 100 mph was possible.

Development paralleled that of the Ford models, with automatic from 1951, power brakes and steering in 1953 and ball-joint independent front suspension in 1954, when overhead-valve engines made their appearance. The Mercury version had a quadrajet carburetter and gave 163 bhp from 4.2 litres, which made it a faster car than the Pontiac, though it could not match the speed of Chrysler's hemis. Ford's 292 Thunderbird unit went into the 1955 line, while with the 'Big Ms' of 1956 a serious attempt was made to give the Mercury an identity. The engines were once again of Thunderbird type (5.1 litres and up to 260 bhp), the options included overdrive and one-shot chassis lubrication, and four-door hardtops were called phaetons, just to be different. Some unattractive Z-shaped side-trim was also introduced on the more expensive models: at the other end of the scale was the austere unadorned Medalist with a detuned 210-bhp engine. Nonetheless, the year's sales still hovered below the quarter million mark.

Cheapest of Chrysler's middle-class contenders was the Dodge, a solid car with a devoted following. It had all the Pontiac's commonsense virtues, only General Motors cared about styling and Chrysler did not. Hence Dodge's sales, running at around 300,000 in 1949, slumped to half this figure in 1954, despite the presence of a modern vee-eight which the Pontiac still lacked.

The 1946 Dodge was a larger more expensive edition of the contemporary Plymouth; the side-valve 230 six had a capacity of 3.8 litres, giving 102 bhp, and the wheelbase was 119½ inches. Dodges, however, could be bought with a four-speed Fluidrive transmission as well as with synchromesh. Also inevitable were the Canadian and *Anversois* Kingsways, alias the Plymouth, while the most expensive models built in Canada had a 228-cubic-inch power unit that was neither Plymouth nor yet quite Dodge! Dodge type!

'Lower outside: higher inside. Shorter outside: longer inside,' proclaimed Dodge's 1949 publicity, but the result was still the same uninspired formula. Dodge, like Plymouth, tried to widen the *marque's* appeal with cheaper short-chassis models, but the idea misfired, though an intriguing variant was the Wayfarer, a genuine two–three-seater roadster in genuine 1930's idiom. Early ones even ran to curtains, but these were too much for Americans and disappeared. So, after 1951, did the Wayfarer. The long-chassis eight-seaters were equally unsuccessful, though Dodge fared better with their hardtops. They confused the issue, however, by calling these Diplomats, just like De Soto's crypto-Plymouths for the export market!

The vee-eight of 1953 was something quite different, being a scaled-down edition of the magnificent hemi with a capacity of 241 cubic inches (3,856 cc). Its 140 bhp was a dramatic improvement on the staid 103 bhp of the six, and only the expensive Coronets could be had with eight-cylinder engines. As for the good old 230 six, it soldiered on, with an overdrive option now available. True automatic and power steering did not make their appearance until 1954, when a complicated line of Coronets and Royals was offered plus a sporty convertible, the Royal 500, using a quadrajet-equipped 241 unit.

The 1955 Flight Sweep Dodges were similar to the parallel Plymouths, though all eights had a capacity of 4.3 litres with outputs as high as 193 bhp. The faithful six was still there in 1956, with a dual-choke carburetter and a surprising 131 bhp, but Dodge, like Plymouth, had a fast car for those who considered the regular eights too tame. There were no special body styles, but the 354-cubic-inch (5.8-litre) power unit disposed of 340 bhp on a 10:1 compression. Dodge also offered a remarkable diversity of station wagons, with two- and four-door as well as six- and nine-seater configurations.

De Soto was still 'the car designed with you in mind', which sounded fine on radio commercials. Towards the end of our period, however, people were wondering if that second person were still plural. An artificial make created in 1928 to bridge the gap between the four-cylinder Plymouth (*née* Maxwell) and the cheaper Chrysler sixes, the De Soto had prospered at the beginning but had never recovered from the Airflow débâcle of 1934. Nor had its sponsors helped, being apparently uncertain whether the breed ranked above or below Dodge in the hierarchy.

The cars lasted the decade with the usual mandatory changes but not much else. 1942's retractable headlamps had gone, leaving De Soto without a cachet. It ran through the whole gamut of engines. What started off with a 3.8-litre (237-cubic-inch) side-valve six ended on a line of vee-eights, with 230 bhp from the standard 5.4-litre type, and options of up to 320 bhp on the ferocious 341 with twin four-barrel carburetters. One of these S24 Pacesetters managed 144 mph, but even this could not make an individual car of the De Soto, since the jazzy gold-and-white finish was also used on the Plymouth Fury. Admittedly the De Soto version was available in ragtop form, but this was scarcely enough.

For the rest, development followed familiar lines: four-light styling in 1949, hardtops in 1950, a 160 bhp hemi-head vee-eight in 1952, Powerflite automatic replacing Fluidrive in 1954 and Flight Sweep in 1955. As befitted Chrysler's number two make, the new order meant the abolition of the six-cylinder range, and the more expensive Fireflites of 1956 could be bought only with automatic and power steering, amenities which made them costlier than the parallel Dodges, at around $2,800. De Soto's sole piece of individuality was the nine-seater Suburban of 1946–8, on a 139½-inch wheelbase. This had a brief vogue while station wagons were still non-U, sales of 19,000 units being assisted by large orders from New York's cab operators. The Suburban's descendants lingered on into 1952, being offered for export as late as 1954—but meanwhile Checker and others had cornered the cab market, and wagons had become respectable. De Soto never made the Top Ten in our period, and the 104,090 cars delivered in 1956 represented the last serious market penetration of a brand name killed off four years later.

Apart from the legendary 5.4-litre hemi-head vee-eight of 1951,

Chrysler's story would be equally uninspired. The much-touted caliper disc brakes were used only on the prestige Imperials, and the rest of the car followed Plymouth or De Soto lines.

1946's range structure embraced two sixes, the Royal and the Windsor, and four eights—the Saratoga, the New Yorker, the Town and Country and the vast Crown Imperial, a Cadillac competitor we shall encounter later. Both the Royal and the Windsor shared the usual flathead six (4.1 litres and 114 bhp), though the more expensive Windsor offered such diversions as long-chassis eight-seaters and a Highlander convertible with tartan trim for Scots Americans. The Saratoga and New Yorker were parallel 5.3-litre straight-eights on a 127½-inch wheelbase. Like the sixes, they could be had with three-speed synchromesh or four-speed Fluidrive transmissions.

The Town and Country, though mechanically similar, was quite different in other respects, featuring a half-timbered body 'with the grace and elegance of a yacht'; by 1948, however, the full mahogany panelling of early models had given way to a mixture of wood and Di-Noc appliqué. Roadster and coupé versions were fortunately withheld, but the four-door sedans and convertibles, the former a six (after 1946) and the latter always an eight, sold surprisingly well—21,671 in their first season alone. Convertible versions were still offered in 1949, the stockbroker's Tudor blending better with the new front end than it had with the rehashed 1942 idiom. 1949's face lift brought nothing more than the standardization of Fluidrive on all cars except the cut-price Royal, though the following season the Crown Imperial's disc brakes made a fleeting appearance on the Town and Country Newport, a quarter-timbered hardtop. Then came the hemi. . . .

This engine was only 100 lb lighter than the straight-eight it replaced. It was also expensive to make and complicated to service; 'two of everything, against one on the Cadillac' was the prevailing grumble. Nonetheless, the Chrysler set new standards of output and torque, and, in Beverly Kimes's words, 'sent the rest of the industry hurrying back to their drawing-boards'. The hemi had immense potential: while the catalogued version was powerful enough, with 180 bhp from 5.4 litres by comparison with the old eight's 135 bhp, experimental units were soon giving 350–400 bhp. Further, there was compensation for all this complexity in long life: a distance of 100,000 miles between overhauls was commonplace, and the vee-eight outlasted both its chassis and its bodywork. A stock New Yorker sedan weighing 4,260 lb attained 100 mph, with 75 mph available on the highest indirect ratio; the 0–30-mph acceleration time was 4 seconds. At $3,403 it was by no means expensive, and by 1952 Chrysler's own Hydraguide full-time power steering was a regular option. True automatic transmission was introduced on the 1953 cars, but it was not until the following year that the company reentered the horsepower race they had initiated. Larger valves and a four-barrel carburetter boosted power to 235 bhp.

Chrysler's engineering was unchallenged; it only needed 1955's Flight Sweep styling to boost sales from a low 101,000 to a creditable 176,039 units. By this time too the sixes had disappeared; the lesser Chryslers used the Spitfire, a smaller hemi-head vee-eight, giving 188 bhp from 4.9 litres. Despite a road weight of 4,300 lb, the latest Windsor would attain 104 mph but was still sold with synchromesh as standard. New Yorkers had the larger 250-bhp engine, and power assistance for everything. The season's main news was, however, the 300, America's most powerful motor-car, and faster than a stock Thunderbird or Corvette.

To look at, the 300 was merely a lowered New Yorker hardtop with an Imperial grille. Manual steering was standard, though with 300 bhp it is not surprising that Powerflite transmission was specified. Mechanical modifications included twin quadrajet carburetters, a racing-type camshaft and twin exhausts. The 300 was bulky, with a length of 219 inches, and heavy, at 4,400 lb, but there was no denying a potential of some 140 mph. 1,692 were sold in 1955, and 1,060 of the 1956 series with tail fins, circular instrument dials and even more power—355 bhp from 5.8 litres. By 1956 all Chryslers had tail fins, pushbutton Powerflite and engines that would have won the horsepower race only a year or two ago. Even basic Windsors had 5.4-litre engines, yielding 235 bhp: the 354 engine went into everything else, with outputs from 280 bhp upwards.

Studebaker had been America's best-selling independent make in 1941, a position they regained nine years later and held until 1954. Their 'amenity' record was mixed: automatic transmissions in 1950, short-stroke vee-eights in 1951, power brakes and tubeless tyres in 1955 and 12-volt electrics in 1956. Overdrive had long been a favourite option, with victories in past Gilmore–Yosemite Economy Runs to justify it. The company bought its automatic transmissions from Borg–Warner yet went to immense pains to develop its own power steering, a curious device driven off the crankshaft by a vee-belt. (It worked but cost too much; hence a hurried switch to the proprietary Saginaw system after only one hundred sets had been completed.) Convertibles were not offered after 1952; the company had dickered for many years with station wagon prototypes before the belated introduction of the Conestoga in 1955, and did not market a hardtop until 1952. However, this last omission did not matter, as the Loewy–Exner Starlight coupé of 1947 was far more exciting.

America's first true post-war designs had in fact appeared in the summer of 1946. Their curved screens and rear windows, short bonnets and long rear decks made one wonder where the engine was, and in fact the box-section Studebaker frame had been engineered for front or rear location. The company actually tested air- and water-cooled flat-sixes before opting once more for the known way. They also tried a torsion-bar front suspension but were scared off it by the prevailing shortage of high-grade steel.

Further, the 'coming-or-going' look had solid advantages. Placing the engine well forward in the frame meant more *lebensraum*, with rear-seat passengers sitting 20 inches ahead of the driving axle and enjoying an excellent ride. Mechanically, there was nothing of moment—Studebaker's established transverse-leaf independent front suspension, hypoid final drive and side-valve six-cylinder engines of four-bearing type. The pre-war President 8 was not revived. We have already encountered the 2.8-litre Champion unit in the 5G of 1945; the 3.7-litre Commander was on similar lines, with an output of 94 bhp. The Champion weighed 2,968 lb in road trim, a coupé cost $1,437, and thanks to superior aerodynamics the little car would do nearly 80 mph, 1 gallon of fuel lasting 21 miles at cruising speeds of 60 mph. As well as the glamorous Starlight with its full wrapround rear window, the range included sedans, a less attractive three-passenger coupé and a convertible. The long-wheelbase Land Cruiser used the Commander engine and was available only in sedan form.

The styling was right from the start. Only the front end was altered between 1947 and 1952. The 1950 and 1951 models had the deplorable if much-imitated guided-missile motif, and the 1952 models featured a shovel nose which did not improve it. The principal chassis change was a switch to a coil-spring front suspension in 1950, when the Commander unit was enlarged to 4 litres. A year later came the little overhead-valve vee-eight engine with wedge-shaped combustion chambers and a capacity of 3,811 cc. This was, as it transpired, a misjudgement; Studebaker utilized higher compression ratios rather than the greater swept volumes adopted by the rest of the industry, but the new eight scored over many of its rivals, since it did not demand high-octane fuel. The output was an adequate 120 bhp, and this engine replaced the big six, though the Champion soldiered on unchanged into 1960.

If anything, Loewy's 1953 Studebakers were an even greater sensation. The driver sat close to the wheel—which he did not on many of the big bulboids. There was no chromium-plated ornamentation, though for all its beautifully balanced looks the Commander version was 17 feet long and 6 feet wide. The star of the range was the coupé, but once again Studebaker had miscalculated, regarding this style as a small-production 'come-on' for their centenary year. Hence, when orders poured in, there were no cars to meet them. The factor that should have saved the company helped to ruin it, along with rustproneness and handling that belied the Studebaker's looks. 'The Commander,' said one report, 'steers like the *Queen Mary* and corners like the *Queen Elizabeth*.' In fact the cars were stable at speed, and the steering was slow rather than inaccurate, as well it might be with nearly six turns from lock to lock.

1954's cars had to be different—and so they were, with unattractive cross-hatched grilles and heavy plated strips down the sides. The styling remained unaltered in 1955, but a wider choice of engines was available. The Champion unit was enlarged to 185 cubic inches (3 litres), while the larger cars (which once again included a President) started the season with a diminutive 3.7-litre eight and ended it with 4¼ litres and 162 bhp, the latter increased to 185 bhp with a quadrajet carburetter. This high-performance version featured in the Speedster, a sporting hardtop with wire-wheel trims, a reinforced frame and an 'ornamental chrome roll bar over the roof panels'. The 160-mph speedometer and the tachometer reading up to 8,000 rpm need not be taken seriously. The regular 1956 line was complicated rather than exciting, with a larger 4.7-litre eight in home-market Presidents: export models, however, managed an easy 95 mph on the old 259 unit. There were also the Hawk hardtops with grilles and instrument panels that would not have shamed those of a British specialist maker.

All Hawks used the President chassis of 120½-inch wheelbase, but there were gradations of performance. The Flight Hawk at $1,986 was a promenade car with the 101-bhp Champion engine. The Power and Sky Hawks used the regular vee-eight units, but the Golden Hawk at $3,061 was a poor man's Chrysler 300, thanks to the 5.8-litre motor inherited from Packard. This gave 275 bhp on a 9.5:1 compression, and the car could be bought with manual-and-overdrive or with Packard's Ultramatic. 0–60 mph took only 9 seconds, and the Golden Hawk could be persuaded up to 130 mph, by anyone brave enough to risk the usual American brakes or lack of them. Surprisingly over 4,000 were sold.

Nash were increasingly preoccupied with small cars. A middle-class line was, however, offered, featuring the long-established overhead-valve six with seven-bearing crankshaft. In 1946 form it gave 112 bhp from 3,848 cc and went into the Ambassador, an orthodox specimen of American engineering which differed from the cut-price 600 in that it had a separate chassis and semielliptic rear springs. Overdrive was an optional extra. The big overhead six featured in such unusual vehicles as the halftimbered Suburban sedan, the British-built Nash–Healey sports cars of 1951–4 and even a line of trucks: the few not exported went to Nash dealers as wreckers. It also found its way into 1949's bath tubs, evolving alongside the smaller types, acquiring the usual driving aids (Hydramatic transmission and power steering) *en route* and assuming the Pininfarina shape in 1952. One of the Healey influences was 1953's Dual Jetfire—or an extra carburetter for the latest 4.1-litre units. At 140 bhp, these were as powerful as some smaller vee-eights.

From 1955 both the Ambassador and the small Statesman shared the same basic hull, though the cheaper model had the old 3.2-litre flathead engine and a shorter wheelbase of 114½ inches. The Ambassador could, however, be had with a vee-eight, even if this came from the rival Packard company. It was a powerful car, giving 208 bhp from 5.2 litres, and was supplied complete with Packard's latest three-speed Twin Ultramatic: manual and overdrive boxes were confined to six-cylinder versions. Nash sales were a low 35,000 in 1956, when much the same models were offered, though American Motors upset the Studebaker–Packard applecart by launching their own eight, a more modest 4.1 litre affair. This was used in the short-wheelbase Ambassador Special, but a year later it would be standardized on all the larger American Motors' cars.

Hudson were another firm who failed to stand the pace. Like Studebaker, however, they had a winner in their first post-war creation. The safe-handling Step-Downs averaged 143,000 cars a year between 1948 and 1950.

Their previous efforts of 1946–7 also showed some deviations from the standard American norm. All models had a 121-inch wheelbase, but unusual features were the splash lubrication (which worked admirably), the wet-plate clutches and the 'triple-safe' brakes with an auxiliary mechanical linkage in case the hydraulics failed. The engines were a pair of old favourites, a 3½-litre six and the well-loved 254-cubic-inch (4,168 cc) straight-eight with roots going back to 1930. Output of the latter was 128 bhp. The Super's prices started at $1,535, and the better-equipped Commodore's at $1,679, though the differential between sixes and eights was once again insignificant, at $100-odd.

Frank Spring's Step-Down series was introduced two years and $18,000,000 later; it featured full unitary construction which 'encircled the passenger space'. The rear wheels were actually mounted inside the frame girders, and a wide 59½-inch track allied to a low build gave the cars new standards of roadworthiness. The price of this was bulk: the Hudson's 124-inch wheelbase was not excessive, but the cars were 207 inches long and 77 inches wide. The driver sat uncomfortably far away from the wide curved windscreen. The basic lineup was the same as before, though the latest six was a pressure-lubricated 4.3-litre unit rated at 121 bhp, and Hudson had their own brand of painless shifting, Drive Master, with a three-position switch offering anything from orthodox synchromesh to an automatic change using only the two upper ratios. Both six and eight were good for 90 mph, and Hudson went into 1950 without any serious changes. In 1950 an inexpensive 3.8-litre Pacemaker on a 119-inch wheelbase was added to the range.

Hydramatics and hardtops followed in 1951, but more important was Hudson's answer to the horsepower race. This was an almost Edwardian solution—the largest flathead six offered for many years, and certainly the biggest specimen to be made in quantity after the Second World War. The Hornet, at 5,047 cc, was quite a package. Even in single-carburetter form with alloy head it disposed of 145 bhp, and with a pair of single-choke instruments (Twin-H Power, in factory jargon) it was eventually worked up to over 170 bhp. The model dominated stock-car racing for three seasons, with 103 major first places.

Racing may improve the breed, but it does not promote sales. Hudson's sales declined: 76,000 in 1952, and 67,000 in 1953. The little Jet was a disaster, and the Step-Downs were not only underengined but outmoded as well. The design was inflexible, so Hudson were left to shuffle the pack with the Wasp, a combination of the Pacemaker's short wheelbase and a 4.3-litre version of the Hornet engine. The company entered 1954, their last year of independence, with four full-sized models—the standard and the Super Wasps, the Hornet and the Hornet Special (which was merely a stripped and detuned Hornet). By contrast, the 1955 Hudsons, though still carrying Wasp and Hornet labels, were Nashes, built at Kenosha. None of them, admittedly, had Nash engines; the Wasp used the 3.3-litre unit from the discarded Jet, and the Hornet had either its own flathead or Packard's vee-eight. A vee-line grille was used in 1956 to distinguish the cars from Nashes, but less than 23,000 were sold, and 1957 was to be even worse, with sales down to 4,000.

A more attractive victim of 1954's merger was the Italia, conceived as a competition special for the Carrera Panamericana. Plans specified a twin-carburetter Hornet engine in a short-wheelbase Jet floor pan, and the construction of a series of 25 cars was entrusted to Touring of Milan. What emerged was a small sports coupé with an inverted-vee front bumper, functional brake cooling ducts in the front wings and chromium-plated wire wheels. The doors opened into the roof. Unfortunately, Hudson cancelled their racing plans, and the Italias, marketed at a high $4,350, used the 114-bhp Jet unit. Top speed was an adequate 95 mph, but the Italia did not commend itself to American Motors' management, and disappeared.

The young Kaiser–Frazer company could not afford even someone else's vee-eight: all the spare cash had been squandered on the Henry-J. General Motors would probably have been cooperative: having already sold them automatic transmissions, they would surely have supplied engines as well. Nor is it true that Kaiser–Frazer's regular six was a proprietary engine. Certainly the tough old 3.7-litre (226-cubic-inch) four-bearing flathead that they used to the end was of a Continental design, but only the first examples were actually purchased from Continental. Thereafter Kaiser–Frazer made it themselves, in a former Hudson engine plant.

Once again, the original plan was more ambitious than what the public received. The initial announcements in 1946 specified two distinct models, sharing only Howard Darrin's slab-sided styling and the 226 engine. The Kaiser-elect featured full unitary construction, all-independent suspension and front-wheel drive, whereas the Frazer was conventionally engineered. The former's heavy steering proved a sufficient deterrent, but the Frazer went ahead, although very slowly. A reporter who visited Ford's former bomber assembly plant at Willow Run in June 1946 spoke of 'rows of hundreds of six-cylinder Continental engines and stacks of chassis frames' but saw only two complete cars and twenty unfinished examples. All of which makes Kaiser–Frazer's 1947 performance—a $19,000,000 profit and 144,000 vehicles delivered—something of a miracle.

It's styling apart, the new model—Kaisers and Frazers differed only in trim and detail—was a straightforward piece of engineering. The engine gave 100 bhp at 3,600 rpm, and the rest of it was close to the norm—Hotchkiss drive, a hypoid rear axle, coil-spring independent front suspension and a three-speed synchromesh gearbox—though early frames eschewed cruciform bracing. The wheelbase was 123½ inches, and the detail work was ingenious—squeeze-trigger door handles, interior safety latches and simple two-spoke steering wheels. Prices started at $1,967. The more expensive Kaiser Super and Frazer could be had with dual-choke carburetters and overdrive, while the Frazer's colour-keyed interiors were most attractive.

The shape survived for four years, though permutations included a taxi-cab, and the Vagabond–Traveler family of 'commercial' sedans with horizontally split tailgates and fold-down rear seats. Even more intriguing—and unique in our decade—was the Virginian, a four-door power-top convertible also available as a padded hardtop. It was also a masterpiece of improvization, having four doors, because Kaiser–Frazer's tooling facilities did not as yet extend to two-door bodies.

The cars that remained unsold at the end of one season were jazzed up and retitled as next year's models. Frazer Manhattans had started life as Kaiser Virginians, and after Joseph Frazer's departure there was no one to object to the reissue of leftover de luxe Kaisers as 1951 Frazers, the last cars to bear the name.

In desperation, the 'real' 1951 Kaisers were announced in March 1950, seeing the company through to 1955 and still looking remarkably up to date, even if the old six had run out of steam. The engine and transmission were basically unchanged, but the wheelbase was shortened to 118½ inches, the curved screen (still divided until 1952) was wide and deep, and the screen pillars were commendably thin. Frames were now cruciform braced.

Variations on this theme were legion. There were the luxury Dragons with 'Dragon vinyl' or painted tops, there were Travelers and cars with Continental spare-wheel kits, not to mention the cut-price Carolina. The $4,400 Dragon of 1953 represented the ultimate antithesis of American mass-production thinking: though the specification was stock Manhattan, the trimmings were near-Docker—gold-plated accessories inside, gold-plated script outside, a gold plaque on the glovebox lid inscribed with the owner's name and a personal letter to the original purchaser signed by Henry J. Kaiser himself. Only 1,277 were sold, and the 1954 Kaiser Specials were merely 1953 Manhattans with new grilles and tail lights.

The last Manhattan looked the same, but a McCulloch centrifugal blower had been grafted onto the old 226 engine. With 140 bhp under the bonnet, a 100-mph Kaiser sedan was a reality, vee-eight or no vee-eight. Alas! public confidence had long since been lost; 7,039 cars were sold in 1954, but barely 1,000 in 1955, by which time all the dead stock had been exhausted, and only the 'blown' sedans were offered.

Though the hearse makers had disappeared, there was still a common-sense seven-passenger sedan that did not have yearly model changes—the Checker, from Kalamazoo, Michigan. Officially there was no private-car manufacture before 1959, but throughout our period 'pleasure' models were available on the taxi-cab chassis. There was even an agent for the *marque* in Berne.

The styling was 1939, but engineering was 1935's finest, which meant a cruciform-braced frame riding on four semielliptic springs, hydraulic brakes and a hypoid rear axle. The engine was the same 3.7-litre Continental used in Kaisers, overdrive was a regular option and the wheelbase was 124 inches. Checkers continued unchanged until 1955, but at the end of our period the A8 was introduced with 1951-type styling, a ball-joint independent front suspension and an automatic option. The regular engine was still the Continental, though a few A8As were made with six-cylinder Nash power units.

1.4   Power Assistance for Everything

In our decade, Cadillac dominated the luxury-car sector.

To begin with, General Motors' prestige Division made nothing else whereas Chrysler's effort was centred on middle-class models, most Packards were modest in appointments and price alike, and the Lincoln took a long time to recover from the Zephyr affair, even if Presidents rode in Cosmopolitans lengthened to 20 feet. Further, Cadillac engineering was kept separate; some of the cheaper bodies might have Oldsmobile and Buick associations, but the *marque* never shared an engine with a lesser breed.

Not that Cadillacs were expensive. 1946's prices started at $1,920 (about £400 at the rate of exchange then!), and even the enormous 75 cost less than $4,000. Nor was production on a modest scale: over 100,000 Cadillacs were delivered in 1950, and thereafter the company never looked back, exceeding 150,000 in 1956, in which year Lincoln sold 48,995 cars, Chrysler's recently established Imperial Division 12,130 and Packard 13,432, though few of these last were luxury items. General Motors could still afford the standards of precision engineering laid down by Henry Leland in 1903. Others could not.

The price of all this was styling in the accepted American mould. The Cadillac did not *look* different—it was merely larger. Further, its evolution followed the familiar pattern—automatic transmissions in 1941, overhead-valve vee-eights in 1949, power steering in 1952 and servo brakes standardized by 1956. Refinements came sooner, because Cadillac's customers were entitled to the best. Cadillac also gave their customers up-to-date styling: curved screens in 1948 changed to the single-panel type in 1951, and the 'dog's leg' idiom in 1954. Equipment relegated to the extras list by lesser firms was standard here—heaters, for instance, from 1949, and 'autronic eye' dippers in 1952. From 1953, all Cadillacs had screen washers and power steering. However, there were some mistakes as well—the sporty Eldorado convertible of 1953 was a shocker.

The 1946 Cadillacs were 1942 models with minimal alterations. The cruciform-braced chassis frame followed the regular General Motors' practice, though Cadillac engineers preferred semielliptics at the back, and Cadillac handbrakes were worked by hand. The excellent three-bearing iron vee-eight with its side-by-side valves had been around in its current form since 1936 and gave 150 bhp from 5.7 litres (346 cubic inches): hydraulic valve lifters and a dual-choke downdraught carburetter featured in the specification, while a three-speed synchromesh gearbox was still available as an alternative to the four-speed Hydramatic. An average Cadillac of the period could attain 95 mph.

Four wheelbase options were available. If the lesser 61s and 62s had Buick-like bodies, the same could not be said of the latest Sixty Specials, lineal descendants of 1938's style leader and still four-light sedans. For ambassadors and the like, there was the 75 limousine on a 136½-inch wheelbase, with lower gearing and larger wheels.

1948 saw Cadillac's version of Futuramic styling, with small tail fins to differentiate it from an Oldsmobile 98. The 75 was unchanged, as were the mechanical specifications. The short-stroke overhead-valve unit with wedge-shaped combustion chambers was introduced a year later. The capacity was 331 cubic inches (5,420 cc), and a gross output of 160 bhp still meant 133 hp delivered to the rear axle. The new car attained 100 mph in commendable silence and took only a little over 30 seconds to reach the 80 mark. Synchromesh was still nominally available, and the limousine's styling was brought into line with the rest of the range. Wheelbase of this latter was now 146½ inches, though for the funeral trade there was a still longer 157-inch 'commercial' chassis.

Thereafter the Cadillac grew steadily in power and refinement. New manifolds and quadrajet carburation gave 190 bhp in 1952, when quadruple silencers were added. The 1953 cars had 210 bhp, would attain 115 mph and took 25 seconds to reach 80 mph; horsepower was also increased from 230 bhp in 1954 to 270 bhp on 1955's 'performance' versions. Six litres and

285 bhp were the order of the day in 1956 though on the Eldorado convertible a high-lift camshaft and a 9.75:1 compression were specified, which meant a formidable 305 bhp. Transmissions kept pace: in 1952 the improved Dual Range Hydramatic was introduced, followed 4 years later by an auxiliary fluid coupling to smooth the car's progress still further. By this time, of course, Cadillacs were too large for Europe; even the basic 62 measured 222 inches from stem to stern, nearly a foot more than a Rolls–Royce Silver Cloud, while the 75 was 22 feet long. It was also the last chauffeur-driven carriage in production in America.

At the beginning of our period, Lincoln was suffering from a dubious heritage. The smaller vee-twelves were non-U and difficult to service, while the cheap Lincolns had Henry Ford's engineering: transverse-leaf suspension and axles. Even such built-in luxuries as electric window lifts could not conceal the Zephyr ancestry of the 1946 models. The cars rode on a 125-inch wheelbase, and the drive went via a torque tube to a hypoid rear axle. After a brief and catastrophic skirmish with semiautomatic boxes in 1942, Lincoln returned to using ordinary synchromesh, though unfortunately it took them several months to discard another of 1942's mistakes, the unreliable 305-cubic-inch (5-litre) engine, in favour of the better although less powerful 4.8-litre. Since 1939, the roofline of the Zephyr-inspired bodies had been raised, and rear-seat headroom was now adequate. Less happy were the box fenders of the current product. Prices started at $1,784, and the twelve-cylinder Lincoln lasted until 1948.

The Continental shared the same mechanics but was wholly individual. Conceived by E. T. Gregorie at the behest of Edsel Ford, it had first appeared as a 1940 model: its most questionable asset (the vertically mounted spare wheel at the rear) had the greatest influence of all. The rest of it, whether in coupé or cabriolet form, was beautiful, albeit ruined by later stylists. 1942's box front fenders had been bad enough, but the segmented die-cast grille of the 1946 models administered the Coup de grâce. Nevertheless the Continental was outstanding—power windows and seats, power tops on convertibles, blue instrument dials, leather trim, attractive colours (including 'pace car yellow', a reminder of the model's recent role at Indianapolis) and even a two-speed axle option in place of the orthodox overdrive. But the humble origins could not be concealed, and at 4,125 lb the car was no lightweight; 90 mph was hard work. The Continental would become a collector's piece almost before the last of 3,334 post-war examples rolled off the lines.

Harold Youngren's 1949 Lincolns followed the latest Ford lines and were available in two series. Both, of course were vee-eights: the latest 5½-litre power unit was common to Ford's heavy trucks. It was of long-stroke (88.9 mm × 111.1 mm) configuration and featured the usual twin water pumps and dual-choke carburetter. The output, at 153 bhp, nearly matched that of the latest overhead-valve Cadillac. The car was, of course, much larger than Fords or Mercurys with an overall length of 220 inches, the brakes were of the duo-servo type, and initially a 3.08:1 overdrive was standard; subsequently this was relegated to the extras list. Heaters and electric window lifts featured on the expensive Cosmopolitan, a whale-like fastback reminiscent of the Tatra and not to everyone's taste. This body was not seen after 1950, and the range included a trunkback sports sedan, a coupé and a convertible. This car retained the 125-inch wheelbase, but there was also a more austere short-chassis version known simply as the Lincoln. This resembled an enlarged Mercury. From mid-1949 Lincoln started to buy Hydramatic transmissions from General Motors. By 1951, this system was compulsory, yet still shown as an extra. The absence of an alternative would only emphasize Ford's continuing dependence on a rival organization!

Lincoln's sales were still only a third of Cadillac's sales and half Packard's. The answer came in 1952 with a modern overhead-valve engine, not unlike General Motors' design but smaller, at 5.2 litres, than the superseded flathead. It also featured the new McPherson ball-joint independent front suspension, while the old bulbous shape changed to something crisper. A 123-inch wheelbase was used for all models, the weight was a little over 2 tons in road trim, and the Lincoln proved a taut-handling vehicle, capable of just over 100 mph on a 3.15:1 axle ratio. A year later the output passed 200 bhp, while the addition of power brakes and steering to the options list led Lincoln to suggest that their car was 'completely powered for modern living'. This one would do 112 mph; for the first time Lincoln sold more cars than Packard. High-lift camshafts extracted 215 bhp from the 1955 edition, which featured a Ford-built automatic transmission; another refinement was one-shot lubrication. The 1956 models, like other Ford designs of that season, were overstyled, but power (285 bhp, from 6 litres) was not lacking, and the care that went into manufacture was shown by the Division's handling of 'factory air'. When air conditioners were specified, the extra weight was countered with heavy-duty tyres and lower gearing.

In 1956 the Continental returned in Mark II form, once again as a two-door coupé and also with a rear-mounted spare wheel. The model's patron was Henry Ford II's brother, William, and the design team included Gordon Behrig of Cord fame. Mechanically it was a stock 6-litre car with all the power options, but a $9,517 price tag allowed plenty of latitude. Component inspection was tougher than usual, special leather for the interior was imported from Scotland, and a radio was standard. Instruments were circular, and the pile carpeting extended even to the boot. The turned aluminium finish of the cylinder heads recalled the old Continental. The car handled well, but yet again it was a type destined for future collectors rather than for present customers. The Mark II's run ended in May 1957, after only 3,012 had been made. In 1974 an Arizona firm announced 'remanufactured' models (not replicas) at a mere $18,000 each!

Chrysler's 'prestige' Imperials were not always as illustrious as they sounded; in the 1930s the label had been worn by an assortment of cheap straight-eights. By contrast, the 1946 Crown Imperial limousines were enormous (the wheelbase was 146½ inches), expensive and very rare, only 1,400 being sold in three seasons. Mechanically, they were elongated editions of the 5.3-litre eight, with styling to match, although the Pennsylvanian coach builder Derham used the chassis for such vehicles as a hunting phaeton for King Ibn Saud. The model's sole claim to fame was the use of caliper-type disc brakes, standardized on Crown Imperials from 1949 but never found on lesser models.

Eight-seater Crowns were made up to 1956, but from 1951 there was also an owner-drive Imperial range with all the power options. These cars had the big hemi engine but were little more than de luxe New Yorkers, and they certainly were not in the Cadillac–Lincoln class. A 1954 Crown cost $6,922, inclusive of servo-assisted brakes and radio, but this was a bad year for Chrysler, who delivered precisely 100 of these cars.

With the advent of Flight Sweep in 1955 Chrysler attempted to boost the Imperial's sales by promoting it to the status of a make and giving it an individual version of the latest grille, not to mention gunsight-type tail lamps. The engine was the latest 250 bhp vee-eight, and power seats, power windows, air conditioning and a radio were regular equipment. The immense limousines likewise prospered under the new idiom, though they were on their way out, as the absence of any styling changes for 1956 indicated. The disc brakes were also discontinued. The short-chassis Imperials soldiered on into 1974, when the energy crisis gave Chrysler a convenient excuse for jettisoning an unprofitable line.

Also on their way out were Packard, hastened to their grave by their 1954 union with Studebaker. Nor was everything made after 1945 aimed at the carriage trade: some were purpose-built taxis. However, the integration of manufacture from 1940 onwards makes it difficult to isolate the Junior from the Senior models.

The magnificent 160 and 180 had been casualties of the war. The manner of their deportation is still unclear, but by 1945 the dies were in the Soviet Union, and their descendants were not the Cavaliers and Patricians of the ensuing decade but Russia's ZIS 110 family. This left Packard with the middle-class Clipper, certainly the best-looking of Detroit's 1942 cars.

Variously ascribed to John Tjaarda, Howard Darrin and Packard's own Vern Gubitz, the model combined full-flow lines with minimal ornamentation and a narrower edition of the traditional grille. Unlike the 1953 Studebakers, Clippers looked equally right as sedans or fastback coupés, and they might have become the nation's new style leaders, had the car been left alone. By 1948, alas, the harm had been done.

Two years earlier, however, the shape remained inviolate, although beneath the surface lurked American stereotype. True, Packard had been using hypoid rear axles longer than anyone else, and their cruciform-braced frames were exceptionally robust, but the suspension and brakes followed accepted lines, and so did the gearboxes. The engines were the two family favourites: a 4.6-litre five-bearing straight-eight that had started life in 1935 in the first 120 and a 4-litre six only two years younger. Packards, like Buicks, were started by depressing the accelerator pedal, chokes were automatic, and other unusual features were the two-speed electric wipers (a godsend in the land of suctions system) and the electrically operated overdrive (which was troublesome). Both six and eight shared the same bodies and the same 120-inch wheelbase, though the eight, at 125 bhp, was appreciably more powerful. Most of the post-war six-cylinder cars, indeed, seem to have been used as taxis, a role for which they were still being produced as late as 1949.

Externally, the Supers and Customs were much the same, but for these models Packard retained the splendid 356-cubic-inch (5.8-litre) nine-bearing engine from the 160 and 180. Sales literature proudly proclaimed a crankshaft weight of 104 lb, and the power output, at 165 bhp, was still America's highest. Sedans rode on a 127-inch wheelbase, but for the carriage trade there was an 148-inch limousine weighing 4,675 lb, far more expensive than a Cadillac 75 at $4,332. This model should not, of course, be confused with the lengthened eight-seater Junior, which also enjoyed a brief post-war run.

1948 saw the Clipper's lines marred by the 'pregnant elephant' treatment. Capacities of the two basic eights were enlarged, and there was also an electrovacuum clutch which was as unreliable as Packard's overdrive, while body styles included the company's first post-war convertible and also the Stockbroker's Tudor Station Sedan with wooden strakes bolted to a conventional metal body. These cars were still being made in 1950, but in the meantime Packard had devised their own automatic gearbox, the Ultramatic. Like pre-1956 Hydramatics, this incorporated a friction clutch and was said to be slip-proof. The low range was operative up to 55 mph, and by 1950 Ultramatic was available throughout the range.

The cars were completely restyled in 1951, with one-piece curved screens and wrapround rear windows; the latest wide grille was a great improvement on the 1948 version and retained vestiges of the Packard radiator. Engines were essentially unchanged, though the expensive Patricians, convertibles and Mayfair hardtops had portholes in their rear wings, and Ultramatic transmission was standard on the Patrician. During the next two seasons servo brakes, power steering and air conditioning made their appearance.

By 1954, of course, Studebaker were in control, but in the meanwhile Packard did their best. An attempt was made to recapture the halcyon atmosphere of the 1920s by turning the Clipper into a separate make and by reserving the Packard label for thoroughbreds; this did not mean nine-bearing engines, for all hardtops and convertibles were Packards, regardless of the engine.

1954's cars were indicative of desperation. Delays with the new vee-eight programme left the company to struggle on for an extra season with the old flatheads, though these put up an impressive performance. Even the old 5.4-litre five-bearing unit gave up to 165 bhp in Clipper form and 185 bhp when fitted to the Packard Cavalier. As for the nine-bearing type, it had been stretched to 5.9 litres and 212 bhp, with the aid of quadrajet carburation and an 8.7:1 compression. Further, it went into a variety of cars. The Patrician was merely the Cavalier on a 127-inch wheelbase, with compulsory Ultramatic transmission, but the Pacific hardtop and Caribbean convertible were gargantuan 'sports' models with an impressive overhang which resulted in a length of 220 inches, quite an achievement considering the modest 122-inch wheelbase. A helicopter could almost be landed on the Caribbean's rear deck! To cap everything, there was once again an ultralong 149-inch chassis, on which Henney of hearse fame (they were still building Packard-based 'professional cars') had mounted a nine-seater limousine body. It was very expensive indeed.

Unfortunately the price of vee-eights and upstairs valves in 1955 was the demise of the Packard grille, though the cars had no affinity with Studebakers. The latest Twin Ultramatic gearbox, reserved for the expensive models, offered an intermediate gear, while Packard's Torsion Level suspension had affinities with Citroën thinking. Torsion bars 9 feet long ran the length of the chassis on each side 'wound up,' as *The Motor* put it, 'anticlockwise to the front, and clockwise to the rear'. The rear levelizer bars were linked to an electric motor, resulting in a slight time lag not encountered on the contemporary Citroën, but generally the system worked well. Clippers were available in De Luxe form (with normal suspension) and as Customs with the new arrangements. Both could be bought with manual gearboxes, and the De Luxe featured a small 5.2-litre engine, whereas Customs used a detuned 245-bhp edition of the 5.8-litre 352 already encountered in Studebaker's Golden Hawk. True Packards had Twin Ultramatic transmission and the 352 unit, with ratings of as high as 275 bhp.

1956 saw a final fling. The 352 engine was standardized, and the company sought yet another gap in the middle-class sector—between Clippers and Packards. Their answer, the Executive at $3,567, did not succeed. At the top end of the range, it was a case of power for everything, and pushbutton control for the Twin Ultramatic, though Packard's buttons were on the steering-wheel spokes. The Caribbean had twin electric radio aerials as well.

Packard (as opposed to Clipper) prices started at $4,395, and not even stripped Clippers with traditional springs and synchromesh could help sales, which were down to 13,432—lower, in fact, than they had sunk since the dark days of 1934.

Preston Tucker managed to build 49 of his rear-engined Torpedos in 1948 and 1949, though whether he could have marketed these at $2,450 is another question. Unleashing the average American motorist in a 120-mph sedan with endemic rear-end breakaway, might have sparked off a wave of Naderism long before Ed Cole created the sporty Corvair. One thing is certain: the Torpedo was not viable in its original 1946 form.

The car used a flat-six of awesome proportions. The capacity was 544 cubic inches (9,750 cc); as if fuel injection and hemispherical combustion chambers were not enough, the valves were hydraulically actuated, being opened by columns of oil. A differential was superfluous—the drive was taken to two separate torque converters, one on each rear wheel. Other advanced features were disc brakes and an all-independent rubber suspension, while Tucker planned headlamps integral with true cycle-type wings, turning with the wheels. These had to be abandoned, as they set up a rudder effect. This was not all. The vast flat-six proved a brute to start, even with 24-volt electrics, and alternative engines of this configuration were no better. Eventually, however, the inventor got what he wanted from Air-Cooled Motors of Syracuse, New York, owners of the Franklin patents who converted a 5½-litre flat-six helicopter engine to water cooling. Admittedly, it had conventional valve gear, but it functioned well, giving 166 bhp at 3,200 rpm.

Most of the other oddities disappeared. The weird transmission arrangements gave way to a transaxle with differential incorporating an electrically selected preselective gearbox of Cord type, but the rubber suspension was retained: this featured equal-length A-arms at the front and trailing links at the rear.

Nonetheless, the Tucker remained a bastion of heterodoxy, with safety features to balance the less-than-predictable handling characteristics. These included a pop-out windscreen and a fully carpeted front compartment with no orthodox facia: the instruments were grouped in a modest 'bobble' in front of the driver. The doors opened into the roof, and there was a third protruding central headlamp. The Tucker was heavy, at 4,235 lb, but it was certainly the fastest catalogued American car of its era. Financial troubles prevented serious production.

1.5   Scaring the Jags Away

To Americans, sports cars were still imported cars. This did not, however, prevent two of the nation's 'big three' from trying their luck in this specialist field.

The story of the Chevrolet Corvette belongs properly to the 1960s, though already the master-touch of Zora Arkus-Duntov had extracted 150 mph from a 1956 car, and the small-block Chevrolet vee-eight was destined for a distinguished competition career. None of this was, however, apparent in 1953's pretty little two-seater.

In spite of the smooth lines of the glassfibre coachwork, the mechanics were uninspiring. A stock frame was shortened to 102 inches and was given outboard rear suspension and an open propeller shaft. The engine was the usual 3.9-litre overhead-valve four-bearing six with three horizontal car-buretters; in this form it gave an adequate 150–160 bhp. Strangely though, it was mated to the inept two-speed Powerglide automatic box—no manual Corvettes would be available until 1955. At $3,513, it was nearly as expensive as a Cadillac, neither transmission nor steering were suitable for a sports car, and door sealing was a constant problem. However, it was quite fast—even the first examples would exceed 105 mph, but, of the 10,000 units scheduled for 1953–4, precisely 3,775 saw the light of day. Nothing really happened until the advent of the 265 vee-eight in 1955. This meant performance options of as high as 225 bhp, and speeds almost in the XK class, which were far too much for the brakes. The 1956 Corvettes were even faster, but annual sales still lagged below 3,500.

The Ford Thunderbird never pretended to be a sports car, which is probably why it succeeded. Presented in 1954 by Henry Ford II and by its creator Lewis Crusoe as 'a personal car', it slotted into a gap between sporty convertibles, such as the Buick Skylark, and the Jaguars. It also retailed for $2,695, at a time when an XK140 cost $3,213.

Once again, mechanical elements were stock, the car featuring the latest ball-joint independent front suspension. But, here the resemblance between the Corvette and the Thunderbird ceased, for the Ford was a large car, weighing 3,200 lb to the Corvette's 2,705 lb: it also measured nearly 15 feet from stem to stern. The sheet metal was Fairlane without the Tiara trimmings, and power assistance was used for brakes, steering and hood, though Fordomatic transmission was an option—many cars were equipped with synchromesh-and-overdrive. Even when automatic was specified, the selector was mounted on the floor, thus setting a new fashion. The car's 292-cubic-inch (4,785 cc) engine was exclusive to the model (though it was offered on Mercurys), and in four-barrel form it gave 193–198 bhp. Most cars wore Continental spare-wheel kits, standardized for 1956. By this time the 292 unit was generally available, so to maintain individuality a new Thunderbird Special was offered. This 5.1-litre 312 could, however, only be supplied with Fordomatic transmission.

The Thunderbird was enthusiastically received, with sales of over 30,000 in the first two seasons. Alas! Ford dropped the model after 1957, in favour of a huge six-seater convertible, devoid of looks and handling alike.

Kaiser–Frazer believed in trying anything once, hence the Kaiser-Darrin 161 of 1953. This Howard Darrin creation was another pretty car; the bodywork was of glassfibre, the doors slid open, and the soft-top was of the three-position type in the best British traditions. The only suitable engine was the 2.6-litre Willys Six, tried in both side-valve and overhead-inlet forms, and even with a supercharger. With the three-carburetter flathead unit, the Kaiser Darrin 161 managed 100 mph, but at $3,668 it was more expensive even than the Corvette, and Kaiser–Frazer's failing finances swept it off the scene after only 497 had been made.

In 1946 Howard Darrin himself had built a sporty five-seater convertible of semiunitary type—metal up to the door sills, and self-coloured glassfibre for the upper works. The torsion-bar independent front suspension was unusual on an American car of the period, and Darrin used power assistance even for the bonnet-opening mechanism. The limited power of the Kaiser-type 3.7-litre Continental six engine was balanced by a modest weight of 2,400 lb. The Darrin was another 100-mph model, but plans for series production did not materialize. The prototype was lost in a flash flood.

Apart from a small batch of GS coupés produced in 1953–4, Chrysler never marketed any dream-car derivatives. Gene Casaroll's Dual Motors, however, made their own version of 1955's Dodge Firearrow roadster, the Firebomb; 117 were sold between 1956 and 1958. Chassis and bodies were put together by Ghia in Turin and shipped back to America for their engines and running gear. The car featured a 115-inch wheelbase, a 260-bhp vee-eight unit and an automatic transmission with Thunderbird-type selector on the floor. Luxurious appointments boosted the price to over $7,500, but among Casaroll's customers were Frank Sinatra and Dean Martin.

By contrast, Briggs Cunningham's main interest was racing, with regular entries at Le Mans in the 1951–5 period. The competition Cunninghams need not concern us here, but the vehicle was designed round a European-type steel-tube frame, a coil-spring independent front suspension was used, and Cunningham favoured a de Dion rear end. The steering was commendably high geared, and initially the breed used the 5.4-litre Chrysler hemi engine with four downdraught carburetters. A two-seater weighing 2,800 lb was timed at 152 mph down the Mulsanne Straight. It attained 100 mph in second, with a 0–60-mph acceleration time of 6.3 seconds.

The touring versions, which appeared in 1952, had some additional X-bracing for their frames and conventional coil-sprung rear ends. The wheelbase increased from 105 to 107 inches to accommodate four-seater bodies; these were made in both closed and convertible forms by Vignale of Turin. The four-carburetter Chrysler engine was standard, and various transmissions were used—Chrysler's Fluidrive, automatic or a three-speed

Cadillac manual box. Only 27 were built before Cunningham elected to concentrate on sports racers.

Frank Kurtis specialized in sports-car kits: in 1949 he offered one which, he claimed, could be put on the road, complete with Ford vee-eight engine, for less than $3,000. Soon afterwards he parted with the design and manufacturing rights to Earl Muntz but was back in business by 1951 with the 500, a light tubular chassis with leading-and-trailing-arm suspension and hydraulic brakes working in 12-inch drums. He also offered a matching glassfibre body, while the customer supplied the engine. Never a thing of beauty the Kurtis was light at 1,900 lb, and road-going examples could achieve 120 mph.

The Californian automobile dealer, Earl Muntz, turned the old-school Kurtis into a fully manufactured—or rather assembled—vehicle. It also put on weight to 3,780 lb. Though the overhead-valve Cadillac was occasionally used, most Muntz Jets had the 1949-type 5½-litre side-valve Lincoln unit with its regular four-speed Hydramatic transmission. The floor pan was integral with the perimeter-type chassis, the bodies were panelled in aluminium and steel, and the brakes and suspension were of Ford origin. Unusual for the period were built-in safety features such as a padded dashboard, a padded roof on hardtop versions and even seat belts. Though one of these five-seater convertibles appeared at the 1952 Brussels Salon, the Jet lost money, and production ceased in 1954 after 394 had been built. The last examples had the later overhead-valve Lincoln unit.

Woody Woodill was a Willys dealer in Downey, California, who built a glassfibre-bodied sports two-seater round Willys mechanical elements in 1952. The bonnet-mounted air scoop was a dummy, the transverse-leaf independent front suspension came off a Jeep station wagon, and Woodill, like Kaiser–Frazer, used the 2.6-litre overhead-inlet valve six-cylinder engine. Willys showed some interest but quickly lost it after the Kaiser merger, whereupon Woodill transformed his operation into a do-it-yourself store. This establishment offered $1,300 Wildfire kits to fit old-type Ford engines and transverse suspensions. Le patron even built a machine in front of a television audience to show that it could be done in 14 hours! A complete version cost $3,260. About 315 Wildfires were sold, with a variety of engines and suspensions.

The stylist Brooks Stevens contributed two vastly different sports models. 1952's Excalibur-J was another victim of Kaiser's uneasy finances. This simple two-seater featured aero screens, cycle-type wings and a Lotus-like grille; the chassis, engine and transmission were those of the six-cylinder Henry-J. The top speed was a surprising 120 mph: reputedly more for a second car using the Alfa Romeo 1900 motor. Though the Excalibur did well in sports-car events, only one more example was built.

Stevens's second effort, the Gentleman, commissioned by J. K. Gaylord in

1 Sophistication in the Bargain Basement: one of over 103,000 Chevrolet Bel Air four-door hardtops, 1956 (*Courtesy General Motors*)

2 Old Henry's Idiom: the 1947 Ford De Luxe Tudor sedan, or 1942 skin over 1935 innards (*Courtesy Nicky Wright*)

3 Italianising a Compact: what Pininfarina did to Nash's Rambler, 1953. Note the Continental spare wheel kit (*Courtesy American Motors*)

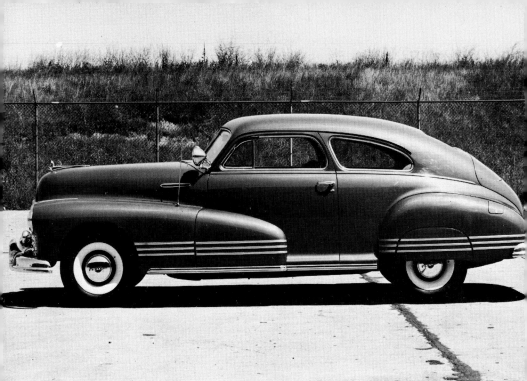

4 Two-door Fastback: Pontiac's 1946 version takes a keen eye to distinquish from a 1942 (*Courtesy General Motors*)

5 1947 Chrysler Town and Country Convertible (*Courtesy Nicky Wright*)

6 Step down to Success: the 5-litre Hudson Hornet as a convertible 'brougham' (*Courtesy American Motors*)

7 Sculptural Beginnings: the 1953 Studebaker Commander Coupe in its original unadorned form (*Courtesy Nicky Wright*)

8 Kaiser's Last Stand: the 1954 Manhattan still looked modern, though the body shape had been around since the spring of 1950 (*Courtesy Nicky Wright*)

9 Standard of the World: Cadillac's 1952-62 series hardtop was called a Coupe de Villé (*Courtesy General Motors*)

10 Nostalgia Road: the 1956 Mk II Continental by Lincoln. This 'remanufactured' edition was offered by an Arizona firm for $18,600 in 1974 (*Courtesy Desert Classics*)

11 The One That Got Away: looking down on the Tucker's pop out windshield. From this angle the short hood is not apparent (*Courtesy Nicky Wright*)

12 Groovy Baby: one of the few 1948 Playboy convertibles that reached the public (*Courtesy Nicky Wright*)

13 First year of the Vee-Eight: Chevrolet Corvette, 1955 (*Author's Collection*)

14 *Adieu, Mme La Traction:* the last 11CV Citroën comes off the lines at Javel, July 1957. Behind can be seen the shovel nose of a DS19 (*Courtesy S A André Citroën*)

15 France's First Two-million Seller: the Renault Dauphine launched early in 1956 (*Courtesy Renault Ltd*)

16 Peugeot by Pininfarina: the indestructible 403, 1955-66 (*Courtesy Automobiles Peugeot*)

17 Fiat with a Fencer's Mask: Simca 8CV saloon, 1949 (*Courtesy Chrysler France SA*)

18 The AFG's Step-child: Dyna-Panhard 120 cabriolet, 1950 (*Courtesy G N Georgano*)

19 *Adieu, Monsieur Weiffenbach:* Delahaye Type 235 by Chapron, 1952 (*Courtesy National Motor Museum*)

20 *Petite Routière:* 1951 Salmson S4-61L cabriolet with hydraulic brakes (*Courtesy Lucien Loreille*)

1955, accounted for five units, though these were the antithesis of the stark Excaliburs. Gaylord's idea of a sports car was 'something that would make a man sell his wife into slavery in order to get one'. Though unable to fit Lucas P100 lamps into his Facel-like vertical clusters, Gaylord did achieve electrically actuated servo brakes, a Facel-type central console between the front seats, colour-coded instruments, wing-mounted inspection lamps for wheel changes at night and an external frost-warning light. The spare wheel rolled out of its locker on serrated rails, like a bier, while the angular coupé body with its heavy tail fins incorporated a retractable metal top: the car's recessed 'breezeway' rear window would later be imitated by Ford. Gaylords used twin-tube frames, conventional suspension with coils at the front and a 'doctored' Hydramatic box which only permitted gear changing at peak revs. The engines were vee-eights by Chrysler or Cadillac, but plans to build this $17,500 masterpiece in series foundered. Reputedly the German coach builder Hermann Spohn made everything far too heavy.

Sterling Edwards's main interest was custom-built aircraft, but he had already constructed more than one sports car when he announced his Edwards America in 1953. The prototype used a Henry-J frame, which was later replaced by a shortened Mercury chassis. Here was a handsome Ferrari-like convertible with wire wheels and luxurious appointments, allied to an American engine with power-for-everything. Oldsmobile, Lincoln and Cadillac units were used at various times, and official Ford interest suggests that the America might have become the Thunderbird. The original list price of $4,994 had been inflated to $8,000 by 1955, which explains why it did not sell well.

The Rockefeller Yankee was marketed in the 1949–52 period. It used a shortened and lowered 1939 Ford frame, with the engine moved back to give a 50–50 weight distribution. Most of the other mechanical elements were Ford—including the higher-geared pre-war type steering—and the car carried sports four-seater coachwork in the English style with a grille reminiscent of the Aston Martin's. A very similar creation was the Story from Portland, Oregon, though this was a two-seater on a shorter 97-inch wheelbase, the chassis, steering and suspension were Willys, and its creator had somehow extracted 113 bhp from a 2.2-litre Ford vee-eight engine with the aid of Offenhauser heads, twin carburetters and a 10.5:1 compression. A price of $3,500 was quoted in 1950. Two years later the Skorpion was produced in California; it was sold in glassfibre kit form to mount on the 722 cc overhead-camshaft Crosley chassis. The frame was the customer's responsibility, but Skorpion were prepared to modify it with a lowered centre-section for an inclusive price of $445.

1.6 Rag, Tag and Bobbi–Kar

As in Europe, the first post-war years were great days for the hopefuls, but of these only Powel Crosley, Jr., achieved any measure of success.

Crosley's crude miniatures with air-cooled Wisconsin engines had been on the market in 1939, struggling through to Pearl Harbour with the help of the family's radio business. During the war, however, Crosley had become involved with Lloyd Taylor's Cobra engine, designed for the Navy, primarily as an air-droppable unit for stationary generators. It was built up from steel stampings, which were copper brazed together, and was said to be frostproof. A fixed cylinder head was unusual for America: so was the overhead camshaft, which had not been seen in an American automobile since the demise of the Stutz in 1935. The capacity of the new small four was only 722 cc, in spite of which 26.5 bhp were delivered at a high 5,400 rpm.

This engine went into a simple channel-section frame with mechanical brakes and a semielliptic suspension, while Crosley's three-speed gearbox featured column shift but no synchromesh. The bodies, like those of the pre-war cars, were angular and ugly, but the machine was compact, with a length of only 145 inches, and it would buzz along quite happily on its 12-inch wheels at 55 mph. Powel Crosley, who was 6 feet 4 inches tall, made great play with the generous legroom, but this was achieved at the price of awkward ingress, not to mention a line of vision making it difficult for a six footer to drive in safety. However, because of the prevailing car shortage and prices in the $800–900 bracket, the Crosley sold quite well—over 32,000 in 1948 alone. Among the styles listed was the Sports Utility, an anticipation of BMC's famous Mini-Moke.

Encountering problems with the Cobra engine, Crosley changed to the CIBA (cast iron block) type in 1949. The car could cope with the extra 12 lb of weight but not with the next move—hydraulic disc brakes. These were efficient enough but were not proof against the American habit of salting highways in winter, which caused them to freeze. A year later Crosley returned to conventional drums, still hydraulically actuated; he was also poorer to the tune of $5,000,000. At the same time the cars were given cantilever rear springing, while the company also essayed a sports model.

The doorless Hotshot on its diminutive wheels might resemble a dodgem car, but it was surprisingly fast—77 mph in normally aspirated form and 90 mph with the optional blower. A Crosley won the Index of Performance at Sebring. On the sports cars, the company used a coil-and-radius arm rear suspension, but, though some 2,500 were sold (and also the engines were supplied to small foreign specialist makers such as Nardi and SIATA), production was down to 4,839 units in 1951. A year later the factory had closed, though not before it had launched the Farm-O-Road, a baby Jeep that could not only plough but also take the farmer to market. Six forward and two reverse speeds might have been an irresistible temptation at $800 for Britons, but never for Americans.

The Crosley's modest success was due to adequate funds and manufacturing facilities. These the opposition lacked, though the Playboy's sponsors did get as far as leasing an old aero-engine plant in Tonawanda, New York, and building some twenty cars there. Like the Crosley, the Playboy rode on 12-inch wheels, but even in its embryonic 1946 stage, it was a more substantial affair powered by a side valve 1½-litre four-cylinder Continental engine, the same make and capacity that had launched W. R. Morris's famous Cowley thirty years previously. There, of course, the resemblance ended, for the Playboy's chassis rode on coil springs at both ends, those at the front being independent, and it had the hydraulic brakes that four-cylinder Morrises would lack until 1932. The engine, likewise, lived at the rear, with a front-mounted fuel tank. The complete two-seater convertible weighed 1,820 lb, and the advertised list price was $950, inclusive of radio. A year later the engine had been moved to the front, in unit with a three-speed Warner synchromesh gearbox common to Studebaker's Champion. Final drive was by hypoid bevel, the suspension was now semielliptic, and a separate chassis had been abandoned in favour of unitary construction. The car was still a convertible, but an all-metal fliptop had replaced the original canvas hood. All this added only $35 to the price.

However, while the Playboy made use of proprietary mechanical elements, the engines were the real problem. Neither the Continental nor the 2-litre four-cylinder Hercules which replaced it were intended as anything but stationary units, and they overheated on the road. The final choice—and certainly the best—was the 2.2-litre Willys four, which cost only $162 delivered, and might have seen the Playboy into production. This, however, did not happen. The plant was sold in 1950, and, despite some curious negotiations with a Chinese Nationalist syndicate, the dies were finally scrapped nine years later.

The Keller (*née* Bobbi–Kar) fared a little better, though it was the same unhappy story of stock promotion schemes, abandoned aircraft factories (in this case Convair of San Diego, though nothing was actually made there), unsuitable engines and an uncertainty as to where to put them. As first planned, the Bobbi-Kar was crude in the extreme, with glassfibre bodywork and a twin-cylinder air-cooled Briggs and Stratton engine driving the rear wheels by chain. Weight was a low 600 lb, but by 1946 the formula was more sophisticated, with a small 1,063-cc water-cooled Hercules four, a steel-tube frame with cruciform bracing and an all-independent rubber suspension. The slab-sided roadster body was of an all-steel construction, and to remove the power plant one merely undid thirteen bolts. The Bobbi-Kar was 132 inches long and required a turning circle of only 27 feet. Deliveries were promised in February 1947, at a bargain $600, but in the meanwhile a new personality had come to the fore, George D. Keller, from the sales side of Studebaker. Henceforward the cars would bear his name.

Rear engines were not immediately discarded, but Keller was a great believer in station wagons. Further, woodies were easy to build, especially if hardware could be bought out, as it (like most other parts) was. The 'factory' in Alabama made only coachwork and seats.

In its definitive form, the Keller was a conventional front-engined machine on a 92-inch wheelbase, with a three-speed synchromesh gearbox and hypoid rear axle. The Torsilastic rubber suspension was used only at the front, with semielliptics at the back, and Keller planned to market his woody at $1,245. After trials with the Hercules, the company switched to the 2.6-litre Continental four, a purpose-built unit. Keller's sudden death of a heart attack brought American operations to a halt, but a few cars were built in Belgium under the name Pullman Super Chief between 1950 and 1954. It was a sad end for a venture which had claimed 1,523 franchises at peak.

Gary Davis's 1947 contribution was an enormous and improbable three-wheeler, also Hercules-powered, with two driven rear wheels. Advance publicity mentioned tubular frames, coil springing and aircraft-type disc brakes, but the actual car featured a channel-steel chassis, conventional semielliptics and drums, although these were hydraulically actuated. Nonetheless, the Davis was quite impressive, with its wrapround screen and rear window, retractable headlamps and bench seat of immense width for four abreast. With these dimensions, nobody could doubt that the car was capsize-proof, but 116 mph from 69 bhp seemed less likely. As for the Davis' ability to move in circles at 55 mph, this was hardly a saleable asset. However, the Securities Exchange Commission took a hand in this venture, and the sponsor was hauled off to jail. Of the 40,000 three-wheelers Gary Davis had planned to make at $995 apiece, only seventeen were actually produced.

The homely little King Midget not only saw production but also pursued a blameless and unsung existence in Athens, Ohio, for about twenty years. The brainchild of two Civil Air Patrol pilots, it was originally sold in dismantled and crated form, since final assembly was conducted on the first floor of the Athens shops, and there was no means of bringing complete vehicles downstairs! Early Midgets were single-seaters, but by 1952 the car had settled down into a standardized two-seater pattern. The air-cooled 377-cc side-valve single-cylinder Wisconsin engine sat at the back of a simple channel-section frame, while the creators' aeronautical interests were reflected in an all-independent suspension of oleo-leg type. The rest of it was primitive—a mechanical cable-operated starter, cycle-type dynamo lighting and single-gear drive, though an option was a two-speed pedal-controlled automatic with vee-belt drive, charmingly explained in the catalogue, 'The automatic transmission means essentially that you have a GO pedal (the accelerator) and a STOP pedal (the brake). The action of the transmission is entirely automatic. The car starts out in low gear, for fast getaways, and shifts automatically into high gear as the speed of the car increases.' A speed of 45 mph was possible on a weight of 500 lb, and $575 bought a standard King Midget. For another $20, there was the Special Show-Room Sports Model in bone white with a red pin stripe, a reverse gear, chromium-plated brightwork and a glass screen.

The others were legion. The Del Mar appeared in 1949 in San Diego, whence it was supposed to issue at the rate of 600 a day. How was not specified, but the car was quite promising, bearing a certain resemblance to a Hillman Minx convertible. Once again it had a Continental four and a three-speed Warner gearbox—one wonders what would have happened to Studebaker's supplies had all these ventures prospered. The front suspension was of the transverse Ford type, but semielliptics featured at the back, and as a compensation for these rustic arrangements Del Mar proposed to fit air-filled aircraft-type shock absorbers. A list price of $1,170 was still too close to Chevrolet. A year earlier T. P. Hall of Convair had taken time out from flying automobile experiments to promote the ground-borne Airway, described as 'a vicinity car for short town transports'! A small air-cooled engine lived at the rear, fluidrive transmission was used, and the body was of mixed plastic and alloy construction. Despite a proposed $700 price tag, Californians continued to commute in Chevrolets. R. C. McCarthy's 1948 Mustang from Seattle was ahead of its time: here was the 1956 Fiat Multipla formula with a rear engine (by Hercules), full forward control and doors on both sides. As befitted a generous carrying capacity, the price was higher, at $1,235.

With gasoline once more plentiful, three-wheelers had even less future. Both the Brogan of 1946 and the Towne Shopper of 1948 were doorless contraptions of dodgem-car type with rear engines and prices in the region of $600. J. V. Martin, already involved in Miles Carpenter's Dart miniatures of 1929, was back twenty-five years later with the Martin Stationette, a bonnetless glassfibre teardrop featuring 'magnetic drive', and as late as 1955 the simply named Tricar offered a rather similar layout with rubber suspension and 'hydraulic' transmission. This one used a Lycoming vertical-twin instead of Martin's 776-cc Hercules, and maximum speed claims were in the sixties, whereas Martin talked of 80.

Sundry attempts were made to put automobiles into the air. Roadable aircraft had long been a preoccupation with Americans; the 1930s had seen the Pitcairn autogiro (photographed in the streets of Washington, DC), and Waldo Waterman's curious high-wing *canard* monoplanes, with Studebaker six engines driving pusher airscrews, but, almost before Japan had surrendered, the Southern Aircraft Co. of Garland, Texas, were back in the business. In their version the empennage—including Lightning-type twin tail booms—was detachable, leaving a three-wheeler saloon with a single front wheel and a vee-eight Mercury engine which drove the rear wheels when not required to drive the propeller. The idea was taken up by Convair's T. P. Hall, who decided to make the two elements independent, mounting a Lycoming flat-six engine in the centre-section of the high wing. This left them with a conventional Crosley-powered four-wheeler, but after a crash in 1947 the idea was abandoned. Robert Fulton's Airphibian reverted to the old scheme of a detachable wing–tail assembly, a single engine and a tractor airscrew. The quadricycle oleo-sprung undercarriage served both functions, and drive, to the rear wheels, was 'hydraulic'. This vehicle turned up at an air display in Britain in the later 1940s.

M. B. Taylor, however, actually sold seven of his Aerocars, though it took him twenty-six years to do so. More ambitious than any of the others, the Aerocar featured a tail boom with a pusher airscrew mounted in the angle of a Beechcraft-style butterfly tailplane. The Lycoming flat-six engine gave an air speed of 110 mph and a ground speed of 67 mph: conversion took only 5 minutes. There was, however, one problem—where to put the wings. Taylor suggested towing them behind the Aerocar on a trailer, but clearly the idea did not appeal.

2 France

2.1 À Bas la Difference

The 1920s had been France's ebullient decade, the 1930s saw stagnation, and 1946–56 would prove both explosive and cathartic.

By 1956, all the dead wood had gone, and with it many a great name. The cumulative shibboleths of years had also vanished. France might not be as receptive to new ideas as Germany, but now the adherents of *traction avant* included Panhard and Citroën, and Renault had espoused the rear engine. If a Frenchman had been told that within twenty-two years *la belle France*, home of the *système* Panhard, would offer precisely one conventionally driven private car—and that no longer made in France—he would have been suitably incredulous. He would also have pointed out to *perfide Albion* that 'the nation of shopkeepers' offered no revolutionary designs beyond Déesses assembled at Slough and Dauphines put together at Acton.

Even if one forgets the 2CV and the Déesse and judges the Renault Dauphine fairly against the standards of 1956, there is still a tendency to dismiss France's efforts on the grounds that each year saw fewer and fewer models.

Because France's recovery was less dramatic—and less generally resented—she has never received the same credit as has Germany. Yet French production increased almost tenfold between 1948 and 1956, and the industry passed its pre-war peak (228,000 units in 1938) sooner than the Germans, with deliveries running at over 254,000 in 1950. It also gave the world more than its share of best-sellers. Of the eleven mass-produced models catalogued in 1956, no fewer than four (Citroën's D family, the Peugeot 403, the 4CV Renault and the Simca Aronde) exceeded 1,000,000, the Renault Dauphine chalked up 2,000,000, and the five millionth *deux-chevaux*, delivered in the spring of 1976, was scarcely noticed. If France exported relatively fewer of her wares than either Britain or Germany—in 1956 her foreign share was 30%, as against Britain's 49% and the Bundes-republik's 48%—it was because she believed in a healthy home market. French manufacturers favoured the safe credo of trying it on the dog, a desirable step when launching anything as revolutionary as the DS19 Citroën. Nine months after the model's introduction, no garages outside Paris fully comprehended its hydropneumatics, so one shudders to think what might have befallen French prestige had Americans been unleashed on the cars so soon.

France faced shortages as serious as those of Germany. During the Second World War friend and foe alike had helped themselves, and though proposed Vichy legislation to outlaw older types (these were named in true civil service detail!) had come to nothing, in February 1946 it was estimated that only about 900,000 of the country's 2,500,000 motor vehicles were still potentially usable: this meant about 300,000 private cars. No wonder that ancient 5CV Citroëns were still a common sight in Paris as late as 1949. The roads were in appalling shape: between the Liberation and October 1945, 680 bridges had been rebuilt, and another 574 were on the short list, but this still left nearly 4,300 improvized river crossings.

Tyres were as scarce as in Italy. Photographs taken in 1945 show Renault trucks standing on their bare rims in Billancourt's despatch bays. The Germans had pillaged the factories: Renault had lost one-fifth of their tooling, and Peugeot's deficit was thought to be between 4,000 and 5,000 machines. Much of what remained was worn out—and had been so in 1939. The Allied Air Forces had paid liberal attention to factories such as Matford's, known to be working for the enemy. Peugeot's Sochaux plant lay in the middle of a battlefield, and Panhard, though escaping serious damage by the RAF, found their Ivry works used for dumping leftover bombs by the retreating Luftwaffe.

There was the added hazard of Resistance Managements, such as those that seized control of Berliet and Voisin. H. T. Pigozzi of Simca was barred for a while from his factory by workers who insisted that he had collaborated with the Germans, Hotchkiss was suspect for 'not having gone slowly enough' during the Occupation, and the unfortunate Louis Renault died in prison at Fresnes in the winter of 1944: his company was nationalized. Ettore Bugatti, whose factories had been requisitioned and turned over to the German Trippelwerke, only just survived the protracted litigation necessary to reestablish his rights at Molsheim.

Governments gave with one hand and took with the other. Pierre Lefaucheux, once entrusted with the management of the new Régie Nationale des Usines Renault, was allowed to make it pay without bureaucratic interference. Yet employers were beset with a multitude of compulsory levies. These, admittedly, kept strikes to a minimum—there was no repetition of the catastrophic stoppages of 1936. Quite the opposite: with generous overtime enforced by law, the 40-hour week was a dead letter. At Simca many workers put in 60 hours. But in 1952 wages tax, family allowances, social insurance, accident liability insurance and contributions to state training schemes all added another 39% to the bill, and this had to be passed on to the motoring public. Further, France adopted the Italian method of collecting tax every time a raw material changed hands; once again, as in Italy, there was no tax rebate on exports. Ford, whose foreign sales decreased from 3,619 in 1950 to 1,490 in 1951, were quick to blame the Government for this.

From the car makers' point of view, the Government was none too generous with steel, either. Ambitious state-sponsored five-year plans called for 1,700,000 new vehicles, with subsidies for such economy items as the 4CV Renault and (initially) the flat-twin Aluminium Française–Grégoire, but these could not be fulfilled: even the amended 1947 target of 136,000 units proved unattainable. Steel supplies were about 40% down on 1938's level, and of this only 6.7% was allocated to car manufacture. Further, there was no allocation at all for new or 'lapsed' manufacturers; Emile Mathis was unable to procure authorization for either of his post-war projects, and Rosengart's revival was delayed until 1951.

The Government also changed the tax structure. Their post-1918 Cyclecar law, aimed at the furtherance of marginal motoring, had bred only an exciting race of small sports cars. Now the authorities discovered that there was a direct relationship between the size of a man's pocket and the size of his car's engine. What is more, they established a clear-cut limit at 16CV (about 3 litres). Below this, a 12–15CV model cost its owner £23 a year: above it, he paid an exorbitant £79. This suited Citroën, for their established front-wheel drive Citroën Six was a 15CV. It was just as fatal for the *grandes routières*, since the Type 57 Bugatti ran to 17CV. The 3½ litres of Delahaye and Hotchkiss were 20CVs, and Talbot's just-introduced Lago Record was a 26CV.

Thus the breed faded away. Home-market buyers could afford neither the price—even a standard 20CV Hotchkiss saloon cost 1,400,000 old francs in 1951, as against 840,000 for a Citroën *quinze* and 851,000 for Ford's 13CV Vedette—nor the upkeep. Nor was there a lasting export market. True, in 1946 Belgian, Swiss and Swedish buyers snatched at anything they could obtain, preferring old and trusted French *marques* to obscure British species such as Armstrong Siddeley or Lea–Francis—but, when the market hardened, most of the British specialists were ready with new models. Their French counterparts were not; the cash had run out. Talbot, admittedly, tried very hard with their excellent 4½-litre cars. In 1947 the Lago Grand Sport was certainly the most powerful (at 190 bhp) and probably also the fastest roadgoing model available anywhere. By 1953 it had to compete with Mercedes–Benz and Jaguar, who could make as many sports cars in a year as Talbot could turn out in a decade.

Every scheme turned to wormwood. Delahaye dispensed with their bread and butter 12CV after 1948, hoping to recoup their losses with the four-wheel drive VLR. The Army accepted this, only to discontinue using it on grounds of complexity. Talbot's bid to stay on the right side of the abyss with the 15CV Baby ended in disaster, and Hotchkiss could not afford the excellent but expensive flat-four Grégoire. Statistics tell their own story: Hotchkiss managed to sell 2,705 cars (most of them the staid old 13CV) in 1951, but by 1953 they were down to 230, in which season Talbot made ten cars, and the combined efforts of Delahaye and Delage produced precisely three.

Even the makers whose products stayed firmly on the safer shore had a tough time. Salmson only just made it to the end of our decade, while Panhard had already enlisted some necessary support from Citroën, and the Ford company took the unprecedented step of selling their entire French operation to Simca.

With the *grande routière* industry also went the great French coachbuilders. Though cut off by currency restrictions from the best English leather, they could still produce extravaganzas on occasion, and up to the early 1950s Chapron, Figoni, Guilloré and (especially) Saoutchik enlivened Salons with their interpretations of the latest slab-sided idiom. A particularly outrageous Figoni creation on a Delahaye chassis, shown in 1948, included in its equipment an ivory-bound copy of the *Guide Michelin* said to be worth 40,000 francs in its own right! Yet in 1955, when Chapron was given the task of building a special long-chassis 15CV Citroën for President Coty, the splendour was only superficial. Among the hardware that graced it were windscreen, bumpers, boot handle and rim trims from assorted French Fords, Chevrolet stop lights, Bentley door handles and a rear window from a 1949 Buick.

To her credit, France protected her industry. French cars were again freely available in Britain from mid-1953, but even Fiat—despite a widening divergence between their own products and those of Simca—did not bother to reestablish their French sales organization until 1958. The brakes were not officially released till two years later, hence the only foreign model readily available at the end of our period was the little Isetta, made under licence by the Vélam concern.

In view of the traditional Gallic preoccupation with subutility devices, it is surprising that the cyclecar made less headway in the country than it did in West Germany. Not even Suez produced any notable echoes, though possibly the French Vespa coupé—which falls outside our period—was an indirect result of that interlude. For every twenty breeds that graced the Grand Palais, there must have been at least fifteen that never got that far—but only the Rovin and the Mochet sold in measurable quantities. The latter, requiring no *permis de conduire*, appealed especially to drivers who had lost theirs through an excess of blood alcohol.

The reason was not hard to seek: that mobile garden shedful, the 2CV Citroën. Crude it most certainly was, but it was properly made and enjoyed the backing of nationwide service. It could transport four Frenchmen anywhere, provided that they were resigned to an inexorable 35-mph gait, halved by any hill. The rolltop and detachable seating also made it an excellent substitute for that classic French car of the 1930s, the elongated five-door *commerciale* with its poor gear ratios. One could not, after all, carry a grandfather clock aboard a Rovin or Poirier.

An intriguing aspect of the depleted range structures of the 1950s was that direct competition between manufacturers almost ceased. A model slotted—not into a gap in one's own range or into a hitherto unexplored sector—but into a hole in the entire French buyer's guide. At the bottom, the 2CV Citroën was unchallenged, as was the Renault 4CV. The Panhard was *pour les initiés seulement*; everyone else was afraid of breaking the gearbox. At the top of the family-saloon market neither the Ford Vedette nor the 13CV Hotchkiss represented serious competition for the Citroën's Six. With the advent of the 403, Peugeot virtually controlled the 1,500-cc class, and their 203, a large and roomy car, had never really conflicted with the 8CV and 9CV Simcas. Simca, for their part, had anticipated the baby Renaults and Citroëns and had backed out of the *topolino* game in time. The only real overlap was between the good old 11CV Citroën *traction* and the upstart Renault Frégate, but here the two personalities—and clienteles—were so opposed that it seems unlikely that either company lost sales to the other. Pierre Lefaucheux undoubtedly authorized the Frégate to carry on the tradition of 11CV family Renaults dating back to the KZ of the 1920s: he also waited for that market to reactivate itself through a combination of increased affluence and the ravages of the car breakers. Sometimes, of course, one maker picked up another's sales—the slow workups of Dauphine and Déesse production during 1956 pushed the Simca Aronde briefly into the No. 1 spot—but true cut-throat competition would not begin until the 1960s.

The new uniformity had some intriguing side-lights. By the mid-1950s, the French purveyors of tuned Panhards and Renaults rivalled Italy's custom-Fiat industry. The Deutsch–Bonnet partnership was already as important—far more so, on the circuits—as SIATA, for instance, while Jean Rédélé's as-yet obscure Alpine would soon become a household word. At a lower level, the bolt-on goody industry was thriving, with emphasis on the in-car of the moment. In Good King Traction's golden days (1946–8), owners were encouraged to decorate their *onze légères* with wrapround rear windows, mock-American grilles and fake bonnets with Buick-style portholes, as well as useful twin-carburetter manifolds and desirable four-speed conversions. A year later it was the 4CV Renault's turn, with suitcases styled to fit the awkwardly shaped front boot, a folding 'Kiss-Ply' picnic table set and even a portable mini-garage for the customer's front garden. SAPRAR, a Renault associate, dispensed these goodies much as Renault Boutiques did in the 1970s.

Further, when France designed for the world, the world liked it. It did not like the Dauphine's handling, but it bought Dauphines. The only clear instance of 'Vanguarditis' was the Renault Frégate—but unlike its British counterpart, it was never more than a second (or third) string in the Régie's lineup. In 1956, 29,000 were made, as against 112,000 4CVs and 78,000 of the new Dauphines. In spite of all her tax difficulties, France's rationalized ranges did keep prices down. In Switzerland in 1949, the 4CV Renault at £335 undercut both the Fiat *topolino* (£395) and the Morris Minor (£410), despite the added attraction of four doors. The Peugeot 203 cost £130 less than a Hillman Minx, and Citroën fans could buy an *onze légère* for only £575. Even in 1953, when the pace had quickened and the sellers' market was over, not only the *deux-chevaux* but the little Renault as well were cheaper than either the Austin A30 or the state-subsidized IFA F9 from East Germany.

2.2   Goddess and Garden Shed

No agonising decisions faced Citroën in 1945. Rear-wheel drive had long been relegated to the *poids lourds*, and the *traction avant* was a respected member of society. It would be bought in Britain purely on the strength of its traditional looks, by those who disliked the Americanized Standards and Hillmans. Teething troubles lay in the past—for the *traction's* eleventh birthday coincided almost exactly with the Nazi surrender. Thus, having outsold the opposition in 1938 and 1939, the 11CV family lasted the new decade out. The last of 708,339 four-cylinder cars (the 7CV was not revived after the war) rolled off the lines in July 1957.

Nor was the design changed much. The 1956 model was identifiable from its 1946 counterpart—but only just. To a Frenchman, the major difference was that the 11 came in a choice of colours and had done so since 1953—before that, it had been uncompromisingly black, with lemon-yellow wheels as the distinguishing mark (in theory) of the large 15/6. At the same time it had acquired a bigger but still inadequate external-access boot. Pendant pedals had appeared in 1949, from the 1954 model year the old eight–nine-seater *commerciales* with swing-up tailgates were back, and in its last eighteen months the Citroën Six (which disappeared in the autumn of 1955) gave the public a foretaste of the Déesse's hydropneumatics, albeit at the rear only. The 11 was also given the new D-series engine of 1956, which boosted power from a long-standing 56 bhp to 60.

The Citroën had a long-stroke (78 mm × 100 mm) overhead-valve engine with detachable cylinder barrels and wet liners, driving forwards via a single-plate clutch and three-speed synchromesh gearbox. The excellent all-torsion-bar suspension was independent at the front, rack-and-pinion steering had been in use since 1936, and the brakes were hydraulic. 6-volt electrics sufficed—12-volt equipment, together with leather trim and a sliding roof, were English heresies, confined to Slough-assembled cars. This machinery lived in a welded-up steel unitary structure, with front horns to which the power pack was bolted. This immensely rigid though rustprone *monocoque* retained its 1934 shape and needed no fancy trim to enhance it; on home-market Citroëns, indeed, radiator shells were painted black. The 1,911-cc four-cylinder 11 (the Light Fifteen to Britons) came on a 114½-inch wheelbase and would do 72 mph. The same engine went into the *Normale* (Big Fifteen) with an extra 7 inches of wheelbase, while at the top of the range and sharing the *Normale's* chassis length, was the 2.9-litre 15/6, with dual-choke carburetter, a twin-plate clutch, vertically mounted front shock absorbers and thicker drive shafts with torque-resistant dampers which were inclined to give trouble. This was good for 80–85 mph, though it was for men only thanks to a turning circle of 46 feet and steering geared at 2½ turns from lock to lock.

The virtues of the design were superb handling and first-class brakes, against which had to be set complicated and tedious servicing schedules (especially for the six), an unpleasing dashboard gearchange requiring full depression of the clutch at all times, and (for Europeans if not for Britons) the *démodé* 1934 styling. There were, of course, those who regarded the Citroën as being in the best Coatalen and Roesch traditions. *Motor Sport* was 'unable to recall any other car as roomy as this which has proved so enjoyable to drive in sports-car style'.

Citroën had already been thinking against the tide in 1938. When *six chevaux* still represented the bottom limit for French family saloons, they had evolved 'a runabout for people in rural areas who cannot afford conventional cars'—in other words, a revival of the Model T Ford theme tailored to national requirements. They actually had some 300 prototypes on the road at the time of the Occupation and had already discarded an outboard-type string starter as being too much for the distaff side. At the 1948 Paris Salon they were ready to show the 2CV to the public, though in his autobiography J. A. Grégoire observes that the factory's original 30-mph parameters were hurriedly uprated to 40 mph after tests of his flat-twin Aluminium Française–Grégoire. Cynical journalists, contemplating the 2CV's uncompromising mass of angles and the corrugated finish in unrelieved grey, dismissed the new baby as 'at best a freak and at worst a joke'—but the formula worked.

Like Volkswagen, Citroën opted for slow-turning horizontally opposed engines and air cooling: the tiny 62 mm × 62 mm (375-cc) flat-twin developed its 9 bhp at 3,500 rpm. For long life, they adopted an all-indirect four-speed gearbox on which top was very much an overdrive, at 5.7:1. For coping with heavy payloads on rough surfaces, they devised a form of independent suspension in which a system of leading arms and horizontal coils linked the two wheels on either side. For durability they used the simplest possible form of unitary structure, welded to a punt-type frame, while for ease of maintenance almost everything could be unscrewed—doors lifted out, bonnet and wings came off in minutes, and the disc wheels had three bolts instead of the usual four or five. To handle indivisible loads, one removed the rear seat, and folded back the cabrio-limousine roof.

In other ways, the 2CV was sophisticated. Combustion chambers were hemispherical; and, though dashboard change was retained, the box had synchromesh on all forward ratios, something that no Volkswagen, Fiat, Renault or Morris owner was offered in 1948—or for several years thereafter. The absence of constant-velocity joints was scarcely noticed when so little power was being transmitted, the 2CV's brakes, unlike those of the contemporary Volkswagen, were hydraulic, and there was, of course, an electric starter. A hand wheel on the dashboard permitted adjustment of the dipped beam as the suspension adjusted itself. The tubular-framed rubber-webbing seats were also adjustable at the shift of a peg, the heater drew warm air off the cylinders (thus obviating some of the Dyna Panhard's odder improvizations), and the wipers were driven off the speedometer cable. The 2CV was not a particularly small car: at 149 inches from stem to stern it was 1 inch longer than the Morris Minor and 7 inches longer than the Renault 4CV. It did, however, recapture the old Jowett theme of a small engine pulling a large payload. At a weight of approximately 1,400 lb, the car cruised on the level at a steady 35–38 mph and would attain 41 mph if pushed. One gallon of fuel lasted 70 miles with careful driving, and even heavy treatment returned 50–55 mpg. The prices of replacements—in the early days, at any rate—matched those of a Model T: a set of piston rings and cylinders cost £7.60, and a pair of front wings £2.70. At a list price which fluctuated between £240 and £300, there was a black market in 2CVs: 1952's output of 500 a week was simply not enough, and the situation was not finally relieved until production was allowed to overflow into the Panhard works at Ivry. If Britons did not like the car, this was largely a matter of snobbery and price: at £565 the 2CV was no more competitive than Fiat's 500C. Other nations bought it: in the 1959–71 period Citroën's Argentinian branch built 55,000.

Like the *traction*, the 2CV lasted throughout our period with no significant changes. In 1954, the capacity was increased to 425 cc, which gave another 3½ bhp and 50 mph on occasion. At the same time a semi-automatic centrifugal clutch was made available, and by the end of 1956 there was a de luxe model (Type AZL) with lockable metal boot, chromium-plated bumpers, wheel trims, spats at the rear, interior lighting and better instrumentation.

The *traction*'s successor took a long time to arrive. As early as 1952, reports were filtering through of all-new cars with inboard brakes, four-speed automatic boxes and 1½-litre flat-six air-cooled engines. In 1954, the Citroën 15H Six's hydropneumatic rear suspension gave a clue to the future, and by the end of 1955 the sixes were no more. The last of 50,518 had been delivered.

At the 1955 shows, the DS19 took the world by storm. Now, after a twenty-one-year run, everyone is so acclimatized to the whale-like shape with its downward-sloping nose, absence of a grille and vast areas of glass—thanks to wraparound screen and rear window and the thinnest of pillars—that the Déesse passes unnoticed. Most people do not realise that this aerodynamically styled saloon has a wheel set uncompromisingly at each corner, which is probably why it looked better than Rover's 1964 anglicization of the same theme. One almost forgets how disconcerting first acquaintance could be since the car rose into the air when the ignition was switched on and sank back again when the engine was stopped. *The Motor*'s summary was perhaps the best, 'The most complicated car made anywhere in Europe; the most comfortable car made anywhere in the world.'

The basis of the new suspension was a system of oleopneumatic struts, applied now at both ends, with metal springs replaced by gas compression. Lockheed fluid at a pressure of over 2,500 psi was used to control the system, the power source being a pump driven by a belt off the front of the engine. No human assistance was needed: the Citroën adjusted itself automatically to road conditions, only sudden humpbacks catching the car unawares.

Nor was this the limit of power assistance. To use it for jacking the vehicle was logical, but hydraulics also took care of the clutch (there was no clutch pedal), the steering, the brakes (inboard discs at the front and conventionally located drums at the rear) and even the four-speed synchromesh gearbox, though the driver retained complete control. The column-mounted gear lever also operated the starter, while the new unitary hull incorporated a plastic roof section. A single-spoke steering wheel recalled Humbers of the pre-1914 era. To assist handling, the latest Michelin X radial-ply tyres were factory equipment, eliminating tyre scrub at the price of a high noise level.

It was all too good to be true, for underneath the spare wheel on its inclined mounting lay the same old long-stroke 1.9-litre engine that Citroën had been using for twenty-one years. But not quite, for the top end featured the 2CV's hemi-head design and a 'hotter' camshaft profile. The output was 63 bhp, sufficient to propel the aerodynamic shape at 80–85 mph. Further, the overdrive top and 'working' third were set close enough, at 3.3:1 and 4.78:1 respectively, to enable the latter to be used to bring the car up to its maximum. The fuel consumption remained constant to the 80-mph level.

The DS19 was expensive (£1,727 in Britain), maintenance was trickier than ever, and many drivers found the tiny brake pedal disconcerting: there was also the question of what happens if the power fails. Thus the next step, revealed at the 1956 Salon, was a simplified version with hydropneumatics confined to the suspension. This ID19 used the *traction*'s 11D engine with a plain Solex carburetter in place of the Déesse's dual-choke Weber. The car was also lighter, so performance was unaffected. By mid-1957 the range was sufficiently broken-in to warrant the demise of the 11CV.

In 1945, the newly nationalized Renault company had a staff of 28,000 employed on truck manufacture, though under the energetic direction of Pierre Lefaucheux they managed to turn out about 12,000 of these in France's first year of freedom. Further, Lefaucheux firmly committed himself to a one-model range, discarding Louis Renault's modernized 12CV, a descendant of the old side-valve 85. Its successor was the 4CV (R1060), developed surreptitiously during the Occupation.

This was quite as outstanding as the *deux-chevaux*, and demand was such that it was still a black-market item in 1950. It was certainly more compact than the Citroën, with a wheelbase of 76 inches and a length of 142 inches, since Renault engineers had opted for a rear engine.

In every respect the 4CV marked a break with the past. All four wheels were independently sprung, by a Germanic combination of coils and wishbones at the front and by a swing axle and coils at the rear. This—and the presence of a captive Ferdinand Porsche at Renault during 1945—has led to the widely held belief that the 4CV was a Porsche design. It was not, though both Porsche and his son Ferry were consulted in the later stages. The 7-inch drum brakes were hydraulically actuated, the steering was by rack and pinion, and full unitary construction was used: this method had, of course, already been applied to pre-war Juvaquatres. The lightweight 15-inch wheels with their spider-type rims were a Grégoire legacy, while yet another departure was the overhead-valve four-cylinder engine, even if its dimensions were classic, at 55 mm × 80 mm for a capacity of 760 cc. This unit drove forwards to a three-speed gearbox with synchromesh on second and top; the output was 19 bhp, sufficient to propel the 4CV at 57 mph. The pull-up starter and choke controls were mounted, Volkswagen-style, between the front seats, but, unlike the Volkswagen and Aluminium Française–Grégoire prototypes, the car had four doors.

Like most rear-engined cars, the little Renault oversteered, but the engine was almost 'unburstable', and it was energetically promoted. Among the more ingenious schemes was a prize (a new 4CV of course) for the child who collected the largest diversity of registration numbers on examples of the model.

By 1949 the tuners were at work, and 4CV derivatives were challenging Dyna Panhards at Le Mans and elsewhere. Renault kept a weather eye on sporting developments. In 1950, the capacity of the engine was reduced to 747 cc, to bring it into the official 750-cc category, and, while touring units never gave more than 21 bhp, the R1063, the first of the high-performance variants, went on sale in October 1952. The crankshaft, connecting rods, sump, flywheel, exhaust ports and valve springs were all special, as was the reinforced suspension. The R1063 could attain over 70 mph, while the 0–50-mph acceleration time was an impressive 15 seconds, compared with nearly 38 seconds for the first saloons of 1947. The ultimate in 'hot' models was introduced three years later, available with four- or five-speed gear-boxes; the latter configuration was even crammed into the standard casing, although this meant dispensing with synchromesh altogether. It also meant speeds of 82, 63, 48, 32 and 22 mph on the admirably spaced ratios, all for the modest increment of £120 in France. Like the little Citroën, the 4CV needed few alterations: better brakes, some minor embellishment of the austere saloon body, telescopic dampers and—towards the end of our period—pressurized cooling, an automatic choke and the Ferlec clutch option for two-pedal driving.

4CV production was quick to work up. By 1949 Renault had edged past Citroën with deliveries of 83,107 cars compared with about 65,000 of their rivals. Something, however, had to be done to bridge the immediate post-Armistice gap, and this was the Juvaquatre, first seen in 1937. It was little more than a gallicized Opel Kadett, even down to headlamp fairings on top of the wings—as irate Nazis had been quick to point out. The construction was unitary, dimensions of the 1-litre four-cylinder side-valve engine were more old fashioned than the Opel's, at 58 mm × 95 mm (those *chevaux-vapeur* again!), and the synchromesh gearbox had three speeds. Suspension was by transverse leaves at either end, the beam rear axle being a legacy from earlier Renaults. Post-war Juvas, admittedly, came with four doors and hydraulic brakes, but the car was no more than a hangover, and it had gone from the private-car range by 1950. Surprisingly, light-van and station-wagon editions soldiered on for another decade: they received the 4CV engine in 1954 and the 845-cc Dauphine unit in 1956.

In 1948 Lefaucheux at long last authorized a 2-litre car, the Frégate, for the faithful questing a replacement for their aged Primaquatre. Ironically, this car was to kill him—he died at the wheel of a Frégate in December 1955.

What appeared in 1951 was the Fiat 1400—the Standard Vanguard for-mula all over again—a bulboid six-seater saloon. The Frégate's width was, however, determined by unusual parameters; the dimensions of the paint tunnel at the Flins factory, where the car would be produced. The engine was a wet-liner overhead-valve 2-litre four with dimensions not unlike those of the Vanguard, at 85 mm × 88 mm. Also comparable was its output of 58 bhp.

For all the front engine and rear drive, the Frégate inherited some features from the 4CV, notably unitary construction, all-independent springing and hydraulic brakes, of the leading-and-trailing type with floating shoes. The styling was more felicitous than that of either Fiat or Vanguard, and the high (4.08:1) top gear was admirably suited to French road conditions, although the high-geared steering was paid for with indifferent low-speed manoeuvrability. A 110½-inch wheelbase made for a roomy car, and the Frégate was not excessively heavy, at 2,408 lb. Alas! the pioneers of the direct top gear had opted for an all-indirect box which whined and was afflicted with a difficult column shift.

Nobody liked the car, but excellent aerodynamics helped it to cruise at 75 mph, and sales were creditable, averaging some 31,000 a year between 1953 and the end of our period. By 1956 it had a direct top, synchromesh on bottom and the 4CV's automatic choke. Alongside the Frégate, from 1951 to 1954, Renault offered the Prairie, a ¾-ton van available in station-wagon form. This retained beam axles and—until 1953—the ancient 2,383-cc 85 flathead engine, ultimately replaced by a detuned Frégate unit.

In 1956, of course, a new best-seller was introduced, the Dauphine. Styled by Boano, it fitted conveniently into a gap between the 4CV and the Simca Aronde. Its advent also coincided with the Suez Crisis, which put its combination of performance (70 mph) and economy (45 mpg) at a premium. While the mechanics were uprated 4CV, the Dauphine featured the three-box system of construction—a welded stress-carrying centre-section to which were bolted the front and rear assemblies. The larger and longer boot gave the car almost 'front-engined' proportions, the front windows wound down where they had slid on the 4CV, and a curved screen improved forward vision. The new 845-cc engine made all the difference, with only an extra 35 lb of weight to balance an additional 9 bhp. And herein lay the rub.

All the Dauphine's notorious tricks, from vicious oversteer to an ability to become airborne in a cross-wind, had been present on the 4CV; but the latter's modest output had discouraged speeds at which these became dangerous. The Dauphine invited fast driving; it thrived on 5,000 rpm and more. Further, standards had changed: when the 4CV appeared in 1946, column shift had been on the way in, and the small car's indefinite floor-mounted lever was preferable to some European attempts at 'four-on-the-wheel'. Thus ten years later critics were disappointed to find that the latest model retained the old soup-stirring action, with feet of lost motion between first and second gears.

In its day, however, the car was a well-deserved best-seller, made under licence in Italy by Alfa Romeo and in Brazil by Willys. In due course, it would become indecently fast, thanks to the ministrations of Amédée Gordini. The 20% increase in sales it brought would finally put Renault ahead of Citroën.

Peugeot were a solid family firm. Their sole concessions to heterodoxy were worm drive—more or less extinct on private cars by the 1940s—and a predilection for column changes with peculiar spring-loaded actions which were 'quickly mastered', as one road-test report put it, 'if one thinks of it as a normal three-speed transmission with an additional gear for main-road cruising'. This it certainly was; on Peugeots of our era third was invariably the direct drive. The company's record was steady rather than spectacular; production built up from 13,807 cars in 1946 to nearly 142,000 in 1956.

Once again a pre-war design bridged the gap. Eschewing the big 402 as too close to Citroën's 11 Normale, the company concentrated on the 1,133-cc 202B. The three-bearing overhead-valve four-cylinder engine was housed in the familiar Peugeot *bloctube* frame, 12-volt electrics were an unusual refinement, and the ratios of the three-speed gearbox were selected by a central lever. Inevitably, there was a worm-drive back end, while the transverse-leaf independent front suspension had been seen on Peugeots since 1932. Early post-war examples retained the starfish-like Michelin Pilote wheels abandoned by Citroën, headlamps were still tucked behind a sloping radiator grille, and the absence of an external-access boot dated the little car. The traditional Peugeot reliability was, however, still present. Changes were confined to semielliptic springs in place of quarter-elliptics at the rear, though during 1946 the 202B gave way to the 202BH with hydraulic brakes. Inclusive of light commercials, the 202 series accounted for nearly 140,000 units all told and its eleven-year run terminated late in 1949, when its successor, the 203, was safely established.

This tough and economical machine would win the 1953 and 1956 Round Australia Rallies. It would be the staple Peugeot for five seasons, disappearing only in 1960. In many ways it perpetuated the old *conduite intérieure avec malle* theme, though this latter component was incorporated neatly into a sloping tail, and the usual welded-up unitary construction had been adopted. Headlamps had vanished into the wings, flanking a grille that was more like a Lincoln than a Plymouth, and the bonnet was of the alligator type. With the 203, Peugeot initiated their geared-up top and column change, and, though the traditional independent front suspension was retained, a live axle and coils were preferred at the rear. The engine was a new and advanced design with hemispherical combustion chambers; its wet-liner construction was a 202 heritage. The dimensions, at 75 mm × 73 mm, were slightly oversquare, but no attempt was made to extract a high output. Nonetheless, the Peugeot's 42 bhp from 1.3 litres could match the 40 bhp of Simca's latest 8CV. Long life counted for more at Sochaux.

Not that the Peugeot was a sluggard, attaining 72 mph and cruising at 65, though the acceleration, never sensational, was not improved by the revised gear ratios adopted in 1954. These left a wide gap between first and second gear, and a more serious one between third and top. Equipment was comprehensive by Renault or Citroën standards: self-cancelling direction indicators, a heater-demister, an internally controlled boot lock and even a sliding roof. A screenwash was added in 1957. The price, at 620,000 francs, once again fitted into the national pattern, falling between the *onze légère* Citroën and the Renault Frégate at 795,000 francs.

Nearly half a million 203 private cars were made, with the minimum of modifications during the model's run. A long-wheelbase station wagon with semielliptic rear springs carried on the *commerciale* tradition, and by 1953 Peugeot had set the tone for future ranges with some pretty, though expensive, three-seater coupés and cabriolets. An all-synchromesh gearbox on 1955 and later 203s represented the sum total of mechanical change.

Meanwhile, the Pininfarina-styled 403 saloon had been introduced in 1955. The maestro had not yet gone angular, and there was nothing significantly Italian about the new car's looks. Nor was there anything remarkable about its specification, though a synchronized bottom gear was standard from the start. It was larger than the 203, with 58 bhp available from a 1½-litre engine on established lines. The 403 upheld the *marque*'s reputation for longevity in both senses and had sold over 1,000,000 by the time it was withdrawn in 1967.

H. T. Pigozzi's Simca firm had come a long way since 1934, when the former scrap merchant started to assemble Fiats in the old Donnet factory at Nanterre. This was an important decade for Simca: beginning with no original designs and an annual potential of perhaps 10,000 units, they ended it with a national best-seller, the Aronde, at least three-quarters French in concept and wholly French in content. Better still, this outpost of the Fiat empire and erstwhile member of the GFA consortium now controlled Unic (long since dedicated to trucks) and would soon gobble up the remains of Talbot.

The first post-war Simcas were, of course, Fiats and no more. The *cinq* was a side-valve *topolino* and the 8CV a *millecento*, still with the old sloping bonnet abandoned by Turin in 1940. This state of affairs continued until 1951, though latterly the French house was always one step ahead of Italy in updating their wares. Thus by 1948 the French *topolino* had become the Simca 6 with overhead valves and full-width grille, while the 1949 8CVs featured not only built-out boots and column shift but also the 'stretched' 1,221-cc engine not adopted until 1957 on the other side of the frontier. Though less than competitive in their homeland—in 1948 a Simca 8 cost £40 more than a 203 Peugeot and £9 more even than an *onze légère*— Simcas were beginning to undercut Fiats abroad. In Switzerland the Simca 8 was already better franc-for-franc value than the 1100E.

A further attraction—which 'marked' Fiat, as BMW would later 'mark' Mercedes–Benz—was the 8 Sport, 'the jewel of the Simca line'. In spite of its high-compression 50-bhp engine, it was never as fast as the Italian 1100S on the Cisitalias (it was too heavy, at 2,016 lb), but the success of Amédée Gordini's special competition Simcas helped sales, as did Pininfarina's

well-balanced interpretation of the contemporary idiom. Perhaps intentionally the coupés and cabriolets resembled the new A6 Maseratis, and the
bodies were built for Simca by Facel Metallon. The style—if not the
mechanics—had a long run, selling some 2,000 units a year. At their peak,
in 1951, Facel were turning out as many as twenty a day. Simca's 1950 sales
were a record 28,988.

By 1952 this figure had more than doubled, to 70,000, thanks to the new
8CV Aronde. Described as the 'first all-Simca', it once again anticipated Fiat
by switching to unitary construction in July 1951. Also anticipated were the
1100-103's pump circulation and hypoid rear axle, while the Simca's saloon
body was curvaceous where Fiat's would be angular. The rest of the
specification followed Fiat ideas, apart from the rear-wheel handbrake. In
its latest form the 1.2-litre engine gave 45 bhp, but the car was heavier than
a Fiat, at 2,300 lb, and needed liberal use of the four-speed gearbox to
achieve the best results, which amounted to 75 mph in top, 53 mph in the
lowish third gear, and a satisfactory 35 mpg. It was still a trifle expensive, at
725,000 francs.

The theme was soon expanded. In 1953 the 8 Sport acquired an Aronde
engine and running gear, while a new windscreen and rear-window treatment was Facel rather than Farina. While Citroën made only saloons (apart,
of course, from the rolltop 2CV), Simca branched out, with a Châtelaine
station wagon and even an American-style hardtop, the Grande Large.
Renault's stripped *affaires* models were matched by the equally austere
Aronde *quotidienne* in 1954, when double-acting dampers, worm-and-
roller steering and a stronger back axle were the principal changes. 1955
cars were higher geared to compensate for smaller 14-inch wheels, while in
1956 the 48-bhp Flash engine was introduced to the public with a
100,000-kilometre workout at Montlhéry autodrome. In the last months of
that year Simca would find an intriguing answer to the fuel shortage by
marrying the hull of the newly acquired Ford Vedette to an Aronde engine.
The resultant Ariane was the Gallic equivalent of a Morris-Oxford, and a
favourite with cabbies.

Ford France came under Simca ownership at the end of 1954, but in the
meantime they had enjoyed a respectable innings (21,078 cars in 1951) with
their 13CV Vedette—*la voiture du nouveau riche*, as cynical Frenchmen
called it. Though peculiar to France, the Vedette was the outward and
visible sign of Ford of America's $18,000,000 subcompact programme
authorized in 1944, and hurriedly dropped in the face of a negative reaction
from dealers. Part of the trouble was undoubtedly the plan to revive the
unloved small vee-eight engine. Fortunately for all concerned, Maurice Dollfus of Ford France liked the American prototype—or at any rate preferred it
to a variation on Cologne's *bückel* theme also being considered at that time.

The Vedette was not ready until 1949, so the French factory ran off a batch of F472A saloons, still wearing the Matford badges, a legacy of 1934's Ford–Mathis deal. These cars used a 1939-type 2.2-litre vee-eight engine and were indistinguishable from 1939's models or, for that matter, from the 22-hp model offered pre-war by Dagenham.

The new car reflected Young Henry's thinking in its Hotchkiss drive, coil spring independent front suspension and longitudinal semielliptics at the rear. The brakes were hydraulic, and the use of a separate cruciform-braced frame emphasized the American origins. The power unit was a slightly smaller edition (2,158 cc as against 2,227 cc) of the old flathead vee-eight 60. The Vedette was compact, with a wheelbase of 106 inches, weighed 2,613 lb and came in two- or four-door saloon forms, the latter of fastback type. 1953 and later editions had stepped backs, pressurized cooling and the option of a four-speed Electrofluide transmission with hydraulic clutch. Other extensions of the range included the Abeille, a stripped five-door commerciale, and the big Vendôme, which used the company's 3.9-litre truck engine in a standard chassis and instilled some hitherto-lacking power into the Vedette. Unfortunately, at 20CV, this had passed the fiscal abyss though a Vendôme was used as the basis for Facel Vega's first—and forgettable—prototype four-door saloon.

Like Simca, Ford had their prestige model, a parody of a grande routière. The Comète of 1951, gave Facel's stylist Brasseur a chance to show his mettle. He rose magnificently to the task with a four-seater fixed-head coupé featuring the famous roly-poly seats that would become a Facel Vega hallmark. All production Comètes had Cotal four-speed electric gearboxes, but beneath this handsome exterior beat the chicken heart of the small vee-eight, and on 66 bhp a speed of 80 mph was hard work. It cost £1,208, and, for this price, nearly two Citroën Sixes could be bought. In 1954, Ford fitted a tuned Vendôme engine, adding wire wheels and the four-speed all-synchromesh Pont-à-Mousson gearbox, but even on a 3.45:1 back axle the ton remained elusive. At this juncture Simca entered the picture.

They inherited something better than the old Vedette, for at the recent Paris Salon Poissy had stepped into line with Dagenham and Cologne. The 1955 cars featured unitary construction, a McPherson ball-joint independent front suspension and bodywork that was more up-to-date than that of Dagenham, with a wrapround rear window. The 12-volt electrics were also new, but the company was stuck with the old vee-eight, though the capacity was up to 2.4 litres, 80 bhp were claimed, and the engine had acquired an 'Aquilon' label.

Simca did not change it: they merely stepped up production from 150 to 200 units a day. They also made much of the de luxe equipment available: the top-of-the-line Régence at £1,035 offered more than a Zodiac, to wit a radio, a foot-operated screenwash and even mock wire wheels. The Simca-built Vedette was made until 1962.

Panhard's complete *volte-face* of 1946—from enormous cars using anti-quated sleeve-valve engines in modern chassis to tiny and rapid flat-twins—was inspired by J. A. Grégoire's brilliant Aluminium Française–Grégoire prototypes, though *la marque doyenne* meddled frighteningly with the latter. As originally conceived, the A.F.G. was an extension of 1937's Hotchkiss–Amilcar theme, with front-wheel drive and a unitary carcass built up around an Alpax dash. The new car, clandestinely tested—as the 4CV Renault had been—during the Occupation, featured a 72 mm × 73 mm (594-cc) air-cooled overhead-valve flat-twin engine, a four-speed gear-box with overdrive top and an all-independent suspension. Official trials revealed the incredibly low weight of 885 lb, a speed of 56 mph and a fuel consumption of 70 mpg.

Prototypes were submitted to all the major French manufacturers, though only Panhard and Simca—the latter on the strength of an enthusiastic report from the great Carlo Salamano in Turin—showed any real interest. Grégoire restyled his functional cabrio-limousine into a more streamlined saloon at Pigozzi's request, but Pigozzi later withdrew from the deal. So did the French Government, who had agreed to finance Aluminium Française–Grégoire production at Nanterre.

Panhard, however, did make the car, though not in the form Grégoire would have wished. In spite of this, it can be regarded as a direct descendant of his 3CV.

The classic unitary construction, the flat-twin engine with its cooling by twin belt-driven fans and the hemi-heads were retained. The cylinders were of light alloy with steel liners, and the four-speed crash-type gearbox had a direct third and an overdrive top. Suspension was by double transverse leaves at the front, with trailing arms and torsion bars at the rear, and the brakes were hydraulic. The light spider-type wheels were of 15-inches diam-eter, and the drive was taken to the front wheels by spiral bevel gears, with constant-velocity joints. The forward mounting of the engine meant, as Panhard were quick to point out, that 75% of available space could be allotted to passengers and another 15% to baggage, thus permitting a four-door body (which Grégoire had rejected as less robust than his two-door type) on an 83-inch wheelbase. Other 'improvements' not sanctioned by Grégoire were the double torsion bars used at the rear of Panhards, and the use of torsion bars to open and close the valves. Not only were Panhard's roller-bearing big ends noisy, they also limited the engine's life, reputedly to 6,000 miles in early days. The gearbox remained a cross which the company and its clients bore less than gladly. The fragile selectors did not lend thems-leves to rough treatment, and it was quite easy to select first and reverse simultaneously. Even 1951's synchromesh did not effect a complete cure. Swiss reactions to the Dyna Panhard were typical: the car was very expen-sive for what it was, the noise levels were too high, and the service was indifferent. Even the much-improved 1954 version found only 66 buyers in the whole Confederacy.

Production took a long time to reach economic levels. The 10,000 mark was not passed until 1950. This is not surprising when it is remembered that Facel Metallon, who built the bodies, undertook basic presswork at Amboise, welded the structures together at Colombes and then sent them on to Ivry, where Panhard installed the mechanical elements!

Nonetheless, in the right hands the Dyna was a rapid little car with admirable road holding. The original X84 with a 610-cc engine weighed 1,052 lb and could manage 60 mph, but by 1950 the 750-cc X85 unit had become available. This increased the weight of a saloon by scarcely 200 lb, yet disposed of 33 bhp; standard cars would attain 71 mph, took 22.3 seconds to reach 50 mph and would cruise happily at speeds beyond the ultimate limits of stock 4CV Renaults or Morris Minors. The 850-cc Type 130 unit which reached the catalogue in 1953 was even fiercer. The normal output was 38–40 bhp at 5,000 rpm, but units fitted to competition cars were a great deal more powerful, and the Bionnier-designed works stream-liners which ran at Le Mans that year were credited with 100 mph.

Improvements included front-wheel handbrakes and single fan cooling in 1949, and synchromesh on second gear from 1952, in which year the com-pany added an exhaust heater of notorious inefficiency, though this was better than no heater at all. 1953's cars had new crankshafts, still of roller-bearing type, as well as alloy pushrods, 'to have the same coefficient of expan-sion as the cylinders, thus reducing noise'. Also listed that year was Panhard's own sports car, the angular two-seater Junior, built up on a box-section frame with tubular cross-members. The twin-carburetter 850-cc engine was standard, though a blower was an option which boosted power to 62 bhp and gave the small car a maximum way above the 90 mark.

From 1954 the 850-cc engine was standardized. At the same time both the original form of construction and the Facel contract were discontinued. Moreover, Panhard had achieved the remarkable feat of persuading their flat-twin to propel six people at 80 mph, and on a modest 42 bhp, too. Like the old Jowett, the new saloon was 'as big as an ordinary ten', in spite of which it still weighed less than 1 ton. Sales climbed to a record 13,000, and Panhard found themselves in the taxi business.

But, if the système Grégoire had gone, light alloys had not. The only steel in the hull was in the transverse tube supporting the front end. Wind-tunnel tests had established a truly aerodynamic shape, the entire wing and bonnet assembly swung up, and the boot was enormous. Further, the Panhard would turn in nearly 40 mpg at cruising speeds of 60 mph, while a lack of flexibility in the overdrive top was balanced by a smooth 10–65-mph accel-eration in the direct third gear. The snags were poor synchromesh and a petrol heater as capricious as the old exhaust type; few people liked the looks. The central protruding spotlamp was incongruous, and the plastic instrument binnacle a nightmare.

Both spotlamp and heater had vanished by 1956. However, though sales and reliability alike improved and though Citroën's injection of cash helped, the alloy carcass was expensive to make. The 1957 season saw a switch to all-steel construction, which meant an extra 440 lb, the equivalent of three passengers. The suspension had to be reinforced, with adverse effects on low-speed handling, though later Dynas were better made. They sold to people who wanted 'something different', yet found the Déesse too bulky and automated.

The only other serious contender was the Rosengart, billed as '*la voiture qui dure*'. Economically speaking, it did not. Four years after its renaissance at the 1951 Salon, the *marque* had disappeared for good.

Even during their vee-eight venture of 1946–7 Rosengart had been testing improved versions of their Gallic Austin Seven, and the definitive 5CV Ariette featured the usual side-valve 747-cc engine with thermosyphon circulation, though its hydraulic brakes and transverse-leaf independent front suspension (with semielliptics at the rear) were amenities that Longbridge never achieved. Like the Belgian Imperia and the 500B Fiat, the Rosengart combined a dashboard-mounted fuel tank with mechanical pump feed. Synchromesh was provided only on third and top, and the car's humble Birmingham origins were camouflaged by slab-sided two-door saloon and cabriolet bodies. A speed of 55–60 mph was claimed on a 5.5:1 top gear, but, despite promises of volume production, only 237 Rosengarts were delivered in 1953. The Swiss, who had been shown the new style at Geneva the previous year, took precisely thirteen.

Undaunted, Rosengart tried again in 1954 with the Sagaie, an Ariette with a more powerful engine, the 748-cc overhead-valve flat-twin air-cooled CEMEC used in police motor-cycles. Liberal use of glassfibre, for wings, bonnet and body saved some 180 lb of weight, and the top speed was over 70 mph. Despite the usual austerity edition—Rosengart called theirs an Artisane—Citroën and Renault continued to prosper as before.

Some traditional purveyors of *conduites intérieures avec malle* still continued to supply them in 1946. Chenard–Walcker staged a brief comeback with their near-Matfords, the Citroën-engined 11CV and the 21CV with the big Ford vee-eight unit. It was rumoured that they were more attracted by mini-cars, but in fact their principal interest was a small front-wheel drive delivery van. This also appealed to Peugeot, who took the company over and continued its development.

Also present was La Licorne. The 1946 editions of their 6CV came with the old 1,125-cc pushrod four. Other features were a forked backbone frame, an independent front suspension by superimposed double quarter-elliptics and the firm's traditional quarter-elliptics at the rear. Few, however, were seen, and fewer still of an obscure 14CV six. This turned up at the 1948 Salon with a Delahaye-like foursome cabriolet body. Statistical returns, however, showed La Licorne as building only trucks, and even these in modest numbers.

Delaunay–Belleville tried rather harder, with a stand at Geneva in 1947, and even a Swiss agent. The 12CV was a classic *conduite intérieure avec malle*; however, its 1934 styling was at war with a grille and front-wing assembly that might have come off a 1940 Ford truck. The mechanical elements were neither modern nor French, being a rehash of Delaunay's French-speaking Type 230 Mercedes–Benz, with a six-cylinder side-valve engine, Mercedes suspension, one-shot lubrication and a Cotal gearbox in place of Stuttgart's synchromesh. This one lingered on into 1950, but not more than 14 were built. Thereafter the shops that had once supplied monster limousines for the last Tsar devoted themselves to Robert de Rovin's mini-cars.

2.3   All *Routières* Great and Small

For all the arid climate, most of the great names reappeared briefly, even Hispano-Suiza, who had abdicated into aero engines as long ago as 1938. Their *merveille d'horologerie*, a front-wheel drive vee-eight, was never produced, but a car with these characteristics did appear, in 1948. Its interlinked torsion-bar suspension had Packard overtones, as had the half-timbered saloon body. A massive grille in the best Hispano tradition concealed no fewer than three radiators in line abreast, but what they cooled was merely a Ford vee-eight, initially the small 13CV, though the bigger 3.6-litre unit was later fitted. No production was apparently contemplated.

Ettore Bugatti's prime piece of horology was his idea of a cycle-car. This involved scaling down a supercharged twin overhead-camshaft sixteen-valve four-cylinder engine to the smallest possible dimensions and then making it rev twice as hard. The Type 68 370-cc unit had a bore of 48.5 mm and a stroke of 50 mm and was designed to run at 7,500 rpm. The four-speed unit gearbox featured a silent bottom gear, and the assembly, its creator wrote, 'was tried out in a motor-cycle to avoid revealing my intentions'.

By contrast, Type 73 was a single-camshaft 1½-litre unit with the traditional three valves per cylinder: the crossflow-type head was detachable, which horrified the purists almost as much as the synchromesh gearbox. There was also talk of a twin-camshaft edition, which emerged in 1951 under the Type 102 designation. Described as 'a sight which would gladden the heart of any Bugattiste', it marked a reversion to a fixed cylinder head, the five-speed gearbox was separately mounted, and there was a transverse-leaf independent front suspension.

Though all these cars were built, and development continued after *le patron*'s death in 1947, the ten Bugattis that actually reached the public were Type 101s or modernized Type 57s with the hydraulic brakes used since 1938. This was the familiar 3.3-litre twin-camshaft straight-eight, essentially unchanged apart from its twin-plate clutch and a choice of three transmissions—four- or five-speed manual or a four-speed Cotal. There was a choice of normally aspirated or supercharged engines, the latter giving 190 bhp at 5,400 rpm. 17-inch Rudge wire wheels and right-hand steering made no concessions to a changing world, but the car did not take kindly to slab-sided styling, and the horseshoe grille looked a trifle lost in the midst of all that sheet metal. A price of over 3,000,000 francs—1,000,000 francs more than was asked for a Type 135 Delahaye—was sufficient deterrent, even to the faithful.

Bugatti stayed away from the circuits until 1956, when it was too late, but Talbot's Antonio Lago ran a full-scale competition department, his slow but dependable 4½-litre single-seaters forming the basis for sports models which were anything but slow. The 26CV Lago Record in standard 1946 form could have been taken for a well-maintained 1936 model, but the capacity of the seven-bearing six-cylinder overhead-valve engine with its hemi-head and twin high-set camshafts had increased from 4 litres to 4,482 cc, and its output was an impressive 170 bhp. The chassis still featured Talbot's established transverse-leaf-and-wishbone front suspension, though coils were used on the long-wheelbase models. Lago likewise remained faithful to the Wilson preselective gearbox. The knock-on wire wheels were filled by brake drums of 14 inches diameter, now hydraulically actuated. Most cars came on the 123-inch chassis, but in 1952 Saoutchik recaptured the old mood with a three-ton limousine for King Ibn Saud. A refrigerator, a lavatory and about 3,600 feet of assorted wiring accounted for most of the weight.

The Record was still offered in 1954, accounting for 353 of the 433 cars sold in 1950, one of the few good years. 1947 saw the magnificent Lago Grand Sport, on a shorter wheelbase, capable of 120 mph in its original 190-bhp form and of appreciably more when the output was boosted to 215 bhp in 1953. This car normally wore handsome two-seater coupé body-work in the Italian idiom, though some unmentionable horrors were perpetrated by Saoutchik and others. Mock-Ferraris were not unknown, and one specimen masqueraded as an 1100S Fiat of the Savio type.

Unfortunately in 1949 Lago persuaded himself that there was a market for what he called 'a class car of modest horsepower, easy to maintain'. The resultant 15CV Baby, according to one critic, 'rode like a brick and sounded and felt like a 5-ton truck'. Both chassis and styling were of authentic 1936 type, but the engine was a new short-stroke (93 mm × 99 mm) 2.7-litre three-bearing pushrod four, with the option of Wilson or synchromesh gearboxes. The wheelbase was 112 inches, but the Baby neither went nor stopped particularly well, and by 1951 its makers were in receivership. The French, however, order such matters better than do the Anglo-Saxons, and a few months later Talbot were back. They were also being more economical, for there was now only one touring chassis—of box-section type with tubular cross-members and a coil-spring independent front suspension—and one body, the familiar four-door sports saloon, hardly improved by its new slab-sided treatment. This sufficed for both Record and Baby, though the retention of the longer wheelbase meant that the wretched four was rendered even more gutless. Shortly afterwards a mysterious Quinze Luxe appeared in the catalogue. This was a six, but the cylinder dimensions were variously quoted as 88 mm × 73.8 mm (which sounded modern enough) and 74.5 mm × 104.5 mm, a clear indication that some 1937 15CV units had been unearthed from a forgotten store. In either form, the Quinze Luxe was hardly ever seen, and by 1955 Talbot were making a final effort with a new 14CV four.

This was an all-new five-bearing 2½-litre with twin Solex or Weber carburetters and an output of 120 bhp. ZF furnished the four-speed all-synchromesh gearbox, the transverse-leaf independent front suspension was reinstated, and the wheelbase was an abbreviated 98½ inches. With a weight of 2,215 lb, the maximum speed approached 120 mph, while the standard body was the elegant 2 + 2 coupé common to later Grand Sports, with a wrapround rear window. The fact that this latter component (and the side-windows as well) were of Perspex suggested that Talbot was scraping the bottom of the barrel, and only 70 14CVs were delivered in the first two years. By 1957 Lago was frantically questing more power; he tried a Raymond Mays conversion of the British Ford Zephyr before settling for BMW's vee-eight. The BMW-powered Lago America represented Talbot's last gasp.

Delahaye had been under Charles Weiffenbach's direction since the nineteenth century. They also had a healthy truck business. Indeed, the indestructible four-bearing overhead-valve six fitted to their sporting Type 135 was found also, in detuned form, in a forward-control 5-ton truck. Even in 1946, the 135 was competitive: the 3,557-cc engine gave 110–130 bhp according to tune, could use the low-octane fuels of the day, and would stand high revs if required. Though most cars used the electrically selected Cotal transmission with its finger-tip gate and the hazardous pleasures of four speeds in either direction, a crash gearbox was still available. Apart from the transverse-leaf independent front suspension, dating back to 1934, the chassis design was early 1930s style, with friction dampers and Bendix cable-operated brakes working in drums of generous diameter. Right-hand drive was standard, as were wire wheels, though steel-spoke equipment was used on the single-carburetter 148, an executive carriage available on an 11-foot wheelbase for those requiring limousine coachwork.

Up to 1948, Delahaye still offered a *conduite intérieure avec malle*, the faithful old 12CV Type 134. This could be bought in 2.2-litre or 2.4-litre forms, the latter disposing of 55 bhp. The rest of it paralleled the 135 and 148, though the manual-gearbox option had synchromesh as a sop to the unskilled. This car sold well in Belgium, and Delahaye were perhaps unwise to discard it. The range was rounded out by the 3-litre D6 Delage, by now very much a poor relation. Cotal gearboxes were standard, as were hydraulic brakes, inherited from the pre-war D6-70. The short-stroke (83.7 mm × 90.5 mm) engine was more susceptible to tuning than the somewhat rustic Delahaye, and a few sports racing editions were built immediately after the Second World War, one of these taking second place at Le Mans in 1949. It was only a token survival, though. Jacques Rousseau was scathing: 'Togged up,' he wrote, 'with heavy wood-framed bodies, they had far less urge: and the awkward access under the diminutive bonnet flanked by the huge wings emphasized the precarious union of a French chassis and the new bulboid style.'

Delahaye's contribution to the latest idiom was a 4½-litre car unveiled at the 1946 Salon. This was not intended as a sports model, and its left-hand steering was indicative of American aspirations. The engine was, however, a promising piece of work, being a seven-bearing development of the 135 unit with dimensions of 94 mm × 107 mm. It gave 125 bhp in single-carburetter form, and another 15 bhp with three downdraught instruments. Other advanced features were a de Dion back axle and (at last!) hydraulic brakes: the Cotal gearbox was standard. Unfortunately, they had forsaken their well-tried transverse-leaf independent front suspension for Dubonnet coils, and the car rolled alarmingly if cornered fast. The 175 also coincided with an unpleasant era in custom coachwork, receiving the same extravaganzas as seen on Mark VI Bentleys at Earls Court. The only difference was that there were no Standard Steel Delahayes! The three-carburetter 175 was invariably produced on an 116-inch wheelbase, but there were also long-chassis 178s and 180s with the 'cooking' unit. Delage versions were announced but never built. Between 100 and 150 of these cars were sold, but by 1951 the company had given it best.

Matters improved when Delahaye won an army contract for their VLR, a variation on the Jeep theme with an all-round independent suspension and a four-cylinder 12CV engine with dry-sump lubrication. This engine was also tried in a low-built tubular space-frame, but the army soon tired of the VLR's complexities.

Delahaye tried once more in 1952 with the splendid 235, Weiffenbach's swansong. The Type 135 engine was given a 'hotter' camshaft, boosting power to 152 bhp, while rearrangement of the three carburetters permitted a lower more fashionable bonnet line. The frame received an extra tubular cross-member, and the bodies were elegant. A lovely coupé with a wide yet not overexuberant grille graced Delahaye's final exhibit at Earls Court. Nor was it just a pretty face: a 235 lapped Montlhéry at 112 mph, and the top speed was in the region of 125 mph. But mechanical brakes in the era of the 300SL and the C-type Jaguar . . . it simply was not viable. In 1954 Delahaye merged with Hotchkiss, and the private-car line came to an end. Less than 400 had been sold in the past four years.

When the army abandoned Delahaye's Jeep, they ordered the Willys version from its French licencees, Hotchkiss of Saint-Denis. On paper, Hotchkiss appeared sound; the cars, publicized under the slogan '*Le juste milieu*', were unspectacular and 'unburstable'. The long reign of an English managing director, Harry Ainsworth, had instilled a degree of Englishness into the product. In 1946 the *marque* still had two Monte Carlo Rally victories ahead of it.

No attempt was made to revive the front wheel drive Amilcars, and the long-established 3-litre 17CV was not reinstated, either. In other respects the 1939 range continued, though the steel shortage delayed production of the standard 13CV four until 1948. This as much as anything else held sales down to 117 units in the first year of peace, for the admirable 3½-litre Type 686 was a 20CV in its native land. Its robust seven-bearing pushrod engine had dimensions of 86 mm × 100 mm and was mounted in unit with a four-speed synchromesh gearbox. The chassis was copybook 1935: cruciform bracing, semiellriptics at each corner supplemented by single-acting hydraulic dampers, Bendix brakes and pressed-steel wheels. There were two stages of tune and three wheelbase lengths, the most desirable Hotchkiss being the short Grand Sport two-door saloon, capable of 100 mph on 125 bhp. The bodies were likewise unchanged from 1939, though the seven-seater was now called the Versailles instead of the Vichy! The four was the same car in miniature, giving 63 bhp from 2,312 cc: an admirable buy for those who still regarded *tractions* as daring. By 1949 hydraulic brakes (which had been tried previously in 1936 and found wanting) were back again, there was a vertical-coil independent front suspension, and the headlamps were receding into the wings. Hotchkiss had also resumed their Grégoire connections with a licence to build his 2-litre Model R.

Grégoire had enlarged his basic front-wheel drive theme 'by tracing the most aerodynamic shape around the smallest area needed for the transport of six people'. Once again the engine was horizontally opposed, with pushrod-operated overhead valves and an alloy crankcase, but the unit was now a water-cooled four. In Hotchkiss form, the dimensions were 86 mm × 90 mm, for a capacity of 2,186 cc, and the output was 70 bhp. The four-speed all-indirect gearbox incorporated an overdrive top, variable-rate coil springing was used all round, and the carcass weight was a mere 187 lb. The steering was, of course, by rack and pinion, and the car attained over 90 mph, with a fuel consumption of 28–30 mpg.

Unfortunately nothing turned out right. People just did not like Grégoire's perfect shape with the grille projecting over the front axle. Women were especially antipathetic. On top of this, Hotchkiss were desperately short of money and only managed to turn out 250 Grégoires. There the matter might have ended, had not an enthusiastic doctor fitted a Roots-type blower to his car. Grégoire himself was so enchanted by this conversion that he bought some sets of mechanical elements from Hotchkiss and produced a series of Grégoire-Sports, mostly Chapron-bodied cabriolets. Later examples had front disc brakes, and this rare car exceeded 110 mph on 125–130 bhp. The supply of components was, however, limited, and Chapron's prices were prohibitive, so Grégoire rationed himself to 15 cars. They took a long time to sell.

Meanwhile the regular Hotchkiss line was still produced, emerging in 1951 as the 1350 and 2050 with a column shift, a Grégoire-type auxiliary rear suspension and a Cotal-box option on the six. Headlamps were now fully recessed, the latest vee-screens were used, and the roof panels were carefully beaten out by hand. The 13CV sold 2,276 units that year, bringing total production up to about 2,700, but what was this compared with 30,928 *onze légères*? Hotchkiss struggled on a little longer: even the 20CV Grand Sport was still listed in 1954, but the restyled Agay and Monceau models exhibited at the Grand Palais that autumn passed unnoticed, and few, if any, reached the public.

The same Salon, of course, saw the début of a new star, the Facel Vega, styled by the same Brasseur who had given France the Ford Comète and the later Simca Sport. The cold wind that had blown away Delahaye's VLR and persuaded Panhard to go it alone was setting Facel Metallon's chief, Jean Daninos, on a new course. His plan was to launch a new *grande routière* and thus to compensate for his recent loss of business. He was to lose a lot more money in the process, but he would also revive the concept of the fast Euro-American hybrid as pioneered by Railton in Britain before the war.

The Facel set many fashions. The famous roly-poly seats have already been encountered on the Ford Comète, but nothing made before (or since) has rivalled the car's aeronautical atmosphere, with aircraft-type levers for ancillary controls, and less important items overflowing onto a console between the front seats, a practice much imitated in later years. Also imitated were the four driving lamps in their vertical clusters. The body was superbly proportioned, with the wrapround rear window matching a curved single-panel screen which had yet to achieve the aggressive 'dog's leg' of subsequent series. Nice touches were the power windows (with a master control on the driver's side) and the matching radio aerials in the tail fins, though only one of these latter was functional. Nobody commented on the left-hand steering: right-hand drive would not be available until 1957.

The body was welded to a robust tubular chassis, with a conventional suspension, by coils at the front and semielliptics at the rear, reinforced by Allinquant telescopic dampers. The brakes were, of course, hydraulic, though there was no servo, and the use of 11-inch drums on a 3,600-lb motor-car capable of nearly 130 mph seemed inadequate. For his engine, Daninos chose one of Chrysler's smaller hemi-head vee-eights, the 4½-litre 180-bhp De Soto. This unit came complete with a Powerflite two-speed automatic transmission, but for enthusiasts the company offered a more expensive alternative, the four-speed Pont-à-Mousson gearbox fitted to later Comètes.

Facel production had scarcely got into its stride by 1956, so neither the splendours nor the miseries were yet apparent, though by the end of our period a slightly larger 4.8-litre engine and servo brakes had been adopted. The cabriolet exhibited at the 1955 Salon never went into production: structural weaknesses led Facel to discourage prospective customers. The only warning note came from that promising market, Switzerland. Here a Facel at 39,500 francs compared unfavourably with such rivals as the 300SL Mercedes–Benz (33,500 francs) and the 507 BMW (34,370 francs). Neither, however, offered the French car's Dornford Yates aura.

Interestingly, there had been an attempt at a Franco-American in 1946 by a most improbable manufacturer, Rosengart. In fact their Super Trahuit, though unrealistic, was far from illogical, since in 1939 a similar front-wheel drive sports saloon had been introduced, evolved by the simple expedient of mounting an 11CV Citroën power pack at the front of their own platform frame. The mock-Plymouth grille was less than felicitous. The post-war edition had a longer wheelbase, to accommodate a 3.9-litre vee-eight Mercury unit. Quite apart from financial problems, people were—and are—very wary of large front-wheel drive cars, and the 1947 Geneva Salon was the big Rosengart's last appearance.

In theory, Salmson were better off than either Talbot or Hotchkiss. Not only did they have a second string (aero engines), but they were also financially sound. The S4E was quite a big car, with a 2.3-litre engine, but it was still only a 13CV, and Salmson made nothing larger. Better still, there was the supporting 10CV S4-61 which explains the sale of some 3,000 traditional *conduites intérieures avec malle* between 1946 and 1951.

The Salmson formula was as firmly established as that of Delahaye or Talbot. The company had been building twin overhead-camshaft four-cylinder engines with hemispherical combustion chambers longer than anyone else, and the present models traced their descent back to the S4 of 1929. Cooling was by pump and fan, and buyers had a choice of synchromesh or Cotal gearboxes, both with four forward speeds. The electrically welded frame incorporated tubular cross-members, and Salmson favoured the unusual combination of a torsion-bar independent front suspension and cantilever springs at the rear. Only the S4E's recessed headlamps suggested a post-war model: those of the smaller S4-61 were outdoors. The wheels were of the 16-inch pressed steel type, but surprisingly there was an umbrella-handle-type handbrake under the dash. On 2.3 litres and 68 bhp, the big Salmson was a *petite routière* capable of 90 mph. The S4-61 was 5½ inches shorter in the wheelbase, had rod-and-cable actuation for its brakes where the S4E used hydraulics and was a little too heavy, at 2,360 lb, to set the Seine on fire. Nonetheless, it managed an honest 75 mph. These models continued into 1951 without change, beyond the provision of hydraulic brakes on the last S4-61s.

The 1951 Randonnée was an attempt at rationalization, using a 2.2-litre alloy engine on traditional lines. The bodywork was restyled, with a new grille and full-flow wings, and Cotal gearboxes were now standard. Financial troubles held production of the latest series down to 63 units, but for 1953 there was a true *grande routière* in miniature from the drawing-board of Eugène Martin. Better still, a French maker had adopted the Italian *granturismo* idiom.

Essentially the engine was a Randonnée unit slightly enlarged to 2.3 litres. The output was 105 bhp, and the 2300S was a handsome little car, apart from its plated bolt-on wire wheels. It would do over 100 mph and distinguished itself in local rallies. Like Lancia, Salmson essayed a roadster version in 1955. They also planned a new streamlined six-light saloon on a 118-inch wheelbase, and prototypes were built by Chapron (who also made the regular coupés) and the Italian firm of Motto. Once again, however, the money ran out, and the Billancourt works closed in February 1957, after 227 of these promising little *granturismi* had been made.

Georges Irat's miniature front-wheel drive sports-cars flitted briefly across the scene in 1946. The latest version was an over-complicated variation on a Grégoire theme, with a cast magnesium structure built up round the fire-wall. The heads and blocks of the new twin-carburetter 1,100-cc flat-four engine were of alloy also, but it was hard to take the Irat seriously. Indeed, a casual glance at the front end suggested that there were no headlights at all, though closer study revealed fragile-looking strip lamps incorporated in the bumper. A year later all this had been discarded in favour of a conventionally driven model with an all-independent suspension, though the new in-line power unit with a capacity of 2 litres featured a light-alloy block, a five-bearing crankshaft and twin chain-driven overhead camshafts. Thereafter the company moved to Bordeaux, where they made diesel engines for trucks. There was, however, a final fling in Morocco in 1952. This time they were promoting 'a desert car' with Dyna Panhard mechanics. Much was made of the car's very basic specification—no starter, simple mechanical brakes and a frostproof engine! In spite of this, the *colons* continued to buy 2CV Citroëns all the same.

Much more serious were the small sports cars of Germain Lambert, who had been at it since 1926 and who sought to perpetuate the Salmson–Amilcar tradition. His clientele was not unlike that of Morgan in England, and he owned the rights to the famous old 1,100-cc overhead-valve Ruby engine. Specifications were a matter of personal preference, but the basic package comprised a simple underslung tubular frame with beam axles at either end, quarter-elliptic rear suspension and mechanical brakes. M. Lambert preferred gravity feed, because it avoided 'the use of pumps and other nuisances', and the cheapest CS model came with a Plexiglass screen. It also was innocent of a starter, irrelevant since Ruby engines used magneto ignition. Outputs ranged from 36 bhp upwards, and blown 'Course' editions could achieve 95–100 mph. A few later Lamberts had streamlined bodies and pontoon front wings which swung up with their bonnets, but even on these the honeycomb radiator (reminiscent of a Darracq or F.N. of the 1920s) remained exposed to view. No Lamberts were made after 1953.

Amedée Gordini left Simca at the end of 1951 and pursued a hand-to-mouth competition career until 1957. This embraced Formula 1 as well as sports-car events and left neither time nor money for the development of street machinery, though Gordinis were exhibited at the 1952 Paris Salon and also in New York the following spring. John Bolster recalls seeing at least one Gordini in road trim. *Le Sorcier*'s ideas embraced a light and simple frame based on two straight-tube side-members, with a torsion-bar independent suspension at each end. The 2LS hydraulic brakes worked in finned drums, five-speed gearboxes were used, and a variety of twin overhead-camshaft power units was tried, the 2-litre six having cylinder dimensions of 78 mm × 75 mm. Both the 1½-litre four and the 3-litre straight-eight were 'square', at 78 mm × 78 mm. Competition models featured Kieft-like all-enveloping coachwork with a central driving position. On 175 bhp the six was said to accelerate to 100 mph in less than 20 seconds, and even with civilised amenities the 235-bhp eight would have been quite something. It would also have been the last example of this once-fashionable configuration that the public could buy. Gordini, however, elected to join Renault in 1957, and his *marque* was seen no longer.

Already Renault and Panhard tuners were becoming manufacturers in their own right. Of the 4CV derivatives, the Autobleu of 1955 was little more than a Renault platform with stylish coupé or cabriolet coachwork by Chapron. Jean Rédélé's Alpine from Dieppe was more serious, but, though the breed launched itself with a bang in 1955 by winning its class in the Mille Miglia, it was as yet little known. Rédélé's *Mille Miles* was a two-seater fastback coupé in glassfibre, and its engine was tuned to give over 40 bhp. The five-speed gearbox had a synchromesh the factory-built sports models as yet lacked, and catalogued models could do 95 mph.

The 'Panhardistes' were more numerous. The REAC from Casablanca was a 1952 ephemeral which carried its crew in a glassfibre turret clearly inspired by an armoured car of the 1920s, while the Marathon was merely Rosengart's version of the German Trippel, with Panhard in place of Zündapp mechanical elements. The Arista first appeared in 1951 as the Ranelagh; either way it was an 850-cc Dyna sports platform with a steel roadster or glassfibre coupé body. Aristas could still be bought in 1963.

The efforts of Réné Bonnet and Charles Deutsch merit closer attention. The partnership built its first special in 1938, though up to 1949 the raw material was the 11CV Citroën. In addition to the DB competition models, there were also sports coupés and cabriolets, using their own forked backbone frames, Citroën front suspension and swing axles at the rear. Four-speed Cotal gearboxes were used, and with a twin-carburetter manifold and alloy head the engine was persuaded to give 71 bhp.

By 1951 Deutsch and Bonnet were fully committed to the Dyna Panhard, with distinguished results. In 1954, DBs won their class in the Mille Miglia, the Index of Performance at Le Mans, and the TT (still a handicap race) outright. Road-going coupés were built up on box-section frames, with light alloy panelling. Mechanics were to order: any engine that Panhard made was available, and some of them in supercharged form as well. By 1955 DB modifications included all-synchromesh gearboxes, overbored 1,000-cc and 1,300-cc engines and glassfibre coachwork built by Chausson. Only the dissolution of the partnership in 1961 brought the DB's career to an end.

2.4   Folies, but not always de Grandeur

Though petrol was not finally derationed until December 1949, few wartime electric cars survived into 1946.

The CGE-Tudor was yet another Grégoire creation featuring the classic Alpax structure and all-round independent suspension, though in this case the motor was bolted to the rear cross-member of the frame, necessitating rear-wheel drive. The attractive little roadster resembled an Amilcar Compound, and a 56-mile range was claimed. Less conventional in appearance was the Faure, with a short sloping Beetle-type bonnet into which were crammed controls, batteries and spare wheel. This fastback coupé had its rear wheels set close together, like the Isetta, to dispense with the need for a differential.

Electricity also bulked large in that outstanding folly, Casimir Loubières's Symetric, which made intermittent appearances between 1952 and 1958. The original version achieved full forward control by mounting the 1,100-cc four-cylinder engine (apparently a Simca) across the front of the car, whence it drove all four wheels through a transmission described as 'infinitely variable thermoelectric'; the ultimate medium consisted of an electric hub motor at each corner in the best 1900 Lohner–Porsche tradition. The space-frame was built up on a tubular backbone which doubled as fuel tank. 'Use sandpaper and polish,' recommended the catalogue, 'to replace dents: anything else can be knocked out or thrown away.' M. Loubières maintained that this structure could be put together in any backstreet *atelier*. Thus his Symetric would sell for the price of a 4CV Renault. It did not happen—but it was at least credible, in contrast with his 1958 sequel with the same four-wheel drive, an atomic-power option, fluorescent rear bumpers, chutes to empty the ashtrays into the road and every possible gimmick from built-in jacks to a built-in electric razor.

Emile Mathis's attempts to recapture past successes were more serious. The original 333 of 1946—three wheels, three seats, 3 litres of petrol per hundred kilometres—was an egg-shaped confection styled by the same Jean Andreau whose aerodynamic Peugeot and Delage saloons had graced pre-war Salons. The car's single rear wheel did not take the drive: the front end was a variation on the Grégoire–Panhard theme with some interpolations of Mathis's own. The 700-cc flat-twin engine was water cooled, with individual radiators built into each cylinder head, in the manner of Frédéric Dufaux's enormous racer of 1905. The suspension was of all-coil type, and the hydraulic brakes worked on the front wheels only, the rear-wheel brake being reserved for parking. In the interests of simplicity, welded-up three-piece construction was to have been utilized; the vehicle rode on Grégoire-style spider-type wheels and weighed only 840 lb. Early claims of 100 mpg were whittled down to 70–75, but Mathis was refused permission to produce this one.

In 1948, he tried again. Ever mindful of his pre-war slogan (*'le poids, c'est l'ennemi'*), he came up with a full-sized 2.8-litre saloon alleged to weigh 1,456 lb. This 666 (the designation signified six cylinders, six seats and six speeds) was an overhead-valve flat-six of 88.9 mm × 76.2 mm bore and stroke. Once again the front wheels were driven, overdrive was operative on all forward ratios, and coil-spring suspension was used. To an oval-tube frame was welded an astonishing body with angular rear quarters and an immense Panoramic windscreen, but evidently it did not work, for at the 1949 Salon Mathis displayed a conventionally driven version featuring a box-section chassis. No complete cars were shown, but the presence of a spinner-type radiator grille in the Studebaker idiom opened up alarming possibilities. A list price more than three times that of an 11CV Citroën, explains why M. Mathis retired to Strasbourg to make light aero engines.

Emile Claveau was a charter member of the academy of projectors. He had been playing with strange motor-cars since 1926, most of them featuring unitary construction, front-wheel drive and an all-independent suspension. His 1946 contribution, billed as *'sous le patronage de Descartes'*, incorporated all three, plus an impressive-sounding twin overhead-camshaft vee-eight of light alloy construction, with hemispherical combustion chambers, magneto ignition and a roller-bearing crankshaft, mounted in unit with a five-speed gearbox. The gearchange was power assisted, though not the brakes, and the suspension was of conventional all-independent layout. The six-seater saloon body was panelled in aluminium, and on 85 bhp from 2.3 litres the Claveau should have gone indecently fast, especially as the dry weight was quoted at well under 1 ton, about the same as a Simca 8. It seems doubtful if this one ran under its own power.

The 4CV Bernardet, another of 1946's models, was rather more practical. This came from the drawing-board of the equally prolific Marcel Violet, but was no cyclecar. It was a substantially built three-seater roadster on a 78-inch wheelbase, with a frameless Vutotal windscreen of the type found on pre-war La Licorne and Chenard–Walcker convertibles. By this time Violet was enamoured of the DKW (or Issigonis) idea of a transversely mounted engine driving the front wheels, and the Bernardet used such an arrangement, the power unit being a water-cooled side-valve four of 798 cc (64 mm × 62 mm). Most of this was fabricated from aluminium castings, but the rest was unremarkable, with rack-and-pinion steering, hydraulic brakes, an all-independent suspension and a four-speed synchromesh gearbox with column shift. The quickly detachable power pack was positioned over the front axle, but the designer's idea of setting the brake and clutch pedals on either side of the steering column must have made the car awkward to drive. Like the front-wheel drive Rosengart, the Bernardet made the rounds from Paris to Geneva and then disappeared. Its sponsors, however, prospered with a line of side-cars.

1947 saw a less probable front-wheel driven device, the Dolo, a super-bubble car with a transparent plastic roof. The bonnet terminated well behind the front wings, Volvo-style, the headlamps were countersunk in curved shrouds, and the rear wings were flush with the body. The rear track was only 35 inches. Other features were an all-independent suspension by torsion bars and an overdrive top gear. The engine was horizontally opposed, with air cooling and overhead camshafts, and alternating-current electrics were unusual for the period. The cars exhibited had 571-cc four-cylinder units, but on paper there was also a 1,143-cc eight with twin carburetters and a top speed of 87 mph. This latter was quoted in Switzerland at 9,500 francs, but even the car's compatriots do not seem to have bought any Dolos.

The Boitel was rather more than a mini-car and dated back to 1938. It used the 584-cc two-stroke DKW twin engine, but mounted it at the back. The suspension followed DKW lines, brakes were hydraulic, and this attractive two-seater was said to do 55 mph and 62 mpg.

The JPW almost made it into production. Conceived during the war by racing driver Jean-Pierre Wimille and Pierre Leygonie, it was yet another egg-shape, though rear-engined this time. The basis was a twin-tube frame reinforced by immensely rigid cross-members, while staggered seating was adopted, the driver being located in the centre ahead of his two passengers. The short frontal bonnet was full of radiator, battery and spare wheel, and plans called for an exciting series of 120-degree vee-six engines, with outputs as high as 220 bhp.

At the 1946 Salon, however, the prototype appeared with a tuned 11CV Citroën unit, though even in this form speeds of 90 mph were attained. At this juncture Maurice Dollfus of Ford France took a hand, setting up a Special Products Division at Poissy to evolve a new version utilizing the maximum number of Vedette components—the 13CV engine, as well as its brakes, gearbox and front suspension. The original Plexiglass screen was abandoned, and the radiator was moved to the rear to give at least some luggage accommodation. The speed went up to 100 mph, but Wimille's untimely death led to the cancellation of the project.

Of the mini-cars, the Rovin, built in the Delaunay–Belleville works at Saint-Denis, was the longest lived, appearing at the 1946 Salon, and still being quoted—if hardly ever seen—twelve years later. Examples were even sold in Belgium and Switzerland.

In its original guise it was the crudest of doorless open two-seaters, with a single centrally mounted headlamp. The rear-mounted 260-cc single-cylinder overhead-valve engine was in unit with a three-speed gearbox. This machinery lived in an all-independently sprung backbone frame, with double transverse leaves at the front, and trailing arms and coils at the rear. The steering was by rack and pinion, and a speed of 43 mph was claimed.

Even at 65,000 francs this was too basic to succeed, and a year later Rovin introduced the D3-series. This one had slab-sided bodywork with doors and hood, floor mounted gear lever and a 425-cc side-valve water-cooled flat-twin engine, developing 10 bhp. By 1950 this had been enlarged to 462 cc and 13 bhp. The car continued in this form to the end, still with three forward speeds, but, though catalogues spoke of 50 mph, the handling was peculiar ('The back end comes round at the least provocation,' one owner complained), and the actual performance was no match even for a *deux-chevaux*. Production figures told their own story: 383 cars in 1948, 395 in 1950 and only 115 in 1953.

The Rovin required a driving licence, but the strange confections fabricated by Charles Mochet in his shed at Puteaux did not. Hence even in 1958 this happy backyard 'manufacturer' had a six-week backlog of orders.

Here was real soapbox motoring. The CM125 was a tiny slab-sided affair with a snub nose *à la* Tatra. Suddenly we were back in 1919, with brakes on the rear wheels only, a three-speed motor-cycle gearbox, a cockpit-mounted hand starter, no differential, quarter-elliptic rear springs (though, curiously, coil spring i.f.s.) and a primitive tubular chassis, at the back of which a 125-cc two-stroke Ydral engine reposed on rubber buffers. On 3½ hp the Mochet was good for 30 mph and cruised at 20 mph. One gallon of petrol lasted 80 miles, while those who required something better could specify a Grand Luxe model, distinguishable by its vee-screen and mock-American grille, for 7,000 francs. By 1954, Mochets were available with electric starters, and all models had external-contracting four-wheel brakes. The wheels themselves, formerly of bicycle type, were now steel-spoke affairs. There was even a 175-cc model capable of 45 mph. For those patient enough to endure an 0–30-mph acceleration time of 20 seconds—and those who had lost their licences and so had no option—the Mochet had much to offer. After all, if anything went wrong, it could merely be turned on its side and investigated. In 1953 M. Mochet announced (but did not produce) an attractive little sports two-seater on conventional lines, using the 750-cc CEMEC flat-twin engine already encountered in the Rosengart Sagaie. Unlike the soapbox, it used a transverse-leaf independent front suspension with swing axles and coils at the rear. The wheelbase was an abbreviated 76 inches, and the car weighed 627 lb.

The Julien was always about to enter production during its two-year career, 1946–8. Chenard–Walcker were allegedly interested, and the state-owned SNCASO aircraft plant at Bordeaux actually built a batch of Julien bodies. There was, however, no money to pay their bill: *ergo*, no Julien.

Despite a very narrow rear track (with a differential) it was quite a handsome little two-seater. The front suspension was independent, with quarter-elliptics at the rear, where the engine and gearbox were located. Brakes were mechanical and uncoupled, and various singles and flat-twins were proposed, with three- or four-speed gearboxes.

Of the other early post-war efforts, Gabriel Voisin's Biscuter found a happy home in Spain, and the Rolux, a straightforward little doorless two-seater with a 125-cc engine and Peugeot-style front-end treatment, had managed to sell some 300 units by 1950. Less lucky was Chausson's 1947 CHS.

This car featured an ingenious form of unitary construction without a single casting; even the brake shoes were pressings. The 350-cc single-cylinder two-stroke engine was water cooled and lived, *topolino* fashion, in front of its radiator, driving the front wheels via a three-speed gearbox and bevel differential. A coil-spring independent suspension was used all round, spider-type wheels once again featured, and the cable-operated four-wheel brakes worked in drums that were a surprising 11¾ inches in diameter. Better equipped than most, the CHS was sold complete with direction indicators and electric wipers. There were, however, no doors, and the little car weighed only 672 lb. Hence the claimed 50 mph seemed credible. Leonard Lord of Austin showed a keen interest in this model but backed out when the Board of Trade refused to allocate him any extra steel. With the A40 just getting into its stride, he was naturally reluctant to make cutbacks elsewhere in the range, so the CHS was shelved.

The 1948 Roussey was more of a potential competitor for the Dyna Panhard; it was a proper little four-seater sports saloon with a generous window area, and what we would now term an Astro roof. Admittedly the vertical-barred grille was somewhat crude; the engine, a 750-cc four-cylinder two-stroke in the Trojan idiom, drove the front wheels by chain.

The early 1950s bred a further crop of oddities. Le Piaf was not unlike a Voisin Biscuter in appearance, having no body, only a large windscreen and hammock seats for two. Drive was taken by chain from the 175-cc engine to the left rear wheel, and its makers also marketed a fully bodied version under the Kover name. The contemporary Atlas–Coccinelle was a doorless glassfibre-bodied bubble car with spur gear drive to one rear wheel, a coil-spring independent front suspension and a cable starter, though surprisingly it had a proper box-section frame with tubular cross-members. 1953's Inter three-wheeler was a near-Messerschmitt with a 175-cc Ydral engine made by the Lyonnais branch of the nationalized aircraft industry, while the dodgem-shaped Vallée hailed from Blois and was notable not only for Neimann-type rubber suspension but also for a four-speed-and-reverse gearbox. Both 125-cc and 175-cc Ydral units were used, but Vallée gave up the unequal struggle in 1956, after a four-year run.

The Galy of 1954 acquired French nationality with the death of its designer, the Belgian Daniel d'Ieteren. The change of scene involved a once-famous name, de la Fournaise, general providers of chassis frames in scissors-&-paste days. Thus it is not surprising that this pleasing coupé, promoted as 'the smallest of the real cars', rode on a tubular frame. Double transverse-leaf suspension featured all round, brakes were hydraulic, and the works were at the rear. Gearboxes had only three forward speeds, but there was a wide choice of engines, two-stroke Ydrals or four-stroke French A.M.Cs in the 175–280-cc range. With the most powerful of these, the Galy attained 60 mph, cruised at 50 mph and was credited with a less-than-probable 95 mpg. The Goggomobil-like closed body had a wraparound screen and a wraparound window of generous dimensions, and in addition to this Vibel there was an open Vistand resembling a toy Jeep. At £294, the Vibel should have been an attractive proposition, but once again the 2CV Citroën proved a better bet. The Galy was not quoted after 1956.

With the Reyonnah, designed by Robert Hannoyer, we encounter the Messerschmitt configuration, a four-wheeler with close-set rear wheels. Unlike the Messerschmitt, it was designed to fold—or rather the front wheels and their outriggers were—bringing the width down to 30 inches which was ideal for the front halls of apartment blocks. The usual 175-cc Ydral engine drove the rear wheels by chain, and in 1952 the company was advertising for a British agent. At 280,000 francs, at a time when the *deux-chevaux* cost 323,000 francs it stood no chance of success at home.

The Poirier originated from the *departement* of Eure-et-Loire. Its makers' normal business was the manufacture and motorization of invalid carriages: they also built 98-cc powered models from scratch. Their XW5, though constructed on the same principles, was a tandem *dos-à-dos* tricycle recommended as 'the ideal runabout for town and country alike', requiring no driving licence and needing the same storage space as a Reyonnah. The 125-cc Ydral engine was at the back, in unit with a four-speed gearbox, final drive was by shaft, and the footbrake worked on all three wheels. There was a hand starter in the cockpit, but Poirier were prepared to fit electric starting for a modest consideration. In spite of deliberately low gearing, this curiosity was said to do 28 mph.

3　Spain

Up to the early 1960s the streets of any Spanish city were motor museums in their own right, more intriguing than Rochetaillée or Beaulieu and rivalling even Reno in their diversity. Alas the standard of 'exhibits' was low: some had lost their identities—Opels with Standard bodies and Fiat radiators grafted onto small Vintage Mathis saloons were among the delights that greeted the visitor.

The Civil War of 1936–8 had demolished Spain's economy and industry, and during the long years of recovery Spaniards had to make do with what they could get. Production was modest: 6,500 cars and commercial vehicles in 1954, and still only 22,000 in 1956, by which time the Fiat-sponsored SEAT plant in Barcelona was beginning to achieve a modest production. Though ENASA's superbly made Pegaso trucks, manufactured in the old Hispano-Suiza works, enjoyed an enviable reputation, Spain was best known for its motor-cycles, a fact which explains the profusion of cycle-cars in our period. These emanated, often in small numbers, from sundry small workshops. Several breeds survived into the 1960s, only to be ousted by SEAT-built 600 Fiats. Until the advent of SEAT, of course, no Spanish factory (or assembly plant) offered a family car comparable with Sweden's Volvo or Australia's Holden, though Eugenio Cortes's Eucort (1,500 made between 1949 and 1951) was a gallant effort. At Pegaso, former Alfa Romeo designer Wilfredo Ricart essayed what he termed 'jewels for the rich', but this engaging digression was likewise doomed to failure. Italy dominated the realm of exotic sports cars, and Britain was firmly entrenched in the lower-price echelons.

Some Spanish cycle-cars had roots going back into the distant past. José Maria Armangué's David had started life in 1913 as a soapbox-Derby type of vehicle, progressing by the early Vintage years into a hairy four-cylinder device with twin-belt drive. A period of eclipse had been followed by some electric runabouts produced during and just after the Civil War, but in 1950 the Barcelona firm was back with a three-wheeled mini-car. Its steel-tube frame had a reinforced backbone, and the single driven front wheel incorporated a telescopic fork, after which the cable-and-bobbin steering came as a shock. Power was provided by a 346-cc single-cylinder two-stroke motor-cycle engine, and the David was available either as a streamlined open two-seater or as a pickup truck. About 60 were made, the last of them in 1956.

Far commoner (5,000 were made in the 1952–8 period) and of more illustrious origins was the Biscuter, brainchild of the irrepressible Gabriel Voisin, who had exhibited a prototype at the 1950 Paris Salon. In its original guise, it was a true buckboard, consisting solely of a wooden frame suspended on four semielliptic springs. To this were added a windscreen and two hammock-type seats. A 125-cc motor-cycle engine drove the front wheels via a three-speed gearbox with no reverse. Voisin claimed to have booked 1,400 firm orders for this vehicle, but no French manufacturer was interested. It was left to the Spaniard Damien Casanova and his Autonacional SA to translate the dream into reality.

In definitive form, the Biscuter featured unitary construction (of Duralumin) and an all-independent suspension by coils and swing axles. The brakes were uncoupled, the pedal working on the differential and the lever on the rear wheels, while the engine was a Spanish-built version of that British favourite, the 197-cc two-stroke Villiers. The car weighed only 532 lb, and measured 101½ inches from stem to stern.

Increasing prosperity and the Fiat 600 undoubtedly helped to put an end to the little car, but the process was accelerated by some lily-gilding. Electric starters were introduced in 1955, and by the end of our period the Biscuter had assumed a new identity as the 20CF, a pretty little coupé in the Lotus idiom, complete with reverse and proper four-wheel brakes. A tiny estate car was the final blow in terms of excess weight and abysmal gearing, and the make vanished from the scene in 1958. Many early ones lingered on, however, as cheap runabouts for self-drive hire at seaside resorts.

None of its rivals could match the Biscuter's popularity. Of the four-wheelers, the 1952 Triver was an extension of the Isetta theme, with a narrow rear track and a side-entrance six-light body. This and the bug-eye headlamps gave it a look of the old 1930 Burney Streamline. The PTV of 1956 was an attractive roadster with a rear-mounted 250-cc two-stroke twin engine, in unit with a three-speed transaxle. The brakes were hydraulic, and all four wheels were independently sprung. 1,250 were sold, though it took six years to achieve this output. The TZ Sider from Zaragoza was actually a four-seater saloon on an 80-inch wheelbase, with a bigger-than-usual 350-cc Hispano–Villiers engine driving the front wheels. A speed of over 60 mph was claimed for this 1956 newcomer, which figured in buyers' guides for many years but was hardly ever seen. The Aleu motor-cycle works's Bambi (1952) and the Junior of 1956 were straightforward three-wheelers with rear engines and single driven rear wheels, as was Kapi's first effort, the charmingly named Chi-Qui of 1950. This resembled a motorized side-car and was fitted at various times with Villiers, Montesa and French A.M.C. engines. By 1955 Kapi had progressed to the less orthodox Platillo

Volante (flying saucer), with single front wheel, on which the engine lived to the right-hand side in the manner of the 1921 Scott Sociable and the 1956 Gordon. Also outside, on the front wing, was the kick starter, and this 9-footer was credited with 60 mph and 100 mpg.

By contrast, the 1952 Orix was a full four-seater with a rear-mounted 610-cc flat-twin engine, probably of Panhard make. It resembled a scaled-down Volkswagen, but only 12 were made. Doubtless its sponsors hoped it would fill the void left by the Eucort, which had expired through lack of funds in 1951.

This little four-door saloon was largely hand built, which explains why at various times its front end resembled those of a 1940 Dodge, a TB14 Alvis of 1949 and (on the last Victoria series of 1950) a contemporary Studebaker enlivened by Buick portholes in the bonnet sides. Beneath the surface, however, it was yet another variation on the dependable DKW formula, initially with a 764-cc twin-cylinder two-stroke engine, and later with an in-line three of 76 mm × 76 mm (1,032 cc). Both versions featured the usual wet multi-plate clutch and three-speed gearbox, the frame was the usual backbone with outriggers to support the body, and the suspension was all-independent, by torsion bars at both ends. Taxi-cabs, station wagons and pickups were also available.

The Sociedad de Automoviles de Turismo, established in 1953, succeeded where Eucort and Orix had failed. Backed by Fiat money and know-how, the company's first product was the Fiat 1400, of which 1,345 were delivered during its initial season. By 1954 SEAT were turning out 35 cars a day, and the seal was set on this venture's success when the 600 was added to its repertory in 1955. By the 1970s SEAT had moved into the First Division, with sales of over 330,000 cars in 1975.

Wilfredo Ricart had already been responsible for the Ricart España cars of the 1920s before moving on to Alfa Romeo. His return to Spain after the Second World War heralded an upturn in the affairs of ENASA, heirs to the Hispano-Suiza concern. Although no attempt was made to revive the famous name, the Z102 Pegaso sports car of 1951 was as much a sensation as Marc Birkigt's 32CV had been some thirty years previously. Made entirely by hand in a 'clinical' atmosphere, it was described in contemporary reports as a 'technical and scientific exercise'. It was certainly an exercise in all-Spanish manufacture; only the Bosch electrics were imported. ENASA made their own version of the ZF differential, and, while most early bodies were the work of Touring and Saoutchik, latter-day styling was entrusted to the Spaniard Juan Serra.

Ricart believed that a poor country should build 'jewels for the rich', and nothing was stinted. The engine was a 90-degree vee-eight, with a pair of overhead camshafts per block, driven by a train of gears. The dry nitrided cylinder liners were a Hispano legacy, the crankshaft ran in five bearings, and the dry-sump lubrication reflected racing practice. The dual-choke downdraught Weber carburetter (there was a four-carburetter option) was fed by mechanical pump; the crankcase, sump and heads were all of alloy. The five-speed all-indirect gearbox, with dog-clutch engagement, was at the rear, in unit with the limited-slip differential, and the basis of the car was an electrically welded platform. The front suspension was independent, by double wishbones and torsion bars: at the rear, a de Dion axle was used in conjunction with transverse torsion bars. The hydraulic brakes (inboard at the rear) worked in Alfin drums 12¾ inches in diameter, and the worm-and-sector steering gear was unbelievably complicated. Initially buyers had the choice of two engines, a supercharged 75 mm × 80 mm 2½-litre which gave 225 bhp at 6,800 rpm and a normally aspirated 2.8-litre with a mere 170 bhp. A Pegaso cost £3,000 (a lot of money in 1951) for Barcelona, but in return for this a purchaser knew that his car had had a 5,000-mile predelivery workout, was guaranteed for three years and would receive *any* retrospective modifications free of charge. The alleged fuel consumption of 25 mpg was wishful thinking, not that it mattered. The Pegaso's actual 17 mpg was not excessive.

In experienced hands, clutchless changes were the order of the day, and the 'seat of the pants' handling, superb brakes and high-geared steering invited comparisons with the Alfa Romeo. Pegasos could achieve 125 mph in top and 100 mph in fourth; to accelerate to 0–100 mph took 35 seconds, admittedly slower than an XK120 Jaguar. In 1953, a stock two-seater recorded 151 mph over the flying kilometre. On the debit side were in-different detail finish, an inacceptable noise level and a voracious appetite for plugs. Still, for fanatics with bottomless pockets, vehicles such as 1953's Thrill Berlinetta with its Perspex rear body section and tail fins ('ten thousand pounds' worth of interplanetary red and black cellulose', as *Auto-car*'s Peter Garnier called it) was almost unbeatable value.

Pegaso variations were limitless, the ultimate in Z102s being the 3.2-litre of 1954. This offered 195 bhp in standard form but was credited with 285 bhp (230 bhp was probably a better estimate) when equipped with magneto ignition and twin Roots-type blowers. On a 3.25:1 fifth gear a top speed of 185 mph was quoted. The last of the family was the Z103 announced in 1956. This big vee-eight dispensed with the overhead camshafts, achieving its 150 mph by the time-honoured formula of more litres—anything from 4 to 4.7 litres according to specification. There was dual coil ignition, and a twin-plate clutch was used to transmit outputs which ran as high as 300 bhp when the biggest engine was specified. The weight was up to around 3,400 lb, and only four Z103s were built, out of a total of perhaps 100 Pegasos. After 1958 Ricart elected to concentrate on trucks once more.

4   Belgium and Holland

In the immediate post-war years Belgium's principal role was as a battle-ground for the major foreign manufacturers. Still a colonial power, she suffered from fewer currency problems than any other European nation, except Switzerland. Thus even in 1949 a Belgian motorist with offbeat tastes could choose between Swedish, East German and Russian cars, as well as from the familiar Austins, Renaults, Fiats, Plymouths and Volkswagen. The relaxation of tariff barriers that had proved the native industry's undoing in the 1920s was now working to Belgium's advantage. By 1950, not only Detroit's 'big three', but also Packard, Studebaker and Willys operated Belgian assembly plants, as did Citroën, Renault and Standard–Triumph. A firm as esoteric as Jaguar found it worth their while to circumvent temporary import restrictions with an assembly line in the former Vanden Plas coachworks. This state of affairs gave the country a painless instant motor industry.

There was thus no point in reviving the great names of yesteryear. F.N. declined to make Aluminium Française–Grégoire light cars, though they negotiated for the rights. The only attempt to revive any of the old makes came, predictably, from M. A. van Roggen, who had gathered up the remains of Imperia and Minerva in 1936 and had achieved a modicum of success in the later 1930s with modified front-wheel drive Adlers. His TA8 Imperia of 1948 was, in effect, an updated Adler using the 1,340-cc three-bearing overhead-valve four-cylinder engine intended for 1940 models of the Hotchkiss–Amilcar. This unit developed 45 bhp and went into a classic Adler structure with a transverse-leaf independent front suspension, a rear suspension by trailing arms and torsion bars, rack-and-pinion steering and hydraulic brakes. The three-speed synchromesh gearbox had the fashion-able column shift, and the Imperia was yet another design combining mechanical pump feed with a dash-mounted fuel tank. The 1939 vee-grille was retained, though composite wood-and-metal construction made the two-door saloon, at 2,128 lb, heavier than the old Amilcars; roadsters were quite pretty. The TA8 was good for 70 mph and could be worked up to 53 mph on the intermediate ratio, but at 117,000 francs belges (£670) it was barely competitive with such imports as the Austin A40, the Hillman Minx and the Fiat-based Simca 8, all of which could be bought for less than £500. After 1949 Imperia concentrated their efforts on the Standard Vanguard, adding a cabriolet to the range. By 1951 the Nessonvaux works were turning out 350–400 Anglo-Belgian cars a month.

Van Roggen, however, still hankered after a Belgian luxury machine in the old Minerva tradition, using Armstrong Siddeley's new 3.4-litre Sapphire power unit. As a second string car, he acquired the rights to an Italian Lost Cause, the 1.3-litre Cemsa Caproni flat-four of 1947. Examples of this car, together with an assortment of Siddeleys, were on display at the Minerva stand in Brussels in 1953. All this ambitious programme achieved was a few left-hand drive Sapphires assembled in Belgium. Meanwhile Minerva was assembling the humbler Land Rover, and in 1954 an extraordinary air-cooled four-cylinder sleeve-valve engine was announced. An impressive 72 bhp were claimed from 2 litres, but, when van Roggen's own contender in the Jeep stakes was announced in 1956, it was found to be conventional and powered by the good old side-valve Continental four. There was spiral bevel drive to both axles, the brakes were hydraulic, and a quick-detachable power pack should have been an attraction. It was not: the C20 had a short life. Customers were far more interested in the latest Standard–Triumph variant, the Francorchamps fixed-head coupé on a Triumph TR3 chassis.

Holland, a less affluent nation with little car-making tradition, had almost nothing to offer. In 1946 the Government considered state-subsidized production of our old friend the Aluminium Française–Grégoire, but nothing came of the project. For the rest, the Hostaco motor-cycle factory built a few versions of the ubiquitous German Fuldamobil, and another mini-car was marketed briefly under the odd name of Shelter. There was also the Joymobile of 1953.

The engine of this device, a four-cylinder Delettrez diesel from France, drove twin gear-type pumps. These in their turn circulated hydraulic fluid through the main frame tubes (reminiscent of the 1890 Peugeots) to twin turbines, one on each axle shaft. By using the same fluid to cool the engine, the designer was able to dispense with a radiator, while reversing the fluid's flow gave either engine braking or a reverse. Fortunately, orthodox hydraulic 'anchors' were provided as well. Interchangeable air-suspension units were fitted at front and rear, and the standard body was a futuristic six-seater saloon of glassfibre construction. Washmobile—Holland's programme included versions with six-cylinder petrol and diesel engines, not to mention disc brakes. A sports car was also considered but never materialized.

By contrast, rally driver Maurice Gatsonides' idea of a sports model was made in limited numbers up to 1951. First seen in the 1946 French Alpine Trial, the Gatso featured an early example of the tubular space-frame. The two–three-seater body resembled an aeroplane fuselage, especially in coupé guise with a sliding bubble-canopy. The central protruding headlamp anticipated both the Tucker and the Rover P4, but the mechanics and suspension alike were old-school Ford; so was the standard engine, a 3,917-cc vee-eight Mercury, which gave 120 bhp in standard form with twin downdraught carburetters and magneto ignition, and an optimistic 175 bhp with an overhead-valve conversion, in which case the top speed was 112 mph. The standard Ford three-speed gearbox was mated to a two-speed back axle, the weight was 2,408 lb, and by 1949 the Girling hydromechanical brakes had given way to full hydraulics.

5 Germany

5.1 The Two Fatherlands

Although spared the ultimate *Götterdämmerung* of which Adolf Hitler dreamed in his last days, Germany was so utterly defeated in 1945 that most Allied observers dismissed her for ever as an industrial power. Bearing in mind the events of 1933, her conquerors went several steps further than they had in 1918, partitioning Germany into two halves with opposing ideologies.

However, the Western half, at any rate, bounced back. In 1951 private-car production almost reached its Hitlerian zenith of 276,000 in 1938. Thereafter it rose inexorably, to 388,000 in 1953 and to a staggering 910,996 in 1956. This last performance put the Bundesrepublik in second place, behind America but ahead of Britain, which had delivered only a little over 700,000 units that year. Exports, at 48%, were still just below the British proportion, but, though this might permit a degree of complacency in Coventry, it still meant that more foreigners were buying German than British.

The growth rate was outstanding: 257% between 1948 and 1949, even though this stabilized at a reasonable 40% in ensuing years. German economists muttered darkly about saturation points, but these did not happen. The worst the manufacturers suffered was a brief cutback in 1950, when sheet steel supplies fell behind the insatiable demands of Volkswagen, Opel and their rivals.

By the mid-1950s Volkswagen headed the best-seller lists in Belgium and Switzerland and had edged Britain out of first place in the American foreign-import stakes. The Beetle had helped Germany to about 40 % of Portugal's new-car registrations. It was also Britain's best-selling foreigner, though the *marque*'s share of the 6,885 units imported that year would not have kept Wolfsburg busy for long.

Nor was the Beetle alone. If BMW had barely recovered from the partition of their empire and if DKW competed against a plethora of local variations on a theme by Rasmussen, Opel, backed by the resources of General Motors, were fighting it out with Fiat for second place in Switzerland. The Mercedes–Benz was once again the recognized transport of the professional classes where import regulations permitted (with a useful line in diesel-engined cabs as a safeguard against recessions!). Less important, though significant, were the products of Carl Borgward's Bremen-based empire and the Kölnische Fords, still independent of Dagenham's thinking.

German recovery stemmed, first and foremost, from the determination of German citizens. The moment the Second World War was over, loyal Opel workers set themselves the task of clearing up the damage, to such good effect that the plant was usable by the end of 1945—even if material shortages prevented the actual delivery of vehicles before the following summer. The Trade Unions, despite their new-found freedom, were cooperative, following the credo of Heinz Nordhoff of Volkswagen that 'if we kill the cow on whose milk we want to live later ... then we shall have no future, and our grandchildren will curse us because we did not think of them but only of the present'. Strikes were virtually unknown. Moreover, the German Government made no attempt to interfere: there would be no repetition of 1938's Schell Plan which rationalized the industry's products, albeit less drastically than some writers would have us believe.

Partition in itself was a formidable blow. Apart from the extreme case of Stoewer, whose home town of Stettin was ceded to Poland, Opel lost both the entire Kadett tooling (sent to Russia as reparations) and their Brandenburg truck factory. BMW, while retaining their Munich headquarters, found themselves without Eisenach, where the six-cylinder cars had been built: the Saxon-based Auto Union group lost everything. Wanderer's base, Chemnitz, even acquired the new and symbolic name of Karl Marx Stadt.

The Allied Air Forces had taken a drastic toll of what was left. The Daimler–Benz complex at Stuttgart lay in ruins, Opel were reeling under nine months of intensive bombardment, and at Bremen Carl Borgward lost 90% of his buildings and 60% of his machinery. Ford's factories were, admittedly, usable and were producing trucks within a month of the Armistice, but more typical of the situation was the plight of the Bosch electrical works, which had been general provider to much of Europe in pre-war days. By 1945 this concern had a work force of only 750, as against the 15,000 they could command at their peak. Even allowing for a happier situation at their branch plants, their maximum potential was 40%. Yet despite bomb damage, malnutrition and restrictions imposed by the Allied Military Government—in 1946 Germans were only allowed to use their cars if their jobs rendered these essential—Bosch was already providing work for 10,000 hands in that year. By the end of 1947 Opel workers were assembling some 150 vehicles a·day, while in the first two-and-a-half years of peace Volkswagen managed to deliver over 20,000 Beetles, an interesting comparison with their total wartime output of 66,000, including *Kübeln* and *Schwimmwagens*.

The Allies, of course, could not afford to be too vindictive. Whatever their feelings about the Third Reich, Germany could not 'live on the parish' as an economic liability. With her railway network out of action she (and the occupying forces) had to be kept mobile. In 1945 it was estimated that at least 25,000 trucks were needed for this purpose, and even in 1947 the shortage was still acute. Of the 40,897 private cars registered in Hamburg in 1938, only 7,147 had survived. The onset of the Cold War accelerated the process: German industry was set to work furnishing vehicles for the Occupying Powers. Some odd hybrids resulted, notably Karmann's Horch-like saloon coachwork for military Humber Super Snipes.

Car manufacture was encouraged. To a certain extent this may have been due to Anglo-American complacency—British engineers, at any rate, had a low opinion of the Volkswagen—but it was also due to a desire to relieve their own tax payers of the burden of Germany. Thus the ban on German products did not last as long as it had after 1918, when the British press refused advertising for 'ex-enemy' goods, and even the respected Mercedes was kept out of Olympia until 1927. Volkswagen were on sale in Belgium by 1947, and a certain number trickled back to Britain, thanks to the special price of £160 arranged for members of the BAOR. There was actually a Porsche stand at Earls Court in 1951, and, though its contents were not on sale to Britons, nor were any other foreign exhibits apart from locally assembled Citroëns and Renaults. The Germans were back in England by mid-1953, a year ahead of our American Allies and of the Italians.

Another reason for German success was the modern thinking that had permeated the country's design studios since 1932. True, the comic-opera VW savings-stamp scheme was still echoing in German courts, as subscribers tried to recover their money or a cut-price car, but this hardly worried Heinz Nordhoff. What Ferdinand Porsche had laid down in 1936 was still entirely viable in 1950—or 1960, for that matter. It might be awkward to gain access to the engine, but, with a nationwide dealer network (Volkswagen had mopped up Adler when Adler abandoned cars for good), this did not matter. What did matter was an 'unburstable' engine (the maximum speed really *was* the cruising speed, even if neither as yet exceeded 60 mph), a frostproof cooling system and a sophisticated chassis capable of withstanding Europe's war-torn roads.

Equally modern by 1946 standards were the Opel Olympia and the 170V Mercedes–Benz, a tough and splendid piece of 1934 styling. It was fortunate for the Western Allies that BMW's upheavals prevented an early revival of their admirable 2-litre.

And while the same might be said of Italy's Fiats, Italy was by no means an industrial nation of Germany's calibre. She lacked the raw materials: further, 90% of her output was in the hands of one company—Fiat. In spite of Albert Speer's gloomy prognostications, German industry recovered quickly, once it was freed from the hopeless task of feeding a war on two fronts. Once this happened, no manufacturer in a position to resume car making was short of a saleable design.

Some, it is true, abdicated—Adler when American aid for reconstruction was not forthcoming, Hanomag into truck production, and Maybach because their cars had formed part of a Germany that no longer existed. However, even Auto Union were back in action at Ingolstadt in 1951, producing 15,000 of their evergreen DKWs that year. Of the other manufacturers, Mercedes–Benz delayed the introduction of post-war designs until 1951, and another decade passed before Volkswagen came up with an alternative to the Beetle. Opel carried on just as if 1939–45 had never happened; unlike Vauxhall, they were even spared the growing pains of the short-stroke engine, which they had been using since 1935. First of the all-new German cars was the 1500 Borgward of 1949, as much a byproduct of the Schell Plan as anything else—under that scheme the company had been 'rationed' to a 2.3-litre six that would hardly have been viable in the arid post-war climate.

Thus the German mainstream showed no new trends; the models were all available in 1939. Few beam axles had been visible at the last pre-war Berlin Show, and such legacies as Volkswagen's rear engine and DKW's front-wheel drive were already proven. During our period Borgward's Goliath and Lloyd would join the front-wheel ranks, while followers of the VW layout would include the best of the miniatures, the Goggomobil.

In some ways Germans were conservative. Their long-standing preference for column shift, for instance, is hard to comprehend. A British writer observed in 1952, 'Gas turbines, pneumatic suspension and plastic bodies are regarded as the domain of scientists and not yet that of the manufacturer.' While this was essentially true of any country at that time, Germany would not lead such trends. They might call their little Lloyd 'the Elastoplast car', but it merely perpetuated the wood-and-fabric body construction of the old DKW.

Since the war, some regrettable gaps had developed. Gone was the entire *blitz und donner* brigade, from the Maybach Zeppelin to the handsome if lethargic straight-eight Horch. Big cars were now manufactured only by Britain and America, so German tastes for the grandiose had to be satisfied by the Type 300 Mercedes–Benz.

By contrast, sports-car enthusiasts fared better. Before the war, there had been the 328 BMW—and nothing else. But, though the 328-based Veritas of our period was a very basic effort in its early form and a financial disaster in its subsequent, fully manufactured guise, there were some outstanding high-performance machines available—the 300SL Mercedes–Benz and the Porsche 356. BMW's own eight-cylinder 507 barely got off the ground, though in old age it would realize more at auction than many a Gullwing!

Germany's mini-cars deserve a book in their own right. The breed was, of course, no German preserve, indeed the country's most successful bubble, the BMW Isetta, originated in Italy. But the Teutonic strain tended to be more practical and more sophisticated.

The first factor undoubtedly derived from a tradition for the utilitarian, going back to the three-wheeled Cyklons and Phänomobils of pre-1914 days, machines innocent of the sporting flavour of their British and French counterparts. In Weimar days, also, there had been tax loopholes which permitted oddities such as the Framo. Of the moderns, successes included the Messerschmitt with its aircraft-type cockpit canopy and handlebar steering, and Goggomobils available with electrically selected preselective gearboxes. Moreover, the Isetta, the Goggomobil and the Messerschmitt *kabinenroller* survived far into the 1960s, even if none of them could match the records of the Fuldamobil, a wandering Jew of a car which penetrated Asia and South America and turned up in Greece, under the Alta name, as late as 1968.

In East Germany, matters pursued a totally different course. The Soviet system of government left no room for private enterprise: nor did it consider private cars of prime importance. Though both the IFA F8 (alias the 1938 DKW) and the EMW (the 1939 BMW 321) were on sale in some western countries as early as 1948, East Germany was not a major car-producing nation. Its best performance in our period was a low 28,145 units in 1956, a figure which falls further into perspective when one reflects that the pre-war potential of DKW alone was in the region of 45,000 cars a year.

Nor were East German citizens car owners. Long after the ancients had vanished from the roads of the West, East Germany still harboured such cars as Adler Trumpfs, if only because new vehicles were tightly 'rationed'—by price. In 1954 the three-cylinder IFA F9 retailed for the equivalent of £350 in western Europe, but to the average East German industrial worker its purchase represented three years' wages. Hence as late as 1962 the country registered only 170,000 cars (one to every fifty inhabitants). By contrast, the ratio in West Germany was one to every 7.2 inhabitants.

East German cars are described alongside their Western relatives, if only because design trends represented a slow-motion and somewhat restricted version of what was happening in Konrad Adenauer's domains. The choice was, of course, limited; in the lower echelons there was the faithful old DKW, while the possession of Eisenach gave the state-controlled industry rights to the 2-litre BMW family. Though development of the latter line ceased with the demise of the big Sachsenring saloons in 1959, the cars East Germany was making in 1977—the Wartburg and the smaller Trabant—could trace their ancestry back to the original DKW—Front of 1931.

5.2   The Bubble that Wouldn't Burst

Best-known of the German miniatures was an Italian with a German pass-port, BMW's version of the Isetta, of which the *Münchner* firm built some 36,000 between 1955 and 1962. BMW wisely discarded the two-stroke in favour of their own overhead-valve vertical-singles of 245 and 298 cc, and with these came a motor-cycle-type positive-stop gearchange. The top speed was, however, above 50 mph. German Isettas were subsequently made in Britain at the old LBSCR locomotive works at Brighton. Three-wheeler editions—sold mainly in England—came later.

The Auto-Kabine marketed by a Vespa agent from Lintorf, J. O. Hoff-mann, had a very short life—the last three months of 1954, during which 113 cars were delivered. Herr Hoffmann had entered the mini-car industry by the simple expedient of buying an Isetta and copying it. To avoid infringement suits, he converted the design to a side-entrance and fitted his own 248-cc flat-twin engine. Neither BMW nor Iso felt that this was enough, and some brisk litigation ended the Hoffmann's career.

Aircraft manufacturer Ernst Heinkel's bubble car followed the Isetta in 1956, but, though its configuration was similar, it started life as a three-wheeler, branching out into a fourth wheel early in 1957. The four-speed gearbox (the Heinkel, like the Isetta, was reversible) was once again of motor-cycle type, but this time the construction was unitary, and the hyd-raulically actuated footbrake worked on the front wheels only. A bell-crank independent front suspension was preferred to Dubonnet, and as an engine maker Heinkel naturally fitted his own overhead-valve single, which was smaller than the Isetta's at 174 cc. Both ends swung up, but on Cabin Cruisers the steering column was attached to the door pillar and thus needed no complicated joints. The Heinkel's home-market run was brief and limited—6,436 units in three seasons—but it fared better abroad. Trojan's English-speaking, albeit left-hand drive version survived into 1965.

Three years earlier, in 1953, Heinkel's one-time rival Willi Messerschmitt had climbed aboard the bubble bandwagon, but all the *Kabinenroller*'s joystick steering and tandem cockpits under a Bf110-type canopy the KR175 was not his own invention. It derived from a cheap means of transport for disabled ex-servicemen devised by Fritz Fend of Rosenheim in 1948. Like Poirier in France, Fend started with a 38-cc moped engine in a hand-propelled invalid carriage, progressing to a properly bodied *mono-posto* bubble using 100-cc units by Sachs and Riedel–Imme. When the definitive version turned up at Geneva in 1953 it still carried the Fend name, though examples were already coming off the lines at Messerschmitt's Regensburg works, where they were regarded as a welcome relief from wholesale unemployment.

The Messerschmitt was a three-wheeled scooter with a single chain-driven rear wheel, clothed in a tubular space-frame. The suspension was of Neimann bonded-rubber type, and the power (an adequate 9 bhp in view of a weight of 341 lb) came from a 174-cc Sachs two-stroke single mounted at the rear. Both the multiple wet-plate clutch and the four-speed gearbox were of motor-cycle type, as were the controls—handlebar steering, twist-grip clutch lever, foot change and kick starter. Both pedal and lever actuated brakes on all three wheels. The windscreen, unlike the canopy, was of proper glass, the rear seat was adjustable, and the little car outperformed rival bubbles, attaining over 60 mph, with a 0–30-mph acceleration time of 8.2 seconds. 99 inches long and only 48 inches wide, the Messerschmitt was a real congestion beater and handled well enough to win praise from *Autosport*'s John Bolster.

From 1955 the car was refined, with car-type throttle and clutch controls, a Siba Dynastart, a complicated auxiliary mechanism which reversed the engine, an improved swing-arm suspension and electric wipers in place of the old cable linkage. Extras included a rear dual seat and even a radio, while more powerful 191-cc engines distinguished the KR200 series. The Messerschmitt reached its peak in 1955, with 11,909 sold, but production continued into the 1960s, and total sales were well over 30,000. The Italian Mi-Val motor-cycle factory toyed with a copy of the KR175, using their own two-stroke engine and a tinted canopy to shut out the Mediterranean sun.

The egg-shaped Fuldamobil pursued a lengthy and complicated career, beginning, appositely, in the German town of Fulda and terminating a good twenty years later in Athens, Greece. Its Hellenic name of Alta was apposite, since previous *alter egos* had been the British Nobel, the Dutch Hostaco and sundry Indian and Chilean species. The 1950 prototype was, however, a surrealist egg, with the slab sides and fastback of an early 1930s trailer caravan, mounted on a tubular three-wheeled chassis with a single driven rear wheel. Mechanics were crude, with chain steering and brakes on the front wheels only. The coupé body was panelled in fabric over a steel frame. This model was still being offered in 1954, later examples using hammered aluminium panels, while various small engines were used (Zündapp, Ilo, Sachs, and Baker *u* Polling). The definitive egg shape, Type S, came from a different factory in 1954. It fell into the bubble class with its 8-inch wheels, and car-type steering was used, though the three-speed gearbox was still on motor-cycle lines, and the original transverse-leaf independent front suspension was retained. The bench seat converted into a bed. The first examples used the 359-cc Sachs engine, but standard units were 200s by Sachs or Ilo. By the end of 1956 the improved S4 was available: this had four electrically selected speeds and uncoupled three-wheel brakes. With a length of 122 inches the Fuldamobil was less compact than its rivals, weighed nearly 800 lb and was credited with a sedate 47 mph. Four-wheel versions were certainly listed in this year, and possibly earlier.

More complicated even than the Fuldamobil saga were the strange adventures of Egon Brütsch, racing motor-cyclist turned bubble-car fanatic. His eggs crop up persistently between 1951 and 1958, sometimes under other names and nationalities—the French Avolette and the Swiss Belcar, for instance. The basic Brütsch type was the Zwerg (dwarf), a tubular-framed *monocoque* three-wheeler with a single driven rear wheel, a rubber suspension, rack-and-pinion steering, mechanical brakes and the now mandatory 8-inch scooter wheels. There was a choice of engine; with a 200-cc 14-bhp two-stroke unit the Zwerg weighed about 400 lb and would attain 65 mph.

By contrast, the Mopetta, actually available in England by 1957, represented more minimal transportation than anything from the cycle-car era. Originally conceived as an amphibian, it was a tiny plastic side-car-shape for one, 69 inches long and 26 inches wide. The 50-cc Ilo moped engine was banished to a lateral pannier. The three forward speeds were selected by a handlebar-mounted lever: with a turning circle of 12 feet, reverse was superfluous. So, of course, was a differential, the drive being taken by chain to the left rear wheel. Sophistication extended to a transparent canopy hood, and to brakes (albeit uncoupled ones) on all wheels. The Mopetta attained 22 mph and 111 mpg; a 100-cc edition with front engine and front-wheel drive was planned. In view of the steering ratio (one quarter-turn from lock to lock) it is perhaps as well that this model did not materialize!

Brütsch's four-wheeler, the Pfeil, was actually in production in 1956, though during a two-year career it was sponsored first by the Bavarian Spatz Fahrzeugwerke and then by the Victoria motor-cycle concern. The Spatz, as the car was known, was on accepted Brütsch lines but with a tubular backbone frame in place of the prototype's less-than-rigid *monocoque*. The rear-mounted engine was the familiar 200-cc Sachs, but the pretty little glassfibre two-seater in 190SL Mercedes style was more civilized than most, with hydraulic brakes, a four-speed gearbox, reversible motor, Porsche trailing-arm front suspension and swing axles at the back. Three-wheeler editions were catalogued, if not sold. Under Victoria management in 1957, the Spatz received that company's own more powerful 248-cc engine and also a five-speed electric gearbox. Some 1,500 assorted Spatz were built.

The earlier (1951) Kleinschnittger from Arnsberg was also a sporting two-seater. With its narrow-section tyres, doorless body and aggressive vee-grille, it could easily be mistaken for a dodgem car. The 125-cc Ilo engine drove the front wheels, and once again we encounter a backbone frame and rubber suspension. The three-speed gearbox incorporated a DKW-type free-wheel, if no reverse. All four wheels were braked, and 2,000

Kleinschnittgers were sold at a price of DM 2,400. An attempt to develop the theme into a 244-cc four-seater with four-speed box came to nothing, though DKW played with the design before settling for their Sonderklasse-based Junior in 1958.

Hermann Holbein's Champion started life in 1948 as a copybook piece of Ganz thinking: a two-seater body not unlike that of the Swiss Rapid, a backbone frame and a swing-axle suspension. The brakes—on the rear wheels only—were mounted inboard, other curiosities being the spectacle-type steering wheel and large-diameter motor-cycle wheels which imparted a spidery look. The engine and gearbox came from the 250-cc twin-piston TWN (German Triumph) motor-bike, and starting was mechanical.

Subsequent managements would transform the Champion into a proper small car. By 1951, it had grown up into a pleasing little rolltop convertible, *topolino*-style, which *The Motor* regarded as 'functional without being crude'. The engine was now a 398-cc water-cooled Ilo twin, mounted in unit with the three-speed all-indirect gearbox and bevel-driven rear axle. The usual rubber suspension made its appearance, the brakes were proper 2LS hydraulics on all four wheels, and electric starting was provided. The introduction of a four-seater station wagon called for a more powerful 452-cc Heinkel engine, but, after some 3,300 of this family had been built, control passed to the Maico motor-cycle factory. The 18-bhp Heinkel was standardized, as was the four-seater saloon coachwork. Later Champions suffered from erratic steering, and in 1957 Maico jettisoned the rubber suspension in favour of an orthodox coil-spring setup. After 1958, they jettisoned cars altogether.

Wilhelm Gutbrod's firm had made Josef Ganz's Standard Superior until his non-Aryan origins had forced him out of business in 1939. Surprisingly, though, his 1950 Gutbrod Superior owed little to his former mentor. Like the Champion's, its body was Fiat-inspired, but there the resemblance ended, for Gutbrod made his own reverse-scavenged 71 mm × 75 mm (593-cc) two-stroke twin with thermosyphon cooling and mounted it over the front wheels, which it drove. The backbone frame, coil-spring independent suspension and steering by rack and pinion were to be expected, as were hydraulic brakes on a Fiat competitor, though the three forward speeds were unsynchronized. The wheelbase was a compact 78¾ inches, and the car cost DM 3,990 (£335) in standard form. Fuel injection was adopted for 1953, when a Jaguar-like sports two-seater made a fleeting appearance: this model was credited with 75 mph. The use of a 663-cc engine in 1952's larger 700 model permitted four seats, and Gutbrod even played with a 900-cc vertical-three. By this time, however, DKW were back in business, and their Sonderklasse at DM 6,040 was uncomfortably close to the DM 5,275 asked for the less powerful Gutbrod. The latter company was out of business by 1954, though later a Norwegian syndicate would attempt to revive the design as the Troll. A total of 7,726 Gutbrod private cars was made.

If the Gutbrod failed to stay the course, Carl Borgward's 'Elastoplast car' from Bremen, the Lloyd, not only enjoyed an eleven-year run but also worked itself into third place behind Volkswagen and Opel. Over 130,000 of the basic two-strokes found buyers, and Borgward managed to hold the price below £300 throughout their career.

Essentially his LP300 of 1950 was a reversion to the original unsophisticated DKW thinking of the early 1930s. Like the DKW, it used a vertical twin two-stroke engine driving the front wheels via a three-speed crash box. Other features shared with the great German archetype were 6-volt electrics, dual coil ignition, gravity feed, a backbone frame, cable-operated brakes and transverse-leaf independent front suspension, though the new engine's capacity of 293-cc represented the minimum sufficient to transport four people at 45 mph. Other economies were forced-draught air cooling and the deletion of the free-wheel; Borgward's engineers preferred a swing axle at the rear, and the DKW-type fabric saloon body was panelled in plywood, with metal corners to give at least some curves. The car was appreciably lighter than a pre-war Reichsklasse DKW—1,063 as against 1,595 lb. The range was expanded to embrace a miniature station wagon and an unattractive little coupé, but increasing affluence dictated more power and refinement. By 1953 the Lloyd had grown into the 386-cc LP400, though a year later it could still be bought for £283, inclusive of hydraulic brakes, telescopic dampers and proper metal panelling. There was also a semi-forward-control mini-bus, the LT500, and the family was continued into 1957. The subutility 250 of 1956 was, however, a total failure, even though it undercut Fiat's twin-cylinder Nuova 500 by about £50, Germans no longer wanted crude bumperless vehicles with only 11 bhp on tap.

The second-generation Lloyd also appeared that year. This 600 used a 77 mm × 64 mm (593-cc) power unit with a chain-driven overhead camshaft and an output of 19 bhp. The weight was held down to 1,232 lb, giving a respectable performance, while a further attraction was a cheap (£17) exchange-engine service. This was certainly needed in America, where the high-revving twins lasted about six months under freeway conditions. Yet rough and crude though it was, the Lloyd was the right car at the right time and added another 176,524 units to the factory's sales.

As the Lloyd grew up, its former mantle was assumed by the Goggomobil, a 1955 newcomer from the Hans Glas agricultural engineering firm in Bavaria. Very much a family business, Glas had made their name with scooters, and the Goggomobil was destined to have the longest run of all the German mini-cars, outliving even the Isetta. When it disappeared in 1966, over 250,000 had been sold, most of these the basic type using a 247-cc air-cooled twin engine of Glas's own make.

Here was a later generation of thinking, with welded-up unitary construction based on a platform frame and with hydraulic brakes. The suspension was classic, with coil springs all round and swing axles at the rear, while Ing. Dompert preferred a rear engine. Goggomobils combined a very quick four-speed dog-clutch gearbox and multiple wet-plate clutch with car-type controls, a differential was provided, and this compact four-seater, 114 inches long, managed 50 mph on just under 14 bhp. Even with the original 296-cc power unit, weight was still only 882 lb. As is so often the case with two-strokes, the advertised fuel consumption of 85 mpg was hard to attain in practice, though 55–70 mpg was creditable enough, and a T300 was quicker to 50 mph than a side-valve *topolino*. At the 1956 Frankfurt Show, Glas exhibited the elegant TS300 coupé with a Getrag electrically selected preselective gearbox. This ingenious device became available on the saloons as well, and, almost alone among the bubble merchants, Glas moved on to proper cars in the early 1960s. Unfortunately this step led them into the arms of the resuscitated BMW empire, and after 1967 Glas was heard of no longer.

Zündapp, whose Volksauto of 1932 had been a Volkswagen ancestor, stayed away from cars until the end of our period. In 1956, however, they took the plunge with a most improbable vehicle, a development of the Delta mini-car already developed by the son of aircraft designer Claude Dornier.

The family which created the Flying Pencil had now produced a non-flying rhomboid, with *dos-à-dos* seating (reminiscent of 1899) and Isetta-style swing-up doors at each end. The engine had to be mounted horizontally amidships (the fuel pump lived on one side of it, and the spare wheel on the other), a formula which crammed four people into a space 7½ inches shorter than the later BMC Mini. The rest of the Delta's mechanics followed accepted principles, with unitary construction, a four-speed constant-mesh gearbox and a strut-type independent rear suspension matched to orthodox coils at the front. Zündapp's Janus version used their own 248-cc two-stroke single, and the car was taken up in England by Kaye Don's Pontiac agency. It looked very strange on the Pontiac stand at Earls Court, but at £556 it was too expensive for Britons, and too heterodox at any price for its compatriots. 1957 was its last year.

A few other ephemerals appeared fleetingly, though one that never reached the public was Hanomag's promising and attractive Partner of 1951. Once again the styling was Fiat-inspired, with rolltop coupé coachwork, though the Partner sat three abreast on separate bucket seats. The design was a synthesis of contemporary small-car thinking, with a Champion-type rubber suspension and a DKW configuration, the 697-cc vertical three-cylinder two-stroke engine driving the front wheels. Sophistication extended not only to hydraulic brakes but also to synchromesh on all three forward gears. On 28 bhp, the Hanomag should have performed well.

Its sponsors, however, preferred to stay with trucks.

Nor was much as yet heard of Hanns Trippel, an amphibian specialist and wartime occupant of the Bugatti works at Molsheim. Oddly his SK10 mini-car of 1951, though a *monocoque*, was not waterborne. It was a Beetle-shaped two-seater coupé on the usual lines—a rubber suspension, rack-and-pinion steering and the hydraulic brakes of the superior babies. The rear-mounted four-stroke engine was Zündapp's 597-cc overhead-valve flat-twin, available in standard (18.5-bhp) or sports (26-bhp) guises, with three or four speeds, both innocent of synchromesh. What looked like fron-tal luggage accommodation was full of fuel tank and spare wheel, and, though a speed of 72 mph was claimed from sports Trippels, few were made in Germany. Rosengart, however, turned out a few in France, where the car was known as the Marathon.

Neither of Hamburg's contenders, the Staunau and the Wendax, made such impression. The former was the brainchild of a refrigerator salesman and featured what Germans called 'mini-Ami' styling, though beneath the surface was the inevitable DKW formula, down to a complete DKW front end wedded to a Gutbrod gearbox. The brakes were hydraulic, and the Staunau was a solid affair with all-steel unitary construction and room for four, in spite of which it weighed only 1,400 lb. This, however, was too much for the original 394-cc water-cooled twin-cylinder Ilo engine, and plans were afoot to instal the larger twin-piston 750 when the company folded in 1951.

If the Staunau's stylistic inspiration was American, the Wendax was posi-tively Japanese in appearance. Built by a motor-cycle manufacturer, it started life in 1949 as a dodgem-type open two-seater, its rear-mounted 400-cc two-stroke engine driving the right-hand rear wheel by chain. The protruding central headlamp gave it some individuality, but at DM 4,860 it cost more than a Beetle. Two years later Wendax had second thoughts. These could easily be mistaken for a Datsun or Ohta on the strength of the ponderous four-door six-light saloon coachwork. The 750-cc Ilo engine drove the front wheels via a four-speed synchromesh gearbox. The WS750 had a torsion-bar independent front suspension, hydraulic brakes and 16-inch wheels, but nothing was heard of it after 1952.

5.3 Joy Through Strength

Volkswagen (333,190 cars sold in 1956) dominated the mass market, as Adolf Hitler had predicted they would. Only the name was different: liberal-minded Germans wanted no part of *Kraft durch Freude* (strength through joy) with its unsavoury *Arbeitsfront* overtones.

The ugly little *Käfer* was giving foreign rivals a hard time, thanks to assembly plants in Australia, Brazil, New Zealand and South Africa; not to mention 55,000 cars sold in America during 1956. As for the home market, the Volkswagen was unassailable and would remain so for many years. Even in July 1964, when the basic design was twenty-seven years old, it accounted for 2,666,950 out of about 8,000,000 private cars circulating in West Germany as well as three-fifths of the country's light-van population. The hundred thousandth Beetle was made in 1952, and the quarter millionth in 1955, but this was only the beginning. 1961 saw the five millionth, and eleven years later Ferdinand Porsche's ageless masterpiece had beaten the Model T Ford's record, with a total of 15,007,034 units delivered. It was no wonder that Wolfsburg's advertising suddenly featured a 1914 Tin Lizzie!

The Beetle represented the apotheosis of the Ganz formula: a simple horizontally opposed air-cooled four-cylinder engine at the rear of a backbone frame, with an all-independent suspension by torsion bars. The unit developed its maximum power at a low 3,300 rpm, and this, allied to a top gear which was very much an overdrive (3.5:1 with a 4.43 axle ratio) made for a long life. On a modest 25 bhp, the 1946 edition needed a long stretch of autobahn to attain 60 mph, but once there the car would putter along happily for ever. The aerodynamic shape helped also, though the Volkswagen was alarmingly sensitive to cross-winds and would give a convincing imitation of a blowout in such conditions. Less worrying were the crude thrashing noises: these were inaudible to occupants. *The Motor* rated the car 'a sound job, which should give long years of service, with the minimum of professional attention'.

Apart from the austere finish (chromium plate was notably absent, and the sole instrument was a speedometer), the cars that rolled off the lines under British control in 1945 were easily recognizable as Beetles. The starter and choke controls were floor mounted, as was the gear lever, the petrol tank was at the front, feeding the Solex carburetter by mechanical pump, and the sole stylistic difference was the divided rear window. Even then, heater–demister units were standard in Volkswagen; the fan-belt warning light was a desirable adjunct on an air-cooled car. The four-speed gearbox as yet lacked synchromesh, and the brakes, working in 9-inch drums, were cable operated. During the war the original 1-litre overhead-valve power unit had been replaced by a 75 mm × 64 mm (1,131-cc) version, as always, with alloy heads. The first post-war cars had the high ground clearance specified for the Russian Front, but this had been dispensed with by the beginning of 1946. By the time the Beetle was freely available in Germany; it cost DM 5,300, but this was progressively reduced. In 1956, a standard saloon sold for DM 3,790 and the De Luxe edition for DM 4,600, which explains the decimation of the bubble cars. Comparable prices were DM

3,096 for a 250-cc Goggomobil, DM 3,350 for the Lloyd LP400 and DM 4,600 for the Maico-built Champion.

Very little was done to the design during our period. Plated side flashes and nave plates were standard for export from 1949 onwards. 1952's refinements included self-parking wipers and ventilating panels on the doors of De Luxe versions, 1953 saw the one-piece oval rear window and 1955 models were recognizable by their twin exhausts. Hydraulic brakes were standard equipment on De Luxe Volkswagens from 1950, synchromesh on the three upper ratios came in 1952, and in 1954 output rose to 30 bhp with the introduction of the 1.2-litre engine. This was giving 36 bhp at the end of our period, enabling Beetles to attain (and to cruise at) 68 mph. The standard saloons, however, retained mechanical brakes until 1962, and crash boxes to the end of the line in 1964.

Though several specialist coachbuilders tried their hand at cabriolets—Hebmüller's two-seater was especially attractive—the catalogued Karmann four-seater did not make its appearance until 1951, and the expensive Karmann–Ghia coupé was a 1955 innovation, the convertible version following two years later. Available from 1950 was the Transporter, a ¾-ton van edition; because of full forward control, it was only 8 inches longer than a saloon and set the tone for a new generation of light commercials. This range included a Microbus much favoured by quiverful families; it also pioneered a phase in the recreational-vehicle movement. Although mobile homes are outside our terms of reference, it is worth mentioning that Westfalia's succinctly named Camping Box of 1952 anticipated foreign competitors by more than a year.

With the Beetle firmly in command, Opel (their 1956 contribution was 188,451 cars) assumed an attendant role. General Motors' German branch, however, filled the position to capacity, steadily increasing their sales from a low 13,000 in 1948, their first full post-war season. As the Nazi era's best seller and the first German *marque* to achieve 100,000 units in a twelve-month, they had a reputation to uphold.

Like the Volkswagen, Opel's 1939 models were modern enough to be competitive, though General Motors' *ausländer* thinking, reflected also in Vauxhalls from the other side of the North Sea, was far removed from that of Porsche or Ganz. Those who shopped at Rüsselsheim-am-Main got a scaled-down American sedan with the added attraction (or demerit) of a unitary hull, straightforward water-cooled overhead-valve engines driving the rear wheels, styling that was 1938 Detroit on the four-cylinder Olympia and 1940 on the six-cylinder Kapitän, hydraulic brakes, conventionally sprung rear ends and the usual coils and wishbones at the front, though the horrible Dubonnet 'knees' had disappeared. The handling was dull at best and revolting at worst. The 1½-litre (80 mm × 74 mm) Olympia, unchanged from 1939, was a compact no-nonsense two-door saloon capable of 70 mph, although Germans were offered the four forward speeds denied to British Vauxhall customers. (Not, however, for long as Rüsselsheim fell into line in 1950.) Three speeds sufficed on the Kapitän, which reappeared in 1949. It used a four-bearing engine best described as short-stroke Chevrolet, and managed 80 mph from 2,474 cc and 55 bhp.

Apart from the gearbox modifications, Opel survived into 1953 with only minor stylistic changes: column shift on both cars and ugly pontoon fenders on the Olympia. Outputs rose gradually, and the Kapitän's front-end treatment changed from 1938 Oldsmobile to 1947 Chevrolet.

The Olympia (now called the Rekord) was still much the same car in 1956, though 1953 had seen a single-panel curved screen, followed in 1955 by a matching wrapround rear window. Oddly, however, no four-door model was offered. The Kapitän, however, had higher aspirations as a cheap rival of the Mercedes–Benz and received the full treatment, which meant not only the new windscreen but also four-light styling with an immense boot, a hypoid rear axle and 13-inch wheels. The output increased to 71 bhp, and the result resembled a 1952 Chevrolet.

The facelift worked, for sales climbed from under 9,000 a year to nearly 45,000. The 1956 edition sold more than 90,000, on the strength of more brake horses, vestigial tail fins and an overdrive option. With two good shots in their locker, Opel could afford to wait another six years before challenging Volkswagen on their own ground.

A long gap separated Opel from the other German–American company, Ford of Cologne. While 1956's sales of 64,873 cars represented their best performance to date, outside Germany the Taunus family still played second fiddle to Dagenham's wares.

Cologne, indeed, took a long time to shake off the old ossifying influences. Admittedly the Taunus had had hydraulic brakes in 1939, while its fastback styling was a preview of the 1944 subcompact, but neither virtue could conceal affinities with the British Prefect. Common to both were the 1,172-cc four-cylinder side-valve engine, three-speed synchromesh gearbox, beam axles and transverse-leaf springs at either end. German cars were fractionally more powerful than their British counterparts, but two doors sufficed. This ancient marched on into 1953 with minimal change.

Meanwhile the 12M of 1952 paralleled Dagenham's Consul and Zephyr, with a similar coil-spring independent front suspension and semielliptics at the rear. Also shared with the British strain were the slab-sided styling, the column shift, hypoid rear axle, full-unitary construction and 13-inch wheels, but Cologne was wasting no time on overhead valves. The good old flathead was boosted to 38 bhp, and that was all. This and a horrible divided grille notwithstanding, the 12M was a commercial success.

Overhead valves were introduced in 1955, though the 1,172-cc engine was still available in original form until 1962. Cologne, however, produced their own version of the new 1½-litre unit: for some strange reason the cylinder dimensions were 83 mm × 71 mm as against the 79.4 mm × 76.2 mm of the British Consul. The German unit was more powerful, at 55 bhp, and the four-speed option (also available with the 12M specification) was something Britons were as yet denied. The latest 15M would do close on 80 mph, though the two-door saloon, at DM 6,375, cost considerably more than a comparable Opel, and Ford, like General Motors, offered nothing with four doors in this class. The 1.7-litre 17M of 1957 would mark the beginning of a sharp upturn in Ford's fortunes.

The reconstituted Auto Union company sold just under 35,000 cars in 1956; though had they been paid a royalty on every DKW derivative then on the market, their income would surely have rivalled Volkswagen's. The DKW formula would remain an international family favourite until an emission-conscious world cast a jaundiced eye on two-strokes in the later 1960s.

The new management at Ingolstadt had refined our old friend; they had also steered it up-market. In 1938 the austere Reichsklasse had matched the Opel Kadett's list price of RM 1,795, while the better-equipped Meisterklasse at RM 2,350 had slotted neatly into a gap between the Kadett and the Olympia. By contrast, the latest Meisterklasse competed directly with the Olympia. In any case, its sponsors had lost much leeway through the partition of Germany. They never caught up.

As early as 1939 the old Auto Union AG had been testing their 900-cc vertical-three; a captured example was on show in England in 1945. However, the car the public was offered in 1950 was merely the faithful 684-cc water-cooled twin, set across the frame, though this latter was now of conventional box-section type. The traditional suspension—transverse-leaf i.f.s and a rigid axle with transverse spring at the rear—was retained, as were the wet multi-plate clutch and the three-speed gearbox with its awkward dashboard-mounted lever. Unlike cheaper imitations, the DKW featured a free-wheel, the steering was by rack and pinion, and the hydraulic brakes were a welcome improvement. The latest bodywork was modern in appearance, with recessed headlamps, a single-panel curved screen and alligator bonnet; it was also of all-metal construction, and a wide range of bodies included some handsome coupés and cabriolets by Hebmüller, not to mention a station wagon, and a *kombi* on the semi-forward-control commercial chassis. The cars were, however, heavier, at 1,785 lb. Single-plate clutches and a four-speed option featured in the 1953 catalogue.

The Meisterklasse was still offered in 1954, but in the meantime the long-delayed 896-cc three-cylinder engine had made its appearance on the Sonderklasse series. This new unit had, of course, to be placed longitudinally, in front of its gearbox instead of behind, but in other respects little was changed. Three speeds sufficed for the home market, but a four-speed gearbox was listed and was usually found on the more expensive variants, which included a four-seater hardtop coupé. On a weight of 1,932 lb, the Sonderklasse was a 75-mph motor-car, though at 34 mpg it was not very economical. It was, however, uncannily smooth except at idling speeds and seldom four-stroked. DKW, like Goliath and Porsche, developed a light Jeep-type 4 × 4 in 1954, their Munga being adopted by the NATO powers, and by 1956 Sonderklasse descendants offered over 80 mph from 38 bhp. Further, a long-wheelbase variant permitted something not obtainable elsewhere, a four-door saloon. There was even a sports DKW; this Monza was a pretty little coupé by the coach builders Dannenhauer *u* Strauss, unusual in Germany because of its glassfibre body. It weighed only 816 lb and was said to do 85 mph. Though a small batch of open roadsters was subsequently put in hand, the factory declined to issue their warranty on the original type, and DKW dealers were equally unenthusiastic. Only ten such cars were built in 1956.

Similar themes were pursued across the border in East Germany, though 'red' DKWs, sold under the IFA name, were both more and less advanced. With the original factory at their disposal, however, the Easterners were able to resume production in 1948.

What they offered was the 1938 Meisterklasse, fabric body, mechanical brakes, and all. Over 26,000 of these were made, the last of them in 1955, and sales in western countries were assisted by prices in the region of £230. Even in West Germany IFA's F8 undercut the new Meisterklasse by DM 1,130. Not that this helped sales, even after the Stuttgart coach builder Karl Baur designed some all-steel coupé bodies with a front-end treatment reminiscent of the pre-war four-cylinder Schwebeklasse.

On the credit side, IFA had their three-cylinder F9 on the market by 1950. Both in appearance and in specification it was very close to the West German Sonderklasse, though the frame and suspension were unadulterated 1939, four speeds were standard from the start, and simple gravity feed was preferred to a mechanical fuel pump. The low-octane fuels of the IFA's homeland restricted output to 28 bhp, while indifferent workmanship proved the car's worst enemy; rubber seals seldom lasted long, crankshafts broke, and there was constant cylinder-head trouble. One-piece screens and rear tanks had made their appearance by 1954, though the dashboard change (never used on West German threes) was not discarded in favour of column shift until the last series of 1955–6. These also featured protective shields around their distributors to prevent 'drowning', another common IFA fault. About 30,000 F9s were made, as well as some 110,000 of the original-type Wartburg which replaced them during 1956.

The combination of roomy six-light bodywork and a longer 96½-inch wheelbase chassis concealed a marked lack of change, though the Wartburg offered centralized chassis lubrication, not to mention an overdrive top gear and one of the better column shifts of its era. Top speed was 65–70 mph, and the car was still catalogued in 1966, by which time it was hopelessly outmoded.

Less impressive was the F8's replacement, the Zwickau P70, made in the former Audi factory. The glassfibre construction of the two-door bodies kept the weight down, but beneath their angular outlines nothing had changed, not even the mechanical brakes. For a Communist product, the Zwickau had a short run—three years and 25,000 units.

Carl Borgward, the great independent, was riding high, even if the 20,993 Isabellas he sold in 1956 represented a drop from 1955's form, leaving the little Lloyd to perpetrate his name. Not that the latter's success was any consolation to Borgward dealers; one of the boss's idiosyncracies was a separate sales network for each of his three makes.

With a devastated factory and no holdover models, Borgward had to start from scratch. This meant trucks until 1948, and only 1,148 cars in 1949. In any case, the old Hansas had never been best-sellers: the company's best performance (20,000 units) had been in 1938, and this total embraced commercial vehicles as well.

Not that his new 1500 saloon produced in 1949 lacked continuity. Like its predecessors, it featured a three-bearing four-cylinder overhead-valve engine of undersquare dimensions (72 mm × 92 mm, 1,498 cc), as well as a backbone frame, although a body platform replaced the outriggers of the old 1100, and fuel was now fed by mechanical pump from a rear tank. The all-independent suspension was likewise unchanged. The company had been using hydraulic brakes since 1928. Apart from a few early three-speeders, all cars had four-speed gearboxes with column shift, and the 1500 managed over 70 mph on 48 bhp. But, while the pre-war Hansas had a certain elegance, the latest model was uncompromisingly slab sided. Surprisingly, a four-door saloon was offered, as were a station wagon and a cabriolet. By 1952 the Borgward had been given a more powerful 1,758-cc engine, and a year later all-synchromesh boxes were standardized.

Sales were modest—around 30,000 between 1949 and 1954—but this did not deter Borgward from some curious side-issues. His personal dislike of shifting gears persuaded him to pioneer automatic transmissions in Europe, the Hansamatic appearing as an option as early as 1950. Wealthier organizations (Rover, for instance) were to learn that such gearboxes are best left to outside specialists, but Borgward took the plunge. Initial reactions were favourable; the box behaved well in hilly country. It also called for careful handling; any attempts to select reverse before coming to an absolute halt were an invitation to expensive noises. For all practical purposes this experiment had been forgotten by 1953, though the company later toyed with electric boxes (and with the British Hobbs system) on the Isabella. Neither reached the public. Though a Kamm-shaped 1,800-cc saloon got no further than the 1952 Frankfurt Show, there was a diesel-powered version of the standard article retailing at DM 9,950. This was well received, since it offered better acceleration and handling than the rival Mercedes–Benz. 68 mph and 46 mpg were an attractive combination, but once again 'the big battalions' won. The 1800D was discontinued in 1954 after only 3,226 had been made.

With the Isabella of 1954, Borgward had a winner, even if the change to full unitary construction was a gamble for a small firm. In other respects it broke little new ground. The engine was a straightforward pushrod four of 75 mm × 84.5 mm (1,493 cc), the clutch was hydraulically actuated, and the gearbox was the all-synchromesh unit fitted to later 1500s and 1800s. Final drive was by hypoid bevel, the front brakes were of 2LS type, and the old transverse-leaf independent front suspension had given way to coils and wishbones. Isabella was offered initially as a two-door saloon or station wagon; she was quite a bulky motor-car, 172 inches long and 66 inches wide. At just under 1 ton dry, she was not exceptionally light, either, but there were no obvious German competitors. The car was roomy, held the road well and managed 78 mph. The optional TS version introduced in 1955 gave over 90 mph from 75 bhp, and the gamble paid off. Over 200,000 Isabellas were sold before the collapse in 1961.

The middle member of the Borgward family was a disaster. The Goliath name had long been associated with primitive three-wheelers, made only in commercial form after 1933, though some vans were sold in *kombi* guise. By contrast, the GP700 of 1950 was a full-sized four-wheeler, intended to bridge the gap between Lloyds and Borgwards and, incidentally, to cash in on the continuing absence of a German-made DKW. This last role the Goliath was never to assume; only 849 were sold in the first season, and thanks to the return of the West German DKW, annual deliveries did not exceed 10,000 during our period.

The GP700 perpetuated many DKW ideas, even down to the capacity (684-cc) of its reverse-scavenged water-cooled two-stroke engine. This drove the front wheels via a four-speed gearbox, but the absence of a free-wheel led to monumental 'snatch'. The single-plate clutch anticipated later DKW practice, and coachwork, welded on to the mandatory backbone, was of all-steel construction. The brakes were hydraulic, and conventional semielliptic springs were used at the rear. The Goliath twin's 24 bhp gave it a slight edge over the Meisterklasse, but this was by no means the whole story. The bodies (apart from a few sports coupés produced as a promotional exercise) were ugly, and a price of DM 6,420 was hardly competitive. While the original model performed well enough, Borgward then took the fatal step of adopting fuel injection.

He also took a long time to do it. An official announcement of 1950 had no immediate follow-up, and, when the new system did arrive, it promptly superseded carburetter versions in the crucial American market. Here the peccadilloes of injection pumps were not backed by an efficient service network, and a frantic salvage operation with carburetter kits left a trail of holed pistons and oiled-up plugs in its wake. The 1953 Goliaths had all-synchromesh gearboxes; two years later the 886-cc GP900 was introduced. It offered 40 bhp with fuel injection and 29 bhp in standard form, but 1956's deliveries of 8,162 cars indicated that the peak had passed. Goliath variations included the usual mini-bus and even a light 4 × 4. In 1957, however, the company switched to an overhead-valve flat-four. A year later this one was rechristened Hansa in a belated attempt to retrieve the tarnished image of the defunct two-strokes.

Adler toyed briefly with a revival of their once-popular Trumpf Junior (over 15,000 sold in 1938). Prototypes of the little 995-cc side-valve four, now with proper synchromesh and hydraulic brakes, were displayed in 1948. The latest Karmann-built saloon bodywork had affinities with that other Adler hangover, the Belgian Imperia. The necessary funds were not, however, forthcoming, and the Frankfurt factory retired into the safer realm of typewriters.

The sole remaining major producer was Fiat, who had taken over the former NSU car works in 1930. As in pre-war days, their German wares differed little from the native strain and included—in chronological order—the 500C, the 1400, the 1900, the 1100-103 and the 600. In our period, their only deviation from the Torinese norm was a pretty Viotti coupé on the 600 platform, an expensive item at DM 8,600. NSU–Fiat were, however, a major force, disposing of 150,000 600s alone in a ten-year run. Despite a sizable German content, this enabled the Italian colussus to rate as Germany's top-selling foreign import.

5.4   For Affluent Burghers

Mercedes–Benz had been general providers to Europe's professional classes before the Second World War and were quick to resume this role. They were assisted by the whale-like proportions of America's new generation, and the stodginess of most British contenders. (The Jaguar was, by contrast, too flashy.) Further, the Stuttgart firm had a healthy line of diesel-engined saloons, a type they had pioneered in 1936. A fuel consumption of 40 mpg has its attractions for business men as well as for taxi drivers. Hence, despite an expensive product (nothing cost less than DM 8,700, even in 1956) they managed to outsell Borgward, DKW and Ford in 1956, with a formidable 68,601 cars. Though their successful racing renaissance should not be discounted, there is no reason to suppose that the upward trend would not have continued without benefit of *Rennleiter* Neubauer. The fact that they quit at the end of 1955 was clear evidence that this extravagance was no longer needed.

Bomb damage cannot be made good overnight, and no private cars left Untertürkheim until 1947. Even then, 1939's formidable seven-model line had shrunk to a single type, and a modest car at that, the good old 170V first seen at the 1936 Berlin Show. This combined technical sophistication—a tubular X-frame and all-independent suspension by double transverse springs at the front and the usual swing axles at the rear—with the staidest of engines, a three-bearing side-valve four, giving only 36 bhp from 1.7 litres. The dimensions, at 73.5 mm. × 100 mm, were traditional, as were the updraught carburetter, the gravity feed and the four-door pillarless saloon coachwork. One-shot lubrication was an expected refinement in this class, though a synchronized bottom gear was an unusual bonus. The brakes were, of course, hydraulic—mechanicals had gone out in 1939 with the antideluvian Nurbürg straight-eight—but the 170V was a heavy car, and its maximum of 68 mph took unlimited patience to attain.

It was, however, a proven workhorse. Thus to the 49,000 already made before the war could be added yet another 91,880, the last delivered as late as 1955. The addition of an overhead-valve diesel in 1949 would increase the total by a further 60,000, thanks to the car's ability to *average* 40 mpg in normal driving.

Over the next few years Daimler–Benz produced various models using two basic engines, two chassis types and two bodies. There were the added complications of hypoid rear axles and column shift, which became general practice in 1952, but basically the S-series announced in 1949 can be recognized by their roomier bodies with central door pillars and external-access boots, bigger 1.8-litre petrol engines, rear tanks and coil-spring independent front suspensions. Further exploration of this family can be daunting; the 170DS of 1952 must not be confused with the later 170S-D, though both had diesel engines, and the latter combined the V-chassis and the S-body.

More exciting things were in store. A line of overhead-camshaft sixes was announced in 1951. The base member of the family, Type 220, was externally distinguishable from the 170S only by headlamps recessed into the front wings, though closer inspection revealed an alligator-type bonnet with fixed sides impeding access. The frame and suspension were unchanged, as was the gearbox with baulk-ring synchromesh on all ratios, and an action which ranks with Rootes' Synchromatic as memorably nasty in a nasty era. The brake drums, a mere 9¾ inches in diameter, were also disconcerting, though they stopped the car in exemplary fashion; final drive was by hypoid bevel. Curiously, 6-volt electrics were retained, but entirely new was the four-bearing engine of 80 mm × 72.8 mm (2,195 cc), its single overhead camshaft driven by duplex roller chain. On 80 bhp, a saloon weighing 2,968 lb attained 90 mph, cruised at 75–80 mph and returned 26 mpg with reasonable driving. The 220 was very flexible, though the extra brake horsepower demonstrated all too clearly the limitations of the rear suspension. On longitudinal corrugations, or on the melting bitumen of an Australian summer, the model's behaviour could be hair raising! Though it lacked the elegance of contemporary Jaguars, the type found over 18,000 customers in three seasons. A few cabriolets and coupés were also made.

The big 300 was aimed at the executive market; it was a much larger car, with a wheelbase of 120 inches. The crankshaft ran in seven bearings, and the 3-litre unit was slightly undersquare, at 85 mm × 88 mm. For the equivalent of £1,695, buyers got a telescopic steering damper (which was desirable, with a useful 38 bhp per ton), bigger brake drums (but no servo) and 12-volt electrics. Undoubtedly the 300 needed all its 125 bhp to attain the magic ton, but the ponderous coachwork made it look heavier than it was; at 3,808 lb it was actually lighter than the rival Mark VII Jaguar, though the handling was slightly inferior, and the column shift was a liability. Jaguars outsold the 300 by three to one, with only 11,430 of the big Mercedes delivered during a ten-year run. An interesting variant was a four-door cabriolet, ideal for presidents of emergent republics, and frequently used by such gentry.

Little modification was found necessary. Recirculating ball steering was adopted in 1952, servo-assisted brakes arrived during 1955, and in the last few months of 1956 the 300C was introduced, with an automatic-gearbox option. Fuel injection was also available, boosting the output to 160 bhp. Mercedes, however, were fully conversant with such devices, and the horrors of the Goliath experiment were not repeated.

Unitary construction first featured on the smaller cars in 1953, with a new slab-sided style which blended successfully with the traditional grille. Better still, the grille was now integral with the bonnet, the whole assembly lifting up to give easier access to the engine. On the new Mercedes system, both front and rear power packs were detachable for major servicing, and rubber insulation eliminated the drumming endemic to lesser unitary species. Steering dampers, likewise, were standardized.

The first of the family to receive the treatment were the side-valve fours and their diesel counterparts, the 180 and 180D supplementing and then supplanting the 170s. Because of a weight saving of 330 lb, the new cars had better acceleration, while the price differential between petrol and diesel types was now only DM 350. Mercedes' domination of the cab ranks is reflected in comparative sales. Over 152,000 180Ds were made, as against a mere 118,000 with the petrol engine.

By the spring of 1954 the 220A had appeared in the same clothing, with 12-volt electrics, revised rear suspension which improved the handling and a servo brake option. This was a fast and smooth car capable of 95 mph, not to mention a 0–50 acceleration time of less than 12 seconds. From 1956 there was the cheaper 219, a 180 with the 220 power unit. Finally, towards the end of the year, the 220A gave way to the 220S, which offered 100 bhp and 100 mph with the aid of two Solex carburetters and had servo brakes as standard. The S family saw the 220 into the early 1960s.

Mercedes–Benz had no competition until 1952, when BMW resumed production at Munich with their 2-litre 501. This was an excellent car spoilt by a clumsy attempt to update the 1936 shape. Worse still, BMW's shaky finances forced them to retain this unhappy piece of bulboid until 1964, a state of affairs which explains the car's meagre sales—8,936 between 1952 and 1958.

The rest of the car was based on the old and well-loved Type 326. Here were the tubular frame with its cruciform bracing, the all-torsion-bar suspension (independent at the front) and the hydraulic brakes. The engine was the familiar 66 mm × 96 mm (1,971-cc) four-bearing pushrod six, giving 65 bhp in single-carburetter form, and as always the four-speed gearbox was separately mounted, though the traditional free-wheel had disappeared in favour of a synchronized bottom gear, and BMW had succumbed to column shift. The car was not much slower than the 220 Mercedes–Benz, but at DM 15,150 it was considerably more expensive, and by the time it reached England BMW fans were appalled to find that they were paying £700 more than the price of the latest 2.4-litre Jaguar. Even boring the engine out to 2,077 cc could not recapture the glories of the 1930s. Hence the company pinned its faith on the new vee-eight with its light-alloy block.

They timed its introduction perfectly—at the 1954 Geneva Show, also the début of the 220A Mercedes. The press enthused over the new short-stroke overhead-valve engine. With 100 bhp available from 2.6 litres, BMW claimed 100 mph from their 502 saloon.

The promise was honoured. Unfortunately, the 502 was merely a 501 with a new engine, and a full-scale eight-cylinder programme was hardly viable on annual sales of around 5,000 units, even with assistance from the motor-cycle division and the successful Isetta. To make matters worse, the management launched an all-out attack on Mercedes–Benz, 'marking' every model in Stuttgart's six-cylinder range. BMW's answer to the 300 was a 3,168-cc engine in the 502 chassis as an alternative to the smaller type. They even endeavoured to outbid Mercedes with the little-known 505, a long-wheelbase limousine styled for them by Ghia–Aigle of Switzerland. This package embraced power windows and division, writing tables and even a cocktail bar, but it never reached the public; only two were built. Frazer–Nash in England and Talbot in France toyed with the eight-cylinder engine, and the BMW saloons actually outsold the 300 Mercedes in the end, with deliveries of over 14,000 cars. The 3.2-litre, certainly, was not only a faster car but one which enjoyed greater prestige in Germany. The outcome was, however, inevitable. Mercedes–Benz had money and a safe bread-and-butter line. BMW had neither.

Across the new frontier there were no shareholders to placate. By the end of 1945 a trickle of BMWs was already coming off the lines at Eisenach. They wore an Awtowelo label and were standard 321 two-door saloons, the cheapest of the 1939 cars. The engine was a detuned 45-bhp edition of the 1,971-cc unit, and the car differed from the 326 chiefly in its shorter 108-inch wheelbase and its semielliptic rear springs. A few of these found their way to the west. From 1948, Eisenach also reinstated a famous model, the handsome two-seater 327 in cabriolet and coupé forms. Alas! though the car was outwardly indistinguishable from its forebears and boasted a twin-carburetter engine, the output was down to 60 bhp, and those hoping for 95 mph were disappointed. 80 mph was about the limit. In spite of this, the 327 (by now called an EMW) outlived the other East German sixes, being made in very small numbers up to 1955.

1950 saw the 340 family (a halfway house between the 326 and the 501 soon to be offered by Munich). It had the 501's full-flow front wings but the 1936-type body. The combination was unhappy and looked positively funereal in estate-car form. Twin dual-choke carburetters raised the output to 55 bhp, even on the 6:1 compression demanded by local petrol, and, though column shift was adopted, the Eisenach engineers retained the traditional 326 gearbox with a free-wheel on first and second, and synchromesh on the two higher ratios. 15,000 of these 340s were made.

In 1956, however, the western world was startled by yet another East German *marque*. The famous name of Horch was revived on a luxury saloon with a remote-control boot lock to protect the fitted suitcases, inspection lamps in the bonnet and boot, heater units built into the front wings and bed-seats.

Those who had attended the 1951 Leipzig Fair knew better. The new Horch Sachsenring was merely a development of the stillborn Type 342 EMW. Under the bonnet was a 2.4-litre seven-bearing six that owed nothing to past Horchs. Though the four-speed gearbox incorporated an overdrive top and the clutch was hydraulically actuated, the rest was pure 326. Output was a modest 80 bhp, and top speed was 90–95 mph. Few of the 1,500 cars built were exported, and soon after the model's introduction the Horch label was dropped. Thereafter East Germany's prestige saloon was a Sachsenring.

Predictably, Carl Borgward had a stab at the prestige market with his 2400 of 1952. This used a 2,337-cc four-bearing overhead-valve six-cylinder engine with hemispherical combustion chambers, delivering 80 bhp at 4,200 rpm. The brakes and steering followed regular practice, and the coil-spring front suspension anticipated his later 1½-litre Isabella. The six-light saloon body had a squared-off Kamm-type tail (a notchback version was available for conservative clients), and full unitary construction was adopted, the lateral reinforcements on the floor doubling as heater ducts. It was 174½ inches long, and in standard form with the three-speed synchromesh gearbox the asking price was a reasonable DM 13,000 (£1,145). For DM 14,000 the car was available with the unfortunate Hansamatic transmission, and herein lay the rub. The failings of this device scared prospective buyers off the manual version which proved to be trouble free. Hence the 2400 scarcely got into production, the 1,132 first-series cars being built by hand. From 1953 the 1800's all-synchromesh four-speed box was standardized. In 1955 the saloon with the Kamm-type back saloon was abandoned, and servo brakes were introduced. At the same time a new 2.2-litre engine made its appearance. As it later featured in the big Borgward of 1960, the experiment had at least served one purpose. Only 356 Second-Series 2400s were made.

5.5   Blitz without the Donner

After the Second World War Germans had a wider choice of sports cars than ever they had enjoyed in Hitler's days.

Sadly, no official attempt was made to revive the 328 BMW. This, however, reflects no discredit on two old BMW hands, salesman Lorenz Dietrich and engineer Ernst Loof, who did much to restore German prestige in the later 1940s with the 78 assorted Veritas cars they made between 1947 and 1952.

In the beginning, Veritas was strictly a secret operation. It had to be, since in Germany's American Zone no cars of over 1-litre capacity could be built. Therefore, until the move to French-controlled Messkirch in 1949, the partners' line was, 'Bring us your old BMW, and we'll make a racer of it.' Most of the basic elements, including the twin-tube frame, were stock 328, and in those days no street models were listed, though for DM 22,000 the dedicated could have a two-seater Rennsport with an all-synchromesh gearbox. What was under the bonnet depended on the wealth and aspirations of the client. In addition to the standard 2-litre, however, Loof and Dietrich could make up a short-stroke 1½-litre version, and, with the aid of special heads and even roller-bearing crankshafts, 125 bhp presented no problems. The touring-car story begins with the Veritas exhibit at the 1949 Paris Salon.

Though rebuilt BMW power units were still offered, Loof designed a new seven-bearing overhead-camshaft engine made for him by Heinkel. The combustion chambers were hemispherical, and square (78 mm × 78 mm) dimensions offered greater potential. Three carburetters were standard equipment, and the output varied from 100 bhp in wet-sump form up to 140 bhp with dry-sump lubrication and a magneto. A five-speed synchromesh gearbox was used, with floor change on sports models, and the frame and suspension were still 328, apart from the 2LS brakes with dual master cylinders and the de Dion back end. Road-going models were the Saturn coupé and Scorpion cabriolet on a 102-inch wheelbase, with ugly grilles in the J2 Allard manner. The long-chassis Jupiter saloon was never built, but for the sportsman there was the Comet with a full-house engine and 92½-inch wheelbase. This was only just a road car; as the catalogue pointed out, hood, screen and even bumpers were easily detachable.

Unfortunately, the sole result of this enterprise was a £70,000 deficit. At Messkirch, Dietrich managed to keep going with a batch of 176 Dyna Veritas cabriolets, but not even Baur's well-proportioned coachwork could conceal the fact that these were just another species of customized Panhard.

Loof had other ideas. The opening months of 1952 found him established in a modest workshop at the Nurbürgring circuit with a staff of 35. The cars he was making were essentially the 1949 models, with their Heinkel-built 2-litre engines available in almost any tune: compression ratios ranged from 7.7:1 up to 12.5:1, and outputs from 98 to 147 bhp. He also managed to build the long-chassis version, this carrying five–six-seater closed or convertible coachwork, with radio and heater as standard. Less than twenty customers, however, had DM 20,000 to spare, and soon afterwards Veritas foundered for good.

Equally precarious was the Porsche operation in its early days at Gmünd in Austria. Despite the *marque*'s meteoric rise, less than 8,000 cars had been made by 1955. The 356 was evolved by Ferry Porsche from his father's Volkswagen, the Porsche's immediate progenitor being the streamliner built for the abortive Rome–Berlin Axis Rally before the war. The first Porsche, an open two-seater, was a cobbled up job, with parts obtained from various sources, but already the germ of the idea was there: a box-section frame integral with the floor and body sides, to which Volkswagen brakes and suspension units were fitted. A twin-carburetter manifold boosted the output of the 1,131-cc Volkswagen engine from 25 to 40 bhp, and the light (1,340 lb) prototype attained 85 mph, though it had to be sold in Switzerland for 7,000 francs to raise funds for further development. Production did not start in earnest until 1950's move to Stuttgart, though the first of the famous coupés had been exhibited at Geneva the previous year.

This had a divided windscreen; the single-panel type was adopted in 1951. There were still close affinities with the Volkswagen, and the standard crash gearbox was used, though Wolfsburg's espousal of hydraulic brakes was a step in the right direction. The engine was linered down to bring it within the 1,100-cc category, but the combination of light weight and better aerodynamics assured plenty of performance without a high level of tune. The steering was phenomenally quick; after acclimatizing oneself to Porsche-type oversteer, one found oneself taking corners 10 mph faster than hitherto. (This happened to me in, of all places, San Francisco.)

The 356 grew up steadily. From 1951, an alternative 1,286-cc unit was offered, giving 44 bhp in standard form and 60 bhp with the optional Hirth roller-bearing crankshaft of the Super models. Parallel 1½-litres were available by 1953, when other improvements included 2LS brakes working in alloy drums, 12-volt electrics and Porsche's own incomparable all-synchromesh gearbox. Engines were by now only distant cousins of the Volkswagen, for Porsche made their own crankcases. The cabriolet was first seen in 1951, and in 1954 the stark open Speedster with its shallow Italian-style screen was introduced; this car was a great favourite with Americans. Plain-bearing cars were given the *Damen* tag, but the 1½-litre was certainly not slow, easily attaining 90 mph with a 0–50 mph acceleration time of 10.6 seconds.

The range was tidied up in 1956 with the 356A series, made only in 1300 and 1600 forms, though roller-bearing crankshafts still featured on Supers, and, as *Autocar* remarked, 'One can learn to drive a Porsche by progressive steps.' For most people the Super 1600's 75 bhp and 110 mph were sufficient, but, for those seeking the ultimate, the twin-camshaft engine already tried in the competition RSKs could now be obtained with standard bodywork in the Carrera, at a formidable DM 18,700. Britons paid £2,856, as against £1,959 for the standard article.

This car featured twin coils, two plugs per cylinder, dry-sump lubrication and a pair of dual-choke Solexes. There was a choice of four axle ratios, and on 100 bhp this ferocious 1½-litre (the old capacity was retained) could attain 125 mph. It was also for advanced students only and accounted for a mere 700 of the 22,500 Porsches sold during its four-year currency, which ended in 1959.

Mercedes–Benz waited until 1951, when the 300S was announced, together with the other overhead-camshaft sixes. Enthusiasts were, however, a little disappointed to see a restatement of the 540K theme rather than a return to the ferocious spirit of the older SS and SSK. In essence the 300S was no more than a short-chassis 300 with an extra carburetter. The bodies—open and closed two-seaters—were in the roadster idiom. The cars were heavy, at 3,832 lb, and murderously expensive—DM 34,500 in their homeland and over £5,000 in Britain. True, they would top 110 mph and were even faster with the 175-bhp fuel-injected engine standardized in 1955, but the days of the maharajah market were long gone, and only 760 of all types were produced between 1952 and 1957.

Disappointment was short lived. The legendary 300SL coupé with its gullwing-type doors burst upon a startled world in 1952. Having cleaned up the sports-car racing season, it then retired to Stuttgart until 1954, when the first of 1,400 production editions went on sale in England at £4,330.

The Gullwing was a tricky and sensitive machine, but its performance was staggering. With the standard gear-set (the ratios were 3.64:1, 5.04:1, 7.17:1 and 12.3:1) the car was good for over 130 mph, 98 mph came up in third and 70 in second, with the 'kick-in-the-back' acceleration that old-timers associated with engagement of the legendary Mercedes supercharger.

The 300SL engine was, of course, normally aspirated and based on the single-cam 3-litre six, though the triple carburetters of prototypes had given way to Bosch fuel injection. Dry-sump lubrication was a racing heritage, and the output was 240 bhp at 6,100 rpm. Tilting the power unit to the left kept the bonnet line low but made maintenance awkward; it also ruled out right-hand drive. The all-synchromesh gearbox had a proper central change, while the much-discussed *flügeltüren* were in fact dictated by the complex-ities of the car's multi-tubular space-frame. The suspension was on classic Mercedes lines and the hydraulic brakes—of 2LS type at the front, with leading and trailing shoes at the rear—worked in finned drums. During 1957, this masterpiece gave way to a roadster.

The 300SL's aerodynamic shape rubbed-off on its stablemate, the 190SL roadster, also launched in 1954. Dismissed by many as 'the answer to the call-girl's prayer', it was certainly not a true sports car. The 1.9-litre four-cylinder engine did, however, run to an upstairs camshaft and was essen-tially a 220 with two fewer 'pots'. It was also more powerful than contem-porary 220s, giving 105 bhp with the aid of twin horizontal carburetters. On this car the engine was vertically mounted, and the gearbox was stan-dard 180 with a floor-change conversion. This pseudosports model would do a surprising 107 mph and took only 10.3 seconds to reach 50 mph. The advent of the 300SL roadster, which it closely resembled, helped sales, and about 26,000 were made before the 190SL was dropped in 1962.

BMW, as we have seen, launched an all-out attack on Mercedes–Benz with their vee-eights, but all this achieved in the way of sports cars was a run of 670 superbly built loss leaders. The 503 and 507 were actually cheaper than their Stuttgart-built rivals, but BMW no longer raced, a further score against the new cars. Both used the 3.2-litre engine with twin dual-choke carburetters, the output of the unit in high-compression form being 150 bhp. This version went into the short-chassis two-seater 507, which had servo brakes as standard and was available with a five-speed gearbox. It did nearly 140 mph on a 3.42:1 axle. The styling, often ascribed to Bertone, was in fact the work of Graf Goertz. The 503 carried heavier-looking 2 + 2-seater coupé and cabriolet bodies, but, apart from a brief skirmish with a Bertone-bodied 3.2-litre in the early 1960s, BMW concentrated thereafter on lighter machinery.

Borgward's sports-car programme was fitful, embracing sundry ferocious 1½-litres with twin overhead camshafts, tubular frames and five-speed gearboxes, but, though Bechem actually won the 1954 Eifelrennen and though further experiments involved fuel-injected sixteen-valve engines developing 135 bhp, no cars went on sale. The nearest the Bremen factory came to a catalogued sports car was 1950's 1500 *sportcabriolet*, merely the standard article in ragtop form with a shorter wheelbase and an extra carburetter. On 66 bhp, it achieved more than 90 mph and 100 mph with the optional 80-bhp unit. This car ended its career in 1954 with the stock 1800 engine; as it cost more than a 220 Mercedes–Benz, it made little impact.

6 Austria

When Adolf Hitler marched into Austria in 1938, that country's private-car industry was already a one-man band. Steyr delivered 6,396 units in 1938 and 6,633 in 1939. There was, however, little future for small manufacturers, and, after the war, with their best export markets in Communist hands, Steyr elected to concentrate on trucks. To keep the name alive (and to save at least some import duty) the company built Fiats under licence, beginning with the old-school 1100 and progressing by 1952 to the 1400–1900 family. The 1900 was also offered with Steyr's own engine, a 1,997-cc pushrod four. The regular five-speed Fiat gearbox with its fluid coupling was retained, though for the 2.2-litre sports model announced at the end of our period the 1400 Diesel's heavy-duty four-speed type was adopted. Only 1,274 of these Austro-Italian hybrids were built in six years, though assembly of other Fiats kept annual deliveries at around the 2,500 mark.

Ferry Porsche's Volkswagen-based sports cars had, of course, originated in the Austrian town of Gmünd, and even after that *marque*'s migration the idea lived on in the Vienna shops of Wolfgang Denzel. Member of a bell-founding family, Denzel was an all-round sportsman who had alternated pre-war between skiing and rallying his 328 BMW. In 1948 he built up some wooden-bodied sports four-seaters on war-surplus Volkswagen Kübel chassis. Soon these specials assumed a less amateurish mien, with sheet metal panelling, and Denzel's own twin-carburetter manifold, also supplied as an accessory to Beetle owners. This gave 38 bhp from a linered-down 1,100-cc engine, though by 1953 capacity was up to 1,284 cc, and Denzels were supporting foreign rallies. The head of the firm himself made the best individual performance in the 1954 Alpine.

Unlike Porsches, Denzels were open three-seaters, utilizing box-section frames reinforced with small-diameter steel tubes, to which the aluminium coachwork was welded. The suspension and drive units were stock Volkswagen, and the standard model's four-speed crash box was preferred. The engines fitted to catalogued Seriensupers retained the standard block, crankshaft and camshaft. The wheelbase, at 82½ inches, was a foot shorter than that of the Porsche, and the car was appreciably lighter than a 356 coupé, at 1,344 lb. In 1955 the firm adopted their own crankshafts, with an output of 65 bhp from the 1.3-litre engine and as much as 86 bhp from the 'stretched' 1,488-cc edition. In its fiercest form with high-lift camshaft, dry-sump lubrication, twin dual-choke Weber carburetters and a narrower two-seater body, the 1½-litre Denzel could attain 105 mph and took 11 seconds to reach 60 mph. Competition from Porsche had driven the make off the market by 1961.

7   Switzerland

Though her motor industry had been moribund by 1927 and dead by 1934, Switzerland assumed a new importance after the Second World War as Europe's free market *par excellence*. From 1952, Geneva replaced Brussels as the Continent's top-ranking motor show; twenty-five years later it would be the only such event staged annually. Hence manufacturers found it a convenient launching pad for their latest creations, which included the Austin Sheerline and Princess in 1947, the Fiat 110-103 in 1953 and BMW's vee-eight family in 1954.

But while Swiss sales reflected the swings and roundabouts of world exports, it stifled any national revival. The country was too small to attract local subspecies, although General Motors produced an austerity Chevrolet using the 2½-litre Opel Kapitän engine with Swiss cab drivers in mind. Swiss coach builders also exerted an unexpected influence, Graber being responsible for the 1956 3-litre Alvis, and Beutler furnishing the inspiration for Bristol's later 406 saloon.

The sole Swiss *marques* to appear during our period were cycle-cars, hardly ideal for a mountainous terrain. Of these, only the 1946 Rapid from Zurich achieved production status. This 350-cc two-seater represented the last work of that German–Jewish genius, Josef Ganz, who as editor of *Motor Kritik* magazine had been one of the Volkswagen's midwives. Ever an advocate of all-independent springing, air cooling, rear engines, backbone frames and aerodynamic coachwork, Ganz had translated his ideas into reality on the Gutbrod-built Standard Superior of 1933. In 1936 he took refuge in Switzerland, where he created quite a stir with a new open two-seater prototype. This used a rear-mounted water-cooled two-stroke single-cylinder engine in unit with a wet-plate clutch, a three-speed gearbox and a differentialless axle. The front and rear sections of the streamlined body swung up to give access to the works, and the vehicle had a remarkable off-road performance—not to mention a formidable noise level. In 1939, Ganz was claiming that his car could be marketed at £95.

Rapid's post-war edition rode on large 19-inch disc wheels and used a complicated twin-piston four-stroke engine of Swiss MAG make, though a mechanical starter sufficed. The company, however, ran into financial trouble, and reverted to making motor-mowers after only 36 cars had been built.

The 1955 Belcar also originated in Zurich, though again its origins were

German: it was a variation of Egon Brütsch's egg-shaped Zwerg three-wheeler. The Swiss edition had hydraulic brakes, while the three-speed gearbox boasted not only a reverse but also a press-button electric shift. The engine was a 197-cc Victoria two-stroke, but, though a factory was built, the money ran out before deliveries got under way.

Willi Salzmann's Soletta was frankly described as a *voiture d'étude*, built by the Agricultural Research Institute at Solothurn. This tiny slab-sided four-seater saloon with glassfibre bodywork used the ingenious Neimann rubber suspension. A rear-mounted 750-cc side-valve flat-twin Condor motor-cycle engine drove the rear wheels via a 4CV Renault gearbox, but, though the Soletta was exhibited at Geneva in 1956 and was later rebuilt with more attractive coachwork, it never went into production. Ing. Salzmann still owned it in 1976.

8 Czechoslovakia

Alone of the Socialist republics, Czechoslovakia faced VE-Day with an established motor industry, one of the happier legacies of Hapsburg rule. Before 1918, Praga, Skoda and Tatra had been respected Austrian makes, though in those times the two latter bore the respective names of Laurin–Klement and Nesselsdorf. In the 1930s, Czechoslovak factories supplied virtually all their country's automobile needs; they had to, since their tariff barriers were among Europe's toughest.

Such policies brought their difficulties. In 1937, eight makers turned out 11,819 cars, of which 9,838 came from 'the big three'. Skoda, Czechoslovakia's number one producer, had a potential of perhaps 5,000 units a year, and, while a healthy business in trucks and ordnance rendered this viable enough for the shareholders, it also meant that the Mlada Boleslav works had to be a general provider on a scale comparable with Austin in Britain or Renault in France, both with a sales potential some twenty times greater than that of Skoda. The 1939 catalogue showed six models, from a 995 cc four up to the 3.1-litre six-cylinder Superb, and two new overhead-valve types were in the pipeline for 1940. There were also four parallel Pragas, three Tatras and five distinct varieties of two-stroke from Aero, Jawa and Z—a clear-cut case of too many models chasing a limited demand. Though there had been some penetration of other central European countries and even sallies into France by 'the big three' (Praga, Skoda and Tatra), exports remained modest.

Thus some rationalization was overdue, regardless of ideology, and this the country's new masters tackled from the start. In 1946, a Czechoslovak citizen had a theoretical choice of seven different models, reduced to five by 1949, the first full year of Communist rule. In 1953 he either bought a Skoda 1200 or did without, and the only change apparent by 1956 was the reinstatement of the large Tatra, a vehicle about as accessible to its compatriots as Russia's ZIS 110.

Rationalization restricted private-car manufacture to two concerns—Skoda and Tatra. Aero reverted to the aircraft industry whence they had come, Praga's activities centred on trucks, and Jawa's on motor-cycles, their first love. Czechoslovakia was, however, better placed in one respect than Britain or France; like Germany, she was a bastion of advanced thinking. Bad roads bred sophisticated chassis, and the majority of pre-war Czechoslovak cars had dispensed with beam axles at either end. Tatra had a long tradition of rear engines and air cooling, and Busek's Aeros had featured front-wheel drive since 1934. Skoda's 1101, the mainstay of the industry in the first post-war years, was still modern enough to be competitive in 1950—yet it descended directly from the Popular of 1933.

Recovery was steady. Though Czechoslovakia did not pass her pre-war zenith until 1948, when some 13,000 cars were produced, she made about 125,000 units in the first ten years of peace; but operations were still on a modest scale. The original 1,100-cc Skodas, which lasted until 1951, accounted for a mere 67,000 cars, by comparison with 53,566 Morris Tens made at Cowley between 1945 and 1948.

Though Aero and Praga were already designated for other purposes, both factories made a few pre-war designs in 1946. Praga revived the 1,660-cc four-cylinder Lady, a typical Frantisek Kec creation with side valves, a three-speed synchromesh gearbox and the styling of a 1936 Buick. Centralized chassis lubrication was a recognized Czechoslovak refinement, but Kec (who had been designing Pragas since 1908) adhered to rod-operated brakes and was content to match his transverse-leaf independent front suspension with semielliptics at the rear. The acceleration was described by one former owner as 'lousy', but the Lady was incredibly tough and could still be encountered in her homeland in 1977.

Aero revived their A30, a front-wheel drive two-stroke twin with an all-round independent suspension, a three-speed crash box, rack-and-pinion steering and, once again, mechanical brakes. This elegant little 1-litre car was offered in Switzerland for 9,500 francs, but very few were made, and fewer still of a new generation intended to replace the faithful twin and the 2-litre A50 four. These were smaller cars than their predecessors, with capacities of 750 cc for the twin-cylinder Ponny and 1,500 cc for the companion four-cylinder Rekord. They were also more compact; the Ponny's wheelbase was 19 inches shorter than that of the A30 at 88 inches. Engines were, of course, two-strokes with deflector-type pistons, but the gearboxes were given synchromesh and an extra forward ratio, and the brakes were now hydraulic. The Ponny roadster was a pretty little car in spite of its 1940-style Plymouth grille, and it would cruise at 50 mph all day. Designer Vladimir Kabes actually won a bet with the editor of Prague's *Auto* magazine, by averaging 51.6 mph over 100 kilometres.

The Aero Minors sold from 1946 to 1951 were not, however, Aeros, though the Aero works built the bodies, the mechanical elements being entrusted to the Walter company. They were in fact direct descendants of the 615-cc DKW-based Jawa Minor, of which a few more were run off after the war; the designer being Jawa's Rudolf Vykoukal. Prototypes were actually built during the war, and the model was preferred to an alternative Jawa project, a rear-wheel drive miniature with differentialless back axle.

Cylinder capacity was unchanged, though output was up to 19.5 bhp; an unusual feature for a water-cooled engine was the cooling ribs on the block. Gravity feed was still standard practice in this class, and the frame was a typical Czechoslovak forked backbone, independently suspended at both ends by transverse springs. In the interests of compactness the radiator was positioned behind the engine, the brakes were hydraulic, and the four-speed gearbox incorporated an overdrive top, but no synchromesh or free-wheel. Though the saloon's top speed was an average 56 mph, special versions, overbored to 744 cc, could move in no uncertain fashion, distinguishing themselves at Le Mans and Spa in 1949. The car was a plain little fastback in the Volvo manner, and BSA toyed briefly with the idea of making it in England. Some 14,000 Aero Minors were sold.

In 1956 the aircraft industry built a brace of mini-car prototypes, the Avia and the Moravan. Common to both were rear-mounted two-stroke twin Jawa motor-cycle engines of 350 cc, four-speed-and-reverse gearboxes and swing-axle rear suspension, though the Avia used trailing links and transverse torsion bars at the front. Sliding doors—and staggered seating with a central driving position on the Avia—suggested some interesting competition for the Isetta, but neither car went into production.

Skoda pursued the same theme from 1945 right up to the advent of the rear-engined 1000MB in 1964. The 1100 family, indeed, survived this *volte-face*, the last cars not leaving the factory until 1971. During this period, about 400,000 of all types were made.

Already established before the Second World War, the Skoda formula included yet another tubular backbone frame, with transverse-leaf springs and swing axles at each end, and a worm-and-nut steering gear. It is intriguing to compare *Autocar*'s panegyric on the 1949 1102 (the road holding was 'quite up to sports-car standards' with 'quick and positive' steering) with a 1958 critique of the subsequent 440 series. 'The suspension,' observed this latter report, 'promotes vicious oversteer, which the vague steering is not well fitted to correct.' Thus do our standards change. . . .

Other features of the design included double-acting hydraulic dampers, a spiral bevel back axle and hydraulic brakes in place of the pre-war mechanicals. Once again centralized chassis lubrication was standard, and the engine was a simple and durable three-bearing pushrod four with the Fiat-like dimensions of 68 mm × 75 mm (1,089 cc). Its output of 32 bhp likewise matched that of Fiat's *millecento*, but cooling was by pump and fan (Turin still preferred thermosyphon circulation), and the carburetter was gravity fed. The four-speed gearbox had wide ratios and synchromesh on third and top only. 1948's 1102 was the same car with column shift, but in 1952 the Skoda grew into the heavier 1200 with slab-sided styling. To compensate for the extra weight, the engine was bored out to 72 mm for a capacity of 1,221 cc, and over 15,000 of these cars were sold before they gave way in

1956 to the 1201 series with single-panel screens, downdraught carburetters and synchromesh on second gear. The output was up to 45 bhp, and saloons were still available in 1962. The 1202 station wagon lasted another nine years.

The 1200s were rather clumsy cars, but for the 440 two-door saloon of 1954 Skoda reverted to more compact dimensions (the wheelbase was 94½ inches) and to the 1,100-cc engine. This model featured a rear tank and mechanical pump feed. Evidently Skoda had taken criticism to heart, for the gear lever was back on the floor, though not for long: the 1956 versions had column shift once again. Hypoid final drive now featured, while the single-panel curved screen was interchangeable with the rear window, an idea which, alas! nobody else copied. In spite of its dubious handling, the 440 was incredibly durable and sold over 75,000 units in the first four years. Under the Octavia name, it was destined for a very long run.

In 1946 and 1947 there were also two 3.1-litre overhead-valve sixes. Of these, the Rapid was merely a rehashed 1939 Superb with the usual frame and suspension: only 21 were made. The same mechanical elements also went into a new Superb, an ugly beast which resembled a 1942 Chevrolet with an 1101 grille grafted onto the bows. The 130-inch wheelbase made it unwieldy as well as unattractive, and nobody was sorry when the new régime made prestige models Tatra's preserve.

Hans Ledwinka could improve on Frantisek Kec's record; he had joined Tatra in 1897 and would not retire until 1951, though his continuous service had been broken by a spell across the border with Steyr in the 1920s. Ledwinka practiced what Josef Ganz had been content to preach: backbone frames, air cooling and rear engines, though curiously he confined this last theme to large cars, with consequences that were often peculiar. But, though the name of Tatra had been synonymous with such devices for twelve years, one last hangover from the old days lingered on into 1949. This was the 1,250-cc T57B, a 1932 development of the original 1923 flat-twin, though it had four cylinders, and the old snub nose had given way to a conventional bonnet and dummy radiator. This assembly, however, swung up complete with the wings, in anticipation of later Aston Martins and Jowetts. The rest of it was typical Tatra, with rack-and-pinion steering and transverse-leaf independent front and rear suspensions. The four-speed gearbox had synchromesh on its two upper ratios, but gravity feed and mechanical brakes showed the design's age. On 25 bhp, this car trundled inexorably along at 55 mph, the antithesis of the big rear-engined T87 with its perfect aerodynamic shape, three-piece curved windscreen and tail fin.

The 87 was no newcomer, either. It had been around since 1937 and was a direct descendant of the 77 which had startled visitors at the 1934 Berlin Show. The central backbone carried the linkages for the four-speed all-indirect gearbox, all wheels were independently sprung, and the air-cooled overhead-valve vee-eight engine, of 75 mm × 84 mm (2,984 cc) hung over the rear axle, placing all passengers safely within the wheelbase. The brakes were hydraulic, and in spite of the enormous overhang the Tatra measured only 187 inches from stem to stern. The advantages of the configuration were a minimum of noise within, and the ability to attain over 95 mph on 72 bhp, while equipment included a radio, a sliding roof and seats convertible into a bed. Defects were a woolly gearchange, a total absence of rearward vision and sudden unpredictable rear-end breakaway. 1,721 T87s were produced between 1946 and 1950, but something more manageable was indicated, and the raw material was already available in the shape of the 1,750-cc T97 flat-four, of which 508 had been made before the war. This duly appeared in 1947 as the Tatraplan (T600).

The main change was the enlargement of the hemi-head engine to 2 litres, which boosted the output from 40 to 52 bhp. The use of torsion-bar suspension at the rear improved the handling, but the Tatraplan's column shift was a nightmare, accentuated by some perversity which reversed the 'gate' positions as well. It was, however, a better-looking car than the T87, thanks to its single-panel screen, and performance was respectable—75–80 mph in top, 57 mph in third, and a thirst of 24 mpg.

4,235 Tatraplans were made, a number being sold in the west. Variations on the theme included the 201 ambulance, the Monte Carlo two-door sports saloon and even two four-door cabriolets by the coach builder Sodomka, one of which was presented to Josef Stalin. There was also an experimental car with a diesel engine. Regrettably, though, the midengined 602 sports model of 1949 never went into production; aerodynamically it was a long way ahead of its contemporaries. Even in four-carburetter form the 2-litre Tatraplan engine gave a modest 75 bhp, yet the car was tested to do 112 mph. Rather similar in appearance was the T605, which appeared briefly in 1956. This was an engaging miniature with wire wheels and an all-torsion-bar suspension. The engine, though still air cooled, was an innovation for Tatra, being a vertical-twin of 75 mm × 72 mm (636 cc); it gave 54 bhp at 7,000 rpm. The weight was a low 1,088 lb, and speeds of over 100 mph suggested a possible rival for the fiercer Dyna Panhards.

The cylinder dimensions, however, told another story. The Tatraplan had been discontinued in 1952, but in 1956 came a new large rear-engined air-cooled vee-eight of 75 mm × 72 mm (2½ litres). This T603 was a real improvement. Not only was it faster (the twin-carburetter engine gave 100 bhp, sufficient to propel the vehicle at 105 mph), but it had also been tidied up, with no fin and a wraparound rear window, while room was saved by placing luggage over the fuel tank at the front. An engaging touch was a second starter button in the engine compartment, an all-coil suspension featured, and other improvements included a synchromesh bottom gear and a hydraulically actuated clutch. Less pleasing was the front-end treatment, with three headlamps concealed behind glass in a parody of pre-war Peugeot styling. Though always a badge of rank in Czechoslovakia, the T603 was exported. 5,992 were delivered during an eight-year run, and developments of the theme were still being made in 1973.

9 Poland

Apart from Czechoslovakia and East Germany, Poland was as yet the only Soviet satellite to have a substantial motor industry. What is more, this had been state controlled since the early 1930s, when the Polish Government signed an agreement with Fiat for the licence production of Balilla variants. At the time of the Nazi invasion, *millecentos* were being built in Warsaw.

The new régime's first car was, of course, the Russian Pobeda, assembly of which began in 1951. Four years later these Warszawas, as they were known, were entirely manufactured in Poland. They were still available, although with overhead-valve engines, as late as 1972.

By contrast, the small front-wheel drive Syrena saloon unveiled at the 1955 Poznan Fair made use of an older but more familiar theme, the DKW. Unlike its German contemporaries, however, the Syrena retained the basic transverse-twin engine, giving 27 bhp from 744-cc.

Like most East European small cars, it was fairly crude, the frame with its A-shaped rear section having some affinities with the Austin Seven. The suspension followed DKW lines, the brakes were hydraulic, and the four-speed crash gearbox incorporated a free-wheel. Prototypes retained the wood-and-fabric construction of pre-war days, but, by the time the Syrena reached the public in 1956, this had been abandoned in favour of a steel structure with a glassfibre roof. The wheelbase was 90½ inches and the Syrena weighed 1,764 lb. It was still being made twenty years later.

10 Italy

10.1 Granturismi Galore

In many respects this was Italy's decade.

Not, be it said in terms of physical output: the 145,800 cars delivered by her industry in 1953 would not have earned her a place in America's Top Ten and, even in 1956 the combined efforts of Fiat, Lancia, Alfa Romeo and the smaller specialists still fell short of 280,000 units, in a year when West Germany delivered nearly a million.

Nor were her exports exactly brilliant. True, the modest overall figures (63,597 cars in 1955 and 78,423 in 1956) must be read against a background of Fiat production in Austria, Germany, Spain and Yugoslavia, but the low 40% ratio compares unfavourably with Britain's worst showing in the 1955 recession. Though in the critical Swiss market Fiat were constantly yapping at VW's heels (the canny Agnellis thought it prudent to launch their revolutionary 600 at Geneva rather than to wait another month for Turin). Sweden revealed a more typical picture. Germany and Britain together commanded 57% of overall sales, whereas Italy's share was a doleful 5%. Nor did the Italians as yet bother much about the USA: in pre-1956 days the industry's impact was confined to 'personal imports' of *exotica* in the Ferrari or SIATA class.

The real trouble was, of course, that there was no supporting make to insure against a disappointing reception such as that accorded Fiat's 1400 in 1950. Swiss or Belgians who distrusted rear engines and air cooling bought Opels instead of Volkswagen, but any disruption at Fiat—or, for that matter, the continuance of an obsolescent model—lost sales for Italy.

'The nation of enthusiasts' was still far from being a nation of motorists. The crowds that lined the route of the Mille Miglia were sampling vicarious pleasures. Not only could they never hope to own one of the snarling £3,500 Ferraris that jostled for the lead, but they would be lucky if they could ever afford any model, for in 1950 only one in every 82 Italians possessed a car. Six years later, the ratio was 1 to 35.8, but the effects of *la dolce vita* would not be felt until the 1960s, and even then the spread of car ownership was largely due to Fiat's minimal twin-cylinder Nuova 500, a 1957 introduction. This not only dashed the hopes of the bubble-car manufacturers (such vehicles were never overpopular in Italy): it also hit successful scooter makers such as Innocenti and Piaggio.

Italy's recovery had, nonetheless, been creditable. Poor and lacking in mineral resources, she had also displayed a genius either for backing the wrong side, or losing out when she was on the side of the angels. While Marshal Badoglio's sellout to the Allies in 1943 had spared the country the full humiliation of defeat, she had been fought over, and her factories extensively bombed. Fiat's newest plant at Mirafiori had escaped serious damage, but the same could not be said of Lingotto, or of Lancia's Turin premises. Petrol and tyres were even scarcer than in France—especially the latter. As late as 1947, 70% of Rome's bus fleet was out of action for want of rubber. The gap was filled by a motley assortment of improvized ancients, from the sedater types of 1750 Alfa to straight-frame Tipo Due Fiats that had first been produced in 1917. The *topolino* went about their duties on wheels taken from superannuated fighter planes. As for steel, the makers took what they could get, which was sometimes old air raid shelters! This commodity was not freed from control until 1948.

Inflation was rampant. A *topolino*, retailing at £125 in 1939, now listed at £329. Nor was the Government helpful. The Italian fiscal system had already virtually outlawed any vehicle with an engine of over 3 litres' capacity, and as late as 1952 the owner of a Fiat 1100 paid an annual tax of £70. This explains the poor sales of larger cars: in 1958 cars of over 2 litres accounted for only ½% of new registrations, and even in the *dolce vita* atmosphere of 1961 their share was still a low 4%. Like France, Italy levied tax on raw materials at every stage of manufacture, and concessions to exporters were unknown. On the credit side, America's Marshall Aid programme was used to turn Alfa Romeo into a volume producer—from 414 units in 1949 to a promising 11,722 in 1956. Fiat received $14,000,000 worth of machine tools from the same source; this prevented any repetition of Edgar Kaiser's 1946 takeover bid.

Fortunately, nothing could deflect Italian makers from the drivers' cars they had always offered: this applied not only to Ferrari and Maserati but also to the more mundane breeds. Cynical Anglo-Saxon journalists wrote of driving positions 'tailored for the average Italian ape', and no small Italian family saloon liked the top-gear dawdling to which Britons were addicted: sometimes Italian choices of gear ratio were baffling (on the 1400 Fiat, for instance), but her engineers produced three of the outstanding touring cars of our period—Vittorio Jano's Lancia Aurelia, Dante Giacosa's 1100-103 Fiat of 1953 and (towards the end of the decade), the best of them all, Orazio Satta's Alfa Romeo Giulietta.

Apart from the brief Mercedes–Benz comeback of 1954–5, Italian cars dominated Grand Prix racing, and, while Alfa Romeo's Tipo 159 was not remotely related to anything the public could buy, Ferrari's sports-car record was highly relevant. Between 1949 and 1956 alone the *marque* won twice at Le Mans, twice in the Targa Florio, and annexed every Mille Miglia bar two: over 30 examples contested the 1951 event. If endemic oversteer, axle tramp and unreliable gearboxes tarnished Maranello's early reputation, Enzo Ferrari's creations were fast assuming the mantle of the much-mourned Bugattis from Alsace.

Most important of all, Milan and Turin became the styling capitals of the world. No longer were all eyes centred on the studios of General Motors and Chrysler in Detroit.

Italians have always had an eye for the body beautiful. Cesare Sala's Isotta Fraschinis were among the happiest interpretations of the long bonnet, slit windscreen school that was prevalent in the later 1920s, and Zagato's contemporary spyder on the supercharged Alfa Romeo chassis must be one of the most imitated styles of all time. Pininfarina's vee-grille, first seen on his 1937 Fiat cabriolets, had been standardized by Fiat themselves on their biggest 1940 cars. Though Italian designers were capable of monumental goofs (Ghia's 1948 1500 Fiat with mock-Buick grille and spats to all four wheels must share the wooden spoon with Boano's 1955 Indianapolis coupé, which matched dummy stub exhausts at the front with equally spurious air intakes in the rear wings), they also produced some gems, from Pininfarina's original Cisitalia coupé to his Lancia Flaminia of 1955–6, a first indication of the new angular idiom. It matters not that others less skilled parodied these creations, as they had Buehrig's 1936 Cord. The Italian influence remained.

Italian designers were hired by foreign firms. The shape (if not the detail execution) of the Bristol 401 was the work of Touring, Boano created Renault's Dauphine, and Pininfarina did his best in 1952 with Nash's uncompromising bathtubs. Vignale's transformation of the Standard Vanguard was the prelude to a long and happy alliance between Giovanni Michelotti and the Coventry firm. In time, Latin creativity would extend behind the Iron Curtain (Vignale's T613 Tatra), to Japan (Michelotti's Hino Contessa) and even to the Argentine, where Pininfarina made a lady of that final Kaiser hangover, the IKA Torino. As yet the pitfalls of pan-Italianism lay in the future; it was not until 1961 that people would remark on the embarrassing uniformity of shape of the 1300–1500 Fiats, the Austin Cambridge and the Peugeot 404, all the work of Pininfarina.

One may wonder how, in impoverished Italy, the specialist coach builders flourished, while their British and French counterparts floundered. It is also startling to encounter a sudden profusion of makes. In 1939, there were precisely four—'the big three' and Bianchi. But, between 1946 and 1956, buyers' guides showed no fewer than 28 road-going breeds, irrespective of firms such as Bandini who built exclusively for the circuits.

There is, however, a world of difference between a serious design, and producing it seriously. At this stage, the Ferrari, Maserati and OSCA factories were first and foremost racing shops: it is doubtful whether as many as 200 Maseratis were sold for street use in our period. Isotta Fraschini's post-war contribution amounted to six cars. Moretti, though they listed saloons as well as sports cars, seldom built two vehicles alike. Of the miniatures, the Isetta was built in far greater numbers in Germany and Britain than in the parent factory at Bresso. As for foreign imports, Italy had, perhaps, Europe's tightest restrictions. Less than 15,000 cars were brought in from abroad between 1945 and 1956 (Britain, who did not relax her rules until 1953 took 34,091 in the same period). Thus Fiat held on to their 90% share of the market.

In any case, Fiats were the only cars most Italians could afford. Of seven Italian models selling for under £1,000 in 1957, the sole non-Fiats were the Abarth coupé at £905 (a Fiat derivative), the Lancia Appia (£790) and Alfa Romeo's Giulietta *berlina* at £895, both the latter undercut (and of course outsold) by the 1100 Fiat at £540. The situation had admittedly been much worse in 1946, when there was only a solitary cheap baby, Fiat's *topolino*, as against five such models in Britain and three even in war-torn France. In the so-called 10 hp class, the faithful *millecento*'s near-solo stand (Lancia's Ardea was far more expensive) contrasted with a whole galaxy of family saloons from Austin, Ford, Hillman, Morris, Singer, Vauxhall and Wolseley. As for the 1½-litre cars, neither the six-cylinder Fiat nor the Lancia Aprilia was cheap by English standards, the former costing £810 if one joined the waiting list (Italians seldom did) or £2,375 on the Black Market. Thus customers craved variety and were prepared to pay for it— even a simple 1100 Fiat cabriolet by Stabilimenti Farina cost nearly double the price of the ordinary pillarless saloon.

The art of camouflaging a Fiat had its gradations. *Elaborazioni* were just what the name implied: fancy interiors, built-in radios, altered wing lines or more doors than Ing. Giacosa had specified (this last was a favourite but seldom successful trick on the 600). About thirty such 600 variations were on display at the 1955 Turin Show.

The next step involved building one's own body. By 1948 the more important firms, such as Touring and Pininfarina, were organized on a series-production basis, the former working in aluminium over a tubular frame, while the latter preferred steel. After the exuberance of early days, designers settled down to more sober lines because, as one coach builder put it, 'If a client is going to pay 2,000,000 lire or more for a body, he wants an assurance that it will not be rendered unfashionable in a few months by some new development of style.'

This was fine until Fiat went unitary in 1950, the disease spreading down the range. With their enormous runs, they could not afford Lancia's extravagance of a special platform-type chassis for the carriage trade. The best they could offer was a non-drivable platform, though by the end of our period this had given way to mere mechanical elements—engine, gearbox and suspension units.

At this juncture, a new make was born; notable ones were by Abarth and SIATA. By the time these specialists had developed the mechanics, the end product was scarcely recognizable as a Fiat, even when it did not (like SIATA's 1951 Rallye) pretend to be an MG.

Coachbuilders would also build their own creations in series for 'chassis' makers. Bertone was responsible for the production of the Alfa Romeo Giulietta coupé, to the tune of 3,500 in the first two years, and Fiat's 1100TV spyders were the work of Pininfarina.

Italy's motorway network, of course, dated back to 1925, and sustained high speeds had ceased to worry her car makers. However, perhaps the country's outstanding contribution was the closed sports car.

Up to 1939, sports cars had been open bodied almost by definition. Exceptions had been either overweight, uninhabitable or special aerodynamic shapes for long-distance racing. Both German and Italian *équipes* had explored aerodynamic shapes, and by 1939 such developments of the theme as Touring's 2½-litre Alfa Romeo and Savio's 508CMM Fiat had reached the market.

After the war, the *granturismo* idiom caught on. The term had originally been applied by Alfa Romeo to their long-chassis supercharged 1750 in 1931, and, though in the debased currency of the later 1970s GT can mean simply an overfurnished saloon with an extra carburetter and some un-necessary scriptitis, to the Italians it meant just what it said—high-speed touring for two (the auxiliary seats were introduced later). By the early 1950s most Italian sports cars sold for street use had fixed tops, largely because these added structural reinforcement to the new generation of *monocoques*. Most of the fiercer 1900 Alfa Romeos carried Pininfarina's coupé coach-work, neither of Fiat's overt sports cars, the 1100S (which had a chassis) and the 8V (which had not) was offered by the factory in ragtop form, and Lancia's delightful Aurelia GT only developed into a roadster in 1955, when the company made a bid for the American market.

10.2   Dr Valletta's Italian Empire

The architect of Fiat's revival was Vittorio Valletta, whose aim was 'to regain our former ascendancy, to reestablish the prestige of Italian technol-ogy and to safeguard the jobs of our skilled labour force'. The measure of his achievement can be seen in a tenfold increase of production between 1947 and 1956, in a comprehensive range covering most European requirements, in two million-sellers—the 1100-103 and the 600—and in a chain of foreign manufacturing and assembly plants in Austria, Belgium, Germany, Spain and Yugoslavia. In the pipeline by 1956 were similar ventures in Argentina and India. The 274,300 Fiats sold in 1956 were a long way from Chevrolet's 1,600,000, and the Torinese colossus still tailed Volkswagen by a round 60,000, but Fiat's significance lay in their command of the home market.

Fortunately, all their 1939 models were modern enough to justify revival, though the big six-cylinder 2800 was scrapped, and the 1100 and 1500 now had 1940-type vee-grilles unfamiliar to Britons. The spearhead of the post-war programme was that delightful miniature, the 500 *topolino*. After nine years, the little car's idiosyncracies had become part of folklore, but the specification was unchanged. The tiny 52 mm × 67 mm (569-cc) two-bearing four-cylinder side-valve engine was mounted well over the front axle, with its radiator behind, the gravity feed was controlled by three-way plumbing on the floor, and there was a four-speed synchromesh gearbox. The transverse-leaf independent front suspension was retained, though since 1938 the quarter-elliptic rear springing had given way to more orthodox semielliptics. Bodies were the familiar fixed-head coupés and rolltop convertibles, and they were still two-seaters pure and simple, a wise decision which kept the weight down to 1,176 lb, thereby enabling the car to do 50–55 mph on a mere 13 bhp. Even in 1951, *The Motor* confessed that 'its road holding under braking and cornering conditions has no more than one equal among British light cars'. Another 122,213 side-valve *topolino* left Turin before any change was found necessary.

Even then, not much happened: the 500B's overhead-valve engine boosted the output to 16.5 bhp and the speed to around the 60 mark, though these improvements justified a deviation, in the shape of a tiny station wagon. The provision of a mechanical fuel pump unfortunately deprived owners of their half-gallon reserve, and only 21,000 B-types were made before this model gave way, late in 1949, to the final C-series with a full-width front-end treatment and recessed headlamps. The attractions of 55 mpg at a steady 50 mph were not to be disputed, and the model remained in production until January 1955, adding a further 376,000 units to an impressive score. Regrettably the 500 reappeared in Britain during its declining months; only fanatics would have parted with £575 for a two-seater, when Morris offered a four-seater ragtop with better performance and comparable handling for £99 less. *Topolino* were also made in Germany by NSU: France's Simca 6 was similar but not identical.

The 1100 (*née* 508C) was an even better car. Its 68 mm × 75 mm (1,089-cc) engine featured overhead valves, the crankshaft boasted three mains to the *topolino*'s somewhat fragile two, the fuel tank was at the rear with mechanical pump feed, the frame was a substantial cruciform-braced affair, and the coil-and-wishbone independent front suspension was superior to either the baby's transverse arrangements or the earlier Dubonnet type still found on the 1500. If the pillarless saloon body rattled and let in too many draughts, the *millecento*'s nominal 32 bhp gave it an easy 70–75 mph, and 36 mpg presented no problems. The standard wheelbase was 93 inches, but there was also the long-chassis six-seater 1100L, popular with Italian cabbies, even though Fiat admirers winced when these gently started off uphill in the high third gear; one of the reasons why later cars dispensed with the fabric universals of the pre-war species.

The six-cylinder 1500 with its short-stroke 1,493-cc engine had been around longer than either the *topolino* or the *millecento* and showed its age, though this car, like its younger sisters, had hydraulic brakes which were supported, in the best Fiat tradition, by the lethal transmission handbrake. Peculiar to the six was the backbone frame with its aerodynamic saloon coachwork supported on outriggers. The four-bearing 1500 was smooth and quiet up to its maximum of 72 mph, but it was no ball of fire, taking 8 seconds longer than an 1100 to reach 50 mph. Despite a modest 30 mpg thirst, it was a 19CV in Italy and a sixteen in Britain, which helped sales in neither country. Only about 8,000 were sold after the war.

Nothing happened to either of the larger Fiats until 1949, when the E-series introduced integral rear boots and, unfortunately, column shift. The 1100, though not the six, survived into 1953.

In 1947, Fiat revived the delightful 1100S sports coupé with bodywork by Savio. With suitable attention to the top end, the engine gave 51 bhp on a 7.5:1 compression, and its maximum speed of 95 mph was not catalogue double-talk but fact, as second and third places in that year's Mille Miglia showed. It was, however, very expensive, at 2,150,000 lire (£1,075), hence only 401 were sold, the last of them in 1952. This one also received the E-treatment, though there was compensation for the unpleasant gearchange in Pininfarina's classic two-plus-two coachwork and in bearings lined in copper–lead alloy. The weight and the price were up, and the gearing down.

The first true post-war Fiat did not appear until 1950, and even then it met with a mixed reception. The bulboid style, although owing nothing to Plymouth, was hardly what one would expect from Turin, and the car was ridiculously overgeared for 1,395-cc. Further, if Giacosa's brief had been 'an American car for Europe', how could this be equated with the worst top-gear acceleration in its class?

The 1400 has, however, its place in history. Its unitary construction set the pattern for future Fiats, the welded structure being built up from the chassis side-members, with a detachable 'wheelbarrow' for the engine and front suspension. The power unit was an orthodox three-bearing pushrod four, though in the interests of long life the dimensions were exaggeratedly oversquare, at 82 mm × 66 mm. The four-speed gearbox (ratios of 4.44:1, 6.98:1, 10.6:1 and 17.1:1 told their own story!) had synchromesh on all but bottom, and column shift. The rear suspension was by a rigid axle and coils, which made for some alarming roll angles. The hypoid rear axle was new on a Fiat. On the credit side, the 1400 was a full six-seater, would hold 70 mph and had the American ability to smooth out really bad surfaces, which explains its ready acceptance and long career in Spain.

The 1900 of 1952 was a prestige edition of the 1400, using a 56-bhp 1,901-cc engine, and some embellishments—a more ornate grille, a larger rear window and the much-publicized Tachimedion average speed calculator. A more important refinement was a five-speed gearbox with fluid coupling: the 4.44:1 fourth was used for normal driving, and fifth, at 3.23:1, was very much an *autostrada* ratio, though the new car was extremely flexible for a four and would start in fourth. It also shared with the later Lampredi-designed 1500s a smoothness which belied the absence of an extra pair of 'pots'; cruising speeds in the low 80s were allied to a fuel consumption of 23–26 mpg. The trouble was that it looked too similar to the 1400, and sales were a low 15,750 in five-and-a-half seasons, as against 120,356 of the smaller type. Fiat did their best to give the 1900 some individuality: with the 1900A of 1954 came the infelicitous Gran Luce two-door hardtop, and 1956's 1900B versions were distinguishable by a new grille, a new rear wing line and servo brakes. Later engines gave 80 bhp: the output of the 1400 was progressively increased from 44 bhp in 1950 to 58 in 1956.

Other derivatives of this family were the Campagnola of 1951, a light 4 × 4 in the Jeep–Land Rover idiom with coil-spring independent front suspension, and the 1400 diesel introduced in 1953. This featured a 1.9-litre unit and larger-section tyres to compensate for an extra 350 lb in weight. It survived alongside the petrol-driven models until 1958.

By contrast, the 8V sports coupé unveiled at Geneva in 1952 can best be described as technicians thinking aloud, its small pushrod vee-eight engine being intended for (though never actually installed in) a luxury edition of the 1900. Only 114 were built, but during its three-year run the 8V was used for sundry experiments, with five-speed gearboxes (tried at Le Mans) glassfibre bodies and gas turbine engines.

This was, nonetheless, an attractive dead-end featuring unitary construction based on a steel tube frame. A coil-spring independent suspension was used at both ends, and the four driving lamps anticipated later American practice. The 70-degree vee-eight engine had oversquare dimensions (72 mm × 61 mm, 1.996-cc), with an alloy block and the lead–indium bearings of later 1100S units. The output of 110 bhp was delivered at 6,000 rpm, there were two dual-choke downdraught carburetters, and the rest of the car was orthodox enough, with a four-speed gearbox, floor change, a hypoid rear axle and hydraulic brakes working in 11½-inch drums. On a weight of 2,350 lb, the 8V managed 119 and 89 mph on its two upper ratios, and a

21 Spanish *gran sport* in the Italian Idiom: a factory-bodied Z102 Pegaso spyder, 1954 (*Courtesy ENASA*)

22 Wingless Messerschmitt: early KR175 Kabinenroller, 1953 (*Courtesy National Motor Museum*)

23 A Brighter Beetle: this 1951 de luxe model has a sun roof and swinging quarter lights, but still the divided rear window (*Courtesy Volkswagenwerk AG*)

24 German Chevrolet: by 1954 the 2½-litre Opel Kapitän had succumbed to the Detroit line (*Courtesy Adam Opel AG*)

25 Silver Diamond: Carl Borgward's 1500 sportcabriolet, 1952 (*Courtesy National Motor Museum*)

26 A Natural for Heads of Emergent Republics: Mercedes-Benz 300 as a four-door cabriolet, 1954 (*Courtesy Daimler-Benz*)

27 The Ageless Porsche: the 356A series was current from 1955 to 1959 but it takes a practised eye to distinguished it from earlier and later species (*Courtesy Porsche*)

28 Last of a distinguished Line: Aero Ponny (*left*) and Record prototypes, 1946 (*Courtesy Milos Skorepa*)

29 Czech Mainstay: the 1951 Skoda 1102 with cabriolet bodywork (*Courtesy Milos Skorepa*)

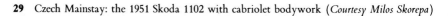

30 Millocento Up to Date: Fiat 1100-103 estate car, 1953 (*Courtesy Fiat*)

31 A Lancia for America: left-hand drive was available on this 1956 B24 spyder (*Courtesy Lancia*)

32 Breaking up Slab Sides: the Alfa Romeo 1900 in 1955 Super form (*Courtesy Alfa Romeo*)

33 The Fiat-tweakers: this 1950 Siata Amica cabriolet is a *topolino* conversion (*Courtesy Fiat*)

34 Classic Ferrari Profile: Vignale's 3-litre 250 coupé for the Paris Salon 1953 (*Courtesy National Motor Museum*)

35 Swedish Made for World's Markets: early PV444 Volvo, 1947 (*Courtesy AB Volvo*)

36 Pure Aerodynamics: SAAB's 92 prototype, 1948 (*Courtesy National Motor Museum*)

37 Armstrong Siddeley Influence: Danish S-1 with flat-twin Jowett Bradford engine, 1950 (*Courtesy Anders Ditlev Clausager*)

38 Rare Russian: a ZIS-110 straight-eight of early post-war vintage with convertible bodywork (*Author's Collection*)

0–60-mph acceleration time of 12.5 seconds. The car was noisy, and not much happened below 3,000 rpm, but, though the 8V's potential as a poor man's Ferrari was never realized, it pointed the way to the delightful 124 coupés of the mid-1960s and dominated the 2-litre *granturismo* class of national events.

A year later the long-awaited 1100-103 was introduced. For this car, Giacosa used the 1400's structural scheme, though mercifully nothing else, apart from the hypoid final drive. Coil-and-wishbone independent front suspension featured at the front, with semielliptics at the rear, and some ingenious detail design enabled four passengers to be located within a short 92-inch wheelbase, on a car only 147½ inches long. The weight, at 1,984 lb, was no higher than on the superseded version, and the main underbonnet change was pump cooling in place of thermosyphon. The output remained conservative, at 36 bhp. No one could accuse the 103 series of elegance—the general effect was that of a foreshortened Mark I Ford Consul, itself an unattractive car—but its performance and road behaviour were as outstanding as had been the 508C's in 1937: a top speed of 78 mph, 0–30-mph acceleration time of 5.4 seconds and a consumption of 40 mpg with gentle driving. A station wagon soon joined the range, and later in the year came the TV (*turismo veloce*) edition, with central cyclop's eye spotlamp and two-tone paintwork. This one would do 85 mph.

The 103 family put Fiat firmly in the best-selling league. They had sold 1,000,000 cars by 1962, and demand was such that the company had to keep it in production long after its successor, the 124, was pouring off the lines in its thousands. Though the last Italian-built 1100Rs were delivered in 1969, the type was still being made in India in 1977. In 1955 a two-seater TV cabriolet with a 'dog's leg' screen, obviously inspired by Ford's Thunderbird, was introduced. Only 571 were built, but it marked the beginning of a long and successful line of spyders, culminating in the midengined X1/9 of the 1970s. Tipo 103 also spearheaded the company's first major attack on the American market for forty years.

Just as successful was the 600, unveiled in February 1955 and destined for a fifteen-year run in Italy, eighteen years in Spain and even longer in Argentina. Domestic plants would account for 1,500,000 cars, and large numbers would be built in Germany, not to mention a whole wave of attractive specials from such firms as Abarth and Moretti.

The birth-pangs of the 600 had been lengthy, dating back to the front-engined overhead-valve 700, 'a halfway house' between the *topolino* and the *millecento* which had been demonstrated to Mussolini in 1940. After trying every possible configuration, however, Giacosa opted for a water-cooled engine at the rear, and the little car's début was a national event almost comparable with the birth of an heir to the throne. No holds were barred, from a brand-new hire-purchase scheme to the split self-sectioning display vehicle that delighted visitors to Geneva that March. Characteristic was some ingenious shoe-horning: the water spaces had been eliminated between the third and fourth cylinders, and the radiator had been mounted beside the engine, but the result furnished room for four people on the *topolino*'s 78¼-inch wheelbase. The weight had scarcely increased, and the length, at 126 inches, was actually 5 inches less than that of the old two-seaters.

With the demise of the 500C, the separate chassis disappeared from the Fiat range. The pushrod-operated overhead valve engine, mechanical fuel pump and transmission handbrake likewise reflected Torinese thinking. Rear suspension was of the 8V type, and the transverse-leaf independent front suspension came from the *topolino*. All the ratios of the synchromesh gearbox were indirect, and at long last the need for three mains on a high-revving small-capacity engine was recognized. The new 60 mm × 56 mm (633-cc) unit was more powerful than that of the 500C, at 21.5 bhp. Nor was the new car gutless: Britons, mindful of the laboured progress of the 1939 four-seater 500s (an English exclusive and one that Turin preferred to forget!), waited apprehensively for road-test reports. But even the first 600s attained 58 mph, cruised happily if unrestfully at 50 mph and took only 32.5 seconds to achieve it. True, it was hardly a bargain at £585 (Italians paid £350), but it was still one of the best babies of the decade, even if siting the heater ducts in the floor backbone rendered the handbrake incandescent to the touch.

Having used his Gucci shoehorn once to good purpose, Giacosa went one better for 1956 with a six-seater mini-bus on the same floor pan. The Multipla theme was, of course, nothing new—Volkswagen's Transporter had shown the way with rear engines and forward control, but the VW was a ¾-ton van, whereas the latest 600 variant measured 138 inches long, 62 inches wide and 62 inches high. Despite a lower top gear (5.38:1 as against 4.82:1 on the saloons), it was by no means tedious to drive. The main mechanical change was a reversion to coils and wishbones at the front. There were also van and taxi-cab versions, the latter enjoying a sizable vogue in Italy.

10.3   Monterosa and Microbo

This was a hard decade for Lancia. Creaky finances were exacerbated by a brilliant and catastrophic sally into Formula I. Enzo Ferrari, it is true, bailed them out, but the ensuing upheaval lost the Lancia family their company. It also introduced a new chief designer, Franco Fessia. Nonetheless, the cars of our period, both old Vincenzo's legacies and Vittorio Jano's newer creations, upheld the Via Monginevro's tradition for 'never making a bad car'.

In 1946 Lancia's offerings were the 1,486-cc Aprilia (new for 1937) and
the 903-cc Ardea, an eve-of-war introduction, both classical essays in unitary construction, with the same combination of a traditional radiator and
fastback saloon styling, together with those pillarless doors beloved of
Italian designers. Common to both models were short-stroke overhead-
camshaft vee-fours of narrow-angle type and surpassing compactness,
6-volt electrics, excellent four-speed gearboxes that neither had nor called
for synchromesh and retained a proper floor shift, worm-and-sector steering, the time-honoured coil-and-sliding pillar independent front suspension
and hydraulic brakes without Fiat's tiresome transmission handbrake.
Apart from their size, the main differences between the two Lancias were
matters of costing: the Ardea made do with gravity feed and semielliptics at
the rear, whereas its bigger sister favoured a mechanical pump and a
transverse-leaf independent rear suspension. Both cars had admirable
power-to-weight ratios: the Aprilia weighed 1,800 lb and needed only an
average 50 bhp to propel it at 80 mph on a high 4:1 top gear. The Ardea's
watch-like 65 mm × 68 mm unit pushed out a useful 29 bhp, and the
complete car was less than 12 feet long. In its Fourth-Series (1949) form
with an extra overdrive fifth gear, it was even better. The range was rounded
out by the traditional long-chassis 'platform' edition of the Aprilia for
specialist coach builders, who made the best possible use of it. Especially
attractive were Touring's two-door saloon (also fitted to Alfa Romeos) and
Pininfarina's cabriolet, though there was also a ponderous six-light style for
the cab drivers. At Geneva in 1948, Pininfarina displayed a restrained four-
light model: this passed unnoticed, though it was the prototype for Jano's
Aurelia.

On 22 October 1949, the last of 31,000 Aprilias rolled off the lines,
accompanied by a farewell note ('your glorious name has made itself known
in the greatest capitals') tucked in the boot. Five months later the vee-six
Aurelia was introduced.

This short-stroke (70 mm × 76 mm) 1¾-litre perpetuated both the
Aprilia's construction and its front springing, but the rest was new. The
full-width styling allowed a wider 60-degree angle for the two banks of
cylinders, and conventional pushrod-operated overhead valves were used,
though combustion chambers were hemispherical. Also new were the 12-
volt electrics, but the real interest came further aft. Jano transmitted his 55
bhp via a divided three-piece propeller shaft to a transaxle incorporating
both the single-plate clutch and the four-speed synchromesh box with overdrive top. His choice of column shift was unfortunate, as it led to complicated linkages. The rear suspension was by coil springs and diagonal wishbones, the wheels being located by single arms ahead of the hubs. The rear
brakes were inboard, the front shock absorbers were incorporated in the
suspension coils, and piston-type dampers were used at the rear. Though not

a spectacular performer, the Aurelia cruised comfortably in the seventies and handled as a Lancia should. A separate-chassis version was offered.

The design was progressively developed. In 1952, the capacity and power went up to 2 litres and 70 bhp respectively and, in 1954's Second-Series cars, to 2,266 cc and about 90 bhp respectively; these second-series cars incorporated a revised rear end with a de Dion axle and semielliptic springs. Other variations on the theme included a 'ministerial' limousine, the B15 on a 128-inch wheelbase which turned the scales at less than 2,900 lb. Right-hand steering was standard, even for the home market.

1951, however, saw the first and perhaps the most successful of the new Italian *granturismi*; it was the nearest approach to a sports car so far marketed by Lancia. This B20 model used a twin-carburetter 74 bhp edition of the 2-litre engine in a shorter 104¾-inch wheelbase, with simple fastback two-plus-two-seater coupé coachwork: the rear seats were very occasional indeed. *Autocar* called it 'a challenging, fascinating car of very great agility', and even early examples would achieve 95 mph. From 1953 onwards 118 bhp were available from a larger 2,451-cc engine, and the GT Aurelia came into its own, attaining 112 mph on its 3.64:1 top gear. A year later the model fell into line with the saloons, acquiring a de Dion rear end, and late in 1955 came the two-seater Spyder, aimed at the American market. It suffered from a lack of structural stiffness and was never as popular as the coupé, though both types outlasted the standard Aurelia. They were still catalogued—and still winning rallies—in 1958.

Meanwhile in 1953 the Ardea had given way to the Appia, a scaled-down Aurelia with the 1100 Fiat's cylinder dimensions of 68 mm × 75 mm. There, of course, all similarity ended, for the little Lancia's engine was a pushrod vee-four of exemplary compactness. Once again money was saved by a conventional gearbox location, outboard rear brakes and semielliptic rear springs. The saloon body used pressed steel only for its structural members: boot lid, doors and bonnet were of aluminium alloy. Hence complexity was not matched by weight; the Lancia was no heavier than the Fiat, and it had much the same overall performance, though the price was £200 higher, at £780. The differential was much greater when the two cars reappeared on the British market in 1955; if there were few buyers for Giacosa's masterpiece at £821, the Lancia at £1,772 cost more than a Mark VII Jaguar! Though more powerful 43.5-bhp engines came with the Second-Series Appias of 1956, sports models were not listed until 1957.

Pininfarina's revolutionary Flaminia saloon prototype had been shown in 1955, but the cars only reached the public at the very end of our period. The capacity of the vee-six engine was almost identical with that of the Aurelia, but in fact had squarer dimensions (80 mm × 81.5 mm as against 78 mm × 85 mm). On a 7.8:1 compression the new unit gave 103 bhp but, though the hypoid transaxle was retained (with a direct top gear), as were the braking arrangements, the rest of it smacked of heresy. The frame was of punt type, with deep box-section side-members, and the sliding-pillar front suspension had been discarded in favour of a commonplace short-and-long-arm setup. Also discarded were the pillarless doors, though the new body's thin pillars gave excellent all-round vision, even if the slab sides and cross-hatch grille displeased the diehards. Thanks to an even weight distribution, the new Lancia held the road in exemplary fashion, but large family saloons have never been best-sellers in Italy, and production tapered off in the middle 1960s.

Alfa Romeo pulled triumphantly out of Grand Prix racing at the end of 1951, spending the rest of our decade in the profitable task of reshaping their image with saloons of superior performance adapted to mass-production techniques. Like Fiat and Lancia, they had an up-to-date design in 1939 and continued to make it for thirteen years, even turning out a handful of civilian models during the war. Perhaps wisely, they abandoned the Gazzella, an exciting wartime prototype: its unitary construction would have been too much for them in the dark days of 1946. This car featured a short-stroke 2-litre six-cylinder engine with the usual twin overhead camshafts, a four-speed transaxle and an all-independent suspension by torsion bars.

Their established 6C-2500, which reappeared after the Second World War, had a similar although more classically dimensioned engine of 72 mm × 100 mm (2,443-cc), with two valves per cylinder actuated by twin chain-driven overhead camshafts. Cooling was by pump and fan, and the four-speed gearbox (column shift was not introduced until 1947) had synchromesh on third and fourth only. A separate chassis was used, but the suspension arrangements were those introduced in 1935: coils at the front, and a swing axle with torsion bars at the rear. Though the single-carburetter 87-bhp *turismo* was regarded as somewhat Buick by the *cognoscenti*—a limousine on a 127-inch wheelbase weighed 3,830 lb, required a 5:1 axle ratio and wore disc wheels—the 118-inch Sport managed 95 mph on 95 bhp, and the triple-carburetter Super Sport, with a speed of 105 mph, was possibly 1946's fastest saloon until the advent of the 2.4-litre Healey. It was also extremely expensive and formed only a small proportion of the factory's output—478 in twelve years, as against 883 Sports and 528 assorted *turismi*. The 145-bhp Corsa was not on sale to the public, any more than were the bizarre *dischi volanti*, with their welded-up space-frames, saucer-shaped *carrosserie* and choice of either a tuned 1900 engine or a new 3-litre six from which over 200 bhp were claimed. The only recorded private customer was the Argentinian dictator Juan Peron.

The 6C-2500 remained the staple Alfa Romeo until 1950, in which year production was down to 325 units. A sudden increase to 1,332 the following year was explained by the first fruits of Marshall Aid: a 1.9-litre four planned for the volume sales it duly achieved, 17,000 leaving the works in the first three years. The 1900 was hardly a thing of beauty: if not as uncompromisingly slab sided as the Singer SM1500 or the Nash Airflyte, its interior was austere to the point of crudity, and from the rear end it bore an embarrassing resemblance to a 1952 Vauxhall. Worse still, the six's column shift had been perpetuated.

This was not the whole story, for the cost saved on presswork had been spent on the mechanics. Under the bonnet was a delightful 82.5 mm × 88 mm four on traditional Alfa Romeo lines, with a five-bearing crankshaft and hemispherical combustion chambers. Carburation was by a downdraught Solex or Weber instrument, and the drive was taken from the four-speed synchromesh gearbox to a hypoid rear axle. The front suspension was unchanged, but a live axle and coils now featured at the rear, the steering was of worm-and-roller pattern, and the 2LS hydraulic brakes, working in 11-inch drums, were made by British Girling. The use of full-width saloon bodywork on a chassis of 106-inch wheelbase made for a full six-seater. Critics noted with pleasure that the traditional Alfa understeer had survived the transformation, and the car was certainly the fastest 2-litre family saloon of its period, topping 100 mph with the optional dual-choke carburetter. At 2,500,000 lire (£1,391) it was not impossibly expensive. Radial-ply tyres were standardized as early as 1952.

Like the Fiat 1400 and the Lancia Aurelia, the 1900 was progressively developed. In 1951 they introduced the light 4 × 4 Matta (which lost the Army contract to Fiat's Campagnola, so that only 2,050 were sold) and the 1900C, a true sports model with centre-lock wire wheels, a 98½-inch wheelbase and a high-compression 100-bhp engine. Pininfarina's fastback coupé edition was especially attractive. 1953 saw a twin-carburetter 100-bhp unit in a high-performance saloon, the 1900TI, with twin exhausts, larger brakes and ventilated disc wheels. This one was good for 110 mph and even more with 1954's 1,975-cc engine. Sports versions offered 115 bhp and five forward speeds with an overdrive top. Early specimens, alas! retained the column shift, resulting, as the late Charles Lam Markmann once observed, in 'the most diabolical change known to man or God'. The lever was back on the floor by 1955. The 1900's run did not end until 1959, though after 1955 it played second fiddle to Satta's magnificent Giulietta.

This was intended as an answer to the 1100TV Fiat and the Lancia Appia, though in fact Bertone's charming Sprint Coupé anticipated the four-door *berline* by a good six months. Mechanically, the formula was scaled-down 1900, apart from an alloy crankcase where the big engine used cast iron. The cylinder dimensions were 74 mm × 75 mm, for a capacity of 1,290-cc, and the car weighed only 1,792 lb. All the Alfa qualities were there: superb handling, brakes to match, an in-or-out clutch and 'seat of the pants' steering. Ratios were well spaced, at 4.55:1, 6.15:1, 9.34:1 and 16:1, and in original single-carburetter form the car would attain 105 mph on 65 bhp. The later twin-carburetter 90 bhp Sprints of 1956 were much faster. Faults were a nasty column shift (though Sprints and open spyders had floor-mounted levers), an umbrella-handle-type handbrake and a marked susceptibility to rust. For the family man the *berlina* of 1955, though tamer, was still the fastest car in its class, with 90 mph in standard form, and 100 mph on the TI series introduced during 1957. 39,055 *berline* of the original series were produced, as well as 22,181 of the parallel sporting types.

Every Juliet has her Romeo, though the male member of the family was marketed as a commercial vehicle. He usually wore an odd little supercharged two-stroke diesel, though a detuned 35 bhp Giulietta unit was an option. Romeo, however, had front-wheel drive, a feature that would not be seen on a true private car until 1972.

Bianchi confined their efforts to motor-cycles, trucks and glassfibre boats during our period, though they were testing a modernized edition of their pre-war S9 in 1949. Infinitely more interesting were the endeavours of the Caproni empire, who had owned Isotta Fraschini since 1933 and now planned a two-pronged attack on the car market. It even seemed that the ambitious schemes of Fabio Rapi and Alessandro Baj might lead somewhere. Rumours filtering out of Milan spoke of rear engines, automatic gearboxes, rubber suspensions, all-wheel drive and even a vast vee-twelve to carry on the tradition of the old straight-eights.

Rumour was not wholly a lying jade. In fact Ing. Baj had propounded all these ideas for a super-car aimed at the Americans, and even what took the road was exciting enough, though the rubber suspension never worked and was soon replaced by a more conventional all-independent system.

The structure of Isotta's 8C Monterosa was based on a platform frame to which bodies were welded. At the rear of this there was a 90-degree overhead-valve vee-eight engine, driving the rear wheels (only) by hypoid bevel. In practice the gearbox was a four-speed preselector with overdrive, and equipment was comprehensive: radio, heater and built-in jacks were all standard, and there was a peculiar system of 'idiot' lights, which reversed the accepted procedure by going *out* when trouble threatened!

Various engine sizes were tried. The first cars had 2½-litre power units, but their output of 103 bhp was inadequate, and the type finally chosen for production was a square (78 mm × 78 mm) 3-litre giving 115 bhp. The long dummy bonnet terminated in a replica of the pre-war radiator. On the first prototype, a whale-like Zagato-bodied saloon, this was non-functional, and cooling was by a pair of ear-type lateral radiators at the rear, but, as a result of constant overheating, the frontal ornamentation was made functional. Later saloons were handsome cars, and speeds of over 100 mph were attained. The great Laurence Pomeroy, who admitted to a healthy distrust of large rear-engined cars, found 'little to criticize . . . in respect of road holding and cornering power'. The Isotta neither oversteered nor became airborne in cross-winds. Unfortunately, nothing could be done about Caproni's ailing finances, and the Italian Government, notoriously generous with lame ducks, decided not to help, either. It was all over by 1950.

With the collapse went the company's second string, Franco Fessia's humbler Cemsa Caproni. This was a potential competitor for the Ardea and the *millecento*, and an interesting one at that. We have already encountered it in Belgium: suffice it to say that its short-stroke overhead-valve flat-four engine drove the front wheels via a four-speed gearbox, the suspension was of the all-coil type, and construction followed Isotta lines. Aeronautical influence was reflected in the liberal use of aluminium alloys, for engine, doors, bonnet, boot lid and even the cross-members of the subframe. On a weight of 1,856 lb and an output of 46 bhp, the little Caproni promised well, though the prototypes were an unhappy stylistic mixture of the 1400 Fiat and the Hillman Minx. Nor was the Belgian débacle the end: Fessia's masterpiece actually got into production in 1961, as the Lancia Flavia.

Above the mini-car level were two other oddities, the Opes of 1946 and the Fusi-Ferro of 1948. The former was an ambitious little saloon with a 700-cc three-cylinder air-cooled radial engine sited in a 'wheelbarrow' and driving the front wheels by worm gear. All-independent suspension was predictable, the gearbox was the fashionable Italian four-speeder with overdrive top, and the frame was of twin-rail type with outriggers for the body. The presence of a transmission brake on an front-wheel drive car was not exactly encouraging, and on the original prototype the driver sat in the middle, albeit the final Ninfea 800 (784 cc and 25 bhp) was more conventionally styled, resembling a cross between a 203 Peugeot and a contemporary Skoda. The Fusi-Ferro was a tiny 1,086-cc straight-eight for which 60 bhp and 85 mph were claimed. All four wheels were once again independently sprung, and it wore curious Perspex-topped six-seater saloon bodywork of very close-coupled type. The press were cynical. 'Curved glass screens,' they said, 'were not viable in Italy.' Nor, it seemed, were funds, for nothing more was heard of Ing. Fusi's *Aurora Otto*.

Most Italian cycle-cars dated from the dark period of 1946–8, and few of them gained much currency, though at least one Volugrafo was sold in Belgium. This one typified subutility thinking: the basis was a tubular frame on which was mounted a one-piece aluminium two-seater body. A 125-cc air-cooled overhead-valve engine was positioned at the rear, driving the left rear wheel by chain, and on a weight of 277 lb the machine achieved 35–40 mph. The Fimer of 1947 was cruder in appearance and featured swing axles at each end. The standard engine was a 250-cc two-stroke twin: the sponsors promised a 350-cc edition for customers in mountainous districts. G. B. Pennachio's Lucciola was a more ambitious affair with *topolino*-style two-seater rolltop coachwork, a curved screen and spatted rear wheels. This car also used a 250-cc engine.

1948 saw contenders from Parma (the 250-cc Atomo three-wheeler coupé with a single driven rear wheel), from Milan (the Volpe) and, improbably, from Palermo, where Ing. Artesi showed his dodgem-like Pulcino (little flea), a four-wheeler with all-independent suspension. The Volpe, which hid patriotically behind a mock Alfa grille, was memorable for a lilliputian twin-cylinder engine of 124-cc and a four-speed pedal-controlled preselective gearbox.

The next wave of miniatures appeared in 1952. These included entries from scooter makers anxious to keep their more sybaritic clients satisfied. Innocenti's 125-cc Lambro did not progress beyond the prototype stage. Iso, however, can claim credit for the first of the true bubble cars.

The Isetta was a little egg on diminutive wheels. 88½ inches long and 52 inches wide, it could be parked end-on between two conventional cars, yet carried two people in reasonable comfort at 40 mph. The basis of the vehicle was a tubular space-frame to which the body panels were attached. The engine, a 236-cc horizontal two-stroke on Trojan lines, with a common combustion chamber for its two cylinders, lived at the rear, and there was a Dubonnet-type independent front suspension. A compromise between stability and low cost was achieved by mounting the rear wheels so close together than no differential was required, but the vehicle was not lacking in sophistication, as is witnessed by the electric starter, the four-speed all-synchromesh gearbox and hydraulic brakes. The Isetta's most memorable feature was, of course, the swing-up front door, to which the steering column was hinged. Curiously, the native version had a short run, terminating in 1955; though Iso toyed with light commercials on similar lines and would later plunge into Euro-American hybrids, subsequent developments were the responsibility of BMW, the German licencees. The contemporary ISSI Microbo may be described as scaled-down Isetta with a single rear wheel, three speeds and a 125-cc engine. The sponsors' full name—Istituto Scientifiche Sperimentale Industriale—suggests that they were seeking a manufacturer rather than proposing to produce it themselves.

The third scooter firm to try their luck were Rumi, makers of the charmingly titled Formichino (little ant). They moved their design ideas from the insect to the animal kingdom with the Panther of 1954, which they were said to be backing. This was a lot more than just a bubble; it was a proper three-seater coupé with front-wheel drive and swing axles all round. 'Phenomenal economy' (90 mpg) was claimed on the strength of a 520-cc twin-cylinder diesel engine; a 480-cc petrol unit was an alternative. These claims were never put to the test, for the Panther's début was also its curtain call.

10.4   The Blood-Red Banner

Britain ruled the American sports-car market, and Italy's 'big battalions' were now primarily concerned with saloons and *granturismi*. This left the blood-red spyders to specialists whose wares were expensive and very bespoke. Foremost of these was Enzo Ferrari.

His prancing-horse symbol had been worn by official Alfa Romeo racing teams in the 1930s. In 1940 he had entered two 1½-litre straight-eights bearing his name in the Mille Miglia, but these were neither true Ferraris nor intended for series production. He did not become a manufacturer until 1947, and even then operations were not very orderly. Batches of five or six cars would be run off at a time, and options were limitless. The first true off-the-peg model was the 250GT of the mid-1950s, and even the Master's own idea of an assembly line would not eventuate until 1958. Further, many sports models, though driven on the road by their devoted owners, were intended strictly for the circuits and thus outside our compass. This applies to the four-cylinder 500–750 family (Ferrari designations are based on the capacity of an individual cylinder) made from 1954 onwards.

The basis of the Ferrari vee-twelve was, of course, Gioacchino Colombo's Type 125 of 1947, a machine neither made in street form nor sold to the public. (The first outside sale, to Gabriele Pesana in 1948, was of an ex-works 125 brought up to Type 166 specification.)

In spite of all the countless variations, all early Ferraris used vee-twelve engines with the blocks set at an angle of 60 degrees and a single chain-driven overhead camshaft per block. Heads were detachable, and coil ignition was fitted to road-going versions. The seven-bearing crankshaft was machined from a solid billet of steel, and the single dual-choke Weber carburetter was fed by mechanical pump. Ferrari, like Lancia, eschewed synchromesh for his five-speed box, fourth gear gave the direct drive, and the clutch was a single plate. The frame utilized tubular side-members, with a robust box-section cross-member at the front, and two tubular ones aft, while front suspension was independent, by transverse leaf with double wishbones. Semielliptics were used at the rear, and final drive was by spiral bevel. The hydraulic brakes worked in alloy drums of generous dimensions, the early bodies were rudimentary open two-seaters, and the handling has been described as 'unforgiving', a tendency accentuated by the factory's habit of installing more and more powerful engines in the same chassis.

Tipo 166, the first catalogued Ferrari, appeared in 1948 and was a Tipo 125 fitted with a 2-litre (60 mm × 58.8 mm) engine. The 'cooking' 89-bhp Turismo was never actually made, so the tamest car that one could buy was the Inter on an 89½-inch wheelbase, which would do about 100 mph on 110 bhp and had, by this time, a form of synchromesh, though only on third and top. Faster still was the Mille Miglia, with three carburetters, 140 bhp and spyder coachwork by Touring. Progressive development led in 1950 to the 2.3-litre Tipo 195 and to the 2,562-cc Tipo 212 a year later. By this time the output was 130–150 bhp according to tune; a 212 two-seater which was tested by *Autocar* went at 120 mph and returned a 0–100-mph acceleration time of 22.5 seconds. The five-speed gearbox required considerable skill, but already the vee-twelve's uncanny flexibility was apparent, and the car would move away from 10 mph on the high (4.28:1) fifth gear. Like Bugatti, Ferrari did not always abandon an old model when a new type appeared; the 166 was still listed in 1953, while the 212 family continued long after the new Lampredi family of cars was established.

1951 saw the arrival of Aurelio Lampredi, and the first of a new series of engines noted for their twin distributors and auxiliary electric pump feed. The chassis, gearboxes and brakes remained much as before, though the America family were true 'big bangers', even the most sedate Tipo 342 disposing of at least 200 bhp from 4.1 litres and attaining an easy 120 mph. The 1953 editions had new four-speed all-synchromesh gearboxes and proved very tractable, ticking over at 700 rpm and returning better than 20 mpg, if driven carefully, but the prices were astronomical (even a 212 cost £3,200 in Italy), and maintenance was complicated. For those who wanted the ultimate, there was always the big Mexico, which had proved itself in the Carrera Panamericana and offered 280 bhp with the aid of three dual-choke Weber carburetters. This one retained the five-speed crash box and a racing-type multi-disc clutch.

By 1954 the Americas had grown to 4½ litres and 300 bhp, and revised braking systems with dual master cylinders were offered to counter complaints of fade. This series culminated (in our period, that is) with the 410 Superamerica of 1955, which developed 340 bhp at 6,000 rpm even in its mildest form and featured a racing clutch. Later models used the 250GT's coil-spring independent front suspension.

The 250GT forms the real genesis of the 'street' Ferrari as it would remain until the early 1970s. This car started off as a smaller 3-litre development of the Lampredi family, the first 250 Sports having 94-inch wheelbases, spyder coachwork, a choice of four- or five-speed all-synchromesh boxes and 2LS brakes with twin master cylinders. The next step was the 250 Europa of 1954, with 200 bhp at 7,000 rpm; this one came with four forward speeds and left-hand drive as standard. In 1956 it was redesigned with a new short-block (73 mm × 58.8 mm) 220-bhp engine; at the same time the original suspension arrangements gave way to coils and wishbones. Maximum speed was anything up to 155 mph according to axle ratio, and the main snag of using a Ferrari for everyday transport in America was the fragility of light-alloy bodies not intended to cope with local parking techniques.

Maserati had built a few sports cars in the early years but had later abandoned this line of business to concentrate on out-and-out racers. Since 1938, however, the company had been under Orsi control, and there were signs of a renewed interest in street machinery with the advent of the A6 at Geneva in 1947. Its single-overhead-camshaft six-cylinder engine, of 66 mm × 72.5 mm (1,488 cc) derived directly from the 1936 racing *voiturette* unit and was a robust pump-cooled affair with a cast iron block and seven-bearing crankshaft. The rest of the mechanics were unremarkable: a four-speed synchromesh gearbox took the drive to a spiral bevel back axle. The frame used tubular side-members and cruciform bracing, while the usual coils and unequal-length wishbones were used at the front in conjunction with a live axle and coils at the rear. The brakes were hydraulic, a 4.4:1 axle ratio was quoted, and the engine was modestly rated—65 bhp at 4,700 rpm. Enthusiasts not deterred by Pininfarina's show coupé with its transparent roof panel and pop-out headlights found the car capable of nearly 95 mph; it 'could be placed in fast corners with a flick of the wrist'. Only 59 A6s (plus a few similar machines with 2-litre engines) were built; among the customers was the Thai racing driver B. Bira. For the next few years Maserati once again devoted themselves to circuit machinery.

Of these sports racers the A6CGS of 1952 is significant, as the basis of the A6G2000 series sold in small numbers from 1954 onwards. Both featured 76.5 mm × 72 mm (1,985-cc) six-cylinder engines with twin gear-driven overhead camshafts, dual coil ignition, electric pump feed and quarter-elliptic rear springing, though tourers used a lower compression ratio, conventional wet-sump lubrication and all-synchromesh boxes. The A6G2000 could attain 118 mph with a 0–60-mph acceleration time of 10 seconds, the bodies were the work of Allemano, Frua and Zagato, and the prices, even in Italy, were not far below Ferrari levels: £2,470 in 1955. This explains why production failed to achieve the proposed 100 units in 1956. The successful 3500GT was not seen until March 1957.

Moretti of Turin were a much humbler firm who never decided what to make, complicating the issue by making most of it themselves. This is probably why they asked for cash in advance. Most of the customers were Italian, though catalogues were printed in French and sometimes in (broken) English.

Nobody took their 1946 début seriously. In *Autocar*'s opinion, the La Cita mini-car was 'rather expensive and too well made to be competitive with Fiat'; this last sentiment must have delighted Vittorio Valletta. There were, however, parallels with the *topolino*, not only in the little Moretti's appearance but also in the application of big-car principles to a tiny two-seater only 118 inches long and weighing 1,019 lb. The engine, initially of 250 cc but later enlarged to 350 cc, was a water-cooled four-stroke twin mounted at the front, and driving the rear wheels via a four-speed box with dashboard change (some reports spoke of five speeds) and a spiral bevel axle. Brakes were hydraulic, suspension was of independent transverse type at the front with semielliptics at the rear, and the radiator was in front of its engine and not behind, as on the Fiat. La Cita was said to do 56 mph and 80 mpg, but nobody expected to hear that 250 Morettis had been sold by 1950.

They had, however, a second string—a 750-cc twin-overhead-camshaft four-cylinder engine, which formed the basis for subsequent developments. By the early 1950s Morettis used single-camshaft engines of 58 mm × 57 mm (592 cc) in conventional chassis with hypoid rear axles. By 1954 the capacity was back at 747 cc, though the standard four-seater sports saloon was a lot more expensive than a *topolino* at 1,260,000 lire (£720).

At this point, models began to appear in frightening profusion. The regular 750 was available with twin upstairs camshafts and five main bearings, in which form the output was 65 bhp; for fanatics there was a GS *barchetta* which looked like a baby Ferrari. In an attempt to attract enthusiasts who wanted a sports Lancia Appia and could not get one, Moretti also offered a larger twin-camshaft 1200 giving 52 bhp on a 6.7:1 compression. The standard article was a two-door saloon styled by Michelotti, but more ferocious editions had twin dual-choke carburetters, floor change and independent rear suspension. To crown everything, catalogues depicted a line of small forward-control trucks, with a choice of almost any engine (except the full-house 750) and the added attraction of a two-speed rear axle. At the 1955 Turin Show Moretti even made a bid for the sporting family market with a four-door saloon using the 27 bhp single-camshaft 750 engine and a 4.875:1 back axle, though this *turismo* does not seem to have gone on sale before 1957. After 1960 Moretti would give up the unequal struggle and join the ranks of the Fiat improvers.

OSCA were more successful: so far from buying Fiat parts, they actually sold their twin-camshaft fours to the Torinese colossus, though not until 1959. This final venture by the Maserati brothers concentrated on competition machinery: there were no 'street' OSCAs as such in our period. The brothers used a steel-tube frame, suspended by coils at the front and by trailing quarter-elliptics with radius arms at the rear; centre-lock wire wheels were regular equipment. Their first engine was an 1,100 of 70 mm × 71 mm with Maserati-style chain-driven overhead camshaft, but twin camshafts were standardized from 1950 onwards. By 1954 the firm were extracting 110 bhp from 1,453 cc, which meant 77 bhp per ton in a two-seater weighing a little over 1,600 lb. This MT4 was to be 'sold freely' from 1955, and the 1956 buyers' guides listed open and closed two-seaters with four-cylinder engines of 750, 1,100 and 1,500 cc. The biggest unit was said to give 125 bhp.

Even less street minded was Enrico Nardi, whose long career as a tuner included work on Ferrari's 1940 straight-eight. His wares featured light multi-tubular frames with transverse-leaf independent front suspensions and (usually) Bugatti-style reversed quarter-elliptics at the rear. Engines were wholly incidental: at various times Nardi fitted motor-cycle units (the Swiss Universal and the 750-cc flat-twin BMW), sundry Fiats, the American Crosley and the French Dyna Panhard. The standard 1956 offering was a tiny *barchetta* with a 747-cc Fiat-based power unit rated at 43 bhp and a four-speed gearbox. The wheelbase was 75¾ inches and claims included 100 mph and a fuel consumption of 35 mpg.

It is doubtful whether Savonuzzi's 1948 SVA, a curious little machine, with a supercharged 813-cc overhead-camshaft four-cylinder engine canted over to the right to lower the bonnet line, rack-and-pinion steering and a de Dion back axle, ever appeared in road-going form, though a racing model did exist, and sports cars were promised. Equally ephemeral was 1950's Italmeccanica, a bid for American sales by racing driver Gigi Platé, who fitted a blown Ford vee-eight engine into an Italian chassis with an all-round torsion-bar suspension and coachwork by Stabilimenti Farina. Platé was before his time.

There remain the Fiat improvers, and of these Piero Dusio was the most important. In the early post-war years his 1,100-cc Cisitalia *monoposti* with their peculiar semiautomatic transmissions achieved considerable success. The touring GS is, however, remembered for the pure lines of Pininfarina's two-seater coupé body, infinitely more attractive than the ugly open and closed sports machinery seen on the circuits.

The Cisitalia's basis was the inevitable space-frame, of chrome molybdenum tubes. Front suspension was independent by transverse leaf; at the rear Dusio used the unusual combination of coils and quarter-elliptics, the latter serving as radius arms. The brakes, steering and gearbox were regular Fiat components, though the gear ratios (3.9:1, 5.2:1, 7.8:1 and 12.3:1) were high and close. Touring editions used near-stock Fiat 1100 units with high-compression pistons and reinforced bottom ends, but for those for whom 50 bhp were inadequate there was the fiercer Mille Miglia type with dry-sump lubrication and a magneto. Thanks to a low build and a wind resistance some 30% less than Fiat's 1100S, the standard coupe would do 106 mph. Unfortunately, *il padrone*'s racing programme led him into bankruptcy and thence to a spell in Argentina helping to get General Peron's motor industry off the ground.

He was back in Turin in 1952, but, like Sherlock Holmes after the Reichenbach Falls episode, he never really recovered his form. At Geneva that March he showed a new two-door saloon, still using the familiar space-frame but in conjunction with a de Dion axle and leaf springs at the rear. The engine, too, was an exciting-sounding affair, a twin-camshaft 2.8-litre four-cylinder BPM marine unit said to give 160 bhp at 5,300 rpm and to propel the latest Cisitalia at 137 mph. On this one, a four-speed transaxle featured, but within a year Dusio had reverted to Fiat themes with the 1,100-cc Volo Radente series, now with orthodox cruciform-braced chassis and stock Fiat suspension units. Though wire-wheel and overdrive options made for an attractive package, the *marque* had lost its cachet. It would be best not to dwell on the 505DF of 1954, a 1900-based hardtop for the carriage trade. Not even the blandishments of a radio and an extra 20 bhp could excuse the mock-Jeep grille with its built-in overriders! The smaller Cisitalias lasted the decade out, together with some custom-bodied 600s of no great merit.

The Ambrosini family's Societa Italiana Applicazione Trasformazione Automobilistiche (to give SIATA their full name) had been in the business since 1926, attaining *marque* status in 1939 with their Fiat 500 sports cabriolet. In post-war years they would do almost anything a customer demanded, from *elaborazioni*, via special cylinder heads (their overhead-valve *topolino* conversion was the most successful of many) to a complete transformation. This would, and did, furnish the customer with a 1400 which looked like one of Hermann Graber's Alvis and went like a Morgan Plus-Four. Nor were they averse to other people's engines: in 1952 they offered their Fiat-based spyder with the Crosley unit. At the same time they announced a sports two-seater with a tubular frame, Chrysler vee-eight engine and a de Dion back axle designed for quick changes of ratio. Even less probable was Mitzi, a mini-car of 1953. This one featured an inclined air-cooled side-valve vertical twin engine at the rear, with spur-gear drive. As Fiat's Nuova 500 was already in the pipeline, the reasons for Mitzi's demise are not hard to seek.

In 1948 it had seemed that SIATA might go independent, for at the Turin Show they displayed the P75, an oddity with a tiny twin-camshaft four-cylinder engine (the crankshaft ran in three roller bearings) mounted at the back of a tubular chassis. A two-speed axle with a self-locking differential and a central driving position completed a bizarre specification, but a year later the company was back in the fold, with the *topolino*-based Amica. The tubular chassis apart, mechanics were 500B, though SIATA inflicted a column shift on their customers and preferred, for some unfathomable reason, the old-type quarter-elliptic rear suspension. The body was a dainty little slab-sided cabriolet modelled on Pininfarina's new Simca 8 Sport, and buyers had the choice of either a tuned stock engine, giving 22 bhp, or a stroked-crank effort with an extra main bearing, which meant 26 bhp from 780 cc. From 1952, Amicas were available with Fiat 1100 or Crosley engines, while by 1956 the name was applied to a straightforward 600 customization.

Also given the treatment was the 1400, which was available as the Daina (a cabriolet or fixed-head coupé), the Barchetta (mock-Ferrari) or the Rallye, a convincing imitation of a TD MG. From 1953, a five-speed gearbox and Borrani wire wheels were optional, and as much as 92 bhp were extracted from the engine in its fiercest form.

Next on the list was the 8V (the SIATA 208), offered in various open and closed forms, including a coupé with an MG-style front end. The 208CS was virtually a racing car, weighing only 1,728 lb and guaranteed to do 124 mph. Quite a few of these eight-cylinder SIATAs found to their way to America, where they sold for less than $5,000. From 1954 onwards, however, the company concentrated on the 1100-103, which emerged as a fast-back with a 52-bhp engine, a floor change and a 4.3:1 axle.

Stanguellini, like OSCA, bothered little with road-going machinery, though they advertised an 1100-based sports saloon with *topolino* front suspension in 1947 and were prepared to convert the chassisless 1100-103 into a pickup to fill a gap in the Fiat range. The Bialbero made from 1951 was a stark open two-seater with a tubular frame, a Fiat-type suspension and latterly *barchetta* styling. Stanguellini's twin-overhead-camshaft engines featured Fiat bottom ends with heavy-duty sumps and dynamically balanced crankshafts; the top ends were their own. 80 bhp were claimed from the 1,100-cc unit, while the 750 (62 mm × 62 mm) was credited with about 20 bhp less. A two-seater weighing 791 lb would top 110 mph, and later Stanguellinis combined a transverse-leaf independent front suspension with 1400-type coil rear suspension.

Carlo Abarth was still primarily a tuner and manufacturer of stainless-steel exhaust systems. This latter business had paid so well that his staff increased from 10 in 1950 to 122 in 1956. On the tuning side, he was best known for his transformations of the 600, which emerged, still looking the same, but with a 'stretched' 747-cc engine incorporating a new crankshaft, pistons, liners, valves and exhaust, not to mention a stronger clutch and a larger radiator. As yet he was content with 44 bhp, in a bomb of a saloon capable of 85 mph. The real 'street rod' 600s would come later.

As early as 1950 he had built a handful of 1100-based sports cars with Porsche trailing-link independent front suspensions, but for several years thereafter there were no Abarth cars as such, merely oddities such as the 1400 Fiat coupé produced in association with Bertone in 1952. This one had cutaway wheel arches and a triple-missile grille. Packard purchased this car for a 'styling study' but fortunately did nothing with it. The real Abarth line started with a pair of ultralow sports racing spyders shown in 1955. Of these, the 1,100-engined 207A went no further, but the 210A with 600 mechanics and Abarth's steel platform frame paved the way for his Zagato-bodied coupés. These beauties used the 747-cc Abarthized Fiat 600 unit with close-ratio four-speed box. Remarkably compact—it was 136½ inches long, and the low roof line necessitated cutouts to give extra headroom—the little car attained 96 mph and would accelerate to 50 mph in 11 seconds. An excellent aerodynamic shape meant 37 mpg at a constant 90 mph. More would be heard of the Austro-Italian wizard in ensuing years.

11   Sweden

Sweden spent the first post-war decade transforming herself—from a major importing nation to a significant exporter. Though still a long way from her 1977 position (one car to every 3.3 persons), her 1954 ratio was, nonetheless, Europe's highest. The logical step was to become self-supporting and thence to find and explore niches in other people's markets. If as yet there was no international Volvo empire, the ingredients were certainly at hand.

The country started with one advantage: private-car production had continued between 1940 and 1945. Volvo had even designed and built their own wood-gas producer. They had gone one better, with a streamlined trailer to carry it. However, though this state of affairs enabled the company to have new models on show by 1944, actual deliveries in the period had been modest, at 1,662 units. In any case, Volvo's annual potential was still the wrong side of 4,000.

Hence imports still loomed large and would continue to do so for many years. In 1950, Sweden imported about 50,000 cars: four years later, Britain alone would contribute 22,239. Nor were native products the best-sellers; they commanded 17.6% of the market in 1952 and 31.3% in 1956, though by this time Volvo had edged Volkswagen out of first place, the *bückel* outselling the Beetle by 26,261 to 23,322. The continuing importance of imports was, of course, due to a changing demand. Pre-war, Sweden had relied heavily on America, and Volvos had consequently been conceived on American lines. This past domination was shaken by the fuel shortage, by higher taxation and by the sheer size of Detroit's latest offerings. Sweden's roads were narrow, and many of them would not allow a brace of Buicks to pass.

1956's statistics were interesting. That year Volvo had made some 35,000 cars, which meant a fair balance of exports. Not that Sweden was a significant force; during the whole of our period she shipped less than 20,000 units, but inroads were being made. Volvo had long been regular exhibitors at Brussels, even if Belgian sales seldom exceeded 200 cars a year. By 1952, SAAB were selling in Finland, and in 1953 they ventured a stand at the Turin Show. By 1956 both Swedish makers had a foot in the American market. Volvo's PV444 was catalogued in 'California' trim (badge bar, bed-seats) at $2,264 all on, and this was the path that led to First Division membership. Twenty-one years later Volvo would be assembling in five countries, including Canada, and would control the private-car side of the Dutch DAF concern.

A bid for SAAB would bring the wheel full circle, for in 1945 Volvo were Sweden's only manufacturers of private cars. Their line of business since 1929 had been no-nonsense sixes in the prevailing American idiom, powered by seven-bearing flathead engines modelled on the proprietary Continental. In current form this unit was of 3,670-cc, developing 84 bhp on petrol for those with the right permits, and a just-adequate 50 bhp on wood-gas for everyone else. Gearboxes were three-speed synchromesh with floor shift, and the rest conformed to the Detroit pattern: cruciform-braced frames, hydraulic brakes, hypoid rear axles and all-steel bodies. Having played with a coil-spring independent front suspension on the 1935 Carioca, an imitation Chrysler Airflow which pleased nobody, Volvo were now in retreat, with semielliptics at both ends. The styling was unkindly summarized as 'a little bit of everything!' The standard PV53 on a 113½-inch wheelbase was a four-light fastback still showing some Airflow influence at the back: the front end was unadulterated 1939 Chevrolet. The long-chassis PV801, usually encountered in taxi-cab form, was modelled on the 1938 Ford vee-eight, with a hint of 1937 Chrysler. Overdrive was available on the smaller car, Volvo's best-seller so far on the strength of 3,900 delivered since 1939.

These sixes were retained in the post-war programme, being updated from 1944 onwards. The PV53 gave way to the PV60 with column shift and, once again, an American-type coil-and-wishbone front suspension. Engines now gave 90 bhp, and the new car was 1½ inches shorter in the wheelbase, though the latest styling (a 1939 Pontiac grille and a 1940 Dodge body) made it look longer. A year later the PV801 became the PV821 with the same mechanical improvements, plus box front fenders in the 1942 Ford idiom; a beam front axle survived on the cabs. The last of 3,500 PV60s was made in 1950; the eight-seaters and their descendants, the PV831 Disponent series, remained until 1958 to the tune of some 7,000 units. Thereafter the Gothenburg factory stayed away from multi-cylinder engines until 1968, apart from some trials with an American-type vee-eight with automatic gearbox, power brakes and power steering. This early-1950s prototype, code-named Philip, was never marketed; its styling was closely based on the 1951 Kaiser. By this time production was running at 6,000 units a year: Volvo had recognized the need for a smaller car.

It was a little unkind to dismiss the PV444, brainchild of Eric Jern and Helmer Pettersen, as 'an American car built down to British standards'. Certainly Volvo's 1944 novelty was purest Detroit to the eye, with its two-door fastback body and ugly grille with box front fenders. The similarity extended within, to the even uglier facia, the plastic horn rim and the cloth upholstery. The concept was likewise American; to the usual coil-spring independent front suspension could be added a live axle and coils at the rear, 6-volt electrics, cam-and-lever steering and a wide-ratio three-speed gearbox, even if Jern and Pettersen preferred a 1937-type central lever to column shift. Quite a few components were imported from America: Wagner furnished the hydraulic brakes, Autolite the electrical equipment, Carter the downdraught carburetter and Delco the telescopic dampers.

Inspiration had, however, come from the far shore of the Baltic, in the shape of the 1939 1.3-litre Hanomag, whence derived the welded-up unitary structure with its forward extensions to take the front suspension. The engine, a straightforward short-stroke (75 mm × 80 mm) 1.4-litre four, featured the pushrod-operated overhead valves already used on Volvo's trucks. Cooling was by pump and fan, with mechanical pump feed, and the output was 40 bhp at 3,800 rpm. On a 102½-inch wheelbase, the PV444 was 172 inches long and weighed 2,128 lb. It outperformed contemporary British 1,500s, attaining 73 mph, with over 50 mph in second. The fuel consumption was a respectable 30–33 mpg. Further, the 444 family would account for 330,000 units up to 1965. In its later years, the *bückeln* (as German speakers called them) would become really winners, preferred by the works team to the more modern 121s. In 1965 Volvo would annex not only the Swedish and Acropolis events but the punishing East African Safari as well.

By this time, of course, the car would do 100 mph on 90 bhp, but this took many years to attain, and the PV444 went through to the E-series of 1954 with minimal change. By now there was also a station-wagon edition, the PV445 Duet, with commercial-type chassis-cowl structure. Volvo's first exploration of the American market in 1956 coincided with the delivery of the hundred thousandth PV444, and to celebrate this the K-type was given 51 bhp in standard form and 70 bhp with twin SU carburetters. In the last months of our period the PV444L, with the 1,580-cc engine, was introduced. Standard models were now good for 85 mph, and the twin-carburetter cars did 10 mph more, returned 27 mpg and took only 10.7 seconds to reach 50 mph. The American magazine *Motor Trend* rated the three-bearing Volvo unit 'as tough a little engine as you will find anywhere today'.

Type 121—the car which would make the name of Volvo famous to motorists throughout the world—was on the market by late 1956, though its fourteen-year run had yet to gather momentum. This was essentially the same formula down to the 6-volt electrics and three-speed gearbox, though an extra ratio was optional and would be standardized in 1958. Volvo had, however, achieved four doors without lengthening the wheelbase, and the styling—best summarized as restrained 1955 Chrysler—was their best to date. On 1,600-cc and 80 bhp, the car attained 90 mph.

Volvo also toyed with sports cars, though these, like Fiat's 8V, were a case of thinking aloud in public. The 1900 was first shown in 1954. It was built up on a twin-tube form of 94½-inch wheelbase, to which the standard running gear was attached. The twin-carburetter 1.4-litre engine was rated at 70 bhp, but three speeds still sufficed. The glassfibre roadster body was specially made in California and featured a detachable hardtop, while the cross-hatched grille had some affinity with Chrysler dream cars of the period. No hood was provided: another notable absentee was a spare wheel, rendered (or so the factory said) superfluous by the new Trelleborg tubeless tyres. Later models were, however, orthodox ragtops, and the car was still listed in 1956, now with five forward speeds and an advertised rev. limit of 7,000. The 1600 engine was never used, and only 67 Volvo Sports were made. The 179, a four-seater fastback coupé version, was seen only in prototype form.

The PV444 was too big and American in concept to appeal to everyone. Thus small-car enthusiasts turned to the car that had been top of the pre-war pops, the DKW: 4,000 were sold in 1939 alone. Since nothing was as yet forthcoming from either Germany, the Swedes determined to make their own.

The first contender—in 1946—was Gunnar Philipsson, Stockholm's Chrysler concessionaire. His plan was to rework the stock 684-cc Meister-klasse with a simplified rear suspension, hydraulic brakes and all-metal bodywork in the latest idiom, albeit with separate front wings. The result, which resembled a cross between a Volvo and Borgward's as yet unborn 1500, offered an extra 8 inches of elbowroom in the rear, but manufacturing difficulties supervened. It was not until 1948 that the idea was taken up by the Svenska Aeroplan AB. Everyone was happy: the Swedes got their updated DKW, and Philipsson got the Stockholm agency for the new car.

SAAB could afford cars. Sweden's wartime isolation had forced her into greater self-reliance, and the Trollhättan company became a Renault or Fiat of the aeronautical world. Not content with having a jet fighter in the air by March 1947, they also offered a modern lightplane (the Safir) and a medium-sized airliner, the Scandia, widely used by the SAS network. Further, both chief engineer Gunnar Ljungström and his stylist Sixten Sason had little use for American ideas.

The basis of the SAAB-92 was a two-door fastback of perfect aerodynamic shape, so successful that it was still in production in 1976. Its construction was geared to aircraft-industry methods, being a welded-up *monocoque* based on a steel floor pan. The dimensions of individual pressings were kept as small as possible.

The mechanics were DKW with a difference. The reverse-scavenged two-stroke twin with its thermosyphon cooling and twin coils was enlarged to 764-cc, while the downdraught carburetter was fed by mechanical pump. The three-speed synchromesh gearbox featured a column shift: it also incorporated a free-wheel, though the lock-out control was hidden under the bonnet, away from the meddlings of the inexperienced. Steering was by rack and pinion, the hydraulic brakes worked in 9-inch drums, and all four wheels were independently sprung, by transverse torsion bars. A 97-inch wheelbase and generous body width gave plenty of elbow room, though headroom was a problem, and so was rearward vision until the rear window was enlarged in 1953. A maximum speed of 65 mph was allied to easy and quiet cruising at around 50 mph. Even in the motorway era the absence of wind noise on SAABs was outstanding.

All was not, however, joy. The car was unforgiving. Understeer could reach alarming proportions with sudden rear-end breakaway. There were other troubles, notably cold starting (critical in a Swedish winter), and starter cables which disintegrated at the slightest provocation. High-geared steering and a Citroën-like turning circle of 39 feet made the SAAB awkward for women. (Fortunately, however, Sason had abandoned the full-spatted front wheels of prototypes, which proved to be magnificent mud-traps!) To cap it all, there was no choice of colour before 1953. All SAABs came in a uniform shade of green.

The Swedes soon acclimatized themselves to the 92's curious ways, rating it 'fairly reliable'. From 1,250 cars in 1950, deliveries climbed to 2,298 in 1952 and 3,424 in 1953, when improvements included an external-access boot as well as the modified rear window. The ten thousandth SAAB was built in March, and 1954 cars featured more power—28 instead of 25 bhp—as well as a carburetter deicer. In 1955 the veteran *rallyiste* Greta Molander annexed the Monte Carlo Rally's Coupe des Dames: her ninth place in the general classification showed that this was no fluke occasioned by a shortage of hardy ladies!

In 1956 came the car that was to make not only SAAB's name but also that of the redoubtable Erik Carlsson, vanguard of the great Scandinavian invasion. With the 93 series SAAB fell into line with other purveyors of the DKW fashion by changing to three longitudinally disposed cylinders.

Externally, there was not much difference. Even the half-spats had disappeared from the front wheels, and there was now a proper radiator grille, a welcome change from the unhappy combinations of horizontal chromium strip hitherto used to break up the unadorned masses of the Saxon shape. Beneath the surface, however, there was an all-coil suspension, that at the rear incorporating an U-shaped dead axle and a Panhard rod. Tubeless tyres were now standard, and the car was slightly longer and wider. The engine, designed by the German Hans Müller, featured a cast iron block and alloy head and was inclined 30 degrees to the left. The crankshaft ran in four ball bearings, and the dimensions were 66 mm × 72.9 mm for a capacity of 748-cc. Rubber-block mounts reduced vibration, and on an output of 38 bhp the SAAB would do over 70 mph. The home-market price was 7,300 kröner (£500): though the car was still undercut by the smaller British and German offerings, it was beginning to be competitive.

SAAB's Sonett sports car, another 1956 introduction, paralleled contemporary Volvo thinking. Once again the formula embraced a separate box-section chassis of shorter-than-standard wheelbase (though that of the SAAB was of light-alloy construction), with glassfibre bodywork. The Sonett was, however, very stark and weighed only 1,100 lb. The engine developed 57.5 bhp on a 10:1 compression, and SAAB hinted at a better-furnished edition 'for personal use, with convertible top and baggage compartment'. Neither version reached the public, though the Sonett attracted much attention, getting its makers off to an excellent start in America. By the time the two-strokes disappeared in 1968, 320,000 cars had been made.

In such company the Mueller–Neidhart project of 1952 passed unnoticed, though plans were afoot for 'a factory in the Low Countries'. Here was a typical mini-car in the German idiom, with forked-backbone frame, all-independent springing of the compressed-rubber type and a rear-mounted DKW engine. Its Cyclop's-eye spotlamp apart, the prototype coupé resembled a baby Porsche. However, though 30% of Sweden's car population was concentrated in her three largest cities, she did not like bubble cars, and nothing more was heard of the Mueller–Neidhart.

12 Denmark and Norway

Denmark has never had a significant automobile industry. Nor has she shown any inclination to protect it, as did Switzerland, even in the face of a relentless decline. Imported machinery sufficed, from the Fords and Chevrolets of earlier days to the small German (DKW) and British (Morris Eight) models which ruled the roost in the 1930s. The DKW's following, indeed, was as strong as in Sweden. Thus it was logical to expect DKW elements in at least one of Denmark's three 1950 prototypes, the DK sponsored by Hohnstedt–Pettersen. In any case, the firm was DKW's Danish concessionaire.

Their stand at the Copenhagen Show has been described as a 'memorial hall', since it contained not only a selection of pre-war DKWs but also a 1939 1.3-litre Hanomag! Also on display was S. A. Mathiesen's idea of what a post-war Meisterklasse should be. The engine, gearbox and transmission were authentic 1938, in spite of which an optimistic 30 bhp were claimed, but the hydraulic brakes and all-steel bodywork were entirely new and made the DK about 200 lb heavier than its German prototype. Worse problems were the supply of engines, and the imminence of the new West German F89, a prototype of which was actually on Hohnstedt–Pettersen's stand. Mathiesen hoped to go into business updating existing DKWs, but this was not to be.

Another front-wheel-drive car was the obscure Erla, a contemporary using a 748-cc water-cooled twin-piston two-stroke engine, probably of Ilo make. The brakes were 2LS hydraulics, the suspension was by 'torsion bars', certainly independent at the front, and the wheelbase of this small saloon was 88½ inches. It was said to do 70 mph, but its sponsors preferred to concentrate on the sale of German Lloyds and Goliaths.

The Sommer family's S-1, yet another 1950 débutante, was a victim of the Government's non-protectionist attitudes. This time the mechanical elements were those of Jowett's Bradford van, with a side-valve flat-twin engine; the prototype car even carried a Bradford chassis serial! Less Jowett-like, however, was the transverse-leaf independent front suspension, the steering gear came off a Javelin, and the 9-inch hydraulic brakes gave stopping powers far superior to those of the Bradford's antiquated arrangements. The wheelbase was longer than that of the British car, at 106 inches, and 42–50 mpg were claimed. As shown at Copenhagen, the S1 looked exactly like a scaled-down Armstrong Siddeley Typhoon, reputedly too much so, since the front end was subsequently restyled. No more Danish Bradfords were made, though the prototype still exists.

The DKR of 1954 hailed from Roskilde and was yet another Mathiesen creation, evolved with assistance from S. R. Olsen. In appearance, the new car was not unlike the contemporary Dyna Panhard, and various engines were explored, including a two-stroke Ilo and a mysterious 'Danish diesel'. The two prototypes, however, used 1,098-cc overhead-valve Heinkel fours driving the front wheels via a four-speed synchromesh gearbox. The all-independent coil-spring suspension was on McPherson strut lines, and the glassfibre four-door saloon coachwork incorporated a plastic undershield as well. Like the Panhard, the DKR was a bulky vehicle (length was close on 16 feet), though it weighed just under 1 ton and was credited with a Panhard-like performance—75 mph and 35–40 mpg. Both the Government and private individuals were invited to subscribe to this venture, with promises of 4,000 cars a year and export business in the Iberian Peninsula. The quoted price matched that of British 1½-litres such as Morris and Vauxhall but was hardly competitive with the German opposition.

Two years later, in 1956, came Norway's sole effort, the Troll. This was based on the defunct German Gutbrod and featured the same two-stroke water-cooled twin-cylinder engine driving the front wheels. The body was a neat glassfibre coupé, and on a weight of 1,320 lb the Troll was supposed to do 80 mph. 'The factory,' said a contemporary report, 'is little more than a shed,' with a staff of seven. Thus it is not surprising that initial plans did not extend beyond a trial batch of fifteen cars. Only five of these had been completed when the money ran out.

13 Russia

In Russia, the automobile was still a badge of rank rather than a possession. Even the steady flow of statistics disseminated by Tass could not conceal the fact that private cars enjoyed the lowest of priorities. In our decade, more and more was seen of Soviet products—in the west as well as in the satellite republics—but Moskvitches and Pobedas took second place to trucks. As early as 1946, Russia claimed to be Europe's largest producer of motor vehicles. If one excluded Britain, this was probably true, but of approximately 108,000 units delivered that year, only 6,289 were private cars. Commercials, indeed, represented 82% of the total in 1950, and a resounding 79% in 1956, though by this time the residual 21% amounted to 97,792 units. The bias, however, remained: the State's first million-year for trucks was 1971, but it was not until three years later than deliveries of Volgas, Ladas, Moskvitches and the rest topped the seven-figure mark.

Exports were entering the picture. The satellite countries, with similar social and economic structures, were sterile soil, but in 1949 Konela of Finland took the first foreign shipment of Moskvitches, followed a year later by Belgium and Sweden. A 1953 barter deal (for herrings!) opened up the Norwegian market, and by 1954 the cars were available in Holland. The bigger Russians also found their way abroad; the 2.1-litre Pobeda sold in Belgium by 1952 for £950 (133,000 francs, as against 108,500 for the rival but locally made Standard Vanguard), while the seven-seater ZIM went on sale in Stockholm in 1954. Avtoexport of Moscow even printed foreign-language catalogues for the enormous ZIS, though in this case customers were surely limited to friendly Heads of State. Not that sales were substantial—the Belgian market took 547 cars in 1951, 388 in 1952 and 507 in 1953—but it was an indication of future trends. In due course the robust Volgas and Ladas, with their comprehensive tool kits and starting handles, would acquire a sizable following, not only because of the bargain prices that are viable only when there are no shareholders to placate but also because they were the spiritual successors to the basic sedans once offered by America—the Dodge Four and Ford's Model-A.

In the Communist world, of course, rivalry does not lie between makes but between individual factories eager to raise their norms. This was a mixed blessing. 'The need,' lamented a Russian journalist in 1955, 'to reach a stipulated production quota at the end of the month results in poor inspection when the speed of assembly is raised.' He added that loose nuts and empty sumps were common faults.

Thus a different brand name meant a different cylinder capacity and status—no more. The most to which the man in the street could aspire was the 1,100-cc Moskvitch, though as late as 1953 there were reputedly no servicing facilities even in Moscow itself. One step up was the Pobeda, the social equivalent of a Pontiac; while those who rated a chauffeur (and some ambassadors) used ZIMs in our period and Chaikas thereafter. The ZIS corresponded to a Cadillac 75 or straight-eight Daimler and was definitely not for sale. There was no true baby car before the introduction of the rear-engined Zaporozhets in 1960; the curious twin-cylinder Bielkas and NAMI 103s of 1956 with their Fiat Multipla layouts and swing-up front doors were purely experimental. The Jeep-based GAZ 67 and 69 4 × 4s, though sold to friendly armies and occasionally encountered in foreign lands, were not and are not at the time of writing commercially available in Russia.

Russian cars were a curious mixture of the well appointed and the austere. In a country with no garages, owners were expected to do their own servicing, and tool kits were far from the bent-wire jacks and clumsy wheel-braces all too often the norm in the west: the Moskvitch 402 boasted no fewer than 39 items. Other practical features were towing hooks front and rear and built-in radiator blinds, spring shackles were robustly attached, and radios and heaters were usually part of the package. Even on early Pobedas, two-speed wipers were standard equipment. By contrast, the colour choice was very limited: all Volgas came with identical interior trim. Nor could a Russian save money by dispensing with music while he drove.

The unhappy Moskvitch has probably attracted more opprobrium—not all of it just—than any other cheap car in history, inclusive of the Wolseley Hornet and the catastrophic Hillman Straight-Eight. The paint, upholstery and carburation came in for complaint, but this Russian-speaking Opel was a great step forward from the Model A Ford derivatives that had been the USSR's staple diet since 1931. These were, of course, still around: the 1½-ton GAZ AA truck was being made as late as 1947, as were the 3½-litre six-cylinder GAZ 11-73 saloons and tourers. The GAZ 67 'Red Jeep' was Ford based even down to the oval radiator badge—with Cyrillic script, of course—and the strip-type sparking-plug connections.

In 1947 form, the Moskvitch 401 was simply a four-door version of the 1938 Opel Kadett, built from tooling seized as reparations after the Second World War. Earlier Russian thinking had, however, followed this direction, since the KIM 10 light car of 1940 had much in common with the smaller products of General Motors. The unitary construction, the Dubonnet knee-action independent front suspension, the hypoid rear axle and the three-speed non-synchromesh gearbox with floor-mounted lever were pure

Rüsselsheim, as were the hydraulic brakes. The three-bearing 1,074-cc side-valve four-cylinder engine developed 24 bhp, and on a 5.17:1 top gear the 401 attained a sedate 57 mph. Road testers echoed the familiar complaints of 'dead' brakes and steering, but there was actually a choice of bodies, the range including a cabriolimousine and a station wagon. The output went up to 27 bhp in 1953, when the Moskvitch was also given synchromesh and column shift.

The 402 of 1956 was slightly better, though Russians were uninterested in styling and were content to ape the 1949 American idiom. The engine, now giving 35 bhp from 1.2 litres, was still a flathead, and the wheelbase, at 105 inches, was only fractionally longer. The old Dubonnet suspension gave way to unequal-length wishbones.

Unkind Western critics dismissed the Pobeda as 'a Communist Standard Vanguard', but they conveniently forgot that the Russian car had been demonstrated to the press in February 1946 and was actually in production fifteen months later. The fastback four-light saloon coachwork was obviously American inspired, but a fairer analysis of the car would be to describe it as an Opel Kapitän-type structure wedded to a 2.1-litre side-valve four of Willys ancestry. Understandably, the drive-line had a look of Ford about it, though the three-speed box had synchromesh on its two upper ratios. 12-volt electrics were a necessity in Russia, the coil-and-wishbone independent front suspension was conventional, and the Pobeda was intended for hard work rather than for the traffic-light Grand Prix. It weighed an even 3,000 lb, was flat out at 65 mph and took nearly 40 seconds to reach 60 mph. Variations on the basic GAZ M20 theme were the four-wheel drive M72 and the Warszawa made under licence in Poland.

The Pobeda was current until 1958, but its successor, the GAZ M21 Volga, reached the public during 1956. The styling was scaled-up Moskvitch 402, with a Buick-like grille, and the engine was a 'square' five-bearing overhead-valve (92 mm × 92 mm) 2.4-litre rated at 80 bhp. Performance was average for its class. A few hundred Volgas were made with American-type automatic gearboxes, but these were reserved for the home market, and in any case proved troublesome. The conventional three-speed manual type was standardized thereafter.

The seven-seater ZIM (GAZ 12) from the drawing-board of A. A. Lipgart looked like a 1942 90-series Buick but was structurally identical to the Pobeda, with a unitary hull and frontal 'wheelbarrow'. The engine, likewise, was a Pobeda with two extra cylinders, giving a capacity of 3,485-cc. The rest of it was copybook 1942 American style, though the three-speed synchromesh gearbox incorporated a fluid coupling. All the usual Russian 'extras' were inclusive, though no division was normally provided, and the wheelbase was a compact 126 inches. Amusingly, the English-language catalogue described the ZIM as 'a comfortable middle-class car capable of developing a speed of up to 120 km/h'. Its career spanned the 1950–9 period.

The revisionist revolution of the 1950s caused some semantic flutterings: in 1956 the Zavod Imieni Stalin (Stalin Motor Works) was renamed the Zavod Imieni Likhachev after a blameless and defunct Minister of Roads and Transport, but to the rest of the world Russia's *voiture d'apparat* remained a ZIS. It was not replaced by the new generation of vee-eights until 1958.

Opinions still differ on the ZIS 110's genesis. Some say that Franklin Delano Roosevelt caused Packard to 'volunteer' the tooling of their prestige 160–180, others that the Russians simply helped themselves. Whichever opinion is correct, the ZIS 110 was hard to distinguish from a 1942 Packard, just as its pre-war counterpart resembled a big Buick dressed up as a 1935 Chrysler. This meant a massive nine-bearing side-valve straight-eight engine, a three-speed gearbox, hypoid final drive, servo-assisted hydraulic brakes, coil spring independent front suspension and a robust chassis, in Packard's 148-inch wheelbase. Prestige called for power windows and whitewall tyres, conversion to metric measurements had reduced the capacity slightly to 5,750-cc, and low-octane fuel dictated a compression ratio of 6.5:1 on which the ZIS unit managed 137 bhp. The car was also built as a seven-passenger parade phaeton, a vehicle Americans had almost forgotten, even in 1942. In 1954 photographs were published of a bizarre sports coupé on a ZIS chassis. The wrapround screen incorporated triangular inserts, and the Russians had adopted Studebaker's 1950 missile-type grille, going one better with a third headlamp in the 'warhead'. Retention of the standard-length chassis resulted in a dream device rivalled only by Rust Heinz's 1938 Phantom Corsair. There is, alas! no evidence of any series production.

14 Great Britain

14.1 Export or Bust

From being a tight little island, Britain was suddenly plunged into the role of general provider.

In 1938 she had exported some 18–20% of her cars, mostly to Commonwealth countries: in Europe only Sweden and Denmark consistently took more than 1,000 units a year. 473 had gone to Belgium, and a low 212 to Switzerland. In 1946, however, over 86,000 of 219,162 new cars went abroad, a year later over 50% were exported, and by the early 1950s only about 35% of the output was destined for domestic customers. Even in 1956, when West Germany had edged ahead, 335,000 of Britain's cars helped to maintain the export drive.

'Export or bust' had been the message of Sir Stafford Cripps, Labour's austere Chancellor of the Exchequer, and Britain's motor industry took it to heart. Everything was available with left-hand drive and metric instruments, even Armstrong Siddeleys, Rovers and the other 'true Brits'. The first few thousand of a new model were invariably reserved for export: Jaguar's revolutionary XK120 never reached home buyers in any quantity, and not at all for the first eighteen months of its life. The same applied not only to American 'specials' such as the Austin–Nash Metropolitan but also to the Singer's SM Roadster, the Sunbeam Alpine and the Rolls–Royce Silver Dawn. The four-seater YT MG was not even quoted in England, while export-only variants were commonplace. From 1948, Ford Anglias destined for overseas used the 1,172-cc Prefect engine.

This method, however, had its snags. Unhappy foreigners had to cope with such teething problems as the Jowett Javelin's self-drowning propensities. This, allied to the linguistic limitations of smaller firms, rendered British cars less than popular in Europe. The Swiss accepted rather than welcomed the breed.

However, customers did not have much choice. Even if a nation's currency were 'hard' enough to allow imports from America, a Buick's 15-mpg consumption was a liability in a fuel-starved world. France, Germany and Italy alike were in no position to make 100,000 cars a year, much less the 200,000 of which Britain was already capable. Coventry's manufacturers might have suffered in the 1940 Blitz, but even Alvis, the worst victims, were back in production by the end of 1946. Rover and Singer transferred their operations to the Birmingham area. Further, such captains of industry as Lord Nuffield, Austin's Leonard Lord and Jaguar's William Lyons personally superintended their export drives. By January 1946, a brand-new Armstrong Siddeley Hurricane was touring America, and six months later Godfrey Imhof was demonstrating the as-yet untried J1 Allard in western Europe. Before the 1948 revolution, Allard had an agent in Prague; Ford Anglias went on sale in Sweden as early as the summer of 1945. The drive was maintained throughout the 1940s. 'Colour,' proclaimed Austin's 1947 advertising, 'comes back to motoring,' but 47,000 of the first 50,000 pastel-hued A40 saloons went abroad, all the same. Britons got the old-fashioned Sixteen, in black with brown leather upholstery.

There were other sacrifices in store. 'The British motorist,' opined *Autocar* in 1945, 'would be loth to have to do without a sliding roof,' but, though there was one on the warmed-over 1939 models of the first two seasons, it was omitted on the new generation of Morrises, Hillmans and Vauxhalls: experience showed that the device let in India's monsoon rains and Kenya's murrum dust. He also had to resign himself to PVC trim. Facias of metal or plastic replaced timber, expensive to 'tropicalize'. Windscreens no longer opened, while traditional styling gave way to variations on obsolescent American themes. Standard's stylist Frank Callaby was instructed to base his post-war shape on the 1941 Plymouth. If Fords and Vauxhalls were overtly American in concept, the influence of General Motors was detectable in Austins and Morrises alike, Rootes cars had a Chrysler look long before Chrysler owned a single share in the British firm, and the Singer SM1500 resembled Howard Darrin's Kaiser.

On the credit side, Britons got independent front suspension and unitary structures, the latter used by all 'the big six' by the end of our period, although larger family saloons (Humber, Standard) clung to separate chassis frames. Hydraulic brakes, confined among 1946's cheap cars to Nuffield, Singer and Vauxhall, were almost universal ten years later, though cautious British engineers were also addicted to the hydromechanical 'halfway house', a system not generally used elsewhere.

Worst of all, the British motorist was hemmed in by a spate of restrictions. Petrol was not finally derationed until 1950, while during the latter part of 1947 an adverse balance of payments caused the abolition even of the meagre basic allowance. Ever-increasing export quotas meant long waiting lists. My family ordered a Morris Oxford in November 1948: it was not ready until 1954, by which time we could no longer afford it. To prevent profiteering, the British Motor Trade Association imposed a twelve-month covenant on all new cars, soon extended to two years. The covenant scheme was still in operation at the beginning of 1953, though by this time only best-sellers and export favourites (Jaguar and MG) were still affected. Even if one waited one's turn, there was no choice of colour or equipment. One took what arrived, only to be saddled with an unwanted radio, which carried its own separate purchase tax.

Purchase tax was not, strictly, a new impost. It had been introduced as long ago as October 1940, when it meant nothing to anyone except a few 'essential users' with Ministry of War Transport permits. Thus its impact was not realized until 1945, at a rate of 33⅓%, thereby inflating the price of a Ford Anglia (£126 in 1940) to £293.

Nor was the rate constant. In 1947 the Treasury dug its own Rubicon, comparable with France's 15CV watershed: anything with a basic price of more than £1,000 paid double tax at 66⅔%. Specialist makers struggled to hold their prices down to £999, and sometimes they succeeded; but, although this was easy for Jaguar, with full order books and a potential of 10,000 units a year, it was harder for Lea–Francis, whose small factory could barely cope with a fifth of this quantity, much less market it. Double purchase tax applied to all goods from April 1951, and, though the rate fell to 50% two years later, it returned to 60% by the end of our period. Those who discovered the loophole of the 'shooting brake', still technically a commercial vehicle, were restricted to a statutory and even less acceptable 30 mph. In any case, by August 1950 station wagons had become cars, and tax had to be paid at the standard rate! The Land Rover's status, however, remained anomalous. No purchase tax was necessary, yet it was not a truck. I recall being stopped by a puzzled constable who was sure that I had committed an offence but could not pinpoint it. It took a High Court case in 1956 to define the position. In 1953 hire-purchase restrictions came into force as an 'economic regulator', to add to the joys of motoring.

Fortunately the horsepower tax had disappeared at the end of 1946, thus freeing designers from archaic stroke-bore ratios: the dimensions of Vauxhall's 1½-litre Wyvern engine changed from 69.5 mm × 95 mm to 79.4 mm × 76.2 mm, though not until 1952. The Government toyed with a sliding scale based on cubic capacity but wisely rejected this in favour of a flat rate of £10 per annum, albeit only on cars registered for the first time. (This was a godsend to purchasers of war-surplus Ford vee-eights—and also to owners of large thoroughbreds impressed by Civil Defence, which conveniently 'lost' their logbooks!) Treasury rating died hard: when petrol rationing returned briefly in the winter of 1956, I was delighted to discover that my 1938 1100 Fiat was still classed as a 12-hp car and thus entitled to more fuel than larger-engined Prefects and Minxes, which were Tens.

Britain's new role of general provider carried other implications. Ranges had to be rationalized, since a firm's steel allocation was assessed against its export potential. Thus the attitude of 'make what you can—somebody's bound to want it' was short-lived, even though the country was riding a seller's market as late as 1952.

Rationalization was certainly needed. In the immediate post-war period the Nuffield Organization ran to ten different engines of three different valve configurations, nine distinct and different chassis and nine body types. Rootes, with four engines and four sets of mechanical elements, were slightly less chaotic, but then both Hillman and Sunbeam–Talbot offered a choice of three body styles, and the Group made no sports car comparable with the MG. Vauxhall had two chassis and two engine variations. By 1949, however, medium-sized Morrises and Wolseleys were almost completely integrated, while Standard had opted not only for a one-model programme but had adapted their Vanguard's mechanics to the prestige Triumph line.

After the seller's market came 'the big squeeze'. There was barely room for six groups at the top. By 1951, the major six had become five, with the Austin–Nuffield merger. Singer, always an uneasy seventh, were stuck with the well-engineered but uncompetitive SM1500. Its annual sales potential was 7,000 at best, and there was no money to update it, *ergo* the company sold out to Rootes in 1956. Standard, next in line for relegation, held on until 1960 before surrendering to the Leyland commercial-vehicle empire. Four years later, Rootes, weakened by a costly baby-car programme, were easy meat for Chrysler of America.

The process repeated itself at more exalted levels, with the difference that specialist firms were not always worth taking over. The happy days of the 1930s, when chassis were chassis and a new model involved some mild shuffling of bores and strokes, were well and truly over. Retooling cost a cool half-million.

Hence the traditionalists were assailed from every side. At least some cars had to be sold abroad, and the cheapest model should be priced below the tax dividing line. Even if these criteria could be met, there were other manufacturers, and not necessarily foreign ones, eager to compete. Citroën and Renault, with long-established assembly plants and a sizable British content, retained their foothold, but otherwise imports were banned until mid-1953, when German and French cars were admitted. A year later the Italians and Americans were back, but even in 1955 imports amounted to a mere 11,131 units, with a sharp drop in 1956. The big foreign-car boom would not gather momentum until 1959.

Of the competitors, 'the big battalions' were bad enough. Nuffield offered MG, Riley and Wolseley, Rootes had Humber and Sunbeam–Talbot, and Standard had got into the act with the purchase of Triumph. Austin, who had always enjoyed a fair share of the formal-carriage market, countered with their poor man's Bentleys, the Sheerline and the Princess. When sales of these traditional items faltered, the American-owned groups took over with their jazzed-up tin sedans (Ford Zodiac, Vauxhall Cresta), a policy soon imitated by BMC's Austin A105. Even if Hawks and Westminsters offered no threat to Alvis, there were competitors nearer home: Jaguar and Rover, with sales large enough to pay for the wood and leather.

Already before the war the redoubtable William Lyons had slaughtered the Anglo-Americans on a combination of price, performance and lower taxable horsepower. Now he and Rover's Spencer Wilks would gradually pick off the opposition. Lea–Francis quit in 1954, Alvis moved up market in 1956, and Armstrong Siddeley had given up by the summer of 1960. Daimler played the role of David against three Goliaths, challenging Rover with their Conquests, Jaguar with their sports models and Rolls–Royce with the eight-cylinder DE36. They lost all three battles, even the Royal Family changed to Rolls–Royces (and to Rovers for personal transport!). A 'palace revolution' at the Radford works in 1956 came too late: four years later Jaguar were in possession of Britain's *marque doyenne*.

The ultraspecialists, however, prospered. Before the war Britain had exported what she made best—luxury carriages and sports cars. Rolls–Royce rode the crest of the wave, thanks to the new factory-bodied Standard Steel Bentleys, of which more than 7,000 had been sold by the beginning of 1955. This latter step was timely, for the specialist coach builders were in decline, and their interpretations of the new bulboid themes were often less than felicitous. By the end of our decade only Freestone and Webb, Hooper, H. J. Mulliner, Park Ward and Young were still active: notable casualties had included Gurney Nutting and Windovers, while Thrupp and Maberly now made only catalogued bodies for Rootes, and Vanden Plas fulfilled the same function for Austin.

The sports car, of course, was synonymous with the green of Britain. Porsche apart, there were no significant German contributions before 1954. Italy's wares, though magnificent, were made in small numbers. High taxation and empty exchequers had eliminated France, and the Chevrolet Corvette was still a bad joke. So British factories made hay.

Britain, however, did not benefit. Jaguar exported 96% of their 1952 output, and 10,621 of the 11,560 TD MGs made that year were destined for overseas customers. But scarcely a year passed without some landmark. Donald Healey set the pace in 1946 with his 2.4-litre, followed by the first XK Jaguar in 1948, Allard's J2 in 1949, the DB2 Aston Martin in 1950, the Austin–Healey and the TR Triumph in 1952 and AC's all-independently-sprung Ace a year later. The evergreen MG, which had introduced Americans to the joys of open-air motoring, was finally modernized in 1955 to become the best-selling MG A. Ancillary industries kept pace with these developments, and by the end of our period radial-ply tyres and disc brakes permitted the new standards of performance to be utilized to the full. The latter system, used on Jaguar's competition cars as early as 1952, had yet to enjoy widespread currency, though they were seen on production Jensens and Triumphs at Earls Court in October 1956.

Also making headway was a new if not specifically British breed—the kit-built sports car. The dollar crisis had administered the *coup de grâce* to the Euro-Americans—home-market Allards made do with the aged flathead Ford vee-eight—but much could be achieved with the 1,172-cc Ford Ten.

Having been around since 1935 this unit already supported its own bolt-on goody industry. Now it went into cheap machinery for trials, club racing and occasional road use: since the customer furnished the secondhand engines and gearboxes, he could also furnish the logbook of the rusted-out saloon or van whence these came. The stark Dellow sold quite well for several years, while Colin Chapman of Lotus used 'backgarden' specials as the jumping-off point for a meteoric career. In 1956 Lotuses and Turners were available in kit form, a method of 'manufacture' which obviated purchase tax even when the components were brand-new.

Mini-cars, by contrast, made little headway in Britain, although an assortment of curiosities were produced during the Suez Crisis of 1956 and struggled on for a few years thereafter. Though the Bond and the more substantial Reliant prospered, they were never a serious challenge to 'the big six'—Britons were too sybaritic and preferred 'real' cars. Just as in France and Germany the *deux-chevaux* and the Beetle played havoc with the Galys and the Gutbrods, so the British cycle-cars had an equally formidable opponent, the Ford Popular. More austere than France's *berlines 'affaires'*, old fashioned in concept and neither fast nor frugal, this boxy little saloon was a full-sized affair costing £414 in 1956, as against £319 for a Bond and £430 for a Reliant. Later, the Italo-German Isetta and the all-German Messerschmitt would enjoy a brief vogue with the Chelsea Set, but by 1959 the Mini would have superseded these, too.

The British family car remained uninspiring. Even in 1956, no mass-production model had all-independent springing, and without exception everything in the under-£1,000 category followed the *système* Panhard, with vertical front-mounted water-cooled engines driving the rear wheels.

Designing for the world had stifled individuality. British roads had called for sophisticated gearboxes in the 1930s, but there was little follow-up after 1945, and by 1956 only Daimler and Armstrong Siddeley remained faithful to the excellent preselective system. Automatics were just beginning to make an impact: at the last Earls Court Show of our period bigger Ford and BMC saloons appeared with Borg–Warner transmissions, following the lead of Armstrong Siddeley, Bentley, Jaguar and Rolls–Royce in the prestige class.

The automatic's power losses were, of course, too much for the 50–55 bhp of contemporary 1½-litre engines. Home-market customers were not interested, and the cost of such transmissions would price the cars out of the best export fields. A fad of 1956 was the Manumatic automatic clutch; in theory it offered the best of both worlds, but it did not last long.

More typically British was overdrive. Not, be it said, the simple American automatic system with its kickdown, but a manually selected device often operative on more than one ratio. Except when the solenoid misbehaved, it worked quite well, and, on overloaded 1½-litre saloons, at least 60% of the available gears had some practical application. It was not however the brightest of ideas to place the selector switch on the steering column next to the turn-indicator switch; a driver anxious to signal a right turn was likely to hole out in overdrive second, never a helpful ratio at any time! The worst excesses of this system lay in the future. Nevertheless, twelve British makes had an overdrive option in 1956, Bristol and Jensen fitting it as standard equipment.

Styling fads came and went. British makers, like their American counter-parts, utilized two-toning and chromium strip to eke out tooling costs. The Phase III Hillman Minx of 1949 lasted into mid-1956 with suitable atten-tion to grille and side-trim. Austin's saloon style changed from six to four lights in 1951, to eliminate a 1940 Chevrolet look which was fine until Chevrolet themselves introduced a brand-new shape. Rootes had a hardtop à l'Américaine in the 1953 Hillman line. As elsewhere in Europe, column shift was a disaster, since four-speed 'gates' were never really viable. Austin, Morris and Rootes all had appalling gearchanges, though those on the three-speed Fords, Vauxhalls and Standard Vanguards were less bad. Fortunately in 1956 there was a swing away from column shifts, Nuffield even essaying a Rolls–Royce-type right-hand change. Razor-edged styling, a British innovation of the mid-1930s, did not sort well with the new bulboid, though in the early post-war years two uncompromisingly tradi-tional shapes—the big Triumph and the Austin Sheerline—were very suc-cessful. The less said of Triumph's Mayflower the better.

However, even if the Beetle, the Dauphine and the 600 Fiat were making inroads into British preeminence by 1956, Britain still offered more variety than any other country—and her best was very good indeed.

14.2   Super Scooters for Suez?

In 1946, Morgan's classic three-wheelers were still in evidence, though sales had already taken a tumble: only 29 had been sold in 1939. The hairy Super Sports with exposed vee-twin engine was a thing of the past, although a farewell batch was sent to Australia shortly after the war.

Surviving models were altogether staider. These retained the Z-section frame, the chain drive to the single rear wheel and the coil-and-sliding-pillar independent front suspension used since 1910, but engines were now the ubiquitous four-cylinder side-valve Fords of 933-cc and 1,172-cc, mounted in unit with three-speed synchromesh gearboxes, also of Ford make. The rod-operated Girling brakes were of the coupled type, and the 10-hp F-Super was quite fast, cruising at 65 mph on a 4.58:1 top gear, but the cars were only a pale echo of past glories. In any case, the four-wheeled models were prospering, especially since the advent of the big Plus-Four in 1950. The last 'trike' was delivered in February 1952.

Some of the Morgan aura, however, communicated itself to the Berkeley, a Laurie Bond creation announced in 1956, and manufactured by Charles Panter's go-ahead trailer-home firm at Biggleswade. This astonishing little four-wheeler resembled a baby Austin–Healey and yet was built up from three sections of bolted-up glassfibre and an aluminium bulkhead. In the nose there was an air-cooled two-stroke motor-cycle engine driving the front wheels by open chains, through the medium of a motor-cycle-type multi-plate clutch and three-speed gearbox. The positive-stop gearchange was column mounted, and the Berkeley used all-independent suspension, by coils and wishbones at the front and swing axles and coils at the rear. The 12-inch wheels carried 7-inch brake drums with hydraulic actuation. Detail work was crude, but the car weighed only 732 lb, attained 65 mph and cruised at 60. Initially a 322-cc twin-cylinder British Anzani engine was fitted, but this gave trouble and was replaced by the 18-bhp Excelsior, of 328-cc. Berkeleys were made in various forms until 1960.

Rather less sporting was Air Vice-Marshal Donald Bennett's Fairthorpe Atom, an egg-shape launched in 1954. The engine was at the rear of a tubular backbone frame: like the Berkeley, the Fairthorpe Atom also featured all-independent suspension, hydraulic brakes, a motor-cycle-type transmission and glassfibre bodywork, in this case a two-seater coupé with curious oval side-windows. Tubeless tyres were standard with the optional 13-inch wheels, a differential was an extra, and the cars were available with a variety of engines, from a 250-cc BSA single, which gave 45 mph and 70 mpg, to their 650-cc vertical-twin, in which case the Atom was good for 75 mph. Fairthorpe also tried the unloved Anzani, finding it 'perfectly satisfactory', but the credit squeeze put an end to this miniature after only 44 had been sold.

Reliant of Tamworth had been in business since 1935, when they had acquired the rights of Raleigh's Safety Seven three-wheeler. To this they had added, in 1939, the recently defunct 747-cc four-cylinder Baby Austin engine. Until 1952, light vans had been Reliant's sole interest, and their Regal tourer used a van chassis, with a short bonnet and enclosed fork for the single front wheel. The rectangular box-section frame, spiral bevel back axle and semielliptic rear springs were Raleigh heritages, the Austin-type engine gave 16 bhp, and the three-speed gearbox was without synchromesh. This and the two rear cylinders projected into the cockpit with adverse effects on front-seat legroom, but the Reliant was a four-seater and boasted coupled hydraulic brakes. The Regal III of 1956 featured a more curvaceous bodywork in glassfibre, a hardtop and synchromesh. Despite uncertain handling and a ride described as 'violent', the Reliant appealed to side-car enthusiasts, while the lower rate of tax compensated for a list price £16 higher than the Ford Popular's. The aged engine soldiered on into 1962 before giving way to Reliant's own overhead-valve unit.

Far less successful was the ugly little Rodley which originated in Leeds in 1954. 'The cheapest four-wheel car in Britain' cost £299 and was a steel-panelled rolltop convertible best described as angular *topolino*, with room in the back for two legless passengers. A 750-cc vee-twin JAP engine lived at the rear, driving the rear wheels by chain, the gearbox was of a motor-cycle type, and only the front wheels were independently sprung. The mechanical brakes and chain-type steering were a little primitive, even in this class.

The mini-car specialist Laurie Bond was almost as prolific as Egon Brütsch, but his first 1948 effort was his most successful, enjoying a seventeen-year run. It arrived at the nadir of Crippsian austerity; thus a specification summarized by the motor-cycling writer C. P. Read as a 'Shakespearian "sans everything" ' was acceptable. Read actually dared to drive an early example from the factory at Preston to Geneva and back. He made it, though the climb over the Jura melted the grease in the rear hubs, 'thus removing what brakes the wheels had'.

The Bond's stressed-skin unitary construction was very light, thanks to the aluminium panelling, though doors were impossible. At the front of this structure lived a coil-sprung fork, and a 122-cc two-stroke Villiers single-cylinder engine which delivered its 5 bhp to the single front wheel via a three-speed gearbox without reverse and a roller chain. That was all. The rear suspension was the responsibility of the fat 16×4 tyres, the rod-operated brakes worked on the rear wheels only, steering was by cable and pulley, and another cable actuated the mechanical starter. Weighing a mere 200 lb, the Bond cost less than £200. Car-type controls soon followed, though the column shift retained positive–stop configuration. By 1950 the capacity was up to 197-cc, with a speed of 43 mph on a 4:1 top gear, and an 80 mpg consumption which allowed 400 pleasure miles a month on the meagre basic ration.

The Bond was steadily refined, acquiring a proper glass screen and a coil-spring rear suspension in 1951. The 1952 C-type had three-wheel brakes and could be obtained with electric starting, while by 1954 the family model offered a child's hammock seat at the back, the latest 8E Villiers engine coping with a weight of 460 lb. A year later came new bonded-rubber springing and part-glassfibre construction. The 1957 Bonds had Siba Dynastarts and reversible engines; the E-type at £340 was quite a pretty little car with a separate steel chassis (doors at last!), winkers, a bench seat 48 inches wide and enough power to sustain a weight that had tripled in eight years. Wider front wings allowed 90-degree turns, though such evolutions were too alarming to be lightly essayed!

Others sought to repeat the Bond's success. 1951 saw the Minnow with a

Morgan-style independent front suspension and a rear-mounted 250-cc Excelsior engine driving the single rear wheel. The alloy-panelled two-seater body had a Vintage look and comprehensive weather protection, but there were no buyers at £468. The same applied to the Pashley, a 1953 offering on Bond lines, with the same Villiers engine driving the front wheel. The equipment was more luxurious: coupled brakes, electric starting, two doors and chromium-plated bumpers at both ends, but Pashley found that powered rickshaws for the Mystic Orient were a better bet. The EECC hailed, improbably, from Totnes in Devon and featured an electrically welded frame as well as an Isetta-style swing-up front door. It was only 105 inches long, weighed 588 lb and used the 250-cc Excelsior engine. Nothing was heard of it after 1954.

Of the small four-wheelers, D. A. Russell's Russon Cars actually sold fifteen two-seaters between 1951 and 1953, despite a price of £491. The formula was familiar—tiny wheels, a rear engine (Villiers, JAP and Excelsior units were all tried), Albion gearboxes, a chain drive and a twin-tube frame. The wheelbase was a generous 80 inches, but the Russon was heavy, at 1,008 lb, as well as expensive. An even obscurer contemporary was the RNW, Villiers-powered this time but with a rubber suspension incorporating swing axles at the rear. R. N. Wellington also offered a special version for disabled drivers, but the Ministry of Pensions preferred their 'official' ACs.

AC had started out with three-wheelers in 1907, but their 1953 Petite (not an invalid car) was a far cry from the original Sociable, with which it shared only a rear engine location and chain final drive. There were two driven rear wheels, and the unitary structure included a rubber-mounted boom for the 346-cc Villiers power unit, its three-speed and reverse gearbox, and the differential. The well-appointed rolltop coupé coachwork was panelled in aluminium, and an unusual refinement was a warning light for neutral. The rear suspension was by coils and trailing arms, but the vee-belt primary drive was a trifle archaic, and, though the Girling brakes were hydraulically actuated, they worked on the rear wheels only. The makers called it 'a full-size car', and it was, 123 inches long and weighing 840 lb. The cruising speed was a leisured 30 mph, but the Petite was noisy and ran very hot, possibly because of overzealous attempts at sound-proofing. Production was running at 20 a week towards the end of 1953, and the Petite was still quoted in 1958—unlike another effort by a specialist manufacturer, Allard's Clipper, of which less than 30 were made.

This 1954 entry shared the AC's layout and transmission arrangements, though it featured a separate cruciform-braced frame and rubber suspension. It was also more curvaceous, being fabricated from self-coloured blue-and-white plastic. Once again the absence of a suitable engine was the main bugbear; various types, including the Anzani, were tried. When Allard gave up the unequal struggle, designer David Gottlieb moved on to Wood Green, where he launched his Powerdrive in 1956.

This time he used a single chain-driven rear wheel and the 322-cc Anzani engine; the result was a miniature convertible in the American idiom. Once again there were three forward speeds, their ratios selected by a pendant Citroën-type lever on the dashboard, and other features were a coil-spring independent front suspension and hydraulic brakes, though the twin-tube frame differed from the earlier Allard type. The dummy radiator grille carried a lion's head motif. One may doubt however, if the maker's claims of 65 mph and 65 mpg were within the Anzani's compass, and most people preferred to part with an extra twenty shillings and buy a Ford Popular. In 1958 the Powerdrive would reappear under new sponsorship with a new name (Coronet) and glassfibre coachwork.

British Anzani themselves explored the mini-car market in 1956 with the Astra, previously sold by Jarc of Isleworth as the Little Horse. This was a baby woody intended for 400-lb payloads rather than for passengers, and only a single seat was normally provided. Apart from the 12-inch wheels, the Astra had a conventional appearance, though the engine (predictably an Anzani, though Jarc Motors had favoured the Excelsior) was disposed horizontally under the floor at the back. The suspension was by swing arm and coil at both ends, and the brakes were hydraulic. For all its utilitarian appearance, the Astra handled quite well and was good for 55 mph. Even in kit form, however, it found precious few buyers.

The Gordon of 1954 hailed from Liverpool and was sponsored by Vernons Pools. Erling Poppe, its designer, had been responsible for the last Sunbeam motor-cycles, but none of their refinement had rubbed off on the three-wheeler. The 197-cc Villiers engine was offset to the right of the backbone frame, which necessitated a lateral bulge to house the chain drive. The front fork was of Metalastik type, with a coil-and-trailing arm suspension at the rear, the bodywork was a composite steel-and-aluminium affair, and a weight of 716 lb called for a 7.76:1 top gear. The Gordon was a very occasional four-seater, but, though electric and kick starters were provided, a reverse was not, and the mechanical brakes were uncoupled. At £270, it was cheaper than most miniatures and survived the Suez boom by about a year.

The Tourette coincided almost exactly with Suez. Its sponsors sold Messerschmitts in Surrey, which explains the presence of Messerschmitt front wheels, brakes, hubs and stub axles on the thirty-odd cars that were built. The vehicle itself was yet another variation on a theme by Egon Brütsch, though like the Swiss Belcar it was not unitary, featuring a tubular frame and bodywork in self-coloured ivory plastic or light alloy (the latter never materialized, so the company hurriedly introduced a choice of three colours!). The brakes were uncoupled, a Siba Dynastart was regular equipment, and once again a 197-cc Villiers engine supplied the power. Prices started at £288.

Also a Suez baby was Laurie Bond's Unicar, made at Boreham by Opperman. This one, like the better-known Berkeley, made liberal use of glassfibre, for the chassis platform as well as for the two-seater coupé body, which had Citroën-type hammock seats and a peg adjustment more civilized than the Berkeley's push-and-pull webbing straps. Mechanical brakes sufficed; as on all Bond designs the suspension was ingenious, with Girling struts at the front and a primitive swing-axle arrangement at the rear. The 322-cc Anzani engine was mounted amidships, driving the solid rear axle via the usual Albion gearbox and roller chain. Despite a 72-inch wheelbase the Unicar was quite roomy, and the weight was an average 728 lb. The vehicle was also very noisy. Once again the Anzani soon gave way to an Excelsior, and towards the end of the Unicar's run it was listed in kit form. There was even a handsome sports coupé, the Stirling, into which Oppermans planned to fit the potent little four-stroke Steyr–Puch 500 unit, but by 1958 the bubble-car boom was over. A year later the standard Unicar had disappeared as well. Only about 200 were made.

The Larmar of 1946 was before its time. Conceived as an invalid carriage, it was also available with conventional controls. In appearance it resembled later Rovins, the front suspension was of Morgan type with swing arms at the rear, and the rear-mounted power pack contained a three-speed gearbox and a 250-cc four-stroke single-cylinder engine. It had a five-year run.

14.3   And Then There Were Five

In 1945 Austin and Morris were still hated rivals, pursued by Ford, Rootes, Standard and Vauxhall. Moreover, it seemed that there might be a new contender in the best-selling stakes.

Denis Kendall, Grantham's Independent MP, entertained dreams of a £100 people's car, with an engine applicable also to a people's tractor. To this end he enlisted the aid of M. C. Beaumont, a veteran protagonist of the small air-cooled radial. The result of their labours was on the road by August 1945.

The Kendall–Beaumont was a curious mixture of sophistication and barbarity. The 595-cc overhead-valve three-cylinder engine was said to have given 25 bhp in bench tests; it was mounted in unit with a three-speed gearbox at the rear of a pressed-steel unitary structure, though the independent front suspension mentioned in preliminary press releases had given way to conventional semielliptics. The simple two-door saloon coachwork incorporated recessed door handles, but Kendalls were innocent of either differential or synchromesh, a mechanical starter was deemed sufficient, and

Kendall, like Citroën on their first 2CV prototypes, hoped to get by with a single headlamp.

Unfortunately the car did not work. There were ideas of using the Douglas flat-twin (which had already proved itself) in place of Beaumont's radial, but at this juncture Kendall discovered the Aluminium Française–Grégoire. This he proposed to market in its original form, with a 595-cc overhead-valve flat-twin engine driving the front wheels, though hydromechanical brakes would be substituted for full hydraulics. By early 1946 the Grégoire had supplanted the original design in Grantham Productions' publicity. 'The minor car with major performance' would appeal to 'the smaller salaried family man, the business man or woman to whom comfort plus economy is essential, and for families who so often say, "We *do* need a second car" '. Initial deliveries were promised in July. Nothing, however, materialized beyond a deficiency of £445,000, though Lawrence Hartnett salvaged the remnants of Grantham Productions and would later try to make A.F.G's in Australia.

Not that these events worried Leonard Lord, whose Austin Motor Company delivered its millionth car just as Kendall's house of cards collapsed. Over half the British cars sent abroad between January and April had been Austins, while at home the *marque* commanded 29% of 8-hp sales cars not to mention a third of the Tens.

In spite of all this, Austin were still making pre-war cars. The 900-cc Eight and 1,125-cc Ten dated from 1939, and the 1½-litre Twelve had received its new alligator type bonnet for the aborted 1940 season. All three used three-bearing side-valve four-cylinder engines of conservative design and rating, downdraught carburetters and wide-ratio four-speed synchromesh gearboxes. Welded box-section frames were common to all Austins, though the Twelve's had a non-integral floor pan, the brakes were rod-operated mechanicals, and suspension was semielliptic. The Austin Eight attained 56 mph and 39 mpg: the Ten was only a little faster on 32 bhp. Radio and heater were regular options on the Twelve, which could also be obtained with a 2.2-litre (79.4 mm × 111.1 mm) engine as the Austin Sixteen. Here was rank heresy, for the valves were upstairs, and the unit disposed of 67 bhp, sufficient to propel the car at 75 mph, though the acceleration was negligible. The Sixteen served as the basis of Austin's first post-war taxi-cab, announced in 1948, and available in limousine form. It differed from the regular version in its commercial-vehicle styling and worm-drive back axle.

In fact the 'new' heresy was of long standing. A four-bearing 3½-litre pushrod six (uncommonly like the large Vauxhall) had been used in Austin's all-new 1939 truck range. It was only a matter of time before it was applied to private cars, though the marriage was not consummated until the 1947 Geneva Show.

Here was even worse heresy. There had been luxurious Austins before, but they had always been of the chauffeur-driven type. Further, the new A110 Sheerline and A120 Princess resembled no previous Austin, with their vee-grilles, vee-screens and razor-edge sports saloon bodies suggestive of poor man's Bentleys. Under their bonnets were the 3,460-cc truck engines in unit with four-speed gearboxes. The hypoid rear axles were a novelty, as was the coil-and-wishbone independent front suspension. Frames were cruciform braced and extremely rigid, the brakes were 2LS hydraulics, and even the basic Sheerline came complete with radio, twin heaters, clock, twin foglamps, twin windtone horns and exposed P100 lamps. Better still, it retailed at a low £1,279. The Princess's triple SU carburetters boosted output to 120 bhp; this model was an altogether costlier affair, featuring light alloy coachwork by the Austin-owned Vanden Plas company. The headlamps were recessed in the wings, and the slab-sided styling was less felicitous than the Sheerline's uncluttered shape, but the car was still much cheaper than a Bentley at £1,917.

The production A125 and A135 had 4-litre engines and an extra 10 bhp. The Sheerline was well enough liked, though it was somewhat undergeared, running out of steam at 50 mph in third. The high level of the appointments was also marred by a nasty steering-column change and ugly rectangular instruments. The Princess weighed almost 2 tons and could achieve 90 mph as against the Sheerline's 80 mph. It was, however, a handful on corners and not overly suitable for the owner–driver. After 1950, Austin wisely gave it a chauffeur-driven image, and single-carburetter manifolds were standardized. The Sheerline's last season was 1954, a long-chassis limousine edition being short lived. The Princess, however, enjoyed a twenty-year run with a facelift in 1951 and an automatic-gearbox option from 1956. A seven-seater model on a 132-inch wheelbase made its appearance in 1953, and the 1957 season would see the rare DM7 sports saloon with automatic transmission as standard.

The Sheerline's basic specification—though not, alas! its styling—was applied a few months later to a replacement for the Eight and the Ten, the 1,200-cc A40. On this one, hydromechanical brakes were used, but the latest three-bearing overhead-valve power unit no longer had to be a ten; the bore was opened up to 65.5 mm, with a shorter 89 mm stroke. The output was 40 bhp at 4,300 rpm. Styling was 1940 Chevrolet with a separate wing line, but the rounded grille was entirely new, the 'Austin of England' script emphasizing the car's export potential. Better still, the new Dorset and Devon saloons were available in a selection of pastel shades, a welcome change from the uniform black-with-brown leather of early post-war days. Unusually for the period, the A40 kept its gear lever on the floor and could be had with a sliding roof. On a weight of 1 ton it was much faster than the Ten, without any loss of top-gear flexibility.

Neither a rolling gait nor uncertain brakes affected the model's popularity in America, despite the unconscious *double entendre* of contemporary publicity ('Let's take the Austin: the car that is always at home'!). A metal station wagon joined the range in 1949, and the Devon was listed until 1952; the last models had column shift and full hydraulic brakes. An interesting if unsuccessful variant was the Jensen-bodied Sports of 1951, a pretty little convertible resembling a scaled-down Jensen Interceptor. In twin-carburetter form the engine gave 50 bhp, and the top speed was close to 80 mph. Unfortunately, nobody wanted pseudo-sports cars any more.

Though Sixteens were still being made for the home market in 1949, its successor had already appeared, one of two new large fours which gave Austin the most comprehensive range of any European manufacturer. The A70 Hampshire was Longbridge's answer to the Standard Vanguard and the Vauxhall Velox, and the formula was the same—an A40 body and a Sixteen engine on a short 96-inch wheelbase. The car was faster than its rivals and turned in a frugal 23 mpg, but the legroom was limited. Handling was like the A40's, only more so.

The companion A90 Atlantic was an attempt at an American-type convertible for Americans, complete with power hood and an appalling parody of Detroit styling—sloping nose, recessed headlamps, a central spotlamp, gold dials on the facia and a Pontiac-type plated streak on the bonnet top. Lamentably, such stylistic excesses demand a long wheelbase, and the A90 ran to a mere 96 inches, although a formidable overhang at both ends gave it a length of 177 inches. The mechanical specification was copybook Austin, only this time they had come up with a hefty 2,660-cc twin-carburetter unit pushing out 88 bhp at 4,400 rpm.

The A90 pitched alarmingly. It was, however, fast enough, attaining over 90 mph on a 3.67:1 rear axle, with a 0–60 mph acceleration time of 16.6 seconds. Even a successful attack on American stock-car records at Indianapolis could not sell the car to Americans: after all, the same $2,460 would buy eight-cylinders, automatic, and a better ride. From 1950 the original BE1 gave way to the BE2, a hardtop with lower gearing. In 1951 the cars were given full hydraulic brakes, but it took another year to clear the stocks on hand. The engine received a new lease of life in the Austin–Healey sports car.

America had already changed to four-light styling: so did Austin on their Hampshire replacement, the Hereford of 1951, a six-seater with an extra 3 inches of wheelbase. The brakes were, of course, hydraulic. Driven in a sedate manner, this was an excellent family saloon, but soggy suspension, low-geared steering and vicious roll oversteer discouraged the enthusiastic motorist. The same applied to the companion A40 Somerset of 1952, though this was lighter and more accelerative than the contemporary Hillman Minx, and the retention of a chassis made it less rustprone. The drophead coupé version was very popular, and the Somerset—like the later

Cambridge—was made under licence in Japan by Nissan. A40 mechanical elements would also form the basis of the Anglo-American Metropolitan.

Stressed-skin unitary construction characterized Austin's long awaited baby car, the A30 of 1952. 136½ inches long and 55 inches wide, it was more compact than the Morris Minor, though in other respects it fell far short of Morris standards. Surprisingly, it survived the BMC merger, continuing alongside the Minor even after this latter had been given Austin's excellent A-type engine, a 58 mm × 76 mm (803-cc) four, giving 28 bhp at 4,700 rpm. The car was lighter than its principal rival, at 1,414 lb, and actually higher geared, though nobody would have known this. Economy was exemplary (45 mpg were commonplace), but a narrow track had been adopted in the interests of compactness, and handling was terrible. Driven to capacity, it displayed a penchant for lying down on its door handles, and on motorways, for which, of course, it was never designed—it was perilous in the extreme. On the credit side, its reliability was proverbial. A higher ratio axle was standardized during 1954, and by 1956 the range incorporated two- and four-door saloons, a station wagon and even an Australian-style coupé utility. Its 1957 replacement, the A35, used a bigger 948-cc engine.

Meanwhile the effects of the Austin–Morris merger became apparent. The new BMC management scrapped the entire Morris engine programme: henceforth Austin's pushrod units would be used. Intriguingly, though, the first car to use the durable 1,489-cc four-cylinder B-type was the MG Magnette, a good year ahead of any Austin!

In 1955 the rest of the Austin range, apart from the Princess, went unitary. Also common to the new intermediate models were simpler and more angular four-light styling and rectangular radiator grilles. Clutches were given hydraulic actuation. The Somerset's replacement was the Cambridge on a 99¼-inch wheelbase, available either with the A40 unit or with the 73 mm × 89 mm 1½-litre B-type. The six-cylinder Westminster was Austin's answer to the Ford Zephyr; the C-type engine had a slightly larger bore of 79.4 mm for a capacity of 2.6 litres and a Weslake-designed cylinder head. The brake drum diameter on the sixes was 11 inches as against the Cambridge's 9 inches, and the speed was in the low nineties. The handling characteristics were described as 'neutral', and sliding roofs were still an option on A50s and A90s. The line continued into 1956 with minimal change, apart from an overdrive option for the A90. Automatic transmission was available for 1957.

There had, however, been a mid-season Austin, the A105. With the C-type engine already offered in Austin, Morris and Wolseley models, this should have been superfluous, but the company needed an answer to the luxury compacts—Ford's Zodiac and Vauxhall's Cresta. Hence the whitewall tyres, the two-tone finish and the twin spotlamps to which were added a twin-carburetter engine giving 102 bhp, a lowered suspension and brake-cooling slots in the wheels. There was also multiple overdrive—on the three higher ratios. This was of questionable value, since direct top overlapped with overdrive third, and direct third with overdrive second. The A105, however, could attain 95–100 mph, returned 30 mpg with gentle driving and helped Austin sell 30,000 medium-sized sixes that year.

Morris pursued an independent existence until 1951. In pre-Austin days, rationalization was not understood, and almost anything could happen in the engine department, even in 1949: side valves for the cheapest cars, orthodox pushrods for MGs, pushrods with twin high-set camshafts for Rileys, and a new programme of overhead-camshaft sixes for the MS-type Morris and its Wolseley cousins. There were other anomalies: the old long-stroke 1,548-cc flathead, long banished from private cars, still soldiered on in Morris 10-cwt vans, yet the parallel Morris-Commercial, also a ½-ton van, used another 1½-litre side-valve engine, the short-stroke type found in the latest Morris Oxfords!

Until 1948, however, Morris themselves were content with a two-model programme, adding about 60,000 Series E Eights and 53,566 Series M Tens to the total. Neither model was changed from 1939, and features common to both were SU carburetters and electric pumps, four-speed synchromesh gearboxes with central change, single-plate clutches (the old Morris wet-plate affair had disappeared), hydraulic brakes and Bishop cam steering. The Series E used a 918-cc three-bearing side-valve engine, while its bug-eye headlamps and alligator-type bonnet with fixed sides no longer looked ultramodern. It managed 60 mph, though not everyone appreciated the ultraflexible gearbox mountings, which caused the lever to 'float' most disconcertingly. The Ten had unitary construction, and its 1,140-cc pushrod engine was pump cooled, whereas the Eight favoured thermosyphon circulation. Designed for independent front suspension, the larger Morris retained semielliptic springs, with an auxiliary torsion bar at the front; this was said to eliminate roll, but did not. The car was listed at £432, and a sliding roof was optional. The Series M Ten would be the first car to be produced in series in India, leading to a whole line of Minors and Oxfords; the 1958 Series III version of the latter was still being turned out in 1977.

The Morris Eight and Ten looked old fashioned alongside Austin's colourful A40s, but at Earls Court in 1948 Britons got their first sight of a brilliant new line, the work of Alec Issigonis and Jack Daniels. Beneath the familiar American bulboid were such modern features as unitary construction, torsion-bar independent front suspension, hypoid rear axles and (on the four-cylinder cars) excellent rack-and-pinion steering.

Star of the collection was the MM-series Minor, a neat little car on an 86-inch wheelbase—shorter than that of the old Morris Eight though in fact the Minor was 4 inches longer, and the only room lost was the result of intrusive front-wheel arches. Better aerodynamics permitted higher gearing, and the new model pulled a 4.55:1 top, as against the Eight's 5.286:1. The price of this was indifferent top-gear acceleration, while for budgetary reasons Issigonis and Daniels had had to discard a promising flat-four engine (which explained the wide bonnet) in favour of the aged 8-hp unit, looking out of place in these sophisticated surroundings. Even a good *topolino* could beat a Minor to 30 mph. Handling, however, set new standards, and the tuners were soon at work on the Minor. Modifications ranged from special cylinder heads to heart transplants, among these latter the Austin A40 and overhead-camshaft Coventry-Climax units. The Minor could take it.

Billed by *The Motor* as 'a very good 8-hp car indeed', the Minor was available as a two-door saloon or as an attractive tourer. A four-door saloon joined the range in 1951 and a station wagon in 1954. Late in 1952 the car was given the engine it deserved, Austin's 803-cc overhead-valve A-type. At the very end of our period, the Minor, like the A30, received the 37-bhp 948-cc unit, which boosted top speed of the 1000 series into the low seventies.

The Minor outlived all the other Cowley designs. The quarter-millionth was delivered in the spring of 1954, the half-millionth in June 1957, and the millionth in January 1961. In October 1970, the last Minor, number 1,582,302, left Cowley, killed off to make room for the uninspired Marina. An era had ended.

Curiously the MO-series Oxford, though built on identical principles, was a stolid vehicle. In scaled-up form the compound curves were less pleasing, and in the 1½-litre category column shift was the order of the day. Further, the side-valve engine, though disposing of an adequate 41 bhp, gave a less than scintillating performance. The Oxford was not excessively heavy, at 2,212 lb, and it was stabler than either A40 or Minx. Sales were 135,000 units up to mid-1954.

The MS-type Six used the Oxford's chassis-body structure, the only major difference being the low-geared and woolly Bishop cam steering. The wheelbase was increased from 97 to 110 inches to make room for a new four-bearing six with a gear-driven overhead camshaft. The cylinder dimensions were the same as those of the Morris Oxford at 73 mm × 87 mm (2,215-cc), and an output of 65–70 bhp sufficed for speeds in excess of 80 mph. On this model the alligator-type bonnet terminated in an authentic 1938 Morris grille, retained, it was said, at Lord Nuffield's request. The MS could outperform, if not outaccelerate, most of the opposition. Unfortunately, the engine was difficult to service, the long bonnet impeded vision, and handling was poor. Unlike its Wolseley relatives, favoured, as ever, by the police, the Morris Six found little favour anywhere, and only about 12,400 had been made when it was quietly dropped in 1954.

BMC rationalization could not, of course, halt Cowley's chassis pro-gramme, and, though all subsequent models used Austin engines, they retained SU carburetters and electric pumps, whereas Austins stayed dog-gedly with Zeniths, fed by mechanical pump. This formula covered the Series II Oxford and Cowley introduced during 1954. Both used longer and lower hulls with wider doors, one-piece screens and larger boots. Into these went Austin engines—in the Oxford's case the 1½-litre B-type—and Morris suspension units. Offset steering made the column shift worse than ever. The Cowley was the same car with an A40 engine and a simplified trim. It was underpowered and underbraked, and sold only 17,400 to the Oxford's 87,400. It was given Oxford brakes in 1955 and the 1½-litre unit for 1957, by which time it had lost its *raison d'être*. At the end of our period the Oxford—but not the Cowley—was available with Manumatic two-pedal drive.

The last true Morris bore the respected name of Isis. It was an elongated Oxford with 2.6-litre C-type six-cylinder engine and was excellent pound-for-pound value: at the end of our period it matched the Ford Zephyr's price of £911, undercutting the Vauxhall Velox by £72 and the Austin A95 by £121. Unfortunately, the low-geared Bishop cam steering was used, and it was a repetition of the MS-type story—too much bonnet and indifferent handling. Overdrive was available in 1956, and automatic transmission on the Series II of 1957, which had a floor-mounted right-hand shift (Morris's first since 1916!) as standard. A speed of 90 mph was possible, but the Isis was phased out in March 1958, after 13,500 had been made.

Ford's British operation would become the last bastion of the Model A idiom—transverse-leaf springs at each end of simple channel-section frames, rod-operated mechanical brakes, four-cylinder side-valve engines, three-speed gearboxes, torque tube drive and a combination of short wheelbase and narrow track which led to a bouncy ride. The unsilenced carburetter air intakes emitted a throaty roar, and an ability to negotiate farm tracks at 30 mph was balanced by strange behaviour on icy roads. The cars were, how-ever, tough and cheap; in 1945 the 933-cc two-door Ford Anglia cost £293, and the four-door 1,172-cc Ford Prefect only £59 more. Both went into 1953 with minimal change, though from 1949 Anglias received new grilles similar to those of 1938 Tens (which style, in unmodified form, was actually used in some export markets), and the Prefect's headlamps vanished apologetically into a parody of Dearborn's 1942 box fenders. Sales of 159,000 Anglias and 380,000 Prefects showed that not everyone was fash-ion conscious: cheap service still counted for more.

The British Ford vee-eight Pilot of 1947 descended directly from the Army's WOA model, itself the old 1937 22 hp with the familiar 3.6-litre engine. Though Dagenham had planned an intermediate 2½-litre unit, this was dropped with the abolition of the horsepower tax. Post-war changes included hydromechanical brakes (mechanical had always featured on the all-British vee-eights) a peculiar bent-wire column shift and a more classical radiator grille. A heater and built-in jacks were standard, and the Pilot was a no-nonsense family saloon capable of 85 mph. Production was a modest 22,189 units, and after 1950 vee-eight units were reserved for trucks, though they were still being supplied to Allard as late as 1954–5.

Ford switched to modern styling at the 1950 Show, with the Consul and Zephyr. In fact, these were several jumps ahead of the parent factory, since they featured 12-volt electrics, short-stroke overhead-valve engines and full unitary construction. The front suspension was of the McPherson strut type first seen on the stillborn Chevrolet Cadet, conventional semielliptics were used at the rear, and the cylinder dimensions were 79.4 mm × 76.2 mm, giving capacities of 1,508-cc for the four-cylinder Consul and 2,262-cc for the Zephyr Six. Both cars had three-speed gearboxes with column change, hydraulic clutches, hypoid rear axles and 2LS hydraulic brakes. The EOTA-series Consul on a 100-inch wheelbase weighed 2,436 lb in road trim and attained a predictable 70–75 mph, but the Zephyr, with 68 bhp under its bonnet, combined an 82-mph gait with a satisfying 23 mpg. The British Fords were more angular than their American counterparts, and a high ground clearance preserved the go-anywhere characteristics of earlier days, but weight distribution was biassed towards the front (the ratio was 58:42 in the Zephyr's case), and fast solo motoring was best undertaken with a sandbag in the boot. Nonetheless, the Zephyr at £930 was one of the better buys in its class, smoother than the fours and easier to maintain than the Morris. Convertibles had joined the range by 1952, the Zephyr's having a curious semi-power-operated hood. Pressure on the button raised it to the *de ville* position, but the process had to be completed by hand. 231,481 Consuls and 152,677 Zephyrs had been made by early 1956, as well as 22,634 of the prestige Zodiac series introduced for 1954. This was the car that started off the sporty compact business in Britain, though it was more 'stock' than, for instance, the A105. The extra money went on two-tone finish, whitewall tyres and fog lamps.

Meanwhile the Anglia and Prefect had been brought into line, with the latest structure and suspensions, though not the hypoid rear axles. 12-volt electrics and 13-inch wheels were used, but the 100E-series engines were still long-stroke 1,172-cc flatheads, albeit with pump cooling and stronger bottom ends. Both models shared the same 87-inch wheelbase: the Prefect had four doors, a different grille and more brightwork. The 100Es were wider and roomier—and nearly as thirsty. Fuel consumption seldom bettered 30 mpg, but once again simplicity paid off, and sales were impressive: 350,000 Anglias and 110,000 Prefects in six years. With the advent of the short-stroke 105E engine in October 1959, the Anglia was demoted, soldiering on into 1962 as the cut-price Ford Popular.

This combination of obsolete specification and bargain price had, of course, been proven on 1954's 103E series. The original Popular went down as well with marginal motorists as had France's 2CV Citroën, though not everyone fancied a 1932 model in a 1938 costume. Ford had taken the 1949 Export Anglia with the old-type 10-hp engine and simplified it: a single screen wiper, virtually no chromium plate (even bumpers had aluminium paint), 1938-style instruments and not many of these, small-diameter head-lamps and no turn indicators or vizors. At the time of its introduction it sold for £391, but for another £75—the price, incidentally, of a three-carburetter conversion for the Zephyr—it could be made almost luxurious. Ford called it 'a real working man's car, a real car designed to fill your empty garage or that piece of road in front of your house', which was fine until borough housing managers fell out of love with the automobile. It was still around in 1959, by which time more than 155,000 had been made. The only new Fords in 1955 were station-wagon derivatives of the Anglia–Prefect family. The Ford Escort at £588 was merely a ¼-ton van with windows—plus a starting handle not offered on saloons—but the Squire, like its American namesake, had woody-style side-trim. Britons were not snobbish when it came to wagons, and the Squire's sales, at 17,812 units, were half the Escort's.

In 1956 the Mark II editions of the larger cars were introduced; they had more power, lightweight cast crankshafts, higher gearing, longer wheelbases and an improved weight distribution. American influences were detectable in the key starting and vestigial tail fins. Capacities were up to 1,703-cc and 2,553-cc respectively, the sixes attaining 85–90 mph on 80–86 bhp. With a multi-carburetter manifold the Zephyr could be persuaded to give over 130 bhp, a recipe which added up to Jaguar performance on the cheap: 100 mph, 0–60 mph in 7.5 seconds and a still-acceptable 22 mpg. The handling was still a very uncertain quantity, however. The sixes were available with Borg–Warner overdrive on all forward gears, but an automatic option was not available until October. This range lasted Ford into 1962, though grow-ing prosperity was reflected in the sales pattern of the Mark II: 301,000 sixes as against 350,000 of the Consul series.

Britain was the only market in which Ford consistently outsold General Motors. The latter's Vauxhall had, however, a loyal following, with average home sales of 30,000 cars a year during our period. The engineering was strictly American: three-speed gearboxes, mechanical pump feed, spongy steering, ultrasoft independent front suspension and overhead-valve engines which, though always pressure-lubricated, had a close affinity with the Chevrolet. Vauxhall, like Opel in Germany, were wedded to unitary con-struction, first seen on the H-series Ten of 1938, while their engineers pre-ferred torsion bars to Dubonnet coils. This was not an improvement, as the suspension rose rather than fell under heavy braking, and the ensuing reverse curtsey was as graceless as the original version. The cars were, nonetheless, quiet and smooth. The flutes on the bonnet top remained throughout our period as the sole link with the elder Pomeroy and the 30/98.

Initially 1940's models sufficed; the 1,203-cc H-series Ten, the 1,442-cc I-type Twelve and the 1,781-cc J-type 14/6, all still with those irritating camshaft-driven wipers and 6-volt electrics. The first post-war Vauxhall Twelves were six-light saloons on a 101¾-inch wheelbase, but from March 1946 the model shared the Ten's structure, the H-type being dropped along with the horsepower tax. The four-bearing Fourteen disposed of 48 bhp, had a larger boot and gave an effortless 70–75 mph on a fuel consumption of 30 mpg. An attractive proposition—while it remained free of purchase tax—was the Utilecon, an estate-car adaptation of the ½-ton Bedford van with 12-hp mechanical elements. This one always wore a Bedford badge and was not regarded by its makers as a private car.

Vauxhall adopted modern styling in 1948 on the L-series, notable for a degree of rationalization alien to Austin or Morris. Both the new models shared the same four-light styling, the same three-speed gearbox and the same 9-inch hydraulic brakes. The wheelbase was a compact 97¾ inches, and the six-cylinder Velox was given cream wheels *à la* Citroën to distinguish it from the humbler Wyvern. Close inspection revealed little change: built-out boots, smaller grilles, alligator-type bonnets, inbuilt headlamps and disc instead of steel-spoke wheels. The Wyvern with the old Twelve engine was frugal (35 mpg) and gutless; on the Velox Vauxhall took advantage of the tax concessions by cramming a 2.3-litre engine into the car. The result weighed just over 1 ton and was one of the faster—and more lethal— family saloons of its day. Driven in a manner suited to its suspension and non-geometry, it would return 30 mpg and was a sound buy, although Vauxhall owners sighed for the old Fourteen's *lebensraum*. These models kept the company going into 1951: despite the continuing fuel shortage, Veloxes outsold Wyverns by seven to five.

The necessary *lebensraum* was forthcoming on 1952's E-types—abbreviated 1949 Chevrolets with lower lines, larger boots and Buick-type side-opening bonnets. The wheelbase was up to 103 inches, and mechanical improvements were hypoid rear axles and a coil-and-wishbone independent front suspension, giving a better ride than the old torsion bars though the irrepressible William Boddy headed his report on the Velox, 'Afloat in a Vauxhall'! The cars shown at Earls Court in 1951 retained the 1948 engines, but by the following spring Luton had fallen into line with Dagenham, adopting identical cylinder dimensions of 79.4 mm × 76.2 mm. Recirculating ball steering was introduced on the 1953 models, together with some additional power to meet the stronger Ford challenge. In Australia, General Motors–Holdens offered the Calèche, an open four-seater Velox built on a special floor pan.

For the rest of our period, Vauxhall relied principally on styling changes. In 1955 the Cresta, their answer to the Ford Zodiac, was introduced; this additional model paid off, giving the company their best-ever year for sixes with 55,673 delivered. 1956's cars had thinner screen pillars and wrap-round rear windows, while Crestas had 'three-phase colour separation'. That year the Wyvern was listed at £724 (£60 more than a Ford Consul), the Velox at £794 and the Cresta at £879. Electric wipers made a belated appearance on the 1957 line.

Rootes' family Ten, the Hillman Minx, was as British as roast beef and is immortal as the Gibraltar apes. It had been around since 1932. Tradition-ally better appointed than either Morris or Austin, it remained a family Ten in spirit throughout our period, though what had started out on VE-Day as a stripling of 1,988 lb less than 15 feet long, had by 1956 put on 140 lb and stretched itself 5 inches. Nor was the car a Ten any more, thanks to the adoption of a square 76.2 mm × 76.2 mm engine which would have been a fifteen under the old laws. Speed, a laboured 65 mph in Phase I days, was now 80-plus for anyone resigned to a peculiar fuel-consumption curve. Personal experience of early overhead-valve Minxes on the empty roads of Suez days showed that fast driving returned a miserable 18 mpg!

The Minx was the classic indicator of British taste. Structurally it changed little, having gone unitary in 1940, but the styling went from the traditional (separate wings and headlamps and steel-spoke wheels) in 1945 to disc wheels and concealed headlamps in 1948, and the full-width idiom (one unkind critic likened a Phase III model to 'a Plymouth on which an elephant has sat') in 1949. The mandatory aesthetic (and protective) chromium strip made its appearance on 1951's Phase V, with an extended boot on the Phase VII of 1954. The 'sculptured' low-line treatment featured on the all-new Mark I of 1956. Gearboxes were always of four-speed synchromesh type—1935's synchronized bottom gear had already disappeared before the war—but column shift, adopted in 1948, was still the order of the day at the end of our period, albeit a little-publicized and inexpensive Special shown at Earls Court in 1956 had a floor-mounted lever once more. Overdrive, much favoured by the Rootes Group, was as yet confined to their costlier models.

The suspension, semielliptic at both ends in 1945, had changed to coils and wishbones at the front in 1949, the Bendix brakes gave way to hydraul-ics at the same time. Engine development kept pace: Phases I to III used the familiar three-bearing side-valve four of 9.8 RAC Rating, with dimensions of 63 mm × 95 mm (1,185 cc). It gave an adequate 35 bhp, increased to 37.5 bhp when bored out to 65 mm (1,265 cc) in 1950. The square 1,390-cc overhead-valve unit was a 1955 departure. In its 1956 Mark I form it disposed of 51 bhp.

Hillman were generous with alternative styles. Even in 1945 there were a traditional drophead coupé and an estate car, though this latter was much more of a van than a car, sold under the Commer brand name until 1950. A further bonus on the otherwise unchanged Phase VI of 1953 was the Californian hardtop coupé. This disappeared in 1956, as a duplication of the Minx-based Sunbeam Rapier.

Rootes paid no attention to the minimal market. Stripped Minx Specials were available from 1955 onwards, but these were never popular. In the same year, however, a dual-purpose vehicle for farmers or tradesmen was introduced in the shape of the Husky, a sawn-off Minx van on an 84-inch wheelbase. The engine was the superseded 1,265-cc flathead, the two-door station-wagon body was austerely appointed, and the floor change was a welcome bonus. Lighter than a Minx at 1,904 lb, the Husky was nippy in traffic, but like most cut-and-shut devices it was lethal on ice. It met with an enthusiastic reception, about 38,000 being sold before it was restyled and given overhead valves in 1958.

Standard paid dearly for their one-model policy, based on American-type saloons for world markets. The Vanguard was certainly no worse than the Vauxhall Velox, the Renault Frégate or the 1400 Fiat, and its four-cylinder engine probably powered more interesting sports cars than any other proprietary unit, the 2-litre Bristol included. Unfortunately, Standard, even with their profitable Ferguson tractor connections, could not afford so radical a step, and they spent much of the decade in what Graham Turner has summarized as 'the search for a partner'.

In 1945, of course, the Vanguard was still in the chrysalid stage, and Standard were concentrating on 1939 types, all with the transverse-leaf i.f.s. which had been one of the sensations of the last pre-War Show. Also common to their range were three-bearing four-cylinder side-valve engines, mechanical pump feed, Bendix brakes, underslung rear springs and spiral bevel back axles. The Standard Eight had cylinder dimensions of 56.7 mm × 95 mm (1,006 cc), cooling was by thermosyphon, and 6-volt electrics sufficed. A four-speed gearbox replaced the earlier three-speed type, and a saloon weighed 1,624 lb. A tourer and a miniature drophead coupé were also listed, though a station wagon never passed the prototype stage. The pump-cooled 1.6-litre Twelve and 1.8-litre Fourteen shared the same chassis and bodies. Initially the larger engine had been reserved for export, reaching the home market only as a result of the tax concessions. Prices were competitive: the Standard Eight cost £346, and the larger saloons £576. This series accounted for some 85,000 cars, over 53,000 of them Eights.

The Vanguard took its bow in the summer of 1947. Production of the older models was run down, though the process took over a year. *The Motor* called the new car 'a turning point in the history of the British motor industry', which it was, though not in the way that Standard had hoped or intended. The scaled-down Plymouth styling with its uncompromising slab sides created a furore.

The heart of the car was a short-stroke (85 mm × 92 mm 2,088-cc) pushrod four with pump cooling: the 1.8-litre unit featured in preliminary announcements was never built in series. Wet cylinder liners made for easy replacement and better bore wear, and the downdraught carburetter with its mechanical pump feed was to be expected. So were the three-speed gearbox and column shift, though a synchronized bottom gear was a feature that no other mass producer offered in 1947. The brakes were Standard's first hydraulics, and coil-spring independent front suspension was used, in conjunction with semiellIptics at the rear. Curiously, though, the Vanguard retained a separate cruciform-braced frame, this and the body being rustproofed at the factory. This layout allowed some latitude in body styles, though the only alternative was in fact a station wagon: cabriolets were confined to the cars built in Belgium by Imperia. The dimensions were comparable with those of the Model A Ford: a wheelbase of 94 inches and a length of 164 inches.

Britain's updated Model A cost £544 on the home market. Handling was bad American with violent tyre howl on corners—but the car was incredibly tough and in great demand for caravan towing. Production worked up quickly, from 38,000 in 1948 to over 56,000 in 1950. By the end of 1950 Vanguards were being manufactured or assembled in Australia, Belgium, India and Switzerland. Even in Canada the price was a competitive $1,895.

On 1950 models the awkward right-hand column change had given way to a left-hand shift, and an overdrive option reduced the fuel consumption from 24 to 30 mpg. Like Austin, Standard changed to a four-light style with a larger boot on the 1953 Series II; at the same time clutches were given hydraulic actuation. A year later Britain's first diesel private car, using Standard's own 2.1-litre engine, was introduced. With the necessary chassis reinforcement the weight went up by 235 lb, and the performance was more lethargic. The reward for this was a frugal 37 mpg, but high initial cost and tiresome regulations on untaxed fuel (even pleasure motorists had to keep logbooks) held sales down to less than 2,000.

The idea was beginning to misfire; there were too many competitors, some with six-cylinder engines. Mark I versions accounted for 185,000 units, but Series II's sales never reached 90,000. Thus the one-model policy went overboard in the summer of 1953. The ensuing 8-hp saloon arrived too late: Austin and Morris had cornered the market, and Standard did not enhance their reputation by offering their baby as a 'stripped' item—shoddy-looking Tygan upholstery, untrimmed door panels and no exterior luggage access. Almost everything was extra, from a second wiper to a kit of tools, while the cavity-style grille looked as if someone had fired a shell into the bows.

This was a pity, for there was nothing wrong with the car. The unitary stressed-skin construction (used as an excuse for that non-opening boot!) had marked affinities with the Austin A30, as had many of the other basics—the 803-cc overhead-valve engine, its four-speed gearbox, the hypoid rear axle and the 2LS hydraulic brakes. The Standard was longer, wider, roomier and more stable than the Austin, and it weighed in at a low 1,484 lb. Its performance was comparable with the Austin's, though not everyone considered that the £25 saving justified the high noise level. Only 37,000 found buyers during the Eight's first season, and the company spent the rest of the period trying to uprate the little car.

The first step in this direction was the 948-cc Standard Ten of 1954, with drop instead of sliding windows, external luggage access (it could be done!) and a plated grille. This was a good performer capable of 70 mph, and by 1955 it was available as a four-door estate car as well. The sliding windows had disappeared by 1956, and for 1957 Standard's own two-pedal control, Standrive, added only £20 to the price of any model. The ultimate *volte-face* would, of course, be the later Gold Star Eight with its triple overdrive. About 175,000 Standard Tens were sold, but it took until 1961 to achieve this figure.

The Vanguard struggled on. The unitary Mark III of 1956 was longer, lower and better looking, and the engine had profited from Triumph's sports-car developments. Heaters and screen washers were standard, though, mindful of good Australian sales, Standard retained the 16-inch wheels.

There was also a sporty compact in the Zodiac–Cresta idiom, though the Sportsman's grille suggested (as was later confirmed) that the car had been conceived as a Triumph. With the aid of twin SU carburetters the output was up from 68 to 92 bhp, dual overdrive was standard, and the Vanguard's rather inadequate 9-inch brakes gave way to drums 10 inches in diameter. To the usual mandatory gimmicks were added two-tone upholstery, ultraviolet panel lighting and two-speed wipers. The Sportsman's 90 mph still left it lagging behind the Austin A105, and it fell between every possible stool. Only 901 were sold.

Singer's protracted struggle against 'the big battalions' came to a sad end in 1956, though the sellers' market had earned them a respite, not to mention a £90,000 profit in 1948. Their first post-war cars were the usual 1939 mixture, though more interesting than most, since the company was wedded to chain-driven o.h.c. and had used nothing else since 1934. Otherwise all was orthodoxy: thermosyphon circulation, mechanical pump feed, synchromesh gearboxes and cruciform-braced frames riding on semielliptic springs. The 1,194-cc Ten saloon had four speeds and hydraulic brakes, and cost £509 in 1946. It was the family's best-seller, with 10,497 units delivered. The 1,525-cc Singer Twelve was an extension of the same theme, with a projecting boot, but it took a long time to get into production and accounted for less than a tenth of the smaller car's output.

The Singer Nine Roadster was a last attempt at the old sporty car idiom. It used a 1,074-cc engine developing 36 bhp, and differed from the saloons in having only three forward speeds and rod-operated brakes. A pleasant if unspectacular car, it was made almost exclusively for export. About 2,500 of the original model were produced, before it gave way to the 4A of 1950 with an extra forward ratio. The last of the 9-hp variants was the 4AB with disc wheels, independent front suspension and hydromechanical brakes; it was also tried with a 1,198-cc engine before Singer settled for a 1½-litre type in the SM Roadster of 1951. An electric fuel pump was used for this model, which did not reach the home market until 1954, by which time it was available in twin-carburetter 80-mph form. Singer even tried glassfibre bodies and a swing-up one-piece bonnet–wing assembly on the SMX of 1953, but this was ahead of its time, and more than one of the six prototypes was rebodied with the standard metal four-seater coachwork.

The SM Roadster's engine derived from the SM1500, the company's mainstay in their last years of independence. Unkind things have been said of the Kaiser-like saloon bodies, but Singer's tragedy was their choice of a shape that did not lend itself to updating. With production and sales potentials equally limited, amortization was a slow business. Thus what was acceptable in 1948 had become hopelessly outmoded by 1953. There followed the inevitable downward spiral, from 6,358 cars in 1951 to less than 2,000 a couple of years later. Singer tried everything: a twin-carburetter option, wood-grained dashboards and plated side flashes—but there was no substitute for retooling.

The car itself was an honest effort. A full six-seater mounted on a cruciform-braced frame of 107½-inch wheelbase, it used a new short-stroke (73 mm × 90 mm) edition of the overhead-camshaft engine; the capacity was later reduced from 1,506 cc to 1,497 cc. Fuel feed was by electric pump, all except the first cars had pressurized cooling, and the ratios of the four-speed box were selected by the usual column lever. Singer favoured coil-spring independent front suspension, and the car handled rather better than most of its contemporaries, with an average performance. At £799, it was too expensive to compete against Wyverns and Oxfords.

By 1955 the SM1500 had given way to the Hunter, a gallant attempt to camouflage the 1948 shape behind a traditional grille crowned by a horse's head mascot. The plastic bonnet top was an SMX heritage, and the package included a screenwash, fog lamps, two-note horns and rim trims—not to mention a price £125 higher than Ford's Zodiac. Singer tried a stripped model (the standardization of tubeless tyres allowed them to dispense even with a spare wheel) and a De Luxe version at a bargain £864.

They even announced the Hunter 75 with a brand-new twin-carburetter ·

twin-overhead-camshaft engine, but it was all to no avail. By January 1956, Rootes were in possession, and, though the new management built a few more Hunters, the 1957 Singer Gazelle was merely a luxury Minx with the appropriate grille. The single-camshaft engine survived into 1958 as a sop to the traditionalists.

Jowett had quit the utility market for pastures new, but the ½-ton Bradford commercial was still available as an estate car. Suddenly we were back in 1930, with the ageless 1-litre side-valve flat-twin under a conventional bonnet, and no concessions to modern styling. The oval facia might have come off a late-Vintage Morris, springs were semielliptic, brakes were mechanical, and the three-speed gearbox had central change. The Jowett was neither quiet nor fast, nor did it stop very well, but the legendary 'big pull' was still there. By 1953 the Bradford was becoming too archaic even for farmers, and Jowett were testing the CD-type with i.o.e., torsion-bar independent front suspension and the Javelin's four-speed gearbox. A two-door saloon version would have been listed, but the company's collapse nipped this one in the bud.

There remains the Lloyd, built almost in its entirety—even down to the steel-spoke wheels—in a small factory at Grimsby which had made rear-engined mini-cars before the Second World War. Though unconnected with its German namesake, the Lloyd was curiously Teutonic in specification: a double backbone frame with outriggers for the body, a 654-cc water-cooled two-stroke transverse-twin engine driving the front wheels, rack-and-pinion steering and all-independent suspension by coils and wishbones. The power unit was of charging-pump type with full-pressure lubrication (no petroil mixtures for Lloyd owners!), and there was chain primary drive, with final drive by helical gears. The brakes were mechanical, but the three-speed gearbox offered the ultimate refinement of synchromesh on all ratios, reverse included. The occasional four-seater body was as sporty as Singer's, but the Lloyd was flat out at 46 mph. At £480, it cost about £100 more than a Morris Minor, which explains why it had become a lost cause by 1951. At least one, however, found its way to Belgium.

14.4   A Touch of Class

In the middle-class sector Rover and Jaguar ruled the roost.

Anyone encountering Rover's first post-war models would find it hard to believe that there had been a war at all. None of the old standards had been lost, and it took a keen eye to spot the differences that had crept in since 1937. Wood and leather predominated within, sliding roofs were part of the package, and so, from 1947, were heaters. The gear lever sat firmly on the floor, rigidly braced to the chassis to prevent 'float', and all cars had one-shot lubrication. The engineering was British right through—orthodox frames with tubular cross-members, underslung at the rear, semielliptic springs, rod-operated brakes and four-speed synchromesh gearboxes with the free-wheeling device used since 1933. All engines were of the o.h.v. pushrod type with pump circulation, and the same style of six-light body was common to all models, though the four-light sports version was not available on the 1.4-litre Rover Ten. This one offered refinement rather than power: the little engine was not really up to hauling a 2,800-lb weight. Further up the range were a 1,496-cc Twelve and a pair of sixes, the 1.9-litre Fourteen and the 2.1-litre Rover Sixteen. This last retailed at £857 and offered an easy 70 mph on a 4.7:1 back axle. Even 1948's box-section frames, coil-spring independent front suspension and hydromechanical brakes left the appearance unchanged, though a single wheelbase now sufficed for all Rovers. There were two engines, a 1,595-cc four-cylinder 60 and the 2,103-cc six-cylinder 75, both with overhead inlet and side exhaust valves.

Car production was still modest, but 1948 had seen the début of the Jeep-type four-wheel-drive Land Rover, using the 60 engine and full hydraulic brakes. Though offered briefly in station-wagon form, for 1949—and again on a more serious basis from 1956 onwards—it does not belong in our story. Suffice it to say that in the early days Land Rovers outnumbered cars by eight to five, and even in 1955, when the legendary P4 ('Auntie') was approaching her zenith, the Solihull factory delivered 13,436 saloons, but nearly 29,000 4 × 4s. The Land Rover joined the ranks of the million sellers in 1976.

Long runs were the order of the day. 'Auntie' herself lasted fourteen years and accounted for over 130,000 units, becoming a part of English folklore. Refined—even the four-cylinder 60 was hard to distinguish from a six— quiet, beautifully made and ponderous if driven in a manner beneath her dignity, 'Auntie' was by no means lethargic. The original 2.1-litre 75 of 1950 would comfortably exceed 80 mph, and the latter-day 2.6-litres could attain 100 mph, although it took several miles of motorway to get there.

In October 1949, she represented heresy, with her slab sides, American-style grille and central Cyclop's eye spotlamp. Traditional Rover customers were not easily convinced that this was the best means of seating six people within an 111-inch wheelbase. Beneath the surface, less had changed; the engine (only the 75 unit was now offered) had two horizontal SU carburetters and electric pump feed, column shift had made its appearance, the wheel size was down to 15 inches, and the curious floor-mounted shepherd's-crook-type handbrake was infinitely preferable to the nasty umbrella-handle used on the Mark V Jaguar. The P4 weighed 3,192 lb and cost £1,106.

Regrettably, Rover had already decided not to proceed with the miniature

M1 of 1947. This car featured a 699-cc four-cylinder engine in a semiunitary structure, self-adjusting hydrostatic brakes and rear springing by a live axle and coils. An obsession with unobstructed floors was reflected in the facia-mounted gearshift, and the car was a Fiat-like two-seater coupé. It was a heavy infant, at 1,512 lb, but this was not its undoing. Like Austin's proposed mini-car, it would have used steel that simply was not available.

The 75 was Rover's staple for four seasons. In 1952 the Cyclop's eye had been deleted; already there had been a switch to full hydraulic brakes. Column change disappeared in 1954, though Rover, unwilling as ever to sacrifice three-abreast seating, compromised with a cranked central lever. At the same time buyers were given a choice of two additional engines, the 2-litre four-cylinder 60 and the 90, a bigger six with a capacity of 2.6 litres which gave 'Auntie' a 90-mph top speed. In 1955 the 75 received a new short-stroke (73 mm x 88.9 mm) unit, and all bodies now incorporated wrapround rear windows. 1956's improvements included two-trailing-shoe brakes at the front: 90's had vacuum servo assistance as well. Rover's answer to the sporty-compact problem appeared a year later: like Armstrong Siddeley, they opted for a fast tourer and a parallel gentleman's carriage. Both used 2.6-litre engines uprated to 108 bhp, but the 105S had an overdrive gearbox, whereas the 105R featured Rover's own automatic transmission. The combination of a hydraulic torque converter, a two-speed-and-reverse gearbox with automatic clutch and overdrive was a little too much, and only a few 105Rs were made in the 1957 and 1958 seasons. Thereafter Rover wisely elected to buy automatics from Borg–Warner.

The real excitement at the 1956 Show was, however, the glassfibre-bodied T3 coupé. Rover had, of course, been testing gas-turbine cars since 1950, but this model was designed as an entity. Its 110-bhp engine lived at the rear, insulating the occupants from noise, heat and smell alike, while four-wheel drive was adopted in the interests of adhesion. With no clutch or gearbox, the new car was 5 seconds quicker to 60 than 'Auntie', but a fuel consumption of 13 mpg was daunting. Neither the T3 nor any other gas-turbine prototype was anywhere near the commercial stage. The car's inboard disc brakes and de Dion rear axle would, however, be seen again on the overhead-camshaft 2000.

William Lyons's SS Jaguars had been the prime success story of the 1930s. Up to 1939 Standard had furnished the engines, and, though sixes were now the responsibility of Jaguar Cars Ltd (the unhappy initials had been dropped for obvious reasons in 1945), they would continue to supply four-cylinder units until these were discontinued in 1949. 1939's deliveries had been an impressive 5,378 Jaguars, and there was no reason to meddle with a successful formula. Only hypoid rear axles distinguished the latest models from their pre-war counterparts.

Structurally, the formula was not unlike that of the Rover, down to frames underslung at the rear and Girling mechanical brakes. The bodies were even better proportioned, with the thousand-pound look that had captivated the public since 1936. The short-chassis 100 two-seater was not reinstated: nor, until 1947, were the drophead coupés.

Jaguar motoring was graduated. At the bottom of the range was the 1½-litre, using an overhead valve edition of the 1.8-litre Standard Fourteen engine, its single carburetter fed by electric pump. As always, it was competitively priced at £684, but the chassis and body were shared with the sixes, and the power-to-weight ratio was deplorable. One step up was the twin-carburetter 2½-litre six (actual capacity was 2,664-cc) which was good for 85–90 mph on 102 bhp and the pleasantest of the bunch from a driver's viewpoint. The 125-bhp 3½-litre always felt a little too fast for its chassis: it also had a 16-mpg thirst, and was a notorious foot-frier. It was also marvellous value, offering 90–95 mph for £991. Jaguar's seven-bearing sixes were very durable and would run 250,000 miles between overhauls, though with the original Duralumin connecting-rods it was advisable to stay below 4,500 rpm.

The 1948 Show, of course, saw the début of the magnificent XK engine, the work of W. M. Heynes, Walter Hassan and Clive Baily. Dimensions were 83 mm × 106 mm (3,442-cc), the twin overhead camshafts were driven by duplex chains, the alloy head incorporated hemispherical combustion chambers, and the output was a formidable 160 bhp. Like the pushrod cars, it used a seven-bearing counterbalanced crankshaft, and it was equally devoid of temperament. Jaguar, however, were not prepared to instal this masterpiece in a saloon until it was fully proven, so the existing sixes were given a facelift, emerging as the Mark V series with new frames upswept at the rear, wishbone-and-torsion bar i.f.s., 2LS hydraulic brakes and new bodies with sloping screens and thinner pillars. Debits were the bolt-on disc wheels, the rear-wheel spats and the useless handbrake, but notwithstanding its spongy feel the Mark V was a very forgiving car and a first-touch starter in all weathers. About 10,400 were sold in three seasons.

By 1951, however, the Mark VII saloon with the XK engine was ready. This model sold 30,989 units in six seasons. Nor was this the end, for the theme carried over into 1961 on Marks VIII and IX.

Viewed from hindsight, the Mark VII was bulboid—despite the inimitable Lyons touch—and much too large. Certainly there was a lot of it—it was 200 inches long and turned the scales at 3,864 lb. By British standards the boot was enormous, and certain aspects of design were American oriented, notably the steering which required 4¾ turns from lock to lock. The De-andre vacuum servo brakes were far from predictable, either.

By the standards of 1951, however, the car was remarkable. It could match almost any American vee-eight on sheer output, and appointments included a sliding roof. On a 4.27 rear axle the Mark VII would cruise all day at 90 mph and exceed the ton if pressed. An ingenious solution to the baggage problem was to divide the fuel supply between two wing-mounted tanks. For those few Britons in a position to secure one, it was a bargain at £1,263. It helped to push Jaguar sales to over 10,000 a year, and by 1953 it could be had (for export only) with a two-speed Borg–Warner automatic transmission. Overdrive followed a year later, though Jaguar always confined this amenity to top gear. Evolution was steady. 1955 saw the M-version with high-lift camshafts and 190 bhp, reinforced suspension and closer gear ratios, while automatic models were given a necessary inter-mediate 'hold'. 1957's Mark VIII had a single-panel curved screen and still more horses, 210 of them.

A year earlier Lyons had unveiled his compact 2.4-litre, the first of all the unitary Jaguars was destined for a thirteen-year run. Its 'destroked' engine had dimensions of 83 mm × 76.5 mm (2,483-cc), developing its 112 bhp at a high 5,750 rpm. Lockheed Brakemaster servo brakes were standard equipment, while the suspension arrangements were entirely new—coils and wishbones at the front and cantilever springs located by radius arms at the rear, with rubber insulating blocks to eliminate the old unitary bugbear of drumming. Overdrive, though not (initially) automatic, was a catalogued option, and the 2.4 offered 100 mph allied to a consumption of 24–27 mpg, better, indeed, than the old pushrod 2½-litres. It was considerably safer than the original 3.4—a pleasure yet to come—which used the same structure and was apt to become airborne at around 95–100 mph. 19,937 Mark I 2.4s were made before the model gave way in 1960 to an improved Mark II version.

In the realms of Rover and Jaguar, 'every car was somebody's car'. For those requiring refinement 'off the peg', Rootes's Humber was still an adequate if uninspired answer.

1946's Humbers were more refined than Hillmans, with hydraulic brakes and a transverse-leaf independent front suspension. A separate cruciform-braced chassis was recognized practice in this class, and side valves were universal. Appearance and appointments alike were traditional, down to opening screens and sliding roofs, though the leather shortage was reflected in the 'twin-trim' upholstery. The cheapest of the family, at £784, was the 1,944-cc four-cylinder Hawk; hailed as a new model, it was merely 1940's Hillman Fourteen with a new identity. For those less worried about the fuel consumption, there was the Snipe, using leftover 2.7-litre engines from the 1936 Humber 18, while still in evidence was the firm's Empire-oriented compact, the 4.1-litre Super Snipe, which offered 2–80 mph in top at the price of 15 mpg. Like the rival 18-85 Wolseley, it was widely used by the police. Finally there was the Pullman, 'ambassador of cars', a seven-seater on an 127-inch wheelbase, with razor-edge bodywork by Thrupp and Maberly.

In 1948 column shift was standardised; it had already been applied to the Mark II Hawk. The Super Snipe and the Pullman were updated with recessed headlamps and narrower grilles, the latter's wheelbase being extended to 131 inches. This 'car designed to be handled by the professional chauffeur', as *The Motor* called it, was good for nearly 80 mph, and changing social circumstances did not prevent sales of some 800 a year. It survived with little change into 1953, though from 1949 there was a supplementary saloon variant, the Imperial, and later Pullmans had synchromesh bottom gears. The same fate attended Super Snipes for the time being, though sales were rather higher: 4,397 were made in 1951.

By contrast, the Hawk sold about 8,000 units a year and merited more drastic treatment. 1949 models received four-light coachwork in the prevailing Chrysler idiom, with curved screens, though a wing line was retained, and the grille was unmistakably Humber. Also new were the coil-spring independent front suspension and hypoid rear axle, and the result was a comfortable if gutless six-seater. The latter weakness was gradually remedied; 1951 saw an increase in capacity to 2.3 litres, and three years later this bigger unit was given the Sunbeam–Talbot's overhead valves. Overdrive was now a catalogued option, and though on a weight of 3,000 lb a scintillating performance could not be expected, the Hawk at least offered 28 mpg. This Mark VI version continued into 1957 without further change.

The Hawk's switch to overhead valves cost little, since the engine was already fitted to Sunbeam–Talbots. Nor did an overhead-valve Super Snipe present much problem when this fell due in 1953; Rootes simply dropped in the seven-bearing 4,138-cc Blue Riband six used in heavy-duty Commer trucks. On 113 bhp, this made light work of hauling the 4,000-lb successor to a once-promising line of compacts.

The rest of the car was overgrown Hawk with the same styling, even down to the hideous half-moon speedometer, though it had a synchronized bottom gear which the Hawk as yet lacked. The result resembled a 1942 American sedan with British trim. It would do 95 mph, but the steering was painfully low geared. The car was too big and thirsty for British motorists, and it never caught on, even when overdrive and automatic options were introduced in 1956. Sales levelled off at about 2,000 a year, and the Super Snipe did not reappear in 1957. The wind of change had already caught up with the Pullman, which was discontinued midway through 1954 after a short run with the overhead-valve engine.

Sunbeam–Talbots were already Sunbeams in Europe—to avoid any confusion with Antonio Lago's offerings—and after 1954 the second half of the name was dropped for good. Either way, the ingredients were Hillman–Humber, though unusually among the badge-engineered *marques* the Sunbeam–Talbot gained in stature during our decade, thanks to the exploits of the works rally team and the old-world charm of the later 90s. The 1946 models, however, had looks and nothing else: the Sunbeam–Talbot Ten was a dressed-up Minx with a proper chassis, and the 2-litre a similarly attired Humber Hawk with a beam front axle and—fortunately—had hydraulic brakes. The bodies were handsome, especially Whittingham and Mitchel's tourers, but behind the ornamental discs lurked steel-spoke wheels, and the cars belonged to the lost world of tennis and bridge. Their makers did well to sell nearly 6,000 between 1945 and 1948.

Nor were the first 80s and 90s very impressive. True, o.h.v. heads had been grafted onto the Minx and Hawk blocks, which meant 64 bhp from the 90 engine; and 2LS hydraulics were now universal. The styling was also felicitous; the lines of the old saloon body had been combined with one-piece curved screens, recessed headlamps and full-flow front wings, into which the traditional Talbot grille blended well. No pretence, of course, was made of seating six, and the boot was a bad joke. The facia was too like that of the Humber Hawk for comfort, and there was no excuse for the dreadful Synchromatic column shift. Another unwelcome survival was the beam front axle, which gave a ride comparable to a lodging-house bedstead. The 90 attained a useful 77 mph, but the sports veneer was thin and the gear ratios agricultural. Sales were 7,500 units in two seasons.

After 1950 the overhead-valve Minx engine was no longer offered, but the 90 went from strength to strength. 1951's Mark II had coil-spring independent front suspension, a hypoid rear axle and a new version of the tough old three-bearing engine with an 81-mm bore and a capacity of 2,267-cc. Competition experience soon dispensed with the rear-wheel spats and led to larger and better-cooled brakes, while the output rose steadily, from 70 bhp in 1951 to 92 bhp at the end of 1956. Overdrive made its appearance on the Mark III of 1955, though floor change was never catalogued. Thirty saloons of the last batch were, however, converted to this specification (Mark IIIS) by Castle of Leicester in 1957. Over 21,000 2.3-litre cars were made, including the scarcer Alpine roadsters of 1953–5.

These were always Sunbeams, not Sunbeam–Talbots, and had the 80-bhp engine from the start. The frame and suspension were reinforced, and the steering was higher geared, though the deplorable gearchange was left untouched. The Alpine name was far more than euphony or wishful thinking, being backed by four Coupes des Alpes in 1953, an Alpine Gold Cup for Stirling Moss, and countless other rally successes. Though the first Alpine recorded a well-publicized 120 mph over the kilometre at Jabbeke, the standard model was flat out at 95 mph.

By 1956 the 90 was becoming old fashioned, so Rootes reverted to the Minx-in-a-party frock formula with the Rapier. It was the 90 story all over again, of gradual evolution into a pleasant fast tourer. What could be bought at the 1955 Show was, however, lots of gimmickry and not much car. This meant a jazzed-up hardtop based on the latest 1,390-cc Minx, with the output boosted to 26 bhp, overdrive on third and fourth, antiroll bars at each end and finned brake drums. The grille, regrettably, was Hillman, but the Rapier was quite fast; early models attained 85 mph, and 1967's twin-carburetter R67 could attain 90 mph.

Of Nuffield's three prestige makes, the Wolseley was as traditional as the Rover, though since the abandonment of upstairs camshafts and back-to-front gearshifts in 1936 it had acquired a 'glorified Morris' label which was not wholly deserved. The pushrod-operated overhead valves, SU carburetters and electric pumps, four-speed gearboxes, hydraulic brakes and Bishop cam steering all, however, bore the stamp of the Cowley design office. In 1945 there were fewer models than of old, but most of these were available with such adjuncts as sliding roofs, opening screens, built-in jacks and reversing lights, while six-cylinder Wolseleys had twin horns, adjustable steering columns and the time-honoured Nightpass system on which the passlamps doubled as the dipped beam. The cheapest of the range was the Wolseley Ten, a chassised edition of the 1,140-cc M-series Morris, while in ascending order (and sharing the same body) were the 1,548-cc four-cylinder 12/48, the 1.8-litre six-cylinder 14/60 and the 18/85, the 'cop's' Wolseley with the twin-carburetter 2.3 litre engine from the old SA-type MG. It paralleled the Humber Hawk at £755.

To this assortment would be added the little overhead-valve Wolseley Eight planned for the 1940 season, and the huge 3½-litre 25 limousine on a 141-inch wheelbase, aimed at Lord Mayors who felt that the current Humber Pullman looked too like the war-surplus species selling at around £400. The Eight was a curiosity; contrary to Nuffield practice everything except the radiator, trim and cylinder head was authentic Series E Morris. Undistinguished the Wolseley might be, but it was a known quantity, and approximately 40,000 of this interim series were sold.

Thereafter rationalization quietly killed the *marque*. It became a badge-engineered patchwork of parts from other Nuffield—and eventually Austin—models, identifiable only by the illuminated radiator badge, fog lamps and trim. It speaks volumes for customer loyalty that this farce continued for a quarter of a century.

1949's offerings were the 4/50, alias the MO-series Morris Oxford with an overhead camshaft, and the 6/80 which bore the same relation to the Morris Six but had a second carburetter since Morris themselves were already using o.h.c. Other advantages of 'Buying wisely, buying Wolseley' were an electric choke, a telescopic steering column, individual front seats and spotlamps—though not the Nightpass. Constabulary support was responsible for sales of 25,000 6/80s in six seasons.

By 1953 the 4/50 had given way to the 4/44, a combination of the future MG Magnette's unitary hull with a detuned 1,250-cc engine from that firm's current Y-type saloon. This car sold nearly 30,000 before receiving the

BMC B-type engine and floor change as the 15/50. The last six of our period, the 6/90, was a Riley Pathfinder with a 2.6-litre C-type unit, Lockheed instead of Girling brakes and column shift where the Riley favoured a right-hand lever on the floor. It outlived the Riley by a couple of seasons, ending up with a semielliptic rear suspension. (The wheel would come full circle in 1958 with the Riley 2.6, a Riley-based Wolseley with a Riley grille!)

Riley were likewise destined for a long and meaningless decline. Yet the car that appeared in 1946 was far more desirable than the hurriedly-put-together 1939s. Though only the 1½-litre was initially available, the long-legged, long-stroke (80 mm × 120 mm) 2½-litre four was back on sale by the end of the year. These cars had nothing in common with any other Nuffield product.

The twin-camshaft high-pushrod engines with their hemispherical combustion chambers were a direct heritage from the old days, as were the classic radiators, even if the filler caps were no longer functional. Much of the old Riley elegance had been recaptured in the new fabric-topped sports saloon bodies. Styling alone might dictate a vee-screen, but the panel on the driver's side opened and would continue to open until 1949. SU carburetters were, of course, used, though the 1½-litre had an AC mechanical pump; the four-speed synchromesh gearboxes were controlled by stubby central levers in the MG idiom. The steering was by rack and pinion, but Riley clung to hydromechanical brakes until 1952. Front suspension was independent, by wishbones and torsion bars. The main difference—apart from 7 inches of wheelbase—between the 2½-litre and its smaller sister was the colour of the Blue Diamond badge: dark blue on 1½-litres, and light blue on the large cars.

The 1½-litre weighed 2,624 lb and attained nearly 80 mph: the steering was heavy but pleasantly high geared. By contrast, the 2½-litre was a true grand tourer. Initially the engine developed 90 bhp, but by 1948 an extra 10 bhp were on tap, and the car cruised at 80 mph with a maximum very close to the ton. Thanks to high gearing, the fuel consumption was a reasonable 20–23 mpg, but a weight of 3,350 lb was reflected in the steering, which was beyond the capabilities of most women at parking speeds and still uncomfortably heavy below 40 mph. A bid for the American market was made in 1948 with a three-seater roadster: this model had column shift and heavy overriders. These Rileys continued into 1953, latter-day improvements being hypoid rear axles and divided propeller shafts. Minor styling changes—the deletion of running-boards and some rather meretricious rear-wheel spats—carried the 1½-litre into the first quarter of 1955, but the big Riley was less fortunate. It received the BMC treatment.

The engine was left alone, and so was the torsion-bar front suspension, but the rest of the 1954 Pathfinder was Austin–Morris: cam steering gear, a live axle and coils at the rear and new full-width bodywork. The brakes

39 Vintage Performance, Modern Styling: Jensen Interceptor cabriolet with six-cylinder Austin engine, 1950 (*Author's Collection*)

40 Entente Cordiale: Bentley 4.6-litre with Facel Metallon coupé coachwork, 1951 (*Courtesy Rolls-Royce Ltd*)

41   Roadgoing Trials Car: a 1951 Dellow two-seater disports itself on Brighton Front; note the fiddle brake (*Courtesy National Motor Museum*)

42   Man and his Machine: Sydney Allard (*left*) with his J2 sports car unveiled at Earls Court in October 1949 (*Author's Collection*)

43 California, Here I Come: a fair American enthusiast and her Austin-Healey 100, 1954 (*Courtesy National Motor Museum*)

44 Grace and pace, if not Space: late model XK120 Jaguar with wire wheels, 1953 (*Courtesy Nicky Wright*)

45 Stylistic Revolution: four-light Whitley from Armstrong Siddeley's 1950 range (*Courtesy National Motor Museum*)

46 Everyone's Favourite Aunt: P4 Rover 75 in original cyclops' guise, 1950 (*Author's Collection*)

47 The Rally Winners: a 1951 Sunbeam Talbot 90 Mk II convertible shows its distinctive air intakes (*Author's Collection*)

48 Wood and Leather: a 1946 Wolseley 18/85 saloon posed outside Hertford College, Oxford (*Courtesy Leyland Cars*)

49 Period U Idiom: though by 1952 Hillman's Minx drophead coupé looked very American (*Author's Collection*)

50 Sporty Treatment, English-style: two-toned Austin A105, 1956 (*Courtesy Leyland Cars*)

51 Export or Bust I: this Phase I Standard cabriolet of 1951 was an exclusive of the Belgian Imperia assembly plant (*Courtesy John Davy*)

52 Export or Bust II: Holden of Australia's Vauxhall Velox Caleche tourer, 1949 (*Courtesy General Motors—Holdens Ltd*)

53 Datsun Evolution: in 1948 the DB series had close affinities with the American Crosley (*Courtesy Nissan Motors*)

54 Emergency Motoring: 1947 Tama Electric using Datsun running gear (*Courtesy Nissan Motors*)

were given vacuum servo assistance, and the right-hand floor shift was a sop to traditional Riley customers. Better aerodynamics boosted the Pathfinder's speed to 100 mph, but it needed to be driven on the gears and appealed neither to enthusiasts nor to the sporty-compact fans, who preferred a six. Overdrive was available on 1956 models, and the last cars reverted to semielliptics at the back, but by early 1957 the model had been dropped. Only 5,152 had been produced, as against 13,840 1½-litres and 8,825 of the 'real' 2½-litres. Subsequent Rileys can be summarized as 'Wolseleys with an extra carburetter hung on'.

MG had been ready to jettison their large saloons in 1940, but sedater customers had to be placated, and in 1947 the charming little YA had been launched. This had long been on the stocks as a VA replacement, a fact to which the presence of elderly prototypes in Oxford attested. The car looked as one would expect a 1941 model to look: a 1939 chassis, body and trim with independent front suspension and rack-and-pinion steering attached. The close-set pedals, cramped interior and tiny boot belonged to an earlier era; we have already encountered the 46-bhp TC-based engine in the Wolseley 4/44. The 16-inch disc wheels anticipated the TD of 1950, built-in jacks were part of the package, and the Y-type was a delight to drive up to 70 mph when one ran out of steam. Surprisingly, about 50% of the 6,158 YAs built went abroad, though the improved YB of 1952 with 2LS brakes and hypoid final drive was strictly a home-market offering. MG fared no better than Austin or Singer with their sports tourer, the cross-bred YT with a 54-bhp twin-carburetter engine. It was never offered in England, and only 877 were exported.

The ZA Magnette which replaced the YB for 1954 was a unitary Austin of Wolseley shape, fitted with a twin-carburetter 60-bhp edition of the 1½-litre B-type unit. Longbridge influences were detectable in the hydraulically actuated clutch and coil front suspension: Cowley contributed the SU electric pump and rack-and-pinion steering. There was some compensation for the curved grille, alligator-type bonnet and ugly facia in the wood-and-leather trim and remote-control gearchange. It attained a useful 80 mph, and, though a Swedish enthusiast described it as 'an indignity to all Magnette owners, and to all who know what a Magnette is', worse things would happen a few years later.

Sir John Black's purchase of Triumph had given Standard a foothold in the middle-class sector, though all he bought was a name. The first post-war Triumphs were nevertheless quite unlike Standards and were worthy upholders of the old company's slogan, 'The smartest cars in the land'. The new 1800 featured a steel-tube frame with tubular cross-members, adopted because it used 'delicenced' materials. The front suspension was Standard's transverse-leaf type, but the brakes were the new self-adjusting Girling Hydrostatics, and the engine was the 1.8-litre pushrod affair supplied to Jaguar.

The four-speed synchromesh gearbox had the same clumsy right-hand column shift found on early Vanguards.

The star item was of course the short-chassis roadster, variously described as a 'skit on American classicism' and 'a built-in headwind'. The vee-radiator sat well back between two enormous headlamps, in front of an impressively lengthy bonnet, while a little dog-kennel of a convertible body was perched over the rear axle. As on the old Dolomite roadsters, there was room for two more passengers in the rumble seat, the lid of which incorporated glass panels and could thus transform the car into a dual-cowl phaeton. Opinions might differ on this Callaby–Turner creation, but it was certainly different, though no great performer on a weight of 2,485 lb. Even less of a ball of fire was the saloon on a 108-inch wheelbase, a careful replica of 1930s' razor-edge styling executed in light alloy panels over an ash frame. The angles were carried over into the wings and even the radiator shell. Both cars sold—mainly at home—to customers who found the new bulboid not to their taste. The saloons fared better: 4,000 with the 1800 engine as against a mere 2,500 roadsters.

Standard's one-model policy told. From 1948, first the roadster and then the saloon acquired Vanguard engines, gearboxes, frames and rear axles, though the open cars kept their transverse-leaf suspension to the end. The saloon, after a brief interlude as the TDA, with a Vanguard engine and Triumph chassis, emerged in 1950 as the Renown, a Vanguard dressed for Buckingham Palace. This duly acquired such Vanguard options as overdrive and was still being made at the end of 1954. The total of 6,501 Renowns produced included a handful of long-wheelbase limousines.

The next step was a luxury light car for the ladies, the Mayflower, which enlivened a dull Earls Court Show in 1949. This was Standard–Triumph's first unitary structure: it also used sundry leftover bits, notably a 1939-type side-valve Standard Ten engine of 1,247-cc and its gearbox, with bottom blanked off and column shift. The hypoid rear axle and coil-spring front suspension conformed with current practice, and the Mayflower was a compact little machine only 153 inches long. Visibility and workmanship alike were excellent, the new model retailed for a bargain £473, and it pottered happily along at 10 mph in top, just like a pre-war Hillman Minx.

Unfortunately, the stylist Leslie Moore had attempted the combination of 'a Queen Anne top and a Mary Anne bottom', and the razor-edge upper works were at constant war with the slab sides. Nor did either idiom lend itself to anything as abbreviated as the Mayflower. The indifferent handling, of course, did not matter in this class, so Triumph were able to unload 34,000 cars in four seasons. Reputedly half of these went abroad. Thereafter Standard's prestige division devoted itself to sports cars.

Those inveterate badge engineers, Daimler, were hard hit by the social changes of the 1940s. Their lesser models had always appealed to retired people on fixed incomes, but such clients defected smartly when the price of a DB18 (£485 in 1939) landed on the tax Rubicon's farther shore.

The DB18 was unlucky, for it was an excellent car by any standards. The 2,522-cc pushrod six-cylinder engine, proven in wartime scout cars, disposed of 70 bhp, fuel feed was by mechanical pump, and Daimler retained their traditional transmission line—four-speed preselective gearbox, fluid flywheel and underslung-worm back axle. Coil-spring independent front suspension had been used since 1938, but rod-operated brakes were still deemed adequate. The latest Mulliner body featured thinner pillars and a larger boot, built-in jacks and a fuel reserve were regular equipment, and the car hauled its 3,475 lb at a quiet 70–75 mph. Sales were a respectable 3,365 units. In 1950 the model gave way to the Consort with the new curved grille. Its disc wheels, hydromechanical brakes and hypoid bevel final drive brought it into line with Britain's upper-middle-class norm.

From 1949 Daimler also offered the delightful Special Sports Coupé. Special it certainly was, with its handsome three-seater convertible coachwork by Barker, now a Daimler subsidiary, but the word sports was somewhat euphemistic. Even with an extra carburetter and 85 bhp, there was insufficient power to propel 3,640 lb of motor-car in a sizzling fashion, although none of the DB18's sure-footedness had been lost. What gave the coupé its charm was the geared-up top, in which it would creep along with 300 rpm showing on the rev counter and then accelerate quietly up to its maximum of 85 mph. 608 people felt that this was worth £2,103.

Most successful of the small Daimlers (over 9,000 sold) was 1953's Conquest: appositely the basic price came out at exactly £1,066! The engine was the usual four-bearing six, but with the more modern dimensions of 76.2 mm × 88.9 mm. The output from 2.4 litres was only 5 bhp more than on the superseded DB18 unit, but the engine alone was 112 lb lighter, and more weight was saved on the latest all-steel body. Also new for the *marque* was the torsion-bar independent front suspension, and the Conquest combined an 80-mph top speed with the traditional flexibility. Eighteen months later came the twin-carburetter 100-bhp Century, a sporty compact which would distinguish itself in saloon-car racing. The presence of Daimler script on the boot lid passed almost unnoticed. Another heresy was the Borg–Warner automatic gearbox available in the latter part of 1956; this would supersede the fluid flywheel before the Conquest family was finally dropped during 1958.

Lanchester sales were even worse hit. Their first post-war LD10 was a scaled-down Daimler with a 1.3-litre four-cylinder engine, though bevel drive and all-steel coachwork by Briggs were money savers, as were the cloth trim and the absence of interior woodwork. It was very expensive at £927—there was seldom a waiting list for Lanchesters—and even more costly after 1949, when the makers switched to a better-appointed Barker coachbuilt body. The LJ200 Fourteen of 1951 was somewhat better: it was a four-cylinder prototype of the Daimler Conquest, though the piston stroke of the 2-litre engine was still an archaic 108 mm. The chassis specification paralleled that of the Daimler, and there was an all-metal edition, the Leda, for export customers. Neither sold.

The last of the line was the Sprite of 1954, in theory an £1,100 small car with automatic transmission as standard. In practice it lost its sponsors £500,000, and only one of the ten cars built is known to have ended up in private ownership. The Hobbs box was one of the better automatics of its period, with four forward speeds and a manual override, and the 1.6-litre engine was two-thirds of a Conquest. The swing-up bonnet–wing assembly was new in this class, and a liberal use of light alloy panels kept the weight down to 2,350 lb. Regrettably, the styling was an uneasy mélange of Series II Morris Oxford and SM1500 Singer. A second version combined Conquest styling and more steel, but it was about 300 lb heavier. Edward Turner's new management swept it out with sundry other cobwebs.

The Jowett Javelin certainly worked: sales were about 25,000 cars, there were rave notices in the press, and a string of rally victories. Gerald Palmer conceived it as the answer to Citroën's *onze légère*, basing the fastback shape on the pre-war Lincoln Zephyr. Like many British engineers, he was working to difficult parameters. The export market called for a good ground clearance (which the Javelin had) and plenty of power, but on 1945 form home-market priorities began with a 10-hp (1,200-cc) engine. Either way the car had to be produced in the antiquated factory at Bradford, though this did not in fact happen. The tax concessions eliminated the small-engined Javelin at the prototype stage, and an injection of capital from the Clore interests not only financed a £250,000 tooling bill but also allowed a redesign in unitary form. The hulls were built by Briggs at Doncaster.

Though seen in the Motor Industry's Jubilee Cavalcades of 1946, the car took a long time to reach the public; some early customers, indeed, wished it had not. Not that the Javelin was a bad design: quite the opposite. Being a Jowett, it had a water-cooled flat-four engine, but the latest edition was an advanced overhead-valve affair with die-cast alloy block and hydraulic valve adjusters. The output from 1,486 cc was 60 bhp. The twin Zenith carburetters were fed by mechanical pump, cooling was by pump and fan, and the Jowett's column shift was one of the few bearable four-speed specimens. Salisbury made the hypoid rear axle, and the excellent rack-and-pinion steering gear was matched by an all-torsion bar suspension on Citroën lines. Moreover, the car was a full six-seater with adequate luggage accommodation. Only the low third gear (rectified on 1952 and later models) could be criticized, while to those nurtured on the British family Twelve the performance was a revelation—80 mph in top, 55 mph in third and a 0–50-mph acceleration time of 15.3 seconds. By 1952 the hydromechanical brakes had given way to full hydraulics, and the 'hydraulic' tappets had disappeared, but the change of image was unequalled in the history of the automobile. Jowett's publicity summarized the situation. Where there had once been allusions to the 'little engine with the big pull', now potential customers were adjured to 'take a good look as it passes you'. The Javelin usually did.

It had also passed beyond its makers' capabilities, even without the protracted teething troubles. Horizontally opposed engines are never very accessible, but the water got in, and Javelins 'drowned' in wet weather. Third gear jumped out, and there were interminable problems with blown gaskets and run bearings. It was not until 1953 that all these difficulties were conquered on the Series III engine, and by that time Jowett were in trouble, with rising prices (£1,207 in 1952) and falling demand. Geared as they were to the Briggs machine, there was no way of asking this huge factory to 'go slow'; meanwhile, hulls were stockpiling at Doncaster. In the end, Briggs stopped production altogether—the Ford takeover came later on and merely prevented any resumption. No Javelins were made after 1953; attempts to bridge the gap with the Jupiter sports car and Bradford replacements came to nothing.

Of the true reactionaries, only AC survived into the 1970s, on the strength of their later sports cars. The touring 2-litre, however, accounted for some 1,300 units in our period. Despite a new streamlined body it was certainly the most Vintage of all.

The engine, dating back to 1919, was the famous old 65 mm·× 100 mm 2-litre wet-liner o.h.c. six, giving 74 bhp in 1947 form with three side-draught SU carburetters. The separately mounted Moss gearbox, also used by Morgan, had synchromesh on its three upper ratios and a proper floor shift. Final drive was now by hypoid bevel, and the frame was a fine piece of 1930's engineering, cruciform-braced and underslung at the rear. Once again, the brakes were hydromechanical and would stay that way until the end of 1951, while independent suspension had no place in the scheme of things. The AC was heavy on the hands at low speeds, but managed 80 mph. An attractive option was a four-seater tourer, but increasing preoccupation with the Ace series pushed the saloons steadily into the background, and very few were sold after 1954.

In 1946 form, the Alvis was equally old fashioned, its mechanical brakes calling for fearsome pedal pressures. The TA14 was merely an updated 1939-type 12/70, with a 1,892-cc four-cylinder pushrod engine in a conventional chassis with semielliptic springs and a hypoid rear axle. Like AC, Alvis now used disc wheels. The weight was 3,135 lb, and 75 mph was the limit, but the TA14 was very flexible for a four and beautifully made. 3,400 were sold, though little was heard of the twin-carburetter TB14, a high-performance version marred by its outrageous roadster bodywork. The

1948 show prototype concealed its headlamps behind the grille, and a cocktail cabinet in one of the doors, but, mercifully, these eccentricities were deleted from production models.

The 3-litre TA21 of 1950 was a big step forward. The front wheels were independently sprung, though the transverse-leaf arrangement of the 1930s had given way to a lighter coil-and-wishbone system. The frame was a robust affair with six cross-members, wheel size was down to 15 inches, and the brakes were 2LS hydraulics. The seven-bearing six-cylinder engine had dimensions of 84 mm × 90 mm, and in its original form with a single dual-choke carburetter it gave 85 bhp at 3,800 rpm, sufficient to propel a heavy saloon at 85 mph. It would stay the staple Alvis until the end in 1967, Alec Issigonis's rubber-suspended vee-eight remaining stillborn. Later cars had twin carburetters, and the zenith was reached in 1954 on the TC21/100, a 100-mph saloon with centre-lock wire wheels. Alas for Alvis, Mulliners of Birmingham, their main source of bodies, had been taken over by Standard–Triumph. Since dropheads came from the Aston Martin-owned Tickford works, the company was in a quandary.

They solved it by turning to Graber of Berne, who had been mounting their own attractive coachwork on 3-litre chassis since 1951. The solitary Alvis shown at Earls Court in 1955 was Graber's TC108/G, a streamlined two-door sports saloon. The employment of a foreign *carrossier*, of course, meant import duty on the finished product, so only thirty Alvises were sold in 1956 and 1957. Fortunately an agreement with Park Ward of London enabled the company to resume serious production in 1958.

Armstrong Siddeley's 'cars of aircraft quality' had to compete with Rover rather than Jaguar and suffered accordingly. Not, however, without their moments of glory, for the 1945 Sixteen, the work of Sidney Thornett and F. W. Allard, was a stylistic sensation comparable with America's Studebaker.

Mechanically, we were back with the upper-class norm. Here was a conventional 2-litre pushrod six with four main bearings, hydromechanical brakes, a hypoid rear axle and, of course, the company's four-speed preselective gearbox, though for the first time since 1932 there was a manual option with floor change. The independent front suspension was of torsion-bar type, and the frame was K-braced. Wire wheels were a seldom-seen option, and appointments were genuine wood and leather. Permanent jacks were standard: radios and heaters were catalogued extras from the start.

Not content with recessed headlamps, however, the Armstrong Siddeley's designers had endowed their car with a modern vee-grille atop which the Sphinx sat in resignation. The bodies, available even in 1946 in a choice of pastel shades, were restrained yet attractive, especially the Hurricane drophead coupé and the Typhoon two-door saloon. The Armstrong Siddeley was a gentleman's carriage with good brakes and a 70-mph top speed;

its worst fault from a driver's viewpoint was a bonnet that appeared to slope uphill! From 1949 a 2.3-litre engine was available; this was standardized a year later, powering such variants as the rare long-wheelbase limousine and the even rarer 'sports station coupé', a variation on the Australian coupé utility theme. Total sales of the family were 12,570 units, and the Eighteen lasted into 1953.

The big 3.4-litre Sapphire of 1953 marked a reversion to a traditional radiator grille; it also slotted neatly into a gap between the Austin Sheerline and the R-type Bentley. The engine was a square-dimensioned (90 mm × 90 mm) 3.4-litre six with hemispherical combustion chambers, and, though the transmission options were retained, both were improved, with a synchronized bottom gear for manuals and electrical selection for the Wilsons. Also new were the recirculating ball steering, the coil-and-wishbone front suspension, and hydraulic brakes working in 11-inch drums. With a length of 193 inches, the Sapphire was more compact than the Mark VII Jaguar, and it was not much slower—90–95 mph with a single carburetter and a genuine 100-mph with the 150-bhp twin-carburetter unit available by the summer of 1953. On the debit side, a gallon of petrol lasted 15 miles, and the front wings were rust-traps.

After 1954, sales fell off. The first 3,750 Sapphires took only a couple of years to sell, but fewer Mark IIs were made in the 1955–9 period, despite such refinements as Hydramatic transmission (built by Rolls–Royce) and a vacuum-servo brake option. Once again there was a limousine on a 133-inch wheelbase, while by 1956 the car was available with variable-rate power steering, adjustable rear dampers and power windows, a near-Cadillac specification. In the meanwhile, however, Armstrong Siddeley had committed delayed hari-kari with the small 2.3-litre Sapphires.

The idea—which anticipated the Rover 105—was excellent in theory. One used the same mechanics for a gentleman's carriage to out-Rover Rover and a sports saloon to turn the tables on Jaguar. Apart from the 111-inch wheelbase, the chassis was that of the big Sapphires, with servo brakes, though the all-synchromesh gearbox now featured a floor change. The rapid 234 used a twin-carburetter four-cylinder edition of the large six; for the 236 the company revived the old long-stroke six-cylinder Eighteen and gave it a Manumatic clutch. Overdrive was offered with either package. The 234 was almost as fast as the Jaguar 2.4, steered better and rolled less. Alas! the bodies were not only ugly they were worse rust-traps than ever. The 234 was rough above 4,000 rpm, and once again the customers wanted six cylinders. Sales, at 803, were less than 5% of the small Jaguar's sales. The 236 accounted for another 603 units, and neither car was quoted after 1958.

Lea–Francis blamed their decline on double purchase tax, though they were still selling a few cars in 1954. Their 1946 offerings had much in common with the TA14 Alvis: beam axles, disc wheels and Girling brakes, as well as a four-speed synchromesh gearbox with central change. The main differences were the Leaf's spiral bevel back end and twin-high-camshaft engine, designed by former Riley engineer R. H. Rose. A 69 mm × 100 mm twelve was available up to 1947, but most cars used the 1,767-cc 56-bhp Fourteen unit, its SU carburetter fed by twin electric pumps. Lea–Francis built their own saloon bodies, though their early woody station wagons were contracted out to a small joinery in the Sussex village of Yapton. In 1949 a torsion-bar front suspension and hydromechanical brakes were introduced, together with an aerodynamic Mark VI saloon for export. This piece of bulboid had a more powerful 65-bhp engine to cope with the added weight, but a year later it had reappeared with a new 2½-litre (85 mm × 100 mm) unit rated at 85 bhp. Later improvements would include hypoid rear axles and (in 1953) full hydraulics, but nothing could arrest the steady decline: 878 cars in 1950, 487 in 1952 and a round hundred in 1953.

The Murad made a fleeting appearance in 1948. The Aylesbury-based firm planned to make their own short-stroke (72 mm × 92 mm) 1½-litre push-rod four-cylinder engine with hydraulic tappets, and the four-speed synchromesh gearbox was separately mounted. The coil-spring independent front suspension and hypoid final drive were predictable, and radios and heaters were part of the package. The styling was a bizarre synthesis of SM1500 upper works, a Holden-like grille and angular wing lines. 'Substantial orders' were reported from an unspecified Scandinavian country, but 1949 started without a sign of any Murads.

14.5   Sports Cars for the World

The T-type MG's contribution to the motoring scene was out of all proportion to the 49,000-odd built in our period. Though only two-thirds of all TCs were exported, the breed reintroduced Americans to open-air fun motoring. Among the USA's racing drivers, John Fitch, Richie Ginther and Phil Hill all cut their teeth on the breed.

Basically the TC was the old TA of 1936 with a conventionally sprung frame, tubular cross-members and open two-seater bodywork with Le Mans-type slab tank. 18-inch wire wheels were fitted, and the brakes were hydraulic. The engine, already in use in 1939, was a 'stretched' M-series Morris Ten unit with 66.5-mm bore and twin semidowndraught carburetters, giving 54 bhp from 1,250-cc. The top speed on a 5.125:1 axle ratio was a little under 80 mph. By 1950 it had given way to the more modern TD.

This model sold even better, averaging 10,000 a year; it had taken four seasons to turn out that number of TCs. Externally it was identifiable by its disc wheels, bumpers (the TC had suffered from American parking techniques!) and coil-spring independent front suspension. It cost little to engineer, being merely a shortened YA chassis with a TC body, the package including the saloon's rack-and-pinion steering. A weight penalty of 170 lbs was easily offset by factory-sponsored tuning kits. Such modifications could extract 97 bhp and three-figure maxima. Blowers, special heads and pistons and high-ratio rear axles were available. Sadly, the TF of 1954 was yesterday's lunch warmed-over, since the new BMC management considered the Austin–Healey 100 'enough sports car' for them and played the MG down. The sloping radiator and padded facia were pretty enough, but even a 1,476-cc 63 bhp engine introduced during 1955 could not save the model. Less than 10,000 were sold.

The MG A was introduced late in 1955 and was based on the aerodynamic two-seaters run at Le Mans that year. The suspension and steering were inherited from the T-series, but Abingdon had resorted to the ubiquitous 1½-litre BMC B-type unit, giving 68 bhp in twin-carburetter tune. At 1,968 lb, the car was heavier than the TD, but at long last MG offered proper luggage accommodation for a modest £844, and no tuning kits were needed to attain the magic 100 mph or an 0–50-mph time of 11 seconds. The MG A survived into 1962: 101,081 were produced, inclusive of the later 1600s and Twin-Cams, and a record 96% were exported. For 1957 the two-seater was joined by a fixed-head coupé, MG's first such style in twenty years.

Quantitatively speaking, Jaguar's contribution was smaller—20,992 road-going XKs up to April 1957. It was, however, technically more exciting. True, the combination of a modern chassis, an aerodynamic shape, civilized appointments and untemperamental mechanics had been found in the BMW 328 of 1936, but the BMW was relatively expensive, even in its homeland. The XK120 at £1,273 (Americans paid from $3,345 to just over $4,000) was, however, priced in the Lyons tradition—below the bounds of credibility. Hitherto twin upstairs camshafts had been considered too noisy and complicated for volume production, and many people regarded 1948's bronze show car as a come-on. The following spring it refuted these suspicions by recording 132 mph over the flying mile at Jabbeke. Standard versions weighed 2,856 lb, attained 120–125 mph and took just over 7 seconds to reach 50 mph. They would also accelerate away in direct drive from 10 mph.

The heart of the XK120 was Jaguar's 3,442-cc twin-overhead-camshaft six, developing 160 bhp. The twin SU carburetters were fed by electric pump, and the rest of it was standard Jaguar practice: a robust box-section frame, hydraulic brakes and the torsion-bar front suspension of the latest Mark V saloons. Only contemporary limitations of brakes and tyres prevented full exploitation of the car's potential, but in any case the XK could outperform any other car on the road. A companion 2-litre four, the XK100, was advertised but never built.

No XK120s reached the home market before March 1950, and very few after that date. In 1951, however, a delightful fixed-head coupé was introduced; a drophead followed during 1953, by which time there was a special-equipment 180-bhp version featuring high-lift camshafts, twin exhausts and centre-lock wire wheels for better brake cooling. Also listed was the racing C-type, fulfilling William Lyons's ambition 'to run the fastest possible scheduled service over the Sarthe Circuit'. A lightweight frame, stark bodywork and a 200-bhp engine added up to 145 mph, and the car was tractable enough for town use. Later models had all-disc brakes, as did the *monocoque* D-type of 1954, with dry-sump lubrication, a triple- plate clutch and even less habitable *carrosserie*. On 250 bhp the car attained at least 175 mph but was for advanced students only.

The rack-and-pinion steering of the competition models had reached the catalogue by 1955, on the XK140, with an output of 190-210 bhp according to specification. The occasional rear seats of the coupés and convertibles spoilt their lines, but special-equipment models would do 130 mph. Overdrive was a regular option; so, from mid-1956, was an automatic gearbox, though only 827 cars were sold with this. Disc brakes would not, however, be fitted to street models until 1957. The twin-camshaft Jaguar Six would still be a major force in 1977, even if the true sports models had succumbed to the combined pressures of inflation, the energy crisis and exhaust-emission rules.

Aston Martin, now under the David Brown umbrella, also raced energetically, though they would not win Le Mans until 1959. The cars, were in a different price bracket: a DB2 cost £2,015 in 1950 and £3,076 in 1956. Only 917 had been delivered by 1955.

In 1947 it had seemed as if the traditional Aston cycle of rich sponsors, heavy losses and reorganizations would continue. Claude Hill's 2-litre (David Brown rechristened it the DB1) owed little to pre-war ideas. The new engine was a short-stroke (82.55 mm × 92 mm) five-bearing four with pushrod-operated overhead valves in place of the accepted overhead camshaft. In twin-carburetter form it gave 90 bhp at 4,750 rpm, David Brown furnished the four-speed synchromesh gearbox and hypoid rear axle, and the chassis was fabricated from steel tube. A coil and trailing-arm suspension featured at the front, with a live axle and coils, located by a Panhard rod, at the rear. The hydraulic brakes worked in 12-inch drums. Aston Martin's drophead coupé with its cutaway doors was one of the more attractive cars of the era, though it could not match the elegant simplicity of Lyons's XK120 roadster. The DB1 weighed 2,520 lb and was good for 95 mph.

Meanwhile David Brown had moved in, and the 1949 Le Mans race saw the first results of the new ownership: a fastback coupé using W. O. Bentley's twin-overhead-camshaft 2.6-litre six-cylinder engine, acquired with Lagonda. The chain-driven o.h.c. and hemispherical combustion paralleled Jaguar thinking, though Bentley was content with four mains. The output was a more-than-adequate 105 bhp at 5,000 rpm, boosted to 116 bhp on the high-compression Vantage version. The bonnet—wing assembly tilted forwards to give access to the works, and the chassis, though similar to that of the DB1, was 9 inches shorter. With an eye to American sales, column shift was a catalogued option, and the Aston Martin managed 110 mph, put an easy 60 miles into the hour on British roads and offered superb road behaviour at the price of a harsh ride and a formidable noise level. Like Jaguar's C-type, the 2.9-litre DB3 sports racer of 1952 with its torsion-bar front suspension, five-speed gearbox, de Dion back axle and inboard rear brakes was not made for street use, though two coupés (for David Brown and his daughter Angela) were built on its successor, the DB3S. These latter cars had four-speed boxes, while cooling problems dictated a return to outboard brakes. On an 87-inch wheelbase the open DB3S weighed only 1,960 lb, attained 141 mph in road trim, took less than 15 seconds to reach 100 mph and was reasonably tractable. Disc brakes were regular equipment on competition Aston Martins by 1956.

By the end of 1953 the DB2 had evolved into the DB2/4 with very occasional rear seats and an early example of the hatchback, an extra 5% of power balancing an increase in weight. All the urge was, however, back by 1955, when a detuned edition of the 2.9-litre engine was standardized, giving as much as 165 bhp in Vantage form. The result was a GT that would match the best available from Italy.

GTs were, of course, hardly in the Frazer Nash tradition, even if chains and dogs had given way to variations on a BMW theme, using the eighteen-pushrod 1,971-cc six made in Britain by Bristol. This was a logical step: the Aldington brothers had held the BMW concession since 1934, and in the later 1930s German imports had steadily ousted the old chain-drive cars.

The company's post-war range was as bespoke as ever, but it could all be summarized by the same essential specification: a frame of large-diameter lightweight tubes with an integral firewall doubling as crash pylon, BMW-type suspension (transverse-leaf and wishbone type at the front, with torsion bars at the rear), rack-and-pinion steering, a spiral bevel back axle and 16-inch wheels with proper ventilation for the 2LS hydraulic brakes. Other BMW heritages were one-shot lubrication and a free-wheel on bottom gear. This last refinement was, of course, deleted from the Le Mans Replica (née High Speed), a stark two-seater in ready-to-race trim, weighing 1,400 lb and capable of 120 mph. Fast Roadsters, Mille Miglias and Targa Florios were better-furnished affairs in the full-width idiom, and from 1953 there was a two-seater coupé with a new lower grille and a radiator blind, available to order with a de Dion back end. All engines had three carburetters, and tune was what the customer specified, from a modest 80 bhp up to some 150-bhp on the last Le Mans Replicas delivered in 1953. Everything was expensive: even a 'stripped' 1952 prototype with the four-cylinder Austin A90 engine and column shift cost twice as much as an Austin–Healey, which explains why the experiment was not repeated. Another car which did not happen was a proposed Le Mans entry using the 3.4-litre hemi-head Armstrong Siddeley unit. At the end of our period Frazer Nash adopted the latest BMW vee-eight and its all-synchromesh box. Only a few of these Continental models were made, and after 1961 AFN Ltd concentrated on yet another foreign import, the Porsche.

Donald Healey and A. C. Sampietro set up in business at Warwick in 1946, making five cars a week, which explains why only 633 of the original 2.4-litres were actually produced. The Healey was, however, the fastest four-seater saloon of its day, putting 102 miles into the hour from a standing start. The recipe was a light cruciform-braced chassis (it weighed only 160 lb), a big lazy engine and a 3.5:1 top gear. Both the engine and gearbox came from Riley's excellent 2½-litre four, though frame and suspension were Healey's own, with coils and trailing arms at the front and Aston Martin-like coil springing at the rear. Brakes were full hydraulic, saloons and roadsters weighed around 1 ton, and a wind resistance estimated at 45% less than that of a stock Riley spelt more than a good performance: a gallon of petrol lasted 25–28 miles. The kite-shaped grille gave the Healey an Italian look, and the only real fault was the familiar Riley disease, heavy controls.

Unfortunately, Healey prices were far too high, and there ensued a constant struggle to find safe niches in the market. 1948's slab-sided Sportsmobile convertible was a failure; equally ugly was the stark Duncan two-seater with its Cord-like grille, its austerities justified by a base price of £998. It gave way in 1949 to Healey's own Silverstone, the answer to the club racer's prayer. This was a simple device with cycle-type wings, a retractable windscreen and headlamps tucked Peugeot-fashion behind the radiator grille: the spare wheel was recessed into the tail and doubled as a bumper. The light-alloy body shell was a weight saver, and, though the Silverstone cost only £25 less than an XK120, it was at least readily available in Britain. It could have saved Healey, had their attention not been diverted by George Romney of Nash Motors.

Romney was on the lookout for something different, and this the Nash–Healey certainly was. Made exclusively for sale in America the car was a combination of a reinforced Silverstone chassis and Nash's 3.8-litre overhead-valve six, tuned to give 130 bhp with the aid of twin SU carburetters. Floor shift and dual overdrive were desirable adjuncts, while the

British-built body featured a fixed vee-screen and a Nash-type grille. At $4,063, however, it still cost more than a Jaguar, and 1952's Pininfarina facelift added shipping complications; chassis now went from Warwick to Turin to receive their bodies, inflating the price to an unrealistic $5,868. Only 506 Nash–Healeys were built, the last of them, with 4.1-litre engines, in 1954. Healey salvaged something from this deal by putting 3-litre Alvis units into their Type G for the home market. It was expensive, at £2,490, and only 25 were sold. The Riley-engined cars had put on weight, too, Tickford's sports saloon scaling 2,800 lb. The *marque* seemed destined to be Jaguar fodder.

The situation was saved by the 100 roadster, on a new twin-tube frame of 90-inch wheelbase. Money had been saved, too, by using a 'lump of iron' instead of the expensive Riley engine. This 'lump' was, of course, the 2.7-litre pushrod four from the defunct Austin Atlantic, now with twin horizontal SUs, electric pump feed, pressurized cooling and Austin's four-speed gearbox converted to floor shift. Semielliptic suspension replaced coils at the rear, and the new slab-sided bodywork had an Italianate elegance totally lacking in the rival Triumph. A price of £1,324 was inviting, but Healey's fifty workers were in no position to cope with the ensuing flood of orders.

Austin, however, were, and agreement was reached within days for volume production at Longbridge. The Austin box gave way to a three-speed all-synchromesh affair with dual overdrive. Centre-lock wire wheels were adopted, while the poor ground clearance was offset by the use of an undershield. The hoppity rear end was no worse than the Triumph's understeer, and the Healey formula of a lazy engine pulling less than 2,000 lb produced an excellent performer capable of 110 mph. About 14,500 were sold before it gave way, at the end of 1956, to the 100/6 with BMC's C-type engine. For the competition-minded, there was the hand-built 100S put together at Warwick. With the aid of a special Weslake head and a stiffer crankshaft, the power was boosted from 90 to 133 bhp, other features being a four-speed close-ratio box without overdrive, a heavy-duty clutch, reinforced and lowered suspension and (remarkably, in 1955) Dunlop disc brakes. The S-type gearbox had found its way on to the standard article by 1956. In addition, Americans were offered a compromise between street and competition models. This 100M ran to 110 bhp and an extra antiroll bar but retained the drum brakes. It cost $3,275.

If the Austin–Healey was right from the start, 1952's other important débutante, Triumph's TR2, was almost a disaster. The strange little car shown at Earls Court was evolved around two objectives: a speed of 90 mph and a basic price of £500. On a weight of 1,708 lb, the first target presented no problems, but the means of achieving it were odd—a 1937 Standard Nine frame, Mayflower suspension and the ubiquitous Vanguard engine in 1,991-cc form. The kindest comment was that it was a pardonable reaction from the equally bizarre TR-X of 1950. Officially a casualty of the Korean War, Walter Belgrove's dream car featured fully aerodynamic roadster bodywork of stressed-skin construction. It also carried power assistance beyond Cadillac levels, with a maze of hydroelectrics operating the hood, windows, retractable headlamps, seats, overdrive and radio aerial. The mechanical elements were stock Vanguard with an extra carburetter, but the TR X was a bulky and vulnerable car 166 inches long, which weighed 210 lb more than the superseded 2000 Roadster. Two of the three prototypes have survived.

Harry Webster of Standard had managed to make the TR2 both drivable and saleable by March 1953: a 124-mph demonstration at Jabbeke 'played it in' in the now-accepted manner. The 88-inch wheelbase was retained, but a new and rigid cruciform-braced frame replaced 1937's dead stock, larger front brakes were fitted, and the output was boosted from 75 to 90 bhp. The longer tail offered greater stability and some luggage accommodation, while, unlike Healey, Triumph opted for four speeds and stayed with them. Other basic features were shared with the Vanguard, and on this functional machine Standard's 'hole-in-the-wall' grille looked right. Triumph had found a winner, to the tune of some 80,000 units produced up to 1962.

Powered by the ultimate in tough engines, the Triumph was simpler than its rivals. It weighed only 2,072 lb in road trim and combined a speed of 105 mph with parsimonious habits. *The Motor*'s overdrive-equipped test car, returned a *mean* consumption of 34 mpg, and, at a steady 90 mph a gallon lasted 27 miles. A high noise level, scuttle shake and low-hung doors were snags, while the understeering characteristics could become vicious in unskilled hands. For those who mastered it, the TR2 was an excellent buy at £787. Factory-fitted hardtops arrived in 1955, and a year later came the TR3 with a few more horses, an eggcrate grille and room for a third passenger, though Triumph never made the mistake of essaying a four-seater. The 1957 TR3A was the first cheap sports car to feature disc brakes—on the front only—as standard equipment.

Three years earlier, Daimler had made a brief sally into the sports-car market with their Century roadster. The ugly body with its wrapround screen and tail fins gave the car a promenade look which was belied by the 100 bhp of the twin-carburetter 2.4-litre engine. Handling was good, too, while the fluid flywheel transmission lent itself to fast changes. The ton came up easily on a 4.1:1 axle ratio, but noise, looks, image and price were all against the sports Conquest, and it faded from the picture in 1955 after only 65 had been built. A further 54 two–three-seater drophead coupés were, however, made on the same chassis in 1956 and 1957.

More logical was Lea–Francis's twin-camshaft sports car. The 1948 Special Sports used a twin-carburetter edition of the 12/14 unit in a shortened chassis: the 14-hp version disposed of 77 bhp. The body was a curious mixture of ancient and modern with a streamlined grille and recessed headlamps, yet retaining a 1935-style humped scuttle look. Only 228 were sold. A 2½-litre edition on the same 99-inch wheelbase followed in 1950; this car had a torsion-bar independent front suspension and a hypoid rear axle. 100 bhp and 100 mph were available, but the car cost £200 more than a Jaguar.

Also a natural in the sports-car stakes was the Jowett Javelin, and a great deal of talent—Laurence Pomeroy, Eberan von Eberhorst of Auto Union fame and Leslie Johnson of ERA—was there to effect the transformation. So, unfortunately, were the merchant bankers who controlled Jowett. What was planned as a simple 1,500-lb car aimed at American enthusiasts, came out the other end as a luxurious 2,000-lb 'three-passenger convertible roadster' with wind-up windows, column shift and no luggage accommodation whatsoever. The output of the engine was boosted to 60 bhp; the space-frame and the front suspension, by unequal-length wishbones, were entirely new. Wheelbase was an abbreviated 93 inches, and the Jupiter had full hydraulic brakes, even in 1950. The swing-up bonnet–wing assembly was a great improvement on the Javelin's awkward engine-room arrangements, but £1,087 was a lot to pay for a 1½-litre, and the familiar teething troubles had helped not at all. By 1953 there were a reliable engine and a proper boot, but it was too late.

Nor could the Jupiter's sales of 300 a year keep Jowett going after the Briggs débacle. Right at the end chief engineer Roy Lunn came up with what should have happened in 1950, the ultralight R4 on a 74-inch wheelbase. The presence of an electric fan permitted a smaller and lower radiator, rear springing was now semielliptic, and the box-section chassis wore a glassfibre *barchetta* body in the Ferrari idiom. With the optional 3.64:1 overdrive 120 mph were claimed, but only prototypes were made.

Of the London makers, AC created a furore in 1953 with John Tojeiro's two-seater Ace. This was another Ferrari-shaped car, metal-bodied this time. The chassis was, however, more sophisticated than that of any Ferrari, with a twin-tube frame, a rigidly braced final drive unit and an all-independent suspension, by transverse leaf and lower wishbones. The 2LS hydraulic brakes worked in Al-Fin drums 11¾-inches in diameter, the wheels were of the centre-lock type, and the synchromesh gearbox had high and close ratios—3.64:1, 4.98:1, 7.21:1 and 12.34:1. The steering was high geared and precise, and the handling was probably the best in its class. In the midst of all this, the poor old 2-litre overhead-camshaft six looked out of place, though in its latest twin-carburetter form it gave 85–90 bhp, sufficient to propel the Ace at 103 mph. A coupé variant, the Aceca, followed a year later.

By 1956 the Ace had found a worthier engine, the 2-litre triple-carburetter Bristol with 35–40% more power. It speaks volumes for the soundness of this design that in later years the Ace coped with a 7-litre engine and also over 400 bhp.

AC were wedded to an old-fashioned engine. So were Allard of Clapham, with the added problem that it was not one they made themselves. They were also an unlucky firm. Before 1949, admittedly, they had little opposition in the high-capacity field, though they suffered, as new manufacturers, from constant supply problems. Though Sydney Allard's faith in large, lightly stressed American engines was justified by events, currency restrictions prevented him from offering the latest vee-eights on the home market. When he won the 1952 Monte Carlo Rally at the wheel of one of his own cars (a unique feat in the Rally's history) he returned in triumph—to a Britain mourning the death of her King. His small car, the Palm Beach, coincided with the faster and better-financed Triumph and Austin–Healey. In the circumstances Allard's post-war output of about 1,900 cars must rate as creditable.

The permutations were limitless. The basic engine was, of course, the 3,622-cc side-valve Ford vee-eight, which could achieve 85–90 bhp, but the Mercury was also used in 3.9-litre and stroked-crank 4.4-litre forms, and all these engines could be had with the Ardun overhead-valve conversion devised by Zora Arkus-Duntov. From 1951, hard-currency customers could specify the 5.4-litre overhead-valve Cadillac. Allard's practice was, however, to ship his cars across the Atlantic in engineless form, and consequently other vee-eights (Chrysler, Lincoln and Oldsmobile) found their way into later models. Types ranged from the stark Js to the luxurious and expensive P2 saloons and station wagons of 1952.

The first post-war Allards were on the road by mid-1946. They featured the simple chassis and rearwards-biassed weight distribution of the company's pre-war 'trials irons', with a divided-axle independent front suspension and regular Ford springing at the rear. Hydraulic brakes and 12-volt electrics were standard, as were Ford-built three-speed gearboxes. Allard offered three wheelbase lengths: 100 inches for the J1 competition two-seater, 106 inches for the touring K1 edition and 112 inches for the four-seater L-type tourer and M1 drophead coupé. Unlike the austere 1938–9 models, the latest cars featured sloping bonnets and striking waterfall-type grilles: in their original guise these upset the cooling arrangements, and production versions had fewer and more widely shaped bars. Though not to everyone's taste, Allards combined standing-start acceleration in the Railton tradition with the Ford's go-anywhere qualities. Production reached over 300 units a year at its peak: the best-selling P1 saloon on the long chassis accounted for 551 examples between 1949 and 1952.

Touring Allards continued with little change until 1952, though later Ms (and all Ps) had column shift; while the divided-axle independent front suspension was still used, now incorporating coil springs. Front-end styling varied: the K2 two-seater shared its grille with the super-sports J2, late P1s had a shorter edition of the original waterfall, and the rare M2X drophead had an A-shape of its own, later used in modified form on P2s.

The J2 of 1949 marked a return to simplicity. The main design change was at the rear end, with its de Dion axle and coil springs. The 2LS brakes worked in 12-inch drums, and the wheelbase was 100 inches. The body was a doorless affair with cycle-type wings and alloy panels, which could be removed without disturbing either floor or facia. Even with a 'cooking' Ford engine this one was good for over 100 mph, but with the 160-bhp Cadillac and a 3.2:1 rear axle ratio, it became a bomb. The prototype attained 130 mph in top, 100 in second and an astounding 80 in first, which meant a 0–60-mph time of 7 seconds. In its revised J2X form with Chrysler hemi engine and quick-change final drive unit, the vehicle offered 215 bhp per ton. The last of the J-series was the aerodynamic JR of 1953. This model sold in America, complete with Cadillac power, for $8,500. A total of 189 J2s and JRs were made.

By 1952 touring Allards were more luxurious, with new twin-tube frames, right-hand floor shift and (on the P2 series) a swing-up bonnet opened by hydraulic pump. The P2 saloon cost £2,568, and the K3 roadster on the 100-inch chassis was a roomy car, seating four abreast. Only 83 of this family were built, but Allard were pinning their hopes on the new compact Palm Beach.

This used a P2-type frame with a live axle and coils at the rear. The body was of full-width type like that of the K3, and engines were the latest British Fords, the 1½-litre Consul and the 2.3-litre Zephyr Six. The car weighed less than a ton, but neither performance nor price could match the opposition. A speed of 90 mph was the limit, even with the Zephyr unit, and the £1,064 Allard had little hope against the TR2 at less than £900. The Palm Beach was withdrawn in 1955, only to reappear a year later with restyled bodywork and a choice of 2½-litre Zephyr or 3.4-litre twin-camshaft Jaguar units. Jaguar's unwonted munificence suggested that they took a dim view of Allard's prospects. They were right: deliveries, now down to a trickle, ceased for good in 1959. Plans for an American edition of the Palm Beach with the 4-litre Dodge vee-eight engine likewise came to nothing, though a prototype was built in 1953 and attained over 120 mph.

HRG were even smaller than Allard, and their best year's showing was 40 cars in 1948. The Halford–Robins–Godfrey partnership had risen to prominence in the later 1930s with a Vintage-style sports two-seater. This car was still being made eighteen years later. The deep channel-section frame rode on quarter-elliptic springs at the front and semielliptics at the rear, and cable-operated brakes were used until 1952. The sole concessions to modern thinking were coil ignition and synchromesh, inherited with the overhead-camshaft Singer engines used since 1939, and these units sat well back in their chassis, 6 inches behind the axle. The bodywork was in the best 1933 tradition, with a 10-gallon slab tank at the rear, feeding the twin SU carburetters by pump—mechanical on the 1100 and electric on the 1500. The power units were extensively modified: HRG's own contributions included new exhaust valves, valve springs, pistons, manifolds and water pumps. This extracted 61 bhp from the 1500 engine, sufficient to propel the 1,625-lb lightweight at over 85 mph. In 1946 the company tried all-enveloping bodies on the 1500 chassis, but these HRG Aerodynamics tended to flex, while the mounting of the spare wheel and fuel tank on opposite sides of the tail led to some interesting problems of weight distribution. The last traditional HRGs were sold in 1955, but already something exciting was on the stocks.

This featured a twin-tube frame with AC-type all-independent springing and dual-circuit disc brakes of Palmer design. Magnesium alloy wheels were fitted, and under the bonnet was Singer's latest twin-overhead-camshaft engine, said to give 108 bhp with twin dual-choke carburetters and some further tuning. Singer also contributed the four-speed gearbox, but the Rootes takeover stopped this promising line of development.

Nothing, however, could shake the Morgan—still the same individual, uncomfortable and taut-handling two-seater it had been in 1936 and would be in 1976. Only 1954's sloping grille marked the passage of a decade, though in fact there was more than one engine change.

The original 4/4s had used the overhead-valve Coventry Climax engine, but in 1946 form the car had a 1,267-cc pushrod four made specially for Morgan by Standard. The rest of it was as before: sliding-pillar independent front suspension, a three-wheeler type chassis underslung at the rear, a separate four-speed gearbox and rod-operated Girling brakes. A two-seater cost £499.

The 2,088-cc Standard Vanguard engine arrived in the Plus-Four of 1951, together with a hypoid rear axle and hydraulic brakes; speed went up from the low seventies to around 90 mph. With the 2-litre TR2 engine, available from 1954, the ton was possible. Finally, in 1956 there was a 4/4 revival, the latest edition using the 1,172-cc side-valve 100E Ford. As the deal included the Ford gearbox, Morgan had recourse to an unpleasing push–pull gearchange, but the traditional handling was there. So, in a light two-seater weighing only 1,540 lb, was a most un-Ford-like fuel consumption of 35–40 mpg.

Also Triumph orientated was the Swallow Coachbuilding Company of Walsall, heirs to Jaguar's erstwhile side-car interests. Their Doretti of 1954 was conceived as a luxury edition of the TR2. It used a robust tubular chassis and roadster bodywork of their own design, though the engine, gearbox, brakes and suspension were stock Triumph. Though the Doretti looked roomier, it was not, since the extra wheelbase length had been offset by moving the engine 7 inches further back in the frame. The price of an extra 450 lb of weight was £115, which explains sales of less than 500 cars. It was all over by the spring of 1955.

14.6 'Take One Scrap Ford Van...'

If comfort, weather protection and painless gear changing meant less than purchase tax at 50% or more, it was surprising what could be done to an old Ford Ten.

Some of these devices were short-lived. Little was heard of Rex McCandless's 1956 lightweight two-seater from Belfast. The chassisless backbone was an ingenious adaptation of farm-tractor techniques, with the engine and gearbox as structural members. The suspension was all-independent, with swing axles at the rear, while the use of a disc transmission brake in lieu of orthodox rear drums emphasized the designer's trials background. The Nordec of 1949, a more substantially bodied roadster resembling a baby Allard, also made a fleeting appearance. The divided-axle independent front suspension accentuated the similarity, and the car was offered with one of its maker's specialities, the Marshall supercharger. The rear suspension was orthodox Ford.

By contrast Kenneth Delingpole and R. B. Lowe managed to sell 500 of their Dellows. Originally conceived as trials mounts built up from second-hand Ford components, the little cars were so well received that by 1950 they were being constructed from scratch.

The formula was simple—an A-shaped tubular chassis, Ford running-gear with longitudinal quarter-elliptics at the back, a stark doorless two-seater body welded to the frame and an engine set well back to give better weight distribution. Creature comforts were minimal, but with double valve springs and a Wade–Ventor blower the engine was persuaded to give 48 bhp. On early Dellows, a fiddle brake was fitted; this device, a favourite with trials drivers, worked the front-wheel brakes when pushed forwards and those at the rear when pulled back. Subsequently coil springs were used at the back, and there was even an occasional four-seater on a lengthened 95-inch wheelbase. Not all Dellow customers were sportsmen; in 1952 a firm of agricultural engineers acquired a fleet of two-seaters for their sales staff. The last model of our period was the ultralight Mark V of 1954, a miniature J2 Allard with rigid axles and coils at each end and the latest 100E Ford engine. Brakes were still mechanical.

Buckler and Paramount represented opposite ends of the Ford spectrum. The former was sold in kit form, in trials or club-racing guise. Multi-tubular triangulated frames and divided-axle independent front suspension were regular practice, with de Dion axles, four-speed MG gearboxes and a choice of MG or Coventry–Climax engines in the DD1 of 1955. The trials-type Mark V was cheaper; a frame and body structure cost £60, to which had to be added £41 for an independent front suspension, £15 for a special radiator (it was positioned behind the engine), £8 for a fuel tank and £17.25 for close-ratio gears and remote control. The rest was up to the customer, who got a free badge if the body were panelled 'to professional standards'.

Paramount Cars of Swadlincote offered no kits, nor were they interested in racing. To them the Ford Ten engine was a convenient basis for an individually styled four-seater roadster with a hint of Healey about it. The twin carburetters were standard, a supercharger was an option, and in 1950 they planned to sell the result for £632.

Once again a twin-tube frame was used, but Ford suspension was discarded in favour of transverse-leaf i.f.s. and semielliptics at the rear. The Ford gearbox sported a remote-control floor-mounted lever, brakes were hydromechanical, and the rear axle was of hypoid type. When the original sponsors ran out of cash, the Meynell Motor Company took over, substituting a BMW-shaped grille for the previous Sunbeam–Talbot style and mounting twin fuel tanks in the full-flow front wings. Finally in 1953 the Paramount moved south under the aegis of a Bedfordshire used-car dealer, though all it gained from migration was a 12-volt electrical system and a price tag of £887. The alternative model with the Ford Consul engine was rather faster, but, apart from the excellent range conferred by the 15-gallon tanks, the car had little to offer at over £1,000, and by mid-1956 yet another dealer, this time in Marylebone, was remaindering off the unsold stocks. Between them, the various Paramount companies made about 120 cars.

During our period, Colin Chapman's Lotus Engineering operated on a hole-and-corner basis. As late as 1953, *le patron* worked for British Aluminium by day and in his Hornsey shops by night. Engines, gearboxes and back axles were the client's responsibility. (This was understandable, since Ford declined to furnish Consul engines to backgarden specialists; when Chapman wanted one it had to be purchased piecemeal from dealers!) Typical of his early work was the Mark VI of 1953, the ancestor of the famous Lotus Seven. It consisted of a multi-tubular frame to which flat light-alloy panels were riveted to give extra strength. A swing axle and coils were used at the front, with a live axle, coils and Panhard rod at the rear. Ford cable brakes were retained, the Ford gearbox was given a remote-control shift, and a weight of 950 lb permitted a 90-mph performance.

By 1954 Lotus had progressed to a true aerodynamic shape with twin stabilizing fins, a de Dion rear axle, inboard rear brakes and Morris rack-and-pinion steering. The Eleven of 1956 was a usable if not overcivilized road car. The specification again depended on the owner's ambitions, the Club edition using the side-valve 100E Ford engine and three-speed box, drum brakes and a conventional rear end with an Austin A30 axle and coil springs. This one was good for 98 mph, but with the 1,100-cc overhead-camshaft Coventry–Climax unit and 75 bhp, the package included a de Dion back end and disc brakes. For those undaunted by a Perspex screen too low to protect a tall driver, no hood, no room for luggage and precious little for one's clutch foot either, the reward was almost magical—125 mph and 34 mpg. After testing this *bolide*, *The Motor* felt that 'the forthcoming coupé model from the same designers is likely to be worth waiting for'. They had to wait till the 1957 London Show.

Other people used old vee-eights. The JBM, made at Horley between 1946 and 1948, was a stark competition two-seater using many second-hand parts. With a four-carburetter manifold, 120 bhp were extracted from 3.6 litres, but plans to build a 'new' JBM with a coil-spring independent front suspension and hydraulic brakes never materialized. The JAG of 1949 featured reconditioned vee-eight mechanics in their own steel-tube frame with coils and double wishbones at the front. Its aluminium-panelled roadster bodies had an Italian look.

Turner of Wolverhampton made a few cars in the early 1950s with twin-tube frames, all-independent suspension and Morris steering, but their first serious effort was the A30 Sports of 1956. An early customer was the singer Petula Clark.

This sports car 'for the enthusiast with limited budget' was far less ambitious than a Lotus. Steering gear was Morris, Turners made the ladder-type frame, trailing-arm rear suspension and glassfibre roadster body, and the rest, apart from the hydromechanical brakes, was pure A30. The factory claimed 80 mph and 45 mpg, and more when the 948-cc A35 engine became available towards the end of the year. The American list price of $2,000 compares interestingly with the $2,269 asked for an MG A.

Coopers of Surbiton were primarily interested in racing cars. They did, however, toy with a few road-going lightweights, including one based on their rear-engined Formula III machine of 1947. Like its racing cousins, this one rode on a pair of Fiat *topolino* front suspension units, and the 'anchors' were likewise Fiat, even down to the transmission handbrake. The frontal grille was inspired by the E-type ERA, and the power was provided by a 500-cc vertical-twin Triumph motor-cycle engine. A later effort—of which several were made—was a stark front-engined two-seater, also Fiat-suspended. With a twin-carburetter Vauxhall Twelve engine, it did over 80 mph.

Racing commitments curtailed the road-going Connaught line after only 27 cars had been built. The sponsors, Rodney Clarke and Mike Oliver, found themselves in 1948 with a Bugatti agency and no Bugattis to sell. Their answer to this hiatus was the L2 Connaught, a 1.8-litre two-seater with a swing-up nose section. Essentially the car was the Lea–Francis Fourteen Special Sports, down to the cart springing and mechanical brakes, though

Connaught extracted 98 bhp on an 8.5:1 compression, sufficient for three-figure maxima. Preselective gearboxes were optional, and the mechanical specification kept pace with the latest Lea–Francis developments—hydromechanical brakes and a torsion-bar independent front suspension, this latter found on the L3 of 1951. This was a stark doorless affair with cycle-type wings and aero screens. There was a choice of five axle ratios, while dry-sump lubrication and a four-carburetter manifold could be specified for racing.

Kieft, Cooper's Formula III rivals, tried sundry sports-car themes, from a rear-engined economy device with a 650-cc BSA twin engine and chain drive to a ferocious *bolide* for the American Erwin Goldschmidt, on which a vee-eight De Soto engine was wedded to a Jaguar gearbox. The regular strain featured tubular space-frames, all-round independent suspension by unequal-length wishbones and brake drums integral with the wheels. MG or Coventry–Climax engines were usually fitted, a peculiarity of sports-racing Kiefts being the central driving position.

This did not, however, feature on the two-seater they showed at Earls Court in 1954, though spider-type alloy wheels did. In road-going tune with twin SU carburetters, the 1,098-cc overhead-camshaft Coventry–Climax four-cylinder unit gave 72 bhp, the brakes were 2LS hydraulics, and the glassfibre-bodied car weighed a low 1,120 lb. It managed 105 mph on test, but in 1956 the company changed hands, and this line of development was abandoned.

Fairthorpe fared better with proper sports cars than they had with bubbles. Their Electron was in production by the end of 1956. Available in kit form, it used the same engine as the Kieft, though the output was up to 84 bhp. The twin-tube frame, coil independent front suspension and the four-speed Moss gearbox were familiar ingredients, while Fairthorpe were another firm who favoured live axles and coils at the rear. As on their mini-cars, the two-seater bodies were of glassfibre, and the Electron could attain 110 mph. It was still in production in 1965.

Far divorced from Kieft or Fairthorpe were the fifteen Marauders sold between 1950 and 1952. These luxury roadsters were cut-and-short P4 Rovers on a 102-inch wheelbase, with high-geared steering and flatter rear springs. Some Rover panels were used in the bodies, the work of Richard Mead, whose father had made the overhead-camshaft Rhode in the 1920s. Customers had a choice of the stock 'Auntie' engine or a 'stretched' 2.4-litre edition with a special head and three carburetters. An alternative to the regular free-wheel was a Handa overdrive operative on all forward gears, selected via the free-wheel's control knob. The recommended practice was to select one's range at the beginning of a journey, though nothing untoward happened if a swap were made in motion. Unfortunately, a car that cost £1,236 in 1950 had passed the £2,000 mark a couple of years later. . . .

The Gordano's Italian-sounding name derived from a stream in its native Somerset. According to its sponsors, 'Never before has such a combination of economy and high performance, light weight and long life, been offered at such moderate cost.' If its price of £995 was realistic, the Gordano was certainly a bargain. These virtues had been attained without the benefit of Ford; the company planned to use a 1½-litre four-cylinder Cross rotary-valve unit developing 90 bhp. This delivered its power to a four-speed transaxle with a plain 'dog' engagement on Frazer–Nash or GN lines. The gear lever was rigidly mounted on the central tubular cross-member of the ladder-type frame, and the problem of tall drivers was tackled by making the pedals and steering-column adjustable. The independent front suspension was of Lancia type, with a rubber-in-shear arrangement at the back. An MG-powered prototype took the road, but it was not purchase tax that eliminated the Gordano. Within a year three of the team—Walter Watkins, Joe Fry and the designer Roderick Gordon Jones—all met tragic ends.

14.7 You Can Only Hear the Clock

The 'best car in the world' went marching on.

True, the men at Crewe kept a weather eye on Detroit, so Rolls–Royce's delightful four-speed gearbox with its right-hand change had disappeared by 1955, replaced by the same Hydramatic as graced $2,200 worth of Pontiac. Nor was the product necessarily bespoke: from 1946 the companion Bentley was offered with factory-built Standard Steel bodywork, and three years later the disease had spread to Rolls–Royce's own Silver Dawn. 820 out of 4,000 Mark VI Bentleys carried custom bodies, but only 303 of the 2,000 R-types that followed them were so equipped.

The big news from Rolls–Royce in 1946 was, of course, the adoption of overhead inlet and side exhaust valves, the best compromise. In other respects the cars were refined rather than modernized. Fuel feed was by twin electric pumps, the four-speed synchromesh box was unchanged, and other features included hypoid rear axles, dashboard-controlled rear dampers, one-shot lubrication, and the successful coil-and-wishbone independent front suspension first seen on the Phantom III in 1935. The frames were cruciform braced, and Rolls–Royce still distrusted hydraulic brakes, though they ventured as far as hydromechanicals, incorporating, of course, the gearbox-driven servo used since 1923. Water pumps were now belt driven, and disc wheels replaced the centre-lock wire type of pre-war models. Capacity of the six-cylinder engine was unchanged at 4,257 cc.

The Bentley was by no means badge engineered. Under the bonnet, the inevitably 'sufficient' brake horses called for twin SU carburetters where the Silver Wraith was content with a single, twin-choke Stromberg, and the

Mark VI's wheelbase, at 124 inches was 3 inches shorter than that of the Rolls–Royce. The Bentley was a likeable car, attaining 92 mph on a 3.73:1 axle ratio, and the standard steel saloon's subsequent reputation as a rust-trap was due mainly to the model's longevity, the chassis outliving wings and door sills. From 1948, left-hand drive (with steering-column shift) was a regular option, and a year later came the export-only Rolls–Royce Silver Dawn, a Bentley chassis and body with the detuned Silver Wraith engine. Though this model was progressively developed until 1955, only 760 were made: hence the subsequent brisk trade in 'false Dawns' converted from the commoner Bentley! 1951 saw a long-chassis Silver Wraith for large bodies.

From 1950 there had been a Phantom IV, but this was only for Heads of State; sixteen were built. Clients included Queen Elizabeth II, the Shah of Persia and General Franco. It used a straight-eight edition of the Silver Wraith engine: the capacity was 5.7 litres, and this B80 unit also found its way into fire-engines and specialist military vehicles. A 145-inch wheelbase left plenty of room for ceremonial bodywork, and the massive Phantom chassis alone weighed 5,300 lb.

The six-cylinder engines were enlarged to 4.6 litres during 1951, the latest 92-bore units making the Standard Steel Bentley a 100-mph motor-car. Also available was the fastest four-seater saloon of its day, the Bentley Continental. The compression ratio went up to 7:1, the radiator was lowered, India produced special tyres to cope with speeds of 115–120 mph, and H. J. Mulliner's two-door fastback marked a return to sanity after the bulboid horrors seen at Earls Court in 1948 and 1949. On a 3.077:1 rear axle the Continental would cruise at three-figure speeds in exemplary silence, and its fuel consumption was still a miserly 20–23 mpg. It was also one of the costliest cars on the market, at £6,929 as against £4,824 for a Standard Steel, and only 208 R-type Continentals were built.

Rolls–Royce's own version of GM's four-speed Hydramatic transmission was introduced on the 1953 models, together with automatic chokes and bigger boots for the standard R-type Bentley and the latest Silver Dawn. By 1954, manual gearboxes were confined to the Continental series, offered from September with still bigger 4.9-litre engines. By the summer of 1955, this unit had been standardized on the Silver Cloud and its Bentley equivalent, the S1.

Here was badge engineering at its most stereotyped. True, one could still buy an individually-styled Rolls–Royce or Bentley: the long-chassis Silver Wraith was exclusive to the former *marque*, and the Continental to the latter. But the sole differences between the Cloud and S-type were the radiator—and £130. Improvements were a new six-port head, a revised short-and-long-arm front suspension with an antiroll bar, and electrically controlled rear dampers. Overall length was up by 8 inches, and the latest Standard Steel bodies retained more than a vestige of a wing line. The automatic box could be overridden, and to all the traditional refinement was added a cruising speed in the low nineties. Rolls–Royce remained as cautious as ever in the face of technical innovation: power steering was not adopted until 1957, and as late as March that year one could specify an S-series Bentley Continental with synchromesh.

At the beginning of our decade, the Daimler was still correct Royal wear. Whatever might be said of Sir Bernard Docker's rule at Radford, the era will be remembered for his 'show spectaculars' on the straight-eight chassis. Among these were the Green Goddess of 1948, an enormous power-top convertible with Facel-type headlamp clusters in the full-flow wings and triple wipers, 1951's gold-plated Hooper touring limousine and 1952's 'touring coupé', a fixed-head version of the Green Goddess with double glazing and lizard-skin trim for everything. Some outside customers' were almost as exotic, notably Saoutchik's 7,400-lb limousine for King Ibn Saud.

The basis of all these—and of 201 other cars including the dignified carriages of the House of Windsor—was C. M. Simpson's eight-cylinder DE36, a development of the nine-bearing 4½-litre made before the war. Externally, the main difference was the new model's curved radiator grille, but the DE36 was enormous, with a 147-inch wheelbase, a track of 63 inches and a weight in the region of 3 tons. Its size was accentuated by the dual side-mounts in cellulosed covers found on most cars, though not on the Docker specials. The cylinder capacity was up to 5,460 cc, and the output of the unit with its twin downdraught SU carburetters was 150 bhp at 3,600 rpm. New at the top of the range was the DB18's coil-spring independent front suspension, though unlike the smaller cars the DE36 had a hypoid rear axle and some necessary Dewandre servo assistance for its hydromechanical brakes. Handling was very sure footed for so elephantine a vehicle, and the clients included the reigning houses of Afghanistan, Ethiopia, Holland, Monaco and Thailand, not to mention President Eduard Benes of Czechoslovakia.

The DE27 was much the same thing, only with a 4.1-litre six-cylinder engine and a 138-inch wheelbase. This model was available in some intriguing variations, of which Daimler Hire's austere DH27 limousines had longer chassis than the eights, at 150 inches. Daimler also made 500 DC27 ambulances for well-heeled municipalities, and there were even a brace of Lanchester versions with tourer bodies by Vanden Plas, for that dedicated Lancunian, the Jam Sahib of Nawanagar. By contrast, the exotic Lanchester Dauphin prototype shown at Earls Court in 1953 was merely a 2½-litre Daimler Conquest with two-door Empress coachwork by Hooper. This experiment was not repeated. The DE27 disappeared in 1952, though the large eight outlived it by about eighteen months.

The next step was to replace the owner–driver Daimler Light Straight-Eights of the later 1930s. Had Daimler acted promptly, this might have succeeded, but the whole Regency story is one of indecision, and, by the time there were cars in the showroom, Jaguar and Armstrong Siddeley had cornered the market.

The original DF300 of 1951 was a straightforward four-bearing six with a capacity of 3 litres on a 114-inch wheelbase, with the Conquest's hypoid rear axle and hydromechanical brakes, though not its torsion-bar front suspension. A year passed without any production, and then came one of the decade's most attractive might-have-beens, a four-seater cabriolet with power top and windows and the overdrive gearbox used in the DB18 Special Sports. The twin-carburetter engine developed 100 bhp, but this one never reached the customers, either, albeit a few cars were made to similar mechanical specification, with 3½-litre power units and Hooper's Empress coachwork.

It was not until 1955 that Regency production got under way, and even then the variety was infinite. There were two engines, a 3½-litre and a new 4.6-litre and two wheelbases, 114 inches for saloons and 130 inches for the vast Regina limousine. Overdrive was available on sports saloons, and servo brakes were part of the 4½-litre package. A year later the range had been tidied up, the owner–driver saloon emerging as the 104 series, with 3½ litres and 137 bhp, a stiffer frame, servo-assisted full hydraulic brakes of two-trailing-shoe type, tubeless tyres and a top speed of 100 mph. Even then matters were complicated by the addition of a Ladies' Model. The presence of labelled switches suggested a low opinion of the female intellect, but the package also included simplified wheel-changing tools, a cigarette case, a gold notepad and pencil and even a telescopic umbrella (reminiscent of Rover's 1932 'Carella'). Even in masculine guise, however, the 104 cost £2,672, nearly £1,000 more than a Mark VII Jaguar, so few men could have afforded a second Daimler for their wives. At the end of 1956, Borg–Warner automatic transmissions were offered on 104s but not on the big 4.6-litre limousines.

Down at Staines, W. O. Bentley had interesting plans for Lagonda, though these did not include the legendary vee-twelve. Its replacement was, however, not without excitement. Under the bonnet was a twin-overhead-camshaft six of 78 mm × 90 mm (2,580 cc), mounted in unit with a four-speed Cotal electric gearbox, whence the drive was transmitted to a hypoid rear axle. Steering was by rack and pinion, and Bentley had plumped for all-independent suspension—by coils and wishbones at the front and torsion bars at the rear. The rear brake drums were mounted inboard, and a saloon was provisionally priced at £1,751.

The Lagonda had everything except the necessary materials to built it—and, sadly, style. Pre-war cars from Staines had been superbly proportioned: they also had the lengthy wheelbases which the 2½-litre lacked. Worse still, its traditional bodies sorted ill with the latest streamlined grille and front wings. Double purchase tax was the final blow, and the Staines factory was closed down in August 1947, without having delivered a single car.

Salvation was, however, at hand in the shape of David Brown, already in control of Aston Martin. Bentley's excellent engine was a natural choice for the Aston Martin DB2 sports car, and in due course the Lagonda was revived, turning up at Earls Court in 1948 with a boxed-in frame and a conventional synchromesh gearbox with column shift. Though sure-footed, it was heavy and, like the vee-twelve, had to be driven on the gears. A price of £3,110 explains why only 520 2½-litres were sold, and there was little demand even with 1953's 2.9-litre engine and the lower, better-proportioned saloon and drophead coupé bodies. The 3-litre was still listed in 1958, but, though the customers included the Duke of Edinburgh, only 267 cars were made. The 4½-litre competition vee-twelve of 1954 was never intended for series production and wore a Lagonda badge on the strength of past associations. The rest of it was DB3S Aston Martin.

If Lagondas combined the worst of both worlds, the Bristol enjoyed a well-merited success. Better still, its BMW-based engine was used by AC and Frazer Nash, not to mention countless small specialists such as Cooper and Lister.

The original 400 of 1947 looked more German than British. The complicated cross-pushrod 2-litre six-cylinder engine, the synchromesh gearbox with its free-wheel on first, the hydraulic brakes and the suspension units were copybook BMW, as were the 16-inch pressed-steel wheels. Refinement was apparent in the wood and leather interior (the BMW's plastic knobs had gone), the one-shot lubrication and the built-in radio. The less-U sliding windows, as Bristol remarked, 'gave extra elbow-room.' The weight was high, at 2,580 lb, but the standard three-carburetter engine propelled the Bristol at over 90 mph, the aerodynamic shape was commendably quiet, and the steering was delightfully precise. Despite a price of £2,723, 700 Bristol 400 saloons were sold.

Until 1950, the 400 was the staple home-market offering, though for export there were the 401, a two-door saloon in the Alfa Romeo idiom by Touring, and Pininfarina's 402 cabriolet. The former was much fussier than the anglicized 401 with factory-built bodywork which had supplanted it by 1951, and the shape had a long career, culminating with the 403 series of 1953.

All Teutonic influences vanished on the 404 of 1954, this car, promoted by its makers as 'the business man's express', being a two-seater coupé with a single-panel curved screen and a 'hole-in-the-wall' grille. The spare wheel lived in the left-hand front wing, but less than desirable was the use of wood framing for bodies in place of the 403's steel tubes. On 125 bhp, the 404 could achieve 110 mph, and American customers were offered something even faster, the Bertone-bodied Arnolt–Bristol two-seater exclusive to S. H.

Arnolt of New York. A high price of $4,250 was justified by the Arnolt's versatility. 'Not even a spark plug change,' insisted the catalogue, 'is needed to go from the supermarket to the starting line.' Bertone's coupé version was even more expensive at $6,390, but the cars were still selling in modest numbers when the parent company abandoned their faithful six in 1961.

Latterly Bristols grew more and more expensive: 1955's 405 series retailed at a swingeing £3,586. Sales fell—to 340 units in four seasons—but this latest four-door saloon cruised at an effortless 90 mph. It shared the 404's styling and body construction, but a tamer 105-bhp unit was fitted, radial-ply tyres and overdrive were standard equipment, and the wheelbase was longer than hitherto, at 114 inches. A drophead coupé was also available.

The Railton, first of the Anglo-American sports bastards, made a token appearance after the war, sixteen cars being built up from parts on hand in Hudson's Chiswick shops. New components could not, however, be brought in except for re-export, and the price of £4,750 asked for the 1948 London Show car explains why this was no longer viable.

Even sadder were the declining years of the Railton's one-time *alter ego*, the Invicta. Banished from Cobham and deprived of the enthusiastic support of the Lyle and Macklin families, it retained only two links with the past: Meadows-built engines and the services of designer William Watson. Ironically, too, Britain's great protagonists of 'top gear for everything' had at last evolved a one-gear car.

Only the 16-inch disc wheels proclaimed the Invicta Black Prince's post-war origins: even the headlamps were out of doors. The rest of it, however, would have alarmed even Preston Tucker. The new engine was a complicated all-alloy affair with seven mains, twin overhead camshafts and a twelve-plug head. The three horizontal SU carburetters were fed by twin electric pumps, and the dimensions were 81 mm × 97 mm for a capacity of 2,998 cc. It gave 120 bhp and needed to, for between this impressive piece of machinery and the hypoid rear axle was a 'hydrokinetic turbo transmitter', offering infinitely variable ratios from 4.27:1 to 15:1. Driver control was confined to a forward-and-reverse switch. The massive X-braced chassis embraced a subframe for the body, the brakes were hydraulic, and all wheels were independently sprung, by transverse torsion bars. Hydraulic jacks, radio and heater were standard. So was a 24-volt dynamotor, and this intriguing car weighed 3,920 lb.

Charlesworth, who were to have built the bodies, went bankrupt, though Airflow Streamlines and Jensen bridged the gap. Endless trouble was experienced with the solenoid-operated reverse, and at a price of £3,890 there was little future for any 3-litre car, especially an untried design. Watson planned to scrap the hydrokinetics in favour of a four-speed Jaguar gearbox, but late in 1949 the money—reputedly £100,000 of it—ran out, and the remains were acquired by Frazer Nash. Only about two dozen cars had been made, but the Aldingtons were surprised to find that Invicta had stockpiled sufficient components for thousands more!

Another Anglo-American specialist, Jensen of West Bromwich, had already moved up-market in 1939 with their Nash-engined 4.3-litre and had elected to continue with them. They could afford to: their other interests included trucks not to mention coachwork for 'the big battalions'. During our period Austin was the principal client: not only the A40 Sports but also the successful Healey 100 family were bodied by Jensen.

The PW of 1946 was just as catastrophic as the Invicta. It may well have been the unauthorized prototype of the Austin Sheerline: affinities are detectable in radiator grille and in the saloon body's razor-edge lines, though the Jensens were masters of their craft and did it much better.

As yet the mechanics had no Austin affiliations: the box-section frame incorporated tubular cross-members, and Jensen favoured a worm-drive back end. The four-speed synchromesh gearbox had an overdrive top, and the brakes were full hydraulic, while suspension was of all-coil type, independent at the front. Jensen, like Invicta, went to Meadows for their engines, square-dimensioned (85 mm × 85 mm, 3,860 cc) pushrod straight-eights for which 130 bhp were claimed. Unpublicized but regrettably present was a fearsome vibration period, and of the seven PWs built (one was a four-door convertible with power top) only four were sold. These were fitted with leftover Nash engines.

At this juncture Leonard Lord offered the company his 4-litre Princess unit. This went into a revised PW with direct top gear and hypoid-bevel rear axle, but even then the car did not sell. The Austin engine, however, fitted admirably into the Jensen scheme: a low-revving power unit pulling a high-ratio rear axle. They would pursue this formula to the end in 1976.

The first of the new generation, the Interceptor cabriolet, shared their stand at Earls Court in 1949 with the revised PW saloon. The slab-sided coachwork with its wrapround rear window and oval grille sat six at a pinch and served as the prototype of the A40 Sports. The frame was the PW's, shortened by a foot, rear suspension was semielliptic, and early Interceptors had hydromechanical brakes, though full hydraulics were soon back again. Initially the specification included a 3.22 rear axle and a direct top gear, but from 1952 overdrive was standard, with selection by a sideways flick of the central gear lever. In this form, the car rode along at an effortless 85–90 mph in the highest 2.85:1 ratio, with a fuel consumption of 20–25 mpg. Admittedly the Austin engine protested if 4,000 rpm were exceeded, but this was hardly ever necessary. The Interceptor was still catalogued in 1957, but sales were modest—only 87 saloons and dropheads all told.

The four-seater 541 saloon was, however, one of the great cars of its era, and a true GT, though once again production was on a modest scale—533 cars between 1954 and 1962. The mechanical elements were the Interceptor's with servo-assisted brakes, but the body, designed by Richard Jensen and Eric Neale, was a handsome glassfibre creation with double-skinned front wings, heater ducts in the wheel arches and an ingenious driver-controlled pivoted blanking plate over the grille. The wheelbase was a short 105 inches, and the weight was kept down to 3,165 lb. At 115 mph in overdrive, the engine was still turning below the recommended 4,000-rpm limit, and this 2.75:1 ratio would take the Jensen up a one-in-ten hill at 80 mph. Apart from some rather rustic indirect ratios, it was an excellent car and well worth the £2,701 asked. At the end of our period, it acquired disc brakes.

15   Australia

15.1   A Dinkum Car at Last

In the first post-war decade the Commonwealth joined the ranks of the manufacturing nations.

Admittedly, registration figures did not show the dramatic increases apparent between 1930 and 1940, when Western Australia's car population rose by 278%, and even the highly industrialized state of Victoria recorded a 66% jump. This latter figure was equalled between 1940 and 1950 in both Tasmania and South Australia, but thereafter the average growth rate slowed, from 55 to 41.3%.

The War, however, had not only accelerated road building: it had also isolated Australia from her normal sources of supply. The number of factories rose from 26,941 in 1939 to 48,719 in 1952. By this time New South Wales alone boasted 19 automobile assembly plants, 158 body builders and 44 accessory makers. Four years later, the industry employed 80,000 people (14,200 of these working for General Motors–Holdens), distributed among 72 manufacturing and assembly units. The all-Australian Olympic firm at Footscray in Victoria furnished one-third of the Commonwealth's tyre requirements.

Nor were these developments untimely, for Australia suffered from a chronic balance-of-payments problem. This was reflected in a stop–go attitude towards imports, which had uncomfortable echoes in Birmingham and Coventry, especially in the middle 1950s. The Commonwealth needed its own motor industry, even if as yet the Holden was not only 'Australia's own car': it was the only native product sold in measurable quantities. Chrysler's all-Australian Royal and BMC's prentice efforts would not appear until 1957, and it would be another three years before Ford of Geelong would offer a real challenge with local versions of Detroit's compact Falcon.

The Holden must stand as the classic example of a national car. Before 1914, Spyker was synonymous with Holland and Martini with Switzerland, but neither make was dominant at home. Even Sweden's Volvo did not become a national best-seller until 1956. Yet the first Holden went on sale in November 1948: in a little over two years 10,000 had been delivered, and 250,000 had been sold by January 1956. By this time General Motors–

Holdens had cornered 26.9% of private-car sales and 23.4% of the truck sector. This latter statistic becomes staggering when one reflects that as yet Holden's only commercials were car-based pickups and panel vans! 1955's new registrations were significant: 45,423 Holdens as against 35,017 BMC products, 17,228 American cars of all makes and only 6,412 (mostly Volkswagen) from Germany. In the 1960s Holden's share of car and commercial sales alike would approach 50%.

Not that the Holden was Australian in concept. The 1956 FE was the first all-native effort, and a car which called for an investment of £A7,500,000. Even in 1977 there was still a 2% 'foreign' content, including ignition keys made in America by Briggs and Stratton. Opinions still differ as to whether the basic theme was Vauxhall or Buick's discarded 1938 compact. Suffice it to say that prototypes were made in America in 1946: the ensuing 'Australianization' involved 237,000 miles of intensive road testing.

The car that emerged was copybook American compact. The full unitary construction followed Vauxhall or Opel lines, but the rest of it conformed to trans-Pacific ideas. The engine was a four-bearing overhead-valve six of 76.2 mm × 79.4 mm (2,170-cc), giving 60 bhp at 4,000 rpm, with a downdraught carburetter, mechanical pump feed and 6-volt electrics. The wideratio three-speed synchromesh gearbox incorporated a steering-column change, the hydraulic brakes worked in 9-inch drums, and the suspension was stock Chevrolet, with coils at the front and semielliptics at the rear. The four-light sedan body with its vee-screen was a lineal descendant of the 1938 Cadillac, but less ornate, and therefore more pleasing, than the Detroit idiom. Australian requirements were reflected in a generous 9½-inch ground clearance and the absence of such northern-hemisphere essentials as turn indicators (scarcely legal in the Commonwealth!) and heaters. The car was truly compact, with a wheelbase of 105 inches and an overall length of 172 inches. It weighed only 2,230 lb.

The Holden was a brisk performer, attaining 80 mph with a 0–50-mph acceleration time of 12.3 seconds. It was also light on fuel, the factory claiming 37 mpg at a steady 35 mph. Handling was terrible, and the brakes 'grabbed' in a disconcerting fashion (they still did, fifteen years later, as I once discovered to my cost), but it was tough, it was cheap (a sedan cost £A675 or about £540 sterling), and parts were reputedly available from any barman in the Outback. In the best GM tradition, owners were encouraged to personalize their Holdens with Air Chief radios, and more regionally oriented gimmickry—Coolaride seat cushions, oil-bath air cleaners and venetian blinds for rear windows.

By 1953 the FX series (this designation was never official) had supplanted locally assembled Chevrolets, though its replacement, the FJ, was unchanged apart from a new grille and stiffer dampers. It was available in a variety of forms from the utilitarian Standard to the Special with two-tone trim, vestigial tail fins and a cigar lighter. Production was running at 50,000 a year, and in November 1954 the first Holdens were exported—to New Zealand. The FX and FJ together accounted for 297,000 cars.

C. R. Lewis's all-Australian FE appeared in the summer of 1956. Its 1953 Chevrolet styling with single-panel wrapround screen made it look more revolutionary than it actually was, though the wheel size was now 13 inches, the clutch was hydraulically actuated, and the latest recirculating ball steering was adopted. In spite of the higher compression and larger inlet valves, engine development did not keep pace with the growing weight, and the FE was never the 'bomb' that the FX had been. It was nevertheless sold further afield—to Malaysia and Thailand. By this time Holden-based specials comparable with England's Ford Ten derivatives were in fashion. Of these, the Maserati-like Ausca disposed of 135 bhp, thanks to twin SU carburetters and a special head designed by Phil Irving of Vincent–HRD fame, while the Tontala was a glassfibre coupé kit which could be mistaken, at a distance, for one of Briggs Cunningham's street models. Such 'backyard beauties', as *The Motor* called them, were not produced on a commercial scale, though in 1956 £A1,350 was quoted for a complete Tontala kit.

Of the other contenders, neither Jean Reville's 1950 Ranger nor the Wiles–Thompson of 1947 reached the public. The former was notable only for the odd choice of engine, a 1.3-litre Lanchester Ten with fluid flywheel transmission, but the latter, a stark unitary four-seater tourer, was intended to retail at a low £A300. Almost everything, including the water-cooled vertical-twin two-stroke engine, was to be of Australian make, but only two prototypes saw the light of day.

A more serious small-car project was started in 1947 by Lawrence Hartnett, one of the originators of the Holden project. Initially, Hartnett's idea was a modernized edition of the 1942 Willys Four, with a locally built body to sell at £A275, but a tour of Europe in 1946 changed his plans. He studied the Volkswagen and the 4CV Renault, before settling on the Aluminium Française–Grégoire. The little air-cooled flat-twin with its front-wheel drive seemed the perfect answer, and Hartnett was fortunate enough to pick up the remnants of the Kendall disaster for a modest sum.

Finding the right design was one matter, but making a car from scratch was quite another. Through the good offices of J. A. Grégoire, supplies of essential components—Bendix–Tracta universals, electrics and clutches—were assured from French factories. Engines, gearboxes, castings and the Kendall-type hydromechanical brakes would come from Britain. Hartnett had even persuaded both Federal Premier J. B. Chifley and the Victorian Government to subsidize the venture, but unfortunately Labour lost the next General Election, and the state administration reneged on their deal. Undaunted, Hartnett personally raised the £A100,000 necessary to finance the project, and production started in 1950.

At last all seemed set fair for the Australian Grégoires, but now the coach builders failed to meet their commitments. Imported bodies carried an uneconomic rate of duty, so the company was reduced to knife and fork methods, putting together the Pacific tourer coachwork by hand. Somehow, 120 cars were completed, but this was the end. Understandably Hartnett decided not to proceed with the larger 2-litre R-type Grégoire, a car he personally liked. He would later build up a substantial empire as the Australian agent for the Japanese Datsun.

16 Japan

16.1 Will the Sun Never Rise?

Even in 1956, nobody spared a thought for the Japanese motor industry. 1956's output of private cars was a paltry 32,000, of which precisely 46 were exported. Total home registrations hovered below the 200,000 level, with annual sales of perhaps 30,000 units, most of them taxis. When Renault remonstrated over Hino's reluctance to pay royalties on their locally built 4CVs, the French Foreign Office remarked that it was 'hardly fair to pick on this poor little country which has such a task to feed hundreds of millions of inhabitants'.

True, things were on the move. In 1950, Japanese truck makers were already circulating brochures in bizarre English, aimed at the ex-Colonial nations of the Far East. But, while Toyota's export drive was aided by a convenient parts interchangeability with the ubiquitous Chevrolet, the 2,401 commercial vehicles shipped in 1956 were not sufficient to frighten Bedford, let alone America's 'big three'.

At home, the industry was hemmed in by the old Automobile Control Laws, not to mention a fiscal code of surpassing severity. As if a 50% sales impost were not enough, circulation tax doubled on a car with a capacity of more than 1½-litres. It was not until 1959 that belated concessions ushered in a new race of 2-litre saloons from Nissan, Toyota and others. Ill-surfaced and tortuous roads necessitated stiff suspensions, compact cars and abysmal axle ratios, while the export picture was not as rosy as it looked. The markets nearest to Japan could barely afford private cars at all, while Australians had no use for untried 1-litre sedans. Any hopes of cashing in on Communist China's 'great leap forward' were ended by the Americans after the outbreak of the Korean War, though this conflict brought compensation in the shape of useful American military orders.

Steel was expensive, and wide sheet had to be imported from America. Thus even in 1953 bodies were still made by hand. A spokesman for the three largest makers (Nissan, Ohta and Toyota) observed that these firms would order dies, 'if each could be assured of a market for 7,000 cars annually'. His wish was not granted: that year's deliveries ran to 8,789 units only, well short of the 1,750,000 Toyotas and 1,500,000 Datsuns sold in 1975. Hence Japanese coachwork continued to resemble parodies of the

1940 American idiom, with awkward angles instead of curves.

However, in spite of French criticism, the ingredients of success were already there. Labour was cheap, and the aircraft industry's wartime record showed what could be achieved. True, the big combines had been carved up, but, if Mitsubishi and Nakajima no longer existed in their 1944 guise, both halves of the former empire were already in the truck business. From the remains of the Nakajima Group, the Fuji Precision Industries, makers of the 1½-litre Prince, emerged. Soichiro Honda might still confine his energies to motor-cycles, but he was also investing $1,000,000 in new American machine tools. By 1956, a major road-building programme had been started, and a year later Prince would exhibit at the Paris Salon. Nor were all the statistics laughable: in 1956 Japan made no fewer than 105,000 commercial three-wheelers. These were, as it transpired, a dead end—even their staunchest protagonists, Mazda of Hiroshima, had given its best by 1973— but it only needed the necessary incentive to turn Nippon's efforts in a better direction.

The cars themselves displayed little originality. If only Datsun wore its Austin Seven origins on its sleeve, Japanese firms were content to build suitable European designs under licence. As well as Hino's Renault, there were 'real' Austins (the A40 Somerset and the A50 Cambridge) from Nissan–Datsun. Isuzu offered a local version of the Hillman Minx, and Mitsubishi tried their luck with assembled Kaisers, a project doomed as much by the cost of right-hand drive conversion as by the tax limit. The only native big cars of our period were the near-Jeeps of Nissan and Toyota (Mitsubishi's vehicle was an authentic Willys–Overland and made under licence). Both the Toyota BJ and the Nissan Patrol used their makers' standard truck engines, the Toyota's bluff bonnet concealing a first cousin of Chevrolet's Cast Iron Wonder. The Nissan's 3.7-litre side-valve six had Continental affiliations, dating back to the company's crypto-Grahams of 1936.

Toyota were Japan's most ambitious makers, their SA-series Toyopet of 1948 featuring a backbone frame, hydraulic brakes and transverse-leaf independent front suspension; later models reverted to beam axles and conventional chassis. They actually essayed some curves, and the grille was a convincing imitation of the 1939 Lincoln–Zephyr. The rest of it was uninspiring; the 995-cc (65 mm × 75 mm) side-valve four-cylinder engine was rather Fiat-like and developed a sedate 27 bhp. It was mated to a three-speed gearbox with column shift, and a speed of 57 mph was predictable on a 6.17:1 top gear.

By 1952 the shape had crystallized into the familiar slab-sided four-door sedan with outrigged semaphore-type turn indicators and a grille reminiscent of the MO-series Morris Oxford, though at least the SF-type had four forward speeds. The 1955 RR Master and RS Crown series promised 'a wholly new standard of driving enjoyment', and the more expensive Crown showed some improvement on the doleful styling, with a wrapround rear window and a fancier grille. Catalogues spoke of agents in Brazil and Turkey, but it was not until 1956 that Toyotas acquired coil-spring independent front suspension and hypoid rear axles. The engine was now an overhead-valve 1½-litre giving 48 bhp, and the Japanese passion for gimmickry was making itself felt. De Luxe Crowns came complete with radio, clock and even a venetian blind in the rear window.

The Nissan Motor Company's Datsuns were very similar to Austins, though as always they featured a worm drive and semielliptic rear springs never seen on any Baby Austin. Longbridge legacies were visible in the 'spit-and-hope' lubrication, the 6-volt electrics, three-speed gearbox, transverse-leaf front suspension and primitive frame. The hydraulic brakes worked in drums a generous 10-inches in diameter, and capacity was up from 722 to 860-cc, but on the usual low gearing—top was even worse than Toyota's, at 6.5:1—45 mph was the limit. Standard saloons still resembled 1934 Singer Nines, but the 1950 De Luxe was a deplorable travesty of the American Crosley, and by 1952 even the cheapest Thrift model had fallen into line. More traditional was the Sports model with 29 bhp under its bonnet. This model featured an MG-style 'humped scuttle' and fold-flat screen.

Serious attempts were made to beautify the Datsun, with a Renault-like grille on 1954 cars. 1955's 110 had full-pressure lubrication, a four-speed synchromesh box and a hypoid rear axle. A German-looking cabriolimousine joined the range, and some necessary chassis reinforcement was provided. But the 860-cc flathead soldiered on: it was not until 1958 that upstairs valves would make their appearance, on the first of the Bluebirds with a 1.2-litre engine reminiscent of the Austin A40.

Fuji Precision's Prince commemorated Crown Prince Akihito. Its origins were humble indeed, deriving from the Tama, a small Datsun-based battery–electric saloon of 1948, but the Prince was more advanced than any Datsun or Toyota, with its platform-type frame and coil-spring independent front suspension. The rear end was even more intriguing, using as it did a de Dion axle and semiellipics. The engine was a 1½-litre pushrod four of 75 mm × 84 mm, and by 1956 this unit was giving 60 bhp in the Skyline form. A detuned 52-bhp version was reserved for smaller Princes. Though Vauxhall influences predominated, the cars had some pretentions to elegance and came with tubeless tyres as standard equipment.

Ohta were an older and more conservative concern. Their 1938 staple had been the OD, a tiny 736-cc side-valve four distinguishable from the Datsun only by its semielliptic front springs and cruciform-braced frame. In post-war guise the cars underwent a parallel metamorphosis, with hydraulic brakes and 903-cc engines. With these changes came the inevitable pseudo-American styling, albeit the PH of 1954 featured a six-light body resembling a foreshortened Checker taxi-cab. 1956's PK was much the same thing and was said to do 56 mph and 47 mpg. A year later Ohta were taken over by Tokyu Kurogane and faded quietly from the scene.

There were still tax concessions for cycle-cars. These had, by definition, engines of 350-cc or less, a length no greater than 3 metres (118 inches) and a width of 1.5 metres. Tax was £1.50 a year, and no driving licence was required. Surprisingly, few such mini-cars were seen during our period: the Subaru, the Mazda Carol and Mitsubishi's Minica were 1959 débutantes. True, Daihatsu's three-wheeled Bee was available in 1954, but a 540-cc engine barred this from the minimal category. This unit was an air-cooled vee-twin, sited at the rear of the car, which was made, incredibly, in four-door saloon form.

A more ambitious contemporary was the Suminoe Flying Feather, hailed by the western press as the Japanese *deux-chevaux*, though the two cars had little in common beyond air-cooled twin-cylinder engines, all-independently sprung wheels and rolltop coachwork. The Suminoe's unit was a hemi-head vee and more efficient than Citroën's, giving 12.5 bhp from 350-cc. It was mounted at the rear of a primitive frame with two close-set side-members. The three-speed gearbox had ratios (7.3:1, 13.5:1 and 24.9:1) that were memorable even by the depressing local standards. The back axle was of the worm-drive type, the mechanical brakes worked on the rear wheels only, and the pram-like aspect of the little vehicle was accentuated by the bicycle-type wire wheels. The Flying Feather came well within cycle-car limits with a length of 108 inches, could climb one-in-five gradients and returned 65 mpg, though the top speed was predictably low, at 40 mph. Nothing was heard of this oddity after 1955.

17 Argentina

By the 1970s, South America's principal car-making nation was Brazil, where Volkswagen alone were turning out 500,000 units a year. In the early post-war years, however, Argentina set the pace; even in 1956 the nearest approach to a Brazilian private car was the Jeep, of which Willys's local branch made 1,473 that season.

As early as 1911 Horacio Anasagasti had attempted to found a motor industry in Argentina, assembling cars from French-built components. Nothing came of this, but the Americans succeeded where Anasagasti had failed; Ford had an assembly plant in the country by 1922, and General Motors followed five years later. By 1931, about 241,000 private cars were in use, and £5,000,000 had been set aside for the construction of an all-weather highway between Buenos Aires and Cordoba. In 1936 there was still only one automobile to every 55 inhabitants, but this was South America's best performance. Hence it is hardly surprising that 1945 saw a struggle for Argentinian orders.

This was short lived, for Argentina was in the grip of a permanent inflation. In 1949 it was admitted that the cost of living had increased by 500% in ten years. Attempts at stabilization led to a swingeing 300% import duty. A Volkswagen selling in Germany for about £400 cost £1,180 in Buenos Aires—and it was still the cheapest model on the market.

Thus local manufacture became a necessity. The achievement of this objective is now history: outputs of 200,000 cars a year were commonplace in the 1970s, but twenty years earlier the scene was one of brave ideas and negligible results. Three-year waiting lists were usual even in 1958.

President Peron's first step was to lure Piero Dusio from Turin with a promise to pay Cisitalia's debts. Dusio was accompanied by Savonuzzi, a former Fiat engineer whose SVA sports car had flitted across the Italian scene in 1948. It was rather like asking Sir Giles Gilbert Scott to design the Slough Trading Estate. Argentina did not want sports cars: still less did it want the flat-twelve Grand Prix Cisitalia, which benefited not at all from its translation. Nor did much materialize from the new factory at Tigre, staffed with Italian immigrant labour. An overhead-valve 3-litre six-cylinder engine was promised but never went into production; Dusio's 1950 Autoar had to make do with an old friend the 2.2-litre Willys Jeep Four.

Apart from Porsche-type trailing-link independent front suspension, there was nothing spectacular about the Autoar. The brakes were hydraulic, and semielliptic springs were used at the rear, though the three-speed synchromesh box could be had with an overdrive operative on all gears. The first 150 cars were metal-bodied station wagons; a two-door saloon was added to the range late in 1951, but by this time Dusio was on his way back to Italy. For the rest of its life (which lasted into the early 1960s), the Autoar was a straightforward pickup powered by four-cylinder Fiat or Willys engines.

A more durable contender was IAME, the State Aircraft Factory at Cordoba. Their ideas of a people's car were European rather than American: in effect, the evergreen DKW formula. The 1952 Justicialista was a two-door saloon or station wagon in the slab-sided idiom, and its 800-cc twin-piston two-stroke engine smacked of Puch or Ilo, but the rest of it was purest Zschopau: petroil lubrication, thermosyphon circulation, a three-speed crash gearbox with low and wide ratios, transverse leaf independent front suspension with a combination of rigid axle and torsion bars at the rear and a backbone frame. The brakes were hydraulic, but IAME, like Goliath and Lloyd, dispensed with a free-wheel. The Justicialista was made in small numbers until 1955, but Argentina had not seen the last of *Das Kleine Wunder*. Cordoba's later offerings would include both a licence-produced East German Wartburg and their own two-door Graciela with Wartburg mechanical elements, while Industrias Automotriz of Santa Fé countered with a local edition of the West German 1000 model.

Unpromising as the Justicialista may have been, its stable mates never strayed off Cloud Nine. The Grand Sport of 1953 was a flashy glassfibre roadster in which a 1,488-cc flat-four Porsche engine was arranged to drive the front wheels. Also of Porsche make was the four-speed all-synchromesh gearbox with overdrive top, and this model turned up at the 1954 Turin Show. Their last effort, unveiled at Paris eighteen months later, was an even more flamboyant 3-litre.

First impressions suggested a home-made replica of Ford's new Thunderbird, though the Argentinian car had a permanent top, a Buick windscreen and a divided rear window which improved neither vision nor appearance. The engine was equally unlikely: an air-cooled 90-degree overhead-valve vee-eight with oversquare dimensions of 80 mm × 76 mm. With the aid of four dual-choke carburetters, this was said to give 125 bhp. Front-wheel drive had been abandoned, but the Porsche-type independent front suspension was combined with a live axle and coils at the rear. The three-speed gearbox and hypoid bevel back end were standard Ford components. Two industrial thermometers under the bonnet of the show car suggested that this was an experiment, and so it proved. Apart from two-stroke designs, all IAME's subsequent efforts were centred on Jeep-type vehicles sold under the Rastrojero name.

Index